Internal and International Migration

Chinese Perspectives

Chinese Worlds

Chinese Worlds publishes high-quality scholarship, research monographs, and source collections on Chinese history and society from 1900 into the next century.

"Worlds" signals the ethnic, cultural, and political multiformity and regional diversity of China, the cycles of unity and division through which China's modern history has passed, and recent research trends toward regional studies and local issues. It also signals that Chineseness is not contained within territorial borders – overseas Chinese communities in all countries and regions are also "Chinese worlds". The editors see them as part of a political, economic, social, and cultural continuum that spans the Chinese mainland, Taiwan, Hong Kong, Macau, South-East Asia, and the world.

The focus of Chinese Worlds is on modern politics and society and history. It includes both history in its broader sweep and specialist monographs on Chinese politics, anthropology, political economy, sociology, education, and the social-science aspects of culture and religions.

The Literary Field of Twentieth-Century China
Edited by *Michel Hockx*

Chinese Business in Malaysia
Accumulation, Ascendance, Accommodation
Edmund Terence Gomez

Internal and International Migration
Chinese Perspectives
Edited by *Frank N. Pieke* and *Hein Mallee*

Village Inc.
Chinese Rural Society in the 1990s
Edited by *Flemming Christiansen* and *Zhang Junzuo*

Chen Duxiu's Last Articles and Letters, 1937–1942
Edited and translated by *Gregor Benton*

Encyclopedia of the Chinese Overseas
Edited by *Lynn Pan*

New Fourth Army
Communist Resistance along the Yangtse and the Huai, 1938–1941
Gregor Benton

A Road is Made
Communism in Shanghai 1920–1927
Steve Smith

The Bolsheviks and the Chinese Revolution 1919–1927
Alexander Pantsov

Chinatown, Europe
Identity of the European Chinese Towards the Beginning of the Twenty-First Century
Flemming Christiansen

Birth Control in China 1949–1999
Population Policy and Demographic Development
Thomas Scharping

Internal and International Migration

Chinese Perspectives

Edited by

Frank N. Pieke
and
Hein Mallee

CURZON

First Published in 1999
by Curzon Press
15 The Quadrant, Richmond
Surrey, TW9 1BP

© 1999 Frank N. Pieke and Hein Mallee

Typeset in Plantin by LaserScript Ltd, Mitcham, Surrey
Printed and bound in Great Britain by
TJ International, Padstow, Cornwall

British Library Cataloguing in Publication Data
A catalogue record of this book is available from the British Library

ISBN 0–7007–1076–0

Contents

Contributors   vii

Acknowledgements   xi

1   Introduction: Chinese and European perspectives on migration   1
    Frank N. Pieke

Part I Chinese internal migration   27

2   The "static" decades: Inter-provincial migration in pre-reform
    China   29
    Diana Lary

3   Internal migration in China: A dualistic approach   49
    Kam Wing Chan

4   Selectivity, migration reasons and backward linkages of
    rural-urban migrants: A sample survey of migrants to Foshan
    and Shenzhen in comparative perspective   73
    Thomas Scharping

5   Migrant Construction Teams in Beijing   103
    Victor Yuan and Xin Wong

6   The floating population and the integration of the city
    community: A survey on the attitudes of Shanghai residents
    to recent migrants   119
    Jinhong Ding and Norman Stockman

7   Issues in the fertility of temporary migrants in Beijing   134
    Caroline Hoy

Part II Zhejiang migrants in Europe and China   157

8   Moving stones from China to Europe: The dynamics of
emigration from Zhejiang to Europe   159
Mette Thunø

9   "To Get Rich Quickly in Europe!" – Reflections on migration
motivation in Wenzhou   181
Li Minghuan

10   Patterns of migration from Zhejiang to Germany   199
Karsten Giese

11   Zhejiang village in Beijing: Creating a visible non-state space
through migration and marketized networks   215
Xiang Biao

12   Chinese organizations in Hungary, 1989–1996: A case study
in PRC-oriented community politics overseas   251
Pál Nyíri

13   Exporting the "Wenzhou model" to Beijing and Florence:
Labour and economic organization in two migrant communities   280
Luigi Tomba

Part III Migration, identity and belonging   295

14   Female autobiographies from the Cultural Revolution:
Returned *Xiaxiang* educated women in the 1990s   297
Nora Sausmikat

15   Separation, reunion and the Chinese attachment to place   315
Charles Stafford

Part IV Conclusion   331

16   Of exceptionalisms and generalities   333
Ronald Skeldon and Graeme Hugo

Index   346

Contributors

Kam Wing Chan is an Associate Professor at the Department of Geography, University of Washington, United States. He is the author of *Cities with Invisible Walls: Reinterpreting Urbanization in Post-1949 China* (Hong Kong: Oxford University Press, 1994).

Jinhong Ding is an Associate Professor at the Population Research Institute, East China Normal University, Shanghai, People's Republic of China.

Karsten Giese is a sinologist and professional interpreter and translator of Chinese and a Ph.D. candidate at the East Asian Seminar, Free University of Berlin, Germany. He is the author of *Landflucht und interprovinzielle Migration in der VR China: "Mangliu" 1989 – eine Fallstudie* [Rural-to-urban and interprovincial migration in the PRC: "Mangliu" 1989 – a case study] (Hamburg: Institut für Asienkunde, 1993).

Caroline Hoy is a Lecturer in Population Geography at the Department of Geography, University of Dundee, Britain.

Graeme J. Hugo is Professor of Geography at the Department of Geography, University of Adelaide, Australia. He is the author of *The Economic Implications of Emigration from Australia* (Canberra: Australian Government Publishing Service, Canberra, 1994).

Diana Lary is Professor of Modern Chinese History, University of British Columbia, Vancouver, Canada.

Li Minghuan is a postdoctoral researcher at the International Institute of Asian Studies, Leiden, the Netherlands. She is the author of *Dangdai*

Haiwai Huaren Shetuan Yanjiu [A study on Chinese associations abroad] (Xiamen: Xiamen Daxue Chubanshe, 1995).

Hein Mallee recently received his doctorate from the University of Leiden, the Netherlands. The title of his dissertation is *The Expanded Family: Rural Labour Circulation in Reform China*. He now works on a poverty alleviation project in China.

Pál Nyíri is a postdoctoral researcher at the Institute for Chinese Studies, University of Oxford, Britain. His book on Chinese migration and Hungary *A sarkany atkel a Dunan* [The dragon crosses the Danube] will be published in Hungarian in 1998.

Frank N. Pieke is University Lecturer in the Modern Politics and Society of China and Fellow of St Cross College, University of Oxford, Britain. He is author of *The Ordinary and the Extraordinary: An Anthropological Study of Chinese Reform and the 1989 People's Movement in Beijing* (London: Kegan Paul International, 1996).

Nora Sausmikat is a sinologist and Ph.D. candidate at the East Asian Seminar, Free University of Berlin, Germany.

Thomas Scharping is Professor of Modern Chinese History with special emphasis on political, economic and social problems at Cologne University, Germany. He is the author of many studies on the political structure, economic development and social change in contemporary China.

Ronald Skeldon, previously a Professor of Geography at the University of Hong Kong, is currently a Visiting Professor at the Institute for Population and Social Research, Mahidol University, Bangkok, Thailand. His most recent book is *Migration and Development: A Global Perspective* (London: Longman, 1997).

Charles Stafford is Lecturer at the Department of Anthropology, London School of Economics, Britain. He is the author of *The Roads of Chinese Childhood: Learning and Identification in Angang* (Cambridge: Cambridge University Press, 1995).

Norman Stockman is Senior Lecturer in the Department of Sociology, University of Aberdeen, and Secretary of the University of Aberdeen Chinese Studies Group, Britain. He is author (with Norman Bonney and Shang Xuewen) of *Women's Work in East and West* (London: University College of London Press, 1995).

Mette Thunø is Lecturer of Chinese at the Department of Asian Studies, University of Copenhagen, Denmark. She recently completed her Ph.D. dissertation entitled *Chinese Migration to Denmark: Catering and Ethnicity.*

Luigi Tomba is an affiliated researcher to the Fondazione GG Feltrinelli in Milan, the Centre of International Politics (CESPI) in Rome and San Marino University. From the latter institution he recently received his Ph.D. in History on a dissertation entitled *Paradoxes of Labour Reform: Chinese Labour Theory and Practice from Socialism to the Market.*

Wong Xin holds a Masters degree in Economics and is Senior Researcher of Horizon Research Group, People's Republic of China.

Xiang Biao is an D.Phil. candidate at the Institute of Social and Cultural Anthropology, University of Oxford, Britain. He has written two unpublished book length ethnographic studies on Chinese migration.

Victor Yuan is Senior Researcher of Horizon Research Group People's Republic of China, Inc., a Ph.D. candidate at Peking University, and vice-president of Beijing Consulting Association.

Acknowledgements

The editors would like to thank all participants in the workshop "European Chinese and Chinese Internal Migrants", which was held in Oxford on 3–5 July 1996. The often very lively discussions during the workshop clarified many important issues and contributed much to making this a better book.

Support for the workshop and the book was provided by the Asia Committee of the European Science Foundation, the Universities' China Committee in London, the Davis Fund and the Faculties of Anthropology & Geography and Oriental Studies of the University of Oxford.

We are particularly indebted to Stephan Feuchtwang, to whom we owe the original idea for the topic of the workshop. Flemming Christiansen and Mette Thunø gave us invaluable feedback on the first drafts of the ESF grant application, and later helped us by agreeing to act as co-applicants.

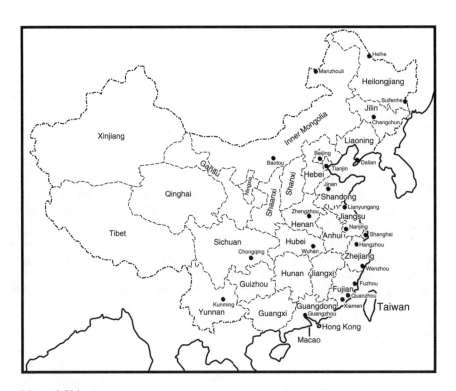

Map of China

Chapter One

Introduction: Chinese migrations compared*

Frank N. Pieke

Introduction

Over the past twenty years, Chinese on the move have gripped the attention of news audiences and scholars both in China and throughout the world. After decades of effective migration controls, the Chinese have regained the freedom to move to destinations abroad and within China itself that offer the prospect of a better life for themselves and their families.

China currently experiences a migration transition in the context of economic and social development similar to the experiences of other developing countries in Asia, Africa, and Latin America. But the current population mobility in China is more than a variation on a universal theme. It would be historically naive to think that the Chinese (or any other people for that matter) suddenly started to migrate with the arrival of Western "capitalist" modernity in 1978 (or 1842, 1912, 1949, or whatever other date one wishes to privilege). Migration has always played an important role in Chinese society, and modernity has a genealogy in China that in part predates the Western incursions of the 19th and 20th centuries.

Chinese migration had, has, and will continue to have its own characteristics. First, the sheer number of people who are involved add up to tens of millions, posing extraordinary challenges to authorities of the receiving areas and countries. Second, the strict controls on internal and international migration of the Maoist period (that have many historical precedents such as the ban on international migration and Han Chinese migration to Manchuria during much of the Qing dynasty (1644–1911)) have not and probably will not be lifted completely. Especially the *hukou*

---

*I would like to thank Hein Mallee, Marcus Banks, Ronald Skeldon and Mette Thunø for extensive suggestions and comments. They have helped me sharpen the argument and avoid at least some of its pitfalls.

1

system (household registration system, see section 2 below) is likely to continue to be a powerful policy instrument to direct and restrict population transfers. Third, patrilinearity, ancestor worship, the importance of the in-group, and the stress on descent and common origin constitute a powerful discourse of attachment to the native area, family and kin that strongly colours Chinese perceptions of migration. This discourse has moreover a profoundly different impact on women, who are routinely expected to *detach* themselves and move away from their native family and community upon marriage. In view of Chinese migration past and present, both universalist modernization theory and Chinese particularism seem equally inadequate.

Recently, the debate concerning Chinese migration has been especially passionate in places that either have witnessed a sudden upsurge in the number of Chinese immigrants (China's large cities, the United States, Australia, Russia, South Africa, Hungary, or Italy), or that, like Britain, live in fear of the imminent immigration of large numbers of (Hong Kong) Chinese. Much serious research is done on Chinese migrations, yet arguably even more is written that merely serves to confirm stereotypical images that say little about the migrants themselves, but much more about the (often not so hidden) agendas of their protagonists. Countless Chinese farmers flocking to the cities of eastern China and the developed world are often portrayed as a Malthusian deluge that has to be forcibly stemmed to protect the collapse of valued ways and standards of living (Ding and Stockman in this volume; De Tinguy 1998; Weiner 1997). Yet on the other hand, successful entrepreneurs in the Chinese "diaspora" are depicted as the vanguard of the alternative transnational modernity of "Greater China", a model to be emulated not only in China itself but also in a western world that threatens to lose the initiative to the "East Asian miracle."[1]

Much work therefore remains to be done before we can assess with any confidence the ramifications of the increased mobility of close to a hundred million people each year. This book grew out of the workshop *European Chinese and Chinese Internal Migrants: Common Themes in International and Internal Migration* held in Oxford on 3–5 July 1996,[2] whose objective was to further the understanding of Chinese migration by comparing migration in China itself with Chinese emigration to Europe, two ostensibly very different areas and contexts. Before I introduce the main themes and results of the workshop and this book, I shall have to say some more about the background and reasons for this particular comparison.

Researchers of Chinese internal migration and Chinese emigration have until now hardly interacted. This book confirms that this division of labour has largely been an artificial one, unnecessarily obscuring the similarities – and some of the equally instructive dissimilarities – between many of the central issues in internal and international migration, such as the social organization of migration, the structure and culture of migrant communities, the role of voluntary associations, the impact of migration on the home communities, entrepreneurship and employment, and the formation of regional and ethnic identities. The fact, for instance, that migrants from the Chinese countryside are shunned in much the same way from the core areas of the global system as from China's core cities may go some way in defusing the more simplistic allegations of either Chinese totalitarianism or European racism that are easily made when talking about migration policies. Resident populations clearly seek to protect their privileges against the (perceived) threat of outsiders, regardless of race, geographical distance, or political system. Similarly, immigration and minority policies elsewhere may provide valuable lessons to governments both in China and Europe, a point I shall return to later on in this essay.

The choice for a comparison specifically with Europe has been a more complex one. The direct overland link between Europe and China through Russia makes certain aspects of Chinese emigration to (eastern) Europe rather similar to migration to China's big cities. In addition, Chinese internal migration is regulated through an internal passport system (*hukou*) that is as variable throughout China as are the immigration restrictions imposed by individual European countries, a situation which invites comparison.

Yet equally important to Hein Mallee and myself as organizers of the workshop and editors of this volume was the worrying state of European Chinese research. Until very recently, students of the overseas Chinese hardly had any contact at all with colleagues in other European countries, and were often almost completely cut off from modern China studies or general migration studies. With the number of European Chinese rapidly approaching the one million mark (Pieke 1998), we can no longer afford to let research on this group linger on in an obscure corner of the academe. *Internal and International Migration: Chinese Perspectives* therefore continues the task started with a recent volume on the Chinese in Europe that took stock of the current state of European Chinese studies (Benton and Pieke 1998).

The final and perhaps most important reason for the comparison is the presence in Europe of large and well-established communities of Chinese from the area around the cities of Wenzhou and Qingtian in south-eastern Zhejiang province. Migrants from this same area in Zhejiang are also found in larger or smaller numbers in almost every city and town in China. The Zhejiang communities therefore not only set the overseas Chinese in Europe off from the better known overseas Chinese communities in Southeast Asia and North America, but also provide a direct link and comparison with migrant communities in China itself. In this book, we have given this comparison ample room with the inclusion of the articles by Mette Thunø, Li Minghuan and Karsten Giese on emigration from Zhejiang to Europe, Xiang Biao's in-depth study of "Zhejiang Village" in

3

Beijing, and Luigi Tomba's comparative study of Zhejiang migrants in Florence and Beijing. Pál Nyíri's article on the Hungarian Chinese community, politically dominated by a minority of Zhejiang immigrants, is also directly relevant to this comparison.

In this chapter I shall discuss some of the main issues raised by the articles and the discussions during the Oxford workshop. For convenience's sake I have grouped these issues into four clusters: (1) Time frame, definitions and methodology, (2) The organization of migration and migrant communities, (3) Rethinking "migration", and (4) Migration policies and policy making. I shall limit the discussion in this introductory chapter to Chinese migration and some of its theoretical ramifications, and leave the comparison with migrations elsewhere in the world to the concluding chapter of Graeme Hugo and Ronald Skeldon, who were the discussants at the Oxford workshop.

Time frame, definitions and methodology

Reading the recent literature on Chinese migration one might easily forget that migration in the People's Republic of China (PRC) did not commence with the official announcement of the reforms policies in December 1978. Diana Lary's chapter defuses this myth by pointing at issues that are either half-forgotten or else often not thought of in the context of migration studies. To name some of the more spectacular examples: the large-scale movements of peasants to the cities in 1956–7 with the speed-up of collectivization; the periodic campaigns to send cadres and intellectuals down to the countryside for ideological remoulding (*xiafang*); the return to the countryside of peasant migrants after 1957 (*huixiang*); and the mammoth campaign forcing high school and university graduates down to the countryside (*shangshan xiaxiang*) between 1968 and 1976 in the aftermath of the Cultural Revolution.

Immense as the population transfers involved in these campaigns were, they were dwarfed by the mobility that is part of the routine state unified job allocation system (*guojia tongyi gongzuo fenpei*, or *fenpei* for short) that is part of the economic plan. Kam Wing Chan draws our attention to the fact that this system continues to be in force, creating a very stable number of about 20 million migrants (or roughly one fifth to one third of the total number of migrants) per year, most of whom move from one city to another. Chan's distinction between such *hukou* (urban registration) and non-hukou migrants is useful, but can easily be interpreted too rigidly and seems to be to a certain extent an artefact of the statistics Chan uses. When looked at from an on-the-ground perspective, the distinction is too inflexible for the 1990s.

First, many non-hukou rural migrants are nowadays legalized by issuing a temporary city registration, or are able to bribe officials into issuing one. Second, there is a considerable grey area of non-hukou, or post-facto hukou urban-urban migration catering for the specific labour needs of state and private enterprises that the official work allocation system does not allow for. This is intimately linked up with the phenomenon that is known as *xiahai* ("to go to sea") in contemporary China: leaving one's allocated state job for private enterprise or employment, which often entails physical mobility. Since the most able and employable in the state sector are tempted most "to go to sea"; xiahai amounts to a domestic brain and skill drain from the ailing state sector, especially in northern and central China, to the booming market sector of the big cities and the south-eastern part of the country. What makes this even more pertinent to this book is that much of the recent migration of urban Chinese to North America or eastern Europe is in fact the international spill-over or extension of domestic xiahai migration and even, as Xiang Biao's (this volume) data on the "border trade" indicate, of rural-urban migration of traders and businesspeople.[3] Pál Nyíri demonstrates that the most successful of these emigrants link up with Chinese state enterprises and act as their representatives abroad. To many well-educated and ambitious urban Chinese, migration to eastern Europe, advanced study in North America, or private sector employment in China itself are alternative paths of social advancement; consequently, they cannot be understood in isolation from each other.

Migration under the state's unified job allocation system entails more than the transfer of labour and skills. The transfer of large numbers of Han Chinese cadres, military personnel, and workers into Tibet is a means to convert military conquest into political gain, although the Chinese government does not appear to aim for full sinicization through migration (Clarke 1994:250). This strategy is by no means unique to China: strengthening border areas through settlement is found in many other places, including Indonesia, the countries bordering on the Amazon basin in South America, and Vietnam. Here too we have to caution against an unduly strict distinction between hukou and non-hukou migration. Xinjiang, Inner Mongolia, Qinghai, and especially Tibet count as hardship posts, and very few workers, cadres, and soldiers who are on a fixed term assignment will stay after the end of their term. Yet in the wake of these "expatriate" communities, large numbers of traders, restaurateurs, and craftsmen have made their way into the border areas to take advantage of the specific demand for better quality or Han ethnic goods and services generated by the "expatriates" (Clarke 1994:246–9).

Turning to non-hukou migration, population mobility outside the plan does not really conform to the common stereotypical image, described and analyzed in the chapter of Ding and Stockman, of the blind inflow (*mangmu liudong*, or *mangliu*) of peasants into the big cities of eastern China unleashed by the market reforms of 1978. First, as is demonstrated by Xiang Biao, voluntary internal migration of specialized traders from the

Wenzhou area already picked up again in the early 1970s.[4] Intriguingly, this corresponds rather closely to the start of *international* migration from Wenzhou to Europe.[5] As with most other phenomena, 1978 is evidently not the watershed that it is made out to be in official Chinese propaganda.

Second and more important, non-hukou migration, like hukou migration, is an extremely heterogeneous phenomenon. The rural-urban or rural-rural circulation of peasant men and women looking for menial employment in construction, manufacturing, farming, or as domestic help in the cities, xiahai urban-urban migration, and the well-organized rural-urban chain migration generated by established migrant communities specialized in specific economic niche activities have very little in common. In sum, migration, or better mobility, in China as elsewhere, emerges as a cover term for a wide range of phenomena. I shall return to this issue in the section on "Rethinking 'migration'" below.

Several contributors to this volume deal with the almost traditional problem of reliable statistical data. Contrary to the situation in many other countries, Chinese researchers recently have published the data from several large scale migration surveys. While none of these surveys is perfect – and indeed surveys can never be perfectly fitted to the tastes of other researchers – the data are plentiful and allow unprecedented quantitative research of Chinese migration.

Most of the problems with official Chinese data are familiar to demographers the world over. Statistics everywhere reflect the preoccupations and world view of their producers, most often the state (Woolf 1989). Statistics are based on facts that individuals are willing to divulge or the state manages and wants to collect. Definitions and classifications are those of the bureaucracy, and aspects of migration that fall outside bureaucratic monitoring remain undetected; more often than not, those tend to be the things independent researchers are interested in most. Yet different bureaucratic agencies have different priorities, and will therefore also use different definitions and methods of data collection. Comparison of different data sets and a careful evaluation of the priorities of the agency responsible for the data may therefore go at least some way in remedying the existing problems.

Many of these points also hold true for research on the Chinese in Europe. European governments are invariably greedy for demographic data on their immigrant population. Yet the problems that come with trying to measure the volume of Chinese immigration to Europe are surprisingly – and revealingly – similar to those that obtain in China itself. Chinese immigration is extremely heterogeneous. It involves many different countries of origin and destination, social classes, migration routes, and time periods. In addition, many immigrants are illegal, and their very business is to remain undetected by the bureaucracy that tries to register their presence. Lastly, European governments and their bureaucratic agencies rarely agree on priorities, definitions and procedures, which makes it almost impossible to construct comparable data sets. Despite the frequent complaints about the incompetence or opacity of the Chinese bureaucracy, we ironically have much more and better data on migration in China than on Chinese migration to Europe.

The organization of Chinese migration and migrant communities

The family often plays a crucial role in migration and circulation. Frequently, migration of one or more members is but one element of a family strategy for social mobility or simply survival. Remittances and return trips home, especially with Chinese New Year, serve to confirm migrants' continued membership of such dispersed families. However, many different configurations pertain. Married men who move to urban areas or even abroad do so to create income for the family, or explore opportunities and prepare for the eventual migration of the whole family. Conversely, middle and upper class Hong Kong heads of household now often send one or more of their dependents to live abroad as an insurance against the possible consequences of the reunification with China, while these "astronauts" (*taikongren* in Mandarin), as they are called in Hong Kong, continue to work in Hong Kong's high wage economy (Skeldon 1994).

Yet, as Caroline Hoy demonstrates, an element of individual ambition is almost inevitably present, especially among young migrants. This is perhaps strongest in the case of women. To unmarried women, migration is not only their contribution to the family purse, but also a way to save money to take with them when marrying into another family. Some young women nowadays even migrate without the consent of their parents. Conversely, as Caroline Hoy's data suggest, young, married women gain more freedom to emigrate with the birth of their first son, which relieves them of the most important familial duty of a daughter-in-law. Upon migration they can even leave their child behind with its grandparents; a pattern, incidentally, that is frequently described among overseas Chinese immigrants in Europe as well. These women truly have the best of both worlds, enjoying the earnings and freedom that are often denied to women in traditional Chinese families, without the double burden bogging down so many other working women. Much like in other strongly patriarchal societies, the impact of migration on gender relations is by no means given: it can be an avenue of empowerment for certain women, but can also simply contribute to the perpetuation of strong, patriarchal families.

A traditional debate in the study of migration is the impact of migration on the home communities. Does migration relieve the home community from its excess labourers, who later return endowed with new skills and capital, or is migration a drain on the home communities that thus become mired in permanent stagnation and backwardness?[6] It is now commonly accepted that home communities are much more than mere recipients of remittances and investment, and a holiday and retirement resort. Home communities are often active in coordinating migration and structuring migrant communities. Back in the village, migrants living in different places meet each other and members of the local elite, who include permanently returned migrants; here, information is exchanged, business partners are found, deals are made, and labour is recruited. Ultimately, however, the issue of the role of the home community and remittances should not be separated from migration itself, as has traditionally been done in the literature. As Massey et al. point out in their discussion of the so-called "new economics of migration," the outcome of migration, including the use to which remittances are put, depends on the original motivations and context of the decision to migrate (Massey et al. 1993:457). Migration motivated by the desire to raise capital for productive investment or to acquire specific skills is likely to have a much different impact on the home community than migration for reasons of, say, income diversification or political exile. Again, further thought on issues pertaining to migration leads to the conclusion that migration actually consists of an extremely diverse bundle of phenomena.

The chapters of Karsten Giese, Li Minghuan and Mette Thunø, especially when read in conjunction with those of Xiang Biao and Luigi Tomba, provide a very detailed case study of how specific villages in southern Zhejiang have come to specialize in migration to western Europe, while others located next door specialize in migration to Chinese cities such as Beijing, while still others do not migrate at all. The origin, destinations, and volume of migratory flows from these areas is determined by the growth and maintenance of specific migration chains, tying together transregional or transnational communities that gravitate around specific native places. Migration from these villages continues despite the fact that reportedly more than 800,000 migrants from other parts of China have flocked to virtually the same area in southern Zhejiang in search of employment. This situation is reminiscent of Hong Kong. From Hong Kong people continue to emigrate to western Europe despite a simultaneous heavy in-migration from the People's Republic and ample employment opportunities in urban Hong Kong's booming economy. These examples vividly illustrate that most forms of migration do not bring the most destitute to the cities: migration requires a certain mind set and access to opportunities and knowledge that are only found in communities that have specialized in migration.

Giese, Li and Thunø describe such highly specialized home communities of well-established migrant communities. Unfortunately, we know much less about the home communities and the role of migration chains in other forms of migration. Migration from the cities in North China to the southern special economic zones or eastern Europe, for instance, seems to be a much more individual affair, although it must be admitted that the role of the home community (or rather the network of kin and friends back home) among such migrants has not yet been systematically investigated. Similarly, short term circulants will most likely have a very different impact on their home communities, although the role of these communities in facilitating and coordinating such migration does not necessarily have to be less active, as is illustrated by Victor Yuan in his chapter on migrant labour squads (*baogongdui*).

A central aspect of migration is the role of family members, kin, and fellow villagers in shaping, directing, and perpetuating migration flows. It is therefore not surprising that networks are crucial to the understanding of migrant settlements and community building, too. Xiang Biao's chapter describes in detail how pioneering Zhejiang migrants in the 1970s and early 1980s fanned out across China in search of opportunities, much in the same way as other Zhejiangese pioneered the emigration to Europe in the second half of the nineteenth century, as described by Mette Thunø. Once these pioneers establish a foothold, they make contact with the home community to recruit labour and business partners. Very rapidly, a strong, internally stratified and organized community grows up around these pioneers, which is able to survive long periods of very limited contact with the home communities (such as between 1930 and the early 1970s in Europe) or strong government repression (such as continues to happen periodically in Beijing).

One would expect different types of migration to produce very dissimilar communities in the destination area. Chain migrants from specialized home communities ought to form close-knit communities that become a permanent feature of the social map in the destination areas, although individual members of these communities circulate back and forth between the home community and the migrant communities in different cities or countries. Continuing this train of thought, individual migration, following the rise and fall of employment and business opportunities, should lead to much more loosely structured communities or even direct assimilation.

Yet this is not necessarily the case. The well-established communities of Chinese chain migrants in northwestern Europe have, until recently at least, displayed a remarkable lack of organization and cohesion (see for instance Pieke 1998 and Thunø 1997 and 1998). Conversely, Pal Nyiri's case study in this book of the Chinese in Hungary indicates that individual migration does not necessarily inhibit the growth of a relatively strong, unified community. Four factors appear to have been decisive here. Until very recently, the Hungarian authorities were hardly concerned with the

9

Chinese community, which was therefore largely left to fend for itself. Second, a minority of Zhejiangese with strong transnational links and access to the PRC authorities came to dominate the community. Third, links with state enterprises back in China were important for business. This provided the PRC authorities, who show an increasing interest in overseas Chinese communities, with the leverage to unite the Hungarian Chinese behind the association of their choice. This combined with the fourth factor, the absence of a significant group of Hong Kong or Southeast Asian Chinese. The latter do not naturally gravitate toward the PRC and provide a check on mainland Chinese dominance in western European countries.

The seeming anomaly of the Hungarian Chinese points to an important issue. If we want to understand an immigrant community (for instance, its degree of closure, the density of its internal structure, its settlement pattern, or the extent of its economic specialization), the nature of the migratory process taken in isolation explains rather little. In itself this is hardly new: the main point of Fredrik Barth's pathbreaking work on the instrumentalist nature of ethnicity was exactly that we have to look at intergroup relations rather than at origins (Barth 1969), but it is a point that is easily forgotten when focusing on migration.

In this spirit, many earlier studies of overseas Chinese communities have stressed the importance of "situational" factors over and above (a stereotype of) Chinese culture (inward looking, collectivist, tied to one's native area) and the specific pattern of migration to which this is supposed to give rise (chain migration of sojourners). In this debate, Lawrence Crissman (1967) is the favourite straw man, while the usual solution called for stresses the socio-economic, political and ethnic context that Chinese migrants find themselves in (Patterson 1974; Hamilton 1977; Thompson 1980).

The example of the Wenzhou communities in European and Chinese cities shows however that the nature of the migration configuration that migrants operate in is an important factor as well. Networks based on chain migration and the connections with the home community give Wenzhou immigrant entrepreneurs a competitive advantage (labour, capital, materials, markets) over potential market entrants from other groups. If competition stiffens, or discrimination and exclusion by the majority population and the state increase, the leaders of these communities have the money and clout to build a strong organizational structure to defend the community against the outside threat and assume many of the functions the state refuses to fulfil. This strong and defensive community structure and ethnic identity serve the purposes of the leaders. The ethnic community is to them a source of cheap and docile labour, and a vehicle to continue their monopolization of certain economic activities. This argument could even be refined to allow for more complex ethnic hierarchies. The case of the Zhejiang community in contemporary Beijing, for instance, demonstrates that the labour used by ethnic entrepreneurs is not necessarily only that of co-ethnics. Co-ethnics are employed in certain positions, while the most menial jobs are given to locals or other migrant groups. Community and ethnicity thus become instruments to segment, and thereby control and exploit the labour force.

When looking at other types of migration in China itself, we find a similar interplay between factors pertaining to the migratory process and the context of settlement. Hukou migrants, by virtue of the nature of their migration (i.e. organized and sanctioned by the state), usually find themselves at the top of the pile in the destination area. In predominantly Han-Chinese areas, they integrate into mainstream society without forming ethnic communities, let alone the native place organizations that were characteristic of pre-1949 migrant communities in Chinese cities. The work unit, or more broadly the bureaucracy, is the source of sustenance of these migrants; here ethnicity neither has much relevance nor is allowed any room to develop. In the case of migration to non-Han areas, however, ethnicity plays a crucial role. Han-Chinese migrants in these areas employ the bureaucratic work unit system to isolate themselves from the local population, most of whom do not have prized state sector employment (Ma 1991). Under these circumstances, not the migrants, but on the contrary the local population are ethnicized as national minorities caught at a lower evolutionary stage. Here ethnicity – or national minority status – is defined by the state and Han-Chinese. As an instrument for exclusion, this ethnicity supports Han Chinese political and cultural control and suppresses the growth of an autonomous ethnic identity.

Lastly, as shown by Ding Jinhong and Norman Stockman, non-hukou migrants to Chinese cities are stereotyped through the imposition of (proto-)ethnic labels. Only certain immigrant groups succeed in carving out their own economic niches. Many other immigrants depend on the majority population – or other ethnic groups – for employment or sustenance and are potentially very vulnerable to discrimination and the exclusion that this may entail. In contemporary China such immigrant groups find themselves at the other side of the Barthian boundary: they are assigned to catch-all discriminatory categories of *mangliu* ("blind flow"), *gongmin* (literally, "working people"), or simply *waidi ren* ("outsiders") that exclude them from mainstream urban Chinese society. Especially worrying is that the state does not seem to take any measures to counter the resultant polarization of urban society. On the contrary, such labels are actively promoted by the mass media; indeed, the category of *mangmu liudong renkou* (the full word usually abbreviated as *mangliu*) started as a bureaucratic term coined by worried planners and demographers. These migrants are defined and excluded by the native population on the basis of the (illegal) nature of their migration. This happens regardless of important differences among these migrants: they hail from all over China, and some are chain migrants who are immediately taken up by firmly established migrants communities, while others are individual migrants without much of a support network.

Pejorative categories such as mangliu have the great danger that they may evolve into enduring stigmas: permanent outcasts of society whose only relevant identity is that they do not belong to the privileged stratum of full citizens. Examples of such exclusionary, catch-all stereotypes (that in certain cases may ultimately be internalized by the people involved and become the basis of ethnic group formation) abound the world over, from Shanghai's Subei people to America's Negroes, or from India's tribals and scheduled castes to western Europe's guest workers and asylum seekers. A similarly exclusionary category in contemporary urban China itself is that of "foreigners" (*waibin, waiguoren, laowai*). This category also derives from official discourse, and has firmly been incorporated in urbanites' conceptions of their society.

At closer inspection, groups of immigrants are defined as much by the nature of their migration as by the circumstances that they create and that are created for them in the receiving society. Yet we should not leave at that: a facile call for an integrated approach to migration and ethnicity merely perpetuates the confusion. Instead, I propose a critical assessment of the analytical value of the concepts of migration and ethnicity themselves, which is what I shall attempt below.

The relevance of migration

In the preceding sections the comparison between Chinese migrants in Europe and China has been pursued in a rather loose, but, to my mind at least, fruitful way. The objective of the exercise has not been to subject unambiguously formulated hypotheses of certain aspects of Chinese migration to the rigours of statistical testing. The objective of comparison has rather been to elucidate certain specific phenomena by contrasting them with partially similar, partially dissimilar phenomena. One further example of such a case by case comparison that has not yet been mentioned are the similarities between the nineteenth century credit ticket system for the recruitment of indentured labour and current human trafficking in southern China (Skeldon 1996:453; Giese, this volume). The patterns of recruitment, the commodification of human beings, and the resulting creation of bonded labour are more than superficially alike. Even the use of contracts and the terms and conditions stipulated therein are broadly similar, although it is difficult to imagine that human traffickers resort to the law to enforce them. This initial comparison may lead us to ask similar questions about other forms of contract migrant labour in China. Teams of labourers recruited by rural governments or state farms that are contracted out to urban work units or construction firms, and nowadays also to the Russian Far East, at closer inspection may reveal more than just a few similarities with 19th century indentured labour. This is not just an academic point, but has disturbing implications for the Chinese Communist Party (CCP) that claims much of its right to rule from liberating China from the yoke of imperialist exploitation.

One result of these comparisons has been to expose the severe limitations of approaches that uncritically use the concept of migration (and, as a corollary, ethnicity), thereby subsuming under one category a whole range of very disparate phenomena. This is not to say that certain migrations do not have much in common. Indeed, certain migrations, such as contract labour migration, may have so much in common that they should be considered of one kind, even when they are usually treated separately in the literature.

When reviewing the chapters in this book, we may therefore draw the preliminary conclusion that certain aspects of certain migrations have surprisingly much in common, and can in fact be thought of as largely identical but for the fact that they happen to be located in different parts of the world. This is especially clear for the various Zhejiang migrant communities introduced in this book. Entrepreneurship, community building, relations with the native population and other immigrant groups in Florence seem remarkably similar to Beijing or Hungary. In this case, it could somewhat speculatively be argued that Zhejiang internal and international migration are parts of one global Zhejiang migration "system" (Mabogunje 1970; Zlotnik 1992). Yet when we proceed with a comparison with other migrations like labour teams in Beijing or hukou migrants throughout China, much of the initial confidence gives way to increasing doubts about the validity of subsuming all under the umbrella category of Chinese migration. Undeniably, these migrations continue to have certain aspects in common, but these rapidly become less in number and relevance as more migrations are included.

The limited explanatory power of migration exposed by an explicit comparative perspective leads us to conclude that a redefinition of the field of migration studies is overdue. At the most fundamental level, migration studies seem biased toward the economics and – more recently – the political economy and sociology of population mobility. An economic view entails that migration is only studied from the perspective of the calculated maximization of scarce resources and opportunities, and mainly in terms of only one of its outcomes: the spatial redistribution of labour.[7] This arguably is the very core and original legitimization for studying migration as a separate topic. Yet by now it is commonly accepted that, when man is reduced to a production factor, much about migration, such as the specific direction and timing of migratory flows, is impossible to explain.

Dissatisfaction with economic theories has led to a shift to the political economy and sociology of migration: the social structures that govern migratory flows and the patterns of insertion of alien groups in established populations. Central ideas here are core and periphery, the growth of a global economy and concomitant migration regimes, chain migration, backward and forward linkages, a focus on households rather than individuals, cultural division of labour, middleman minorities, and ethnicity.[8] The preceding sections of this chapter have mainly been concerned with these sociological aspects. It has been exactly this, however, that has led us to conclude that there actually seems to be very little that unites the many phenomena that are grouped together under the umbrella of migration. Upon reflection, the sociological critique of economic approaches increasingly renders the concept of migration itself analytically irrelevant.

This long term impact of the sociological perspective is not altogether infelicitous. What is commonly called migration is, after all, *just* people changing residence and it is important that we again start seeing things in perspective. Yet migration need not be discarded altogether. In my view, a two-pronged approach is needed for the "reinvention" of migration as an analytical concept.

First, the turn from spatial mobility per se should not be weakened but rather strengthened further. As a first step, I suggest that we study the entire configuration of mobility itself in the context in which it takes place both in the sending and the receiving society. Such *migration configurations* consist of people moving between at least two places, but often, as in the case of the Zhejiang migrants, several places. Frequently, the behaviour of migrants continues to be defined by this transnational migrant community, even when they stay in remote places for years. Migrants actively maintain and promote their position in this community, for example, through lavish funerals, the building of houses, or the purchase of land. At the same time, they depend on the home communities, for example for labour and credit. A specific migration "stream" is in fact a spatially dispersed community (or collectivity) that is continually reinforced.

A migration configuration incorporates much more than just people and locations: flows of information, goods, money, and other resources are at least as important as the migrants themselves. The configuration also includes the niches which the migrants carve out and the specific institutions and networks they use and develop for making the movements possible. The articles in this book illustrate the extremely broad range of institutions and networks constituting a migration configuration. They include kinship and community ties, formal immigration barriers and commercial human traffickers, state agencies and individual officials, the configuration of ethnic groups that migrants encounter, airlines, railways and shipping companies, and even law firms, human rights groups, and anti-immigration activists.

A call for a migration configuration approach in itself is nothing new. In 1974, the anthropologist David Parkin in effect did exactly the same in an influential article on Luo migration and ethnicity in East Africa (Parkin 1974). Parkin's article was not unique: it built upon an a long anthropological tradition that studied the social relations in which migratory flows were embedded (Eades 1987). In addition, important anthropological case studies exist of individual migration configurations, where the anthropologist conducted fieldwork both in the sending and in the receiving community (see, for example, Banks 1992 and 1994; Eades 1993; Watson 1974, 1975, 1977a, and 1977b).

The related term "migration system" is used by demographers and geographers (Boyd 1989; Fawcett 1989; Mabogunje 1970; Skeldon 1994 and 1997; Zlotnik 1992), and their approach obviously has much in common with what I am proposing here. Yet there is an important distinction. My understanding of the term "migration system", as it is used by geographers and demographers, is that it describes aggregate connections through migration between one or more countries (regions) of origin with one or more countries (regions) of destination. A system consists of many individual migratory flows that are often completely independent from each other and that are bundled together for some external analytical purpose. My anthropological approach is somewhat different. A migration configuration is actor centred: it describes a transregional or transnational community in which people are embedded and the established practices that inform and structure that community. A migration system describes migration as it appears to an outside observer; a migration configuration is the social reality that the migrants themselves operate in. Clearly, the two approaches complement each other, yet their fundamental epistemological difference makes it impossible (and undesirable) to merge them into a integrated approach. Zhejiang migration illustrates this rather abstract point. Earlier, I said that Zhejiang migration to Europe and within China can be seen as elements of a global Zhejiang migration system. This may not be all that self-evident for Zhejiang migrants themselves, who usually are embedded either in a European or or an internal migration configuration. Both exist side-by-side, yet largely invisible to each other.[9]

Their differences aside, both anthropologists and geographers and demographers seem to appreciate insufficiently that both a "system" and a "configuration" approach ultimately problematize migration as a core analytical concept. Migration is just *one* aspect of the total system or configuration. Conversely, migration systems or configurations are not of one type, but cover a broad range of phenomena that have little (if anything) in common but the largely contingent fact of spatial mobility of some of the people involved.

This first element of my proposal for the future of migration studies thus entails a turn even further away from mobility itself to the social and political context in which it takes place. Yet we should not forget that the fact of geographical mobility is not without significance to the migrants themselves. The second element of my proposal is therefore exactly the reverse of the first: a fresh, anthropological look at mobility as a discursively constituted event. The chapters by Nora Sausmikat and Charles Stafford in this book take a first step in this direction. They suggest that migration studies should pay more attention to the fact that geographical mobility involves human beings rather than mere human bodies. Leaving one's native soil for an alien environment is a profound biographical event and experience that often permanently changes migrants' conception of themselves and their place in society, even after returning to their native area; similarly, cultures invest mobility with a specific significance and meanings that we shall be looking for in vain in population statistics.

In a recent article on migration and mobility among Chinese students in Britain and villagers in Shaanxi Province, Xin Liu points out that travel and distance in space also represent distance and travel up or down the social hierarchy: mobility is discursively connected with power and wealth. Migration is seen as a sign and avenue of success, staying behind means poverty and backwardness (Liu 1996). To this I would like to add the point that what constitutes success and what migrants thus hope to achieve by moving away is also discursively constructed and therefore varies with time and place. The Red Guards who signed up for the countryside did not expect wealth but glory and revolutionary redemption, while many "economic" migrants leave home not only for the money but also for "freedom" and "adventure": migration to them is a way to break loose from the shackles of their native community and find their own destiny elsewhere.

This cultural approach to migration does not ask what migration does, how it comes about, or how it is structured, but is concerned with how migratory experiences are tied into the web of ongoing discourses of belonging, separation, and achievement. The anthropological input makes it possible again to look at migration as a phenomenon worth while studying in its own right rather than just as an adjunct of, say, the inequalities of the world economic system, modernization, or simply the workings of the national or international labour market. This is well illustrated by Mette Thunø's chapter. It has by now become commonplace to acknowledge the importance of chain migration and backward and forward linkages that direct and perpetuate migratory flows. Yet this structural logic of migration is reinforced by an equally important *cultural* logic of migration (Pieke 1992, 1998). In home communities such as those in Zhejiang or Hong Kong's New Territories, emigration is about as natural as breathing. For generations, young males (and increasingly females) have done nothing but follow in their parents' footsteps to areas often a continent away. Chain migration is not simply a matter of the superior opportunities provided by the chain; even more importantly, a powerful local culture of migration, or *habitus* as Thunø following Bourdieu prefers to call it, steers all but the most independent of mind toward the promised land.[10]

Yet discursive practices inform migratory experiences even where anything but a culture of migration is present. Nora Sausmikat reminds us that migration is an experience that often has a profound biographical impact. The migratory experiences of youths sent down to the countryside during the Cultural Revolution were cause for great personal anxiety and introspection. Migration is an emotionally charged event. Ultimately, it is through these powerful emotions, which colour the experiences of separation and reunion, that people (re)constitute both their selves as migrants and the communities that they belong to. In my opinion, these discursive practices that are part of *all* types of migration receive insufficient attention in studies that focus on the structural or systemic aspects of migration.

The importance of shared migratory experiences should, however, not lead us to believe that these experiences always create or reinforce bonds between people. The experiences of send down youths continue to alienate them from society as much as they integrate them into networks of people with similar experiences. A similar argument can no doubt be made for many other migrants: a lack of integration in mainstream society is often a matter of conscious choice rather than the result of majority exclusion. On the other hand, many people actively resist bonding with fellow migrants. They find the demands of a tight knit network of fellow migrants oppressive, feeling that these people are mired in exactly that conservative past that they themselves have escaped through migration.

Many different discursive practices inform experiences of mobility. Charles Stafford shows how the identification with a certain place (village, house) is discursively constructed through the large and small rites of separation and reunion that punctuate individual lives from the earliest childhood on. Through Stafford's micro-analysis, we are in a better position to appreciate the strength of the Chinese ideology of territorial ties that resurfaces in the frequent recollection by overseas Chinese of separation from one's native place and the hardships suffered while abroad in an alien land. By recounting these (partially imagined) common experiences, ties among migrants and with the home community are reinforced and an imagined transnational community of fellow villagers is perpetuated. Similarly, Chinese governments and opposition movements frequently (and often literally) cash in on the same discourse of separation and exile to re-incorporate overseas Chinese communities into the Chinese nation (Duara 1997; Nyíri, this volume; Pieke 1998). Intriguingly, the Chinese concept of the perpetual territorial bond (*guxiang*) is used to imagine deterritorialized communities.

In this section I have attempted to create a framework for the analysis of the importance of migration as one aspect of social practices. I concluded that the importance of the fact that people change residence can by no means be assumed; its relevance within specific migration configurations has to be assessed on a case by case basis. The bare fact of spatial mobility by itself explains little about the specific structure of migration systems. However, mobility recaptures centre place in the analysis of discursive practices that both inform and follow from changes of residency.

While not providing a watertight solution to all problems of migration studies, my two pronged approach goes at least some way in reaching a more comprehensive assessment of migratory experiences. I suggest that future research should, at least for the time being, abandon its focus on migration as the core variable. Instead, we should, as a first step, construct a typology of migration configurations that each produce different types of ethnicity, employment, entrepreneurship, impact on home communities, migration culture, and cultural meaning of migration. Each type should then be studied in isolation from the others as a unique social configuration.[11]

The new typology I have in mind is likely to cut across the established distinctions between, for instance, commuting, circulation and migration, sojourning and settling, legal and illegal migration, or, as I have shown in this introduction, internal and international migration. The articles in this book suggest several of these new types. Transnational communities of fully specialized middleman minorities, such as the Zhejiang Chinese, are one obvious candidate. For this type of migration configurations the term diaspora would be appropriate in those cases where a discourse of exile and return to the homeland are especially prevalent (Cohen 1997). Another category of migration configurations could be that of privileged, highly qualified workers such as hukou migrants in Tibet or Western and Japanese expatriates in Beijing. The active recruitment by governments or companies of an ethnically distinct underclass of labourers who are (initially at least) denied the full rights of citizenship could be yet another type of migration, which subsumes phenomena as diverse as the 18th and nineteenth century slave trade and subsequent trade in indentured labour from China and India, contracted work teams in China both before and after 1949, and Mediterranean guest workers in Western Europe in the 1960s and 1970s.

The existence of independent migration configurations and the limited role of mobility could be a solution of the conundrum of migration theory. In the words of Massey and his collaborators:

> Our systematic review of empirical studies of international migration in the North American system has produced little substantial evidence that would lead to the rejection of any of the theoretical models I have surveyed. On the contrary, each model

received at least some empirical support, suggesting that each theory captures an element of truth. (Massey et al. 1994:738–9).

So far so good. The solution offered to this paradox on the pages that follow is however less convincing. Massey et al. propose an integrated and global approach to migration, set in motion by "[t]he penetration of markets into peripheral nations [that] disrupts noncapitalist modes of social and economic organization and causes widespread labor displace-ment, creating a mobile population" (p. 740). This in turn sets in motion processes that lead to dual labour markets, the rise of core global cities and peripheral backwaters, the growth of migration chains, cultures of migration, the creation of ethnic economic niches, and other processes summarized as the cumulative causation of migration.

Quite apart from the fact that this reconstruction is historically and anthropologically uninformed (how does one account for migrations that took place in societies before the penetration of markets?), it is flawed in that it treats migration as a unitary phenomenon, rather than just one aspect of a whole range of migration configurations. Many theories of migration are all true not because of the multifacetous nature of migration, but because many different social configurations impel people to change residence. One theory describes a certain range of such configurations (or even just a specific stage of the development of such a configuration), but has little (or perhaps nothing at all) to say about other such configurations that are better explained by other theories. The challenge ahead is to determine which theories apply best to which configurations, rather than trying to force all types of migration and migration theories into a single Procrustean mould.

Policies and policy making

From my discussion of the relevance of migration as an analytical concept follow a couple of recommendations for policy making. Most generally stated, migration can be the corollary of many qualitatively different configurations, and a unitary set of policies regarding immigrants, emigrants and overseas nationals is therefore unwarranted. One obvious example that comes to mind are the British restrictions of Hong Kong immigration during the countdown to the 1997 handover, which were to the detriment of the British economy. They confused the "astronaut" migration of Hong Kong's upper and middle classes with traditional chain migration form Hong Kong's New Territories or the mass exodus of working class residents from other, much poorer former colonies. Similarly, chain migration from fully specialized home communities cannot be brought to a permanent halt by migration restrictions, but only – and at great cost – be slowed down and forced into illegality. Temporary circulation or permanent immigration of contract labourers, on the other hand, can probably be effectively halted by sufficiently raising the cost and risk of immigration and employment. However, not the individual circulatory migrant, but the organizations that facilitate their migration and the employers that hire them should be targeted in order to have any chance of success.

For the government of the People's Republic of China my approach can also be translated into a couple of recommendations. In general, one of the great dangers and weaknesses of the current regime in China is that it is not taking the migrant population seriously. Migrants are still mainly considered a nuisance rather than a normal component of any society, traditional or modern. The state thus does not give itself the ideological and policy space to tie migrants back into mainstream society. Caroline Hoy in her chapter shows that this has led to the embarrassing situation that the Beijing city authorities have to rely on the governments of migrants' areas of origin to enforce such a basic policy as birth control.

Migration in China, as elsewhere, is extremely heterogeneous. Cracking down on individual migrants or migrants' contract work may temporarily have the desired effect of ridding the cities of their "super-fluous" people, but cannot hope to bring a permanent solution. Instead, it would be wiser to pass on the costs of infrastructural investment needed to accommodate them to the migrants themselves and the organizations that facilitate their migration. There are signs that is already happening: China's larger municipalities charge hefty fees for the issuance of a temporary or permanent residency permit with the explicit objective to weed out the undesired migrants from the desired ones.[12] Other policy instruments may however also be made to bear on this issue, such as taxation of agent and middleman fees or the wages of individual migrants.

In the final analysis, however, the choice of policy instruments hinges on the type of migration that is involved.

Xiang Biao's section on Beijing government's failed attempts to control the Zhejiang Village illustrate that this community of specialized chain migrants cannot be controlled through periodic crackdowns. Yet in designing policy instruments to come to grips with such communities, the PRC government is well-advised *not* to look first to western concepts such as multiculturalism. The PRC's own overseas Chinese experience (exemplified by Nyiri's description of the Chinese community in Hungary) may provide valuable clues how the authorities, through measured and conditional endorsement and support, can coopt the elite of seemingly intransigent migrant communities in a flexible and often highly effective way.

Ultimately, the Chinese state's problem with migrants must be traced back to the inability of China's bureaucratized system of administration and control to keep up with the changes wrought by the reforms. Groups like migrants that position themselves outside the formal bureaucratic structure simply cannot be governed using the old instruments of bureaucratic supervision and control. Yet the Chinese authorities, especially at the national level, are curiously unwilling to try out other, less direct instruments.[13]

The main reason that the PRC authorities are a lot more sophisticated in their dealings with overseas Chinese communities than with the migrant communities back home appears to be that abroad the Chinese state cannot possible hope to achieve a monopoly of state power, but competes with Taiwan, Hong Kong and, most importantly, with the local national governments. Such arenas of what I propose to call *multicentred state power* goes quite far in explaining the organizational and discursive complexity of overseas Chinese communities and politics. Yet Chinese cities are perhaps not all that different. As mentioned before, Caroline Hoy demonstrated how the Beijing government needed to enlist the cooperation of the government of the home area of migrants to enforce the birth control policy. Similarly, both Victor Yuan and Xiang Biao illustrate the active interest that governments of emigration areas take in migration and migrant communities. As many China scholars have commented, China's political system is decentralizing rapidly. Yet the data presented by Hoy, Xiang and Yuan show that decentralization does not necessarily lead to the imminent break-up of China. Quite on the contrary, it has spawned new forms of political integration that make cities and other localities arenas for multicentred state power. One result of this has been that migrant communities – and especially their elites – are nowadays as "amphibious", i.e. rooted as much in the area of origin as in the area of destination, as they were during the Ming dynasty (1368–1644) and Qing dynasty (1644–1911; Strand 1995:401–3; see also Mote 1978:101–19; Rowe 1990:81).[14] Apart from their own overseas Chinese policies, the Chinese authorities are therefore well advised also to look at late imperial ways of dealing with urban elites, which combined a reliance on a considerable degree of self-government with government recognition of professional organizations (Strand 1995:412–3). Chinese cities have (again) become extremely heterogeneous social spaces that cannot be run in a unified top-down fashion. Until the Chinese authorities come to terms with this, they will find the problem of migration elusive.

On this point I would also like to take issue with Dorothy Solinger, who in an otherwise excellent article on Chinese migration concludes that assimilation of migrants would ultimately be the best solution, although admittedly a difficult one in the current context (Solinger 1995). While arguably providing a desirable solution in the long term, successful assimilation seems impossible to achieve in the short or medium term, given the current unequal access to resources, power, and privileges. A more practicable policy objective would therefore be a Chinese-style accommodation between the differences and conflicting interests between migrants and non-migrants. This could be done by acknowledging that immigrant communities are a permanent feature of urban life and integrating them *as communities* into a new urban polity. Immigrant associations, in cooperation with the governments of the areas of origin, should be officially recognized – under the condition that they conform to certain standards of internal democracy and transparency of administration – by the government of the area of destination. They should also be given the freedom to manage the affairs of their community as long as they stay within the law. For purposes of coordination, supervision and taxation, these associations should become members of an overarching organization, not unlike a Chinese Chamber of Commerce in overseas Chinese communities or pre-1949 cities, that regularly meets with representatives of the local administration. This model thus envisages a blend of the old and the new. Combining multicentred state power with the hierarchical socialist bureaucracy, and the necessity of supervision and control with the need for autonomy and self-government, this could be a workable compromise for all parties involved.[15]

References

Banks, Marcus. 1992. *Organizing Jainism in India and England*. Oxford: Clarendon Press.

Banks, Marcus. 1994. "Why Move? Regional and Long Distance Migrations of Gujarati Jains." In Judith M. Brown and Rosemary Foot, eds, *Migration: The Asian Experience*. Basingstoke: Macmillan in association with St Antony's College, Oxford, pp. 131–48.

Boyd, Monica. 1989. "Family and Personal Networks in International Migration: Recent Developments and New Agendas." *International Migration Review* 23, no. 3, pp. 638–70.

Clarke, Graham. 1994. "The Movement of Population to the West of China: Tibet and Qinghai." In Judith M. Brown and Rosemary Foot, eds, *Migration: The Asian Experience*. Basingstoke: Macmillan in association with St Antony's College, Oxford, pp. 221–57.

Cohen, Robin. 1997. "Diasporas, the Nation-State, and Globalisation." In Wang Gungwu, ed. *Global History and Migrations*. Boulder, Colorado: Westview Press, 1997, pp. 117–43.

Crissman, Lawrence W. 1967. "The Segmentary Structure of Urban Overseas Chinese Communities." *Man* n.s. 2, no. 2, pp. 185–204.

De Tinguy, Anne. 1998. "Chinese Immigration to Russia: A Variation on an Old Theme." In Gregor Benton and Frank N. Pieke, eds, *The Chinese in Europe*. Basingstoke: Macmillan, 1998, pp. 301–19.

Eades, Jeremy. 1987. "Anthropologists and Migrants: Changing Models and Realities." In Jeremy Eades, ed. *Migrants, Workers, and the Social Order*. ASA Monographs 26. London: Tavistock, pp. 1–16.

Eades, J.S. 1993. *Strangers and Traders: Yoruba Migrants, Markets and the State in Northern Ghana*. Edinburgh: Edinburgh University Press for the International African Institute, London.

Fawcett, James T. 1989. "Networks, Linkages, and Migration Systems." *International Migration Review* 23, no. 3, pp. 671–80.

Gallin, Bernard and Rita S. Gallin. 1974. "The Integration of Village Migrants in Taipei." In Mark Elvin and G. William Skinner, eds, *The Chinese City between Two Worlds*. Stanford: Stanford University Press, pp. 331–50.

Hamilton, Gary G. 1977. "Ethnicity and Regionalism: Some Factors Influencing Chinese Identities in Southeast Asia." *Ethnicity* 4, pp. 337–51.

Liu, Xin. 1997. "Space, Mobility, and Flexibility: Chinese Villagers and Scholars Negotiate Power at Home and Abroad." In Aihwa Ong and Donald Nonini, eds, *Ungrounded Empires: The Cultural Politics of Modern Chinese Transnationalism.* New York: Routledge, pp. 91–114.

Ma, Rong. 1991. "Han and Tibetan Residential Patterns in Lhasa." *The China Quarterly* 128, pp. 814–35.

Mabogunje, Akin. 1970. "Systems Approach to a Theory of Rural-urban Migration." *Geographical Analysis* 2, no. 1, pp. 1–17.

Massey, Douglas S., Joaquín Arango, Graeme Hugo, Ali Kouaouci, Adela Pellegrino and J. Edward Taylor. 1993. "Theories of International Migration: A Review and Appraisal." *Population and Development Review* 19, no. 3, pp. 431–66.

Massey, Douglas S., Joaquín Arango, Graeme Hugo, Ali Kouaouci, Adela Pellegrino and J. Edward Taylor. 1994. "An Evaluation of International Migration Theory: The North American Case." *Population and Development Review* 20, no. 4, pp. 699–751.

Mote, F.W. 1978. "The Transformation of Nanking, 1350–1400." In G. William Skinner, ed. *The City in Late Imperial China*. Stanford: Stanford University Press, pp. 101–53.

Ong, Aihwa and Donald Nonini, eds. 1996. *The Cultural Politics of Modern Chinese Transnationalism*. New York: Routledge.

Patterson, Orlando. 1975. "Context and Choice in Ethnic Allegiance: A Theoretical Framework and Carribean Case Study." In N. Glazer and D.P. Moynihan, eds, *Ethnicity: Theory and Experience*. Cambridge, Mass.: Harvard University Press, pp. 305–49.

Parkin, David. 1974. "Congregational and Interpersonal Ideologies in Political Ethnicity." In Abner Cohen, ed. *Urban Ethnicity*. ASA Monograph no. 12. London: Tavistock, pp. 119–57.

Pieke, Frank N. 1996. *The Ordinary and the Extraordinary: An Anthropological Study of Chinese Reform and the 1989 People's Movement in Beijing*. London: Kegan Paul International.

Pieke, Frank N. 1998. "Introduction." In Gregor Benton and Frank N. Pieke, eds, *The Chinese in Europe*. Basingstoke: Macmillan, pp. 1–17.

Redding, S. Gordon. 1993. *The Spirit of Chinese Capitalism*. Berlin: Walter de Gruyter.

Rowe, William T. 1990. "Success Stories: Lineage and Elite Status in Hanyang County, Hubei, c. 1368–1949." In Joseph W. Esherick and Mary Backus Rankin, eds, *Chinese Local Elites and Patterns of Dominance*. Berkeley: University of California Press, pp. 51–81.

Skeldon, Ronald. 1994. "Reluctant Exiles or Bold Pioneers: An Introduction to Migration from Hong Kong." In Ronald Skeldon, ed. *Reluctant Exiles? Migration from Hong Kong and the New Overseas Chinese*. Armonk, N.Y.: M.E. Sharpe, pp. 3–18.

Skeldon, Ronald. 1994. "Hong Kong in an International Migration System." In Ronald Skeldon, ed. *Reluctant Exiles? Migration from Hong Kong and the New Overseas Chinese*. Armonk, N.Y.: M.E. Sharpe, pp. 21–51.

Skeldon, Ronald. 1996. "Migration from China." *Journal of International Affairs* 49, no. 2, pp. 434–55.

Skeldon, Ronald. 1997. *Migration and Development: A Global Perspective*. London: Belhaven Press.

Solinger, Dorothy. 1995. "The Floating Population in the Cities: Chances for Assimilation?" In Deborah S. Davis, Richard Kraus, Barry Naughton and Elizabeth Perry, eds, *Urban spaces in Contemporary China: The Potential for Autonomy and Community in Post-Mao China*. Cambridge: Woodrow Wilson Center Press and Cambridge University Press, pp. 113–39.

Strand, David. 1995. "Conclusion: Historical Perspectives." In Deborah S. Davis, Richard Kraus, Barry Naughton and Elizabeth Perry, eds, *Urban spaces in Contemporary China: The Potential for Autonomy and Community in Post-Mao China*. Cambridge: Woodrow Wilson Center Press and Cambridge University Press, pp. 394–426.

Thompson, Richard H. 1980. "From Kinship to Class: A New Model of Urban Overseas Chinese Social Organization." *Urban Anthropology* 9, no. 3, pp. 265–93.

Thunø, Mette. 1997. Chinese Migration to Denmark: Catering and Ethnicity. Unpublished Ph.D. dissertation, Department of Asian Studies, University of Copenhagen.

Thunø, Mette. 1998. "Chinese in Denmark." In Gregor Benton and Frank N. Pieke, eds, *The Chinese in Europe*. Basingstoke: Macmillan, pp. 168–96.

Voets, S.Y. and J.J. Schoorl. 1988. "Appendix 1: Deelonderzoek demografie" [Appendix 1: Research project demography]. In Frank N. Pieke, *De positie van de Chinezen in Nederland* [The position of the Chinese in the Netherlands]. Leiden: Documentation and Research Centre for Contemporary China, pp. 157–191. Translated as Peng Ke (Frank N. Pieke), *Helan Huarende Shehui Diwei*. Zhuang Guotu, trans. Taibei: Zhongyang Yanjiuyuan Jindaishi Yanjiusuo, 1992, pp. 179–222.

Watson, James L. "Restaurants and Remittances: Chinese Emigrant Workers in London." In George M. Foster and Robert V. Kemper, eds, *Anthropologists in Cities*. Boston: Little, Brown and Company, pp. 201–22.

Watson, James. 1975. *Emigration and the Chinese Lineage: The Mans in Hong Kong and London*. Berkeley: University of California Press.

Watson, James L. 1977a. "The Chinese: Hong Kong Villagers in the British Catering Trade." In James L. Watson, ed. *Between Two Cultures*. Oxford: Basil Blackwell, pp. 181–213.

Watson, James L. 1977b. "Chinese Emigrant Ties to the Home Community." *New Community* 5, no. 4, pp. 343–52.

Weiner, Myron. 1997. "The Global Migration Crisis." In Wang Gungwu, ed. *Global History and Migrations*. Boulder, Colorado: Westview Press, 1997, pp. 95–115.

White, Lynn T. 1994. "Migration and Politics on the Shanghai Delta." *Issues & Studies* 30, no. 9, pp. 63–94.

Woolf, Stuart. 1989. "Statistics and the Modern State." *Comparative Studies in Society and History* 31, no.3, pp. 588–604.

Yin, Alexander Chien-chung. 1981. "Voluntary Associations and Rural-Urban Migration." In Emily Martin Ahern and Hill Gates, eds, *The Anthropology of Chinese Society*. Stanford: Stanford University Press, pp. 319–37.

Zlotnik, Hania. 1992. "Empirical Identification of International Migration Systems." In Mary M. Kritz, Lin Lean Lim and Hania Zlotnik, eds, *International Migration Systems: A Global Approach*. Oxford: Clarendon Press, pp. 19–40.

Notes

1 Intriguingly, this assessment is shared by scholars who otherwise are in diametrically opposite camps, ranging from virulent postmodernists such Ong and Nonini (1996) to the critical Confucianist Tu Wei-ming (1994) and proponents of culturalist explanations of economic success such as Gordon Redding (1990).

2 The workshop was made possible by financial support from the Asia Committee of the European Science Foundation, the Davis Fund for Chinese Studies of the University of Oxford and the Universities' China Committee in London.

3 The term "spill-over" is chosen here to highlight the fact that these international migrants are drawn from the same social strata and migrate for essentially the same reasons as their domestic counterparts. These internal and international migration flows can be thought of as constituting one migration configuration (see section 4 below). I do not wish to imply that this international migration flow is fully identical to internal flows. Distance, immigration restrictions, cultural and linguistic barriers present the international migrant with some specific challenges that internal migrants only have to face to a lesser degree.

4 Lynn T. White (1994) similarly concludes that migration to Shanghai recommenced in the early 1970s.

5 For Dutch data, see Voets and Schoorl 1988:162–4.

6 See Scharping, this volume for an overview of this debate.

7 This is qualified but not fundamentally discarded by the so-called new economics of migration (see Massey et al. 1993 pp. 436–40 and 457–8).

8 For an authoritative overview and assessment of the main theories of migration, see Massey et al. 1993 and 1994.

9 Conversely, a migration configuration may be part of several migration systems. The fact that migrants from one particular village live both in Europe and in the US will probably be irrelevant to the analyst who is interested in either the North American or the European migration system.

10 By no means do I make the claim to have invented the term culture of migration (see Massey et al. 1993:452–3). What I do believe that is new here, is that the culture of migration to us is an aspect of the cultural, social psychological, and discursive processes that make migration a form of human social action rather than a mechanical act.

11 While constructing this typology, or applying it to different empirical cases, we should be aware that even in a single village several distinct types of migration configurations may be present. For a Chinese case, see Gallin and Gallin 1974, p. 349.

12 Interviews in Shanghai, September 1996 and Zhongguo Qingnian Bao 15 April 1997, p. 7.

13 I have written extensively about this in the context of urban reform in the late 1980s and the Chinese government's inability to deal with the 1989 People's Movement in any other way than forcible suppression (Pieke 1996, chapters 4 and 6).

14 The similarities between contemporary and pre-1949 Chinese migrant communities are real and important. We should, however, be careful not to extend this comparison too far. In the past, elites were amphibious and largely autonomous because of a *lack* of state presence both in the cities and in the country; nowadays, migrant communities and their elites benefit from what is almost an oversupply of multicentred state power.

15 On this point we have to note here that migrants' associations either function as the interface between a group and the state, as we envisage here, or else to defend this group against threats by competitors or the state. Simply condoning associations is therefore not enough, as this can easily backfire when the state is seen as repressive or predatory. Alexander Yin (1981:331), for instance, shows that a migrant association in Gaoxiong, Taiwan, during the Japanese period was founded to defend the group against the Japanese police. His description of the Penghu migrant community in Gaoxiong is also instructive in comparison with the Zhejiang Village in Beijing, especially the former's role in election vote canvassing that foreshadows what can happen in the PRC if the political system loosens up.

Part I

Chinese internal migration

The "Static" Decades: Inter-provincial migration in Pre-Reform China

Diana Lary

Introduction

A general assumption behind the interest in the current waves of migration in China is that it is an unprecedented phenomenon, and that virtually no migration took place in China between the communist victory in 1949 and the start of reforms in the late 1970s. This assumption is true in the case of international migration, but it is not true of migration within China. Millions of people migrated during those three decades, and for a host of different reasons.

The impact of these earlier migrations on the current movements has not adequately been assessed, and yet it must be there. The current migration is not simply a "natural" consequence of economic development, a mechanical reenactment of the migrations that accompanied early industrialization in Europe, when peasants moved to work in the new factories, having previously been rooted in their villages. Without denying that this upsurge in migration is directly linked to the economic boom of the 1980s and 1990s, I would like to highlight some of its historical connections with prior migrations.

Antecedents

There are two sets of antecedents to the present migrations. In terms of labour migration, present migration is a return to interrupted internal migration flows, which started in the late Qing (1644–1911), to the coastal cities and to Manchuria.[1] Over several decades, millions of peasants moved in temporary and permanent migrations to the new cities and to the empty lands of Manchuria. Shandong, a populous, poor province in Northeast China, supplied the largest number of migrants, both to the cities and to

Manchuria[2] Some of the migrants were recruited directly by Chinese and foreign companies who wished to employ them, others were recruited by labour bosses as contract workers. Both forms of recruitment involved highly localized recruitment, and strong personal ties in recruitment.

The present migration continues many of the practices associated with those migrations, such as temporary contract labour and recruitment through personal connections. The main purpose of migration was to earn money, to be paid in remittances to families at home. There were strong elements of chain migration, the process in which prior migration creates further migration through the establishment of migration chains, lines of personal connections along which later migrants move to join former migrants (Lary 1997).

The second set of antecedents comes from the pre-reform period of Communist China, the period in which migration was restricted and controlled and yet millions of people moved.[3] Many of the people who moved during the restricted period did so involuntarily, or for reasons they later regretted, and the migrations tended to produce scars and resentments (Sausmikat, this volume). The parents of the present generation of migrants who were migrants themselves, or know people who moved, must have passed on less than enthusiastic, or actually negative accounts of their experiences, especially of moving to the border regions. This has created an antipathy to movement in those directions. On the other hand the fact that the cities were off limits to peasants after the Great Leap Forward (1958–1961) gave them an allure that only forbidden places can exercise.

These two pressures, one repelling and one attractive, have helped to fuel the return to movements, which are explicitly short term, involve overwhelmingly young people and whose economic stimulus is to provide money for the family at home. The present migrations are just as much a repudiation of the types of migration which occurred in the "static decades" as they are a return to pre-Communist patterns of migration.

The long period of controlled and restricted migration also helped to inject a sense of urgency in the present migration. After three decades of restrictions, many feel it is essential to move now, when it is possible, against the possibility that restrictions will be reimposed. One notable example of this desire to seize the opportunity while it is there is the "fever to go abroad" (*chuguo re*), which since the early 1980s has gripped many young Chinese. The young people who have left China over the past fifteen years have been spurred to do so by the knowledge that for three decades their parents could not go abroad.

The "static" decades

We now turn to look at the migrations that did occur during the three "static" decades between 1949 to 1978. The most visible migrations were driven less by pragmatic economic concerns than by the ideological beliefs of China's leaders and the policies that those beliefs produced. Many of these policies were designed to promote rapid economic growth through state planning. Because these migrations were often involuntary, because many of them caused hardship to the migrants and because many of them failed, they have come to be seen as embarrassments at best, and disasters at worst. These perceptions lie behind the impression that "true" migration only started after 1978.

We should not accept that this hindsight is completely accurate. At the time, many of these migrations were presented as epic, heroic movements, designed to transform man and nature. They were accompanied by the kind of high flown hyperbole often associated with migrations, whether the exodus from Egypt or the search for democracy and liberty in the USA. Their participants started out filled with appropriate exhilaration.

Other movements in the "static decades" were more sober, being the implementation of the idea, which had been current in China since the 1920s and 1930s, that China's population problems could only be solved by moving large numbers of people out of densely settled areas into underpopulated regions. Others still were voluntary or spontaneous, proof that the individuals and groups could still find ways to move, and that the control of the state was not as absolute as it seemed.

One animating idea of state initiated migration was the desire to erase the stigma of shame attached to migration in the late Qing and the Republic (1911–1949). China's international export of coolie labour had come to be seen as a deep humiliation, which had to end. The flight from China around the Communist takeover was seen as desertion or treachery. Both kinds of international migration had to stop. Within China, the chaotic movement of migrants into the cities and to Manchuria, and the refugee movements of wartime were all seen as manifestations of a people without leadership or self-respect. This chaotic milling about was also to stop. The sociologist Fei Xiaotong was one of the many Chinese intellectuals who saw the outmigration of peasants as a tragedy, a sign of rural crisis and a process which could never resolve rural China's fundamental problems (Fei 1946: 40–2).

Pre-1949 migrants were seen as victims of imperialism and feudalism, forced to migrate by poverty, torn away from their proper place, their home. Ironically for a revolutionary government, this distaste for migration revived the traditional view of migration, that none ever willingly left home, and that people who did leave were mere sojourners expecting to return home. Formal steps to limit migration were not taken immediately after 1949; in fact the *hukou* (household registration) regulations which required people to stay at home, unless they were given explicit permission to move, did not come in to full force until the early 1960s (Chan, this volume).

The Communists believed that in a planned society migration, like other aspects of life, should only take place if it was officially sanctioned. Only those, whom the state needed to be away from their homes, should migrate; everyone else should stay at home. The migrations that received formal approval were cloaked in a revolutionary guise, of serving socialism wherever the state demanded. This format appealed to lofty principles, and encouraged idealistic and zealous believers in socialism to move. Other forms of migration were restricted. Economic concerns within migration were those which fulfilled state goals; other economic concerns were submerged.

Migration restrictions did not mean the end of migration. In fact a great number of people did move, though their numbers are dwarfed by current movements. According to People's Republic of China (PRC, 1949–present) statistics, in the period from 1949 to 1978 twenty-five to thirty million people moved between provinces and changed their hukou (Peng 1992:422). If intra-provincial migrations, short term movements without hukou change and unofficial migrations are included, then the figures leap up. One authoritative source estimates that at the highest point of migration, between 1958 and 1960, thirty-two million people migrated annually, or a rate of forty-nine per thousand (Wei 1988:60). The full scale of the migrations is impossible to state, since the actual numbers cannot be pinned down, but this imprecision does not lessen the size of the migrations. What is more significant is that the scale was not revealed at the time. The present growth in migration has to be seen in the context of its predecessors, that is, not only as absolute growth, but also as growth in visibility; we now see what was once hidden.

The sources of migrants were clearly differentiated in the "static" years between urban and rural migrants. The urban population moved principally at the behest of the state, as willing or involuntary participants in projects of socialist construction. Increasingly tight controls restricted and eventually prevented spontaneous movement. Peasants were less restricted. Though it became more difficult over time, and eventually impossible, for them to move into the cities, movement from one rural area to another was much easier. Some peasant migrations were involuntary, others state sponsored but with an element of choice, and a great number spontaneous.

Looked at in hindsight, many of the migrations which took place during the "static" decades made little economic sense. The commandist policies of which the migrations were part were often misguided and often wasted precious human, material and financial resources. The policies caused hardship both to the migrants and to their families; their starkest contrast with earlier migrations, and with contemporary migrations, is that they did not yield remittances to the migrants' families, the classic stimulus for migration. The bad experiences of many migrants gave a new negative image to migration, which derived from the use of migration as a means of fulfilling state goals which overrode the interests of the migrants.

Many of the migrations were painful. People were thrown without preparation into new environments, separated from family and friends. The most painful aspect is that many of the migrations were conceived by the authorities as permanent, life sentences which gave migrants no hope of returning. Though this was not necessarily the actual outcome, the desolation of permanent separation is one of the most acute memories for those who moved. The literature of scars which describes the experiences of the Cultural Revolution is full of stories of the horrors of migrations which seemed at the time to be banishments (Sausmikat, this volume).

Stages of migration

In the first few years after they took over, the Communists had to organize various migrations of relocation, which involved great numbers of people. Refugees had to be resettled, who were displaced either directly by the Civil War between the Communists and the Nationalists between 1947 and 1949, or indirectly by the ensuing economic collapse in the developed areas of China. Workers who had left economic hardship in Manchuria after the Japanese collapse had to be got back to get the economy going again. Huge numbers of demobilized soldiers had to be resettled, both the victorious Communist troops and defeated GMD troops.

There was also a major transfer of officials and cadres from North to South (*nanxia*), a response both to the need to find jobs for revolutionary loyalists, and to bring the turbulent southern provinces under the control of loyal cadres. Northern cadres, old revolutionaries and soldiers, followed the victorious armies southwards and took over key bureaucratic positions. This movement was in effect a new version of the imperial law of avoidance, which stipulated that officials might never serve in their native provinces, but with a variation. It was a one-way movement; there was no parallel northern transfer (*beishang*) that had occurred in 1928, when Southerners who supported the Guomindang moved into important positions in Nanjing and in northern provinces.

Altogether about 130,000 cadres were appointed in this way. (Shen and Tong 1992:149–50). Over twenty thousand people were sent into Guangdong between 1949 and 1952, at the behest of the Party Central Committee, to take up "important" jobs at the provincial, district and county level; about half of them were demobilized soldiers, the other half civilians. They were there to deal with a "complicated political atmosphere" (Peng 1992:158). "Complicated" meant the presence of Guomindang remnants and local guerillas; more generally it meant governing a people who had not been under a strong central government since the Qing dynasty. Other southern provinces were given similar treatment. Seven thousand northern cadres were transferred to Yunnan, most of them to hold high and middle level administrative positions (Zou 1990:207). Guizhou got eight thousand, also destined for high positions within the province (Pan 1988:171).

As the resettlement migrations were winding down, another migration was getting under way, not planned by the government. Peasants were pouring into the cities. Kam Wing Chan discusses the huge movements of peasants into the cities and back again to the rural areas; he estimates urbanization and counter flows at 186 million between 1952 and 1978, of which seventy million was net rural to urban (Chan 1989:366). The flood of peasants into the cities was an ideological problem for the Communist leadership, whose development strategy was posited on rural revolution, on bringing a better life to peasants; this did not mean letting them run away to the cities. These rural to urban migrations became even less tenable with the start of the Great Leap Forward, whose aim was to transform the rural areas into productive, cheerful places; there could be no reason for peasants to leave rural paradises. The ideological thrust of the Leap, coupled with the sheer size of the rural to urban migrations, were the stimuli for increasing restrictions on migration to the cities, which helped to bring the full hukou system into being by the late 1950s.

The migrations that took place from the start of the First Five Year Plan (1953–1957) to the end of the Great Leap Forward (1958–1961) are the ones which bear most strongly the imprint of policies of socialist transformation, of the attempts to engineer a new society. This period was followed by the "bad years" of the latter stages of the Great Leap Forward or "Second Leap" (1960–1961) and the period of recovery (1962–1965), which were characterized by refugee migrations, forced departures of people who could not be fed in a given area and return migrations of people who had settled earlier in stricken regions. The "Second Leap" and the recovery were followed by the turmoil of the Cultural Revolution (1966–1976) that led to a new upsurge in forced migration.

Each of these periods produced its own characteristic migrations, though there were always regional variations which cut across periods. These migrations will be discussed under separate headings. In many cases, these are categories used in Chinese statistical compilations; we follow these categories for convenience, though always with the awareness that some are arbitrary, and that many migrations straddled two categories or more. We also add some categories that do not occur in official statistics, namely punishment migrations and flight migrations.

These were often huge migrations, involving millions of people, many of them organized by the government, some involuntary, some made voluntarily but without sober consideration. "Without sober consideration" refers to the people animated by idealism, persuaded by political propaganda, who moved because they truly believed they would be serving socialism to do so. Their enthusiasm and their often unrealistic expectations is a characteristic of many migrations, internal or international, and is often essential to a migration: without some such enthusiasm most people would stay at home. The regret that often followed the idealistic young migrants in China was the not unlike the disappointment felt by the many Europeans, who failed to find the promised land in America.

Migration to Strengthen the Borders

One of the dominant forms of migration promoted by the Communist government was relocation to the border regions, the strengthening of the borders (*zhiyuan bianqiang*). This policy was not initially based on fears of invasion. Until the early 1960s, China did not see settling the borders as an issue of national defence, since most of the lands to be settled bordered the fraternal Soviet Union. The stress was on bringing new land into cultivation, opening up the wilderness, and at the same time solving China's population problem by redistributing people. A second objective, not stated publicly, was to weaken the possibility of minority agitation by diluting the minority populations with Han settlers.

There was no easy way to get people to go to regions which were regarded as wild and inhospitable. Coercion was not the ideal way to get people to go, and so the movement was glossed with a veneer of patriotism, of service to socialism. Exile was transformed into glorious sacrifice.

The Communist plans to settle China's border lands were not new. Reformers concerned about population pressure had developed plans since the late Qing to populate the Northeast and the Northwest. They saw the adverse effects of having China's huge population concentrated in a small part of the country, and saw massive, utopian advantages in moving people into the empty lands (Peng 1992:477–80). The difference between the two periods was that the reforms of the Nationalist period (1912–1949) stayed on paper. No means were found for turning them into reality.

Border settlement involved a huge movement of people. It peaked in the late 1950s, and petered out in the early 1960s. The Northeastern (Manchurian) borderlands were one of the prime destinations. Between 1949 and 1961, 5.1 million people moved to Heilongjiang: the "Great Northern Waste" (*Beidahuang*), the Daxing'anling Mountains, or the Daqing Oil Fields (Xiong 1989:79). In the second half of the first Five Year Plan a huge scheme was put together by the Ministries of the Interior, Labour, and Agricultural Settlement to relieve overpopulation by settling areas such as the Great Northern Waste. The projects were started by military settlers, who were joined by rural poor from North China, especially Shandong; between 1952 and 1958, eighty-nine per cent of the new settlers came from Shandong (Xiong 1989:155).

Young peasants were given the choice of either migrating and serving socialism by pioneering in the wilderness, or dragging out a pedestrian life at home. Their migrations were a new form of movement, but they had elements of past migrations; in the 1920s and 1930s, millions of Shandong peasants moved to the Northeast to settle on the land.[4] The major difference was that the new generation of migrants were not independent, but were organized by the state.

The Northwest border lands figured almost as large as the Northeast in central plans; they were to be filled up by Han (i.e. non-minority) Chinese from two sources. One was the army, the settlement of demobilized soldiers, both PLA and Guomindang (Li 1989:512). The second source were the overpopulated east coast and the Yangzi Valley. Between 1949 and 1966, over six million people moved to Xinjiang alone, well over half of those between 1953 and 1960. Of those who moved through state organization, many were from the lower Yangzi provinces. (Zhou Chongjing 1990:140). This pairing of origins and destinations followed the pattern of traditional migration flows, such as Shandong/Manchuria and Shanxi/Inner Mongolia.

The migrations to the Northwest borderlands were migrations to non-Han areas; they contributed to dramatic shifts in the ratio of indigenous people (minorities) to Han. Xinjiang's population, for example, went from an almost entirely indigenous population to one in which Han accounted for well over a third of the population. The percentage of Han in the population has gone from seven per cent in 1949 to forty per cent in 1984; eighty-nine per cent of this increase can be attributed to in-migrants and their children (Zhou Chongjing 1990:138). In Inner Mongolia the Han/Mongol ratio rose from 6:1 to 12:1 between 1958 and 1968. Fewer people moved to Tibet, which was protected by its altitude (Heberer 1989:93). The settlement of such vast numbers of Han in the autonomous regions is a telling indicator of what autonomy really means; the authorities of the autonomous regions have no authority over migration, though migration in such numbers is very likely to dilute and even destroy the indigenous cultures (Heberer 1989:97–8).

The plans to settle people in the borderlands did not work out as intended. In the first place, the authorities were not able to attract a high enough calibre of migrants. The migrations did not consist exclusively of planned and organized migrants. In several periods, especially in the early 1960s, organized migrants to Xinjiang were outnumbered by *"zifa"* migrants, that is migrants who moved spontaneously, without official permission. These people were poor peasants from Gansu, Sichuan, Shaanxi and Anhui (Zhou Chongjing 1990 142): not the people who would raise the population of Xinjiang to the desired heights of excellence.

Secondly, the migrants themselves were often disappointed. Among the organized migrants, the conditions for settlement were less idyllic than they had been led to anticipate. Though many people settled permanently, revolutionary hyperbole alone could not make the border regions attractive. The realities of isolation, backwardness, harsh climate and lack of amenities ("civilization"), which had deterred major spontaneous migrations at earlier stages, could not be overcome by zeal alone. Many people would not stay; with or without permission they flocked home. The rate of return migration to one of the largest sending provinces, Shandong, went as high as fifty percent per annum, a figure which probably does not even include all those who came home without permission (Peng 1992:341).

The failures of some of the migrations were due to inadequate planning, the inability of bureaucrats to put a concrete shape to the glowing promises of political leadership. Though migrants were promised better conditions in their new homes, they often arrived to find that few preparations had been made for them. Inadequate provisions made harsh conditions intolerable. The movements were only organized at the departure end; at the reception end little preparation was made. The chains of personal connections, which had made earlier migrations to the Northeast possible by taking care of immediate needs, was not replicated in organized migrations.

There was also recognition that many Han were unwilling to settle permanently away from home. They disliked the natural environment; they detested the cold of the Northeast, feared the high altitude of Tibet and hated the great open spaces of Xinjiang and Inner Mongolia. The indigenous inhabitants did not make them welcome; they understood very well that the migrations were intended in part to weaken their hold over their homelands.

The settlement policies have led to a situation in which Han outnumber minorities in many areas, though this numerical superiority may be deceptive. Settlement does not mean that Han settlers think of themselves as permanently detached from their native provinces; they may think of themselves as exiles.

Relocation for socialist progress

A basic tenet of early socialism in China was that the interests of the collective take precedence over those of the family or individual. As China modernized after 1949, many people found themselves obstructing grand schemes of improvement. They lived in the path of urban and industrial development, in the way of railways, roads and dams. Without legal requirements to go through processes such as formal expropriation and compensation, the new government was able to clear people to make way for progress.

In cities all over China people were moved to allow the building of edifices, squares and roads. Plazas were carved out of city centres, parks created and large public buildings erected. The exceptions were Nanjing and Guangzhou, already improved by Guomindang planners, and Dalian and Changchun, built as expressions of modernity in Japanese imperial style. The total number of people moved for urban improvement is unknown, but was probably not on the scale of people moved to make way for redevelopment since the early 1980s.

The largest group of people moved for the sake of progress were those relocated to make way for dams. Dams were potent symbols of progress; they involved the control of water, and the bending of nature to man's will. Since 1949, 2,500 large and middle-sized dams have been constructed in China, involving the relocation of at least five million people (Peng 1992:408). Local resettlement may not seem like migration, but the uprooting could be as severe as a long range move, and almost always had negative connotations: the loss of housing, good land, extended family support, or graves.

One of the most famous early dams was the Sanmen Dam on the Yellow River. This triumph of engineering was deeply flawed; it silted up almost immediately, but not before 600,000 people had been relocated (Domenach 1995:9–10). The largest dam project, in the Three Gorges on the Yangzi, is still to come; it will dislodge at least a million people.

Shandong, like many other provinces, went through an orgy of dam building. It seemed ideally suited for dams, an arid province plagued with chronic water shortages, and yet with enough hills to make dam building possible. In 1956 and 1957, 27,704 small dams were built. During the Great Leap Forward, the province built 150 large and middle sized dams, and another 5,600 small ones (Dangdai Zhongguo Congshu 1989, volume 1:159 and 181–2). The majority of the displaced population of 1.2 million people were resettled in the immediate locality, though not on good land, since none was available.

Dam building turned out to be an example of the triumph of grandiose ideas over common sense. Dams built without proper planning, and without reference to the history of water supply, were useless. The Ming Tombs Reservoir outside Beijing, on which the elite of the country laboured, has no source of water to fill it. This at least was a neutral outcome, except for those displaced. In other areas the dams caused actual damage. In Shandong some interfered with the water table, and reduced rather than increased the supply of water. Others helped to leach salts and alkalies to the surface, and made once fertile land almost unproductive (Dangdai Zhongguo Congshu 1989, volume 1:182).

Migrations to serve progress had other aspects as well. The government was committed to spreading the intellectual and technical talent of China more evenly than it had been before. Educated youth were relocated through a system which combined the lofty needs of socialist construction with baser forms of preference. This was the state unified job assignment (*guojia tongyi gongzuo fenpei*, or *fenpei*) system. Though its initial intentions were high-minded, based on disinterested ideals, it was susceptible to manipulation. When jobs were assigned to school and college graduates, the more desirable jobs, in the cities, tended to go to young people who had attracted favourable attention from their teachers and had good class backgrounds; the less desirable jobs, away from the cities, went to young people who had either upset their school or university authorities, or had bad class backgrounds. The fear of a bad fenpei exercised enormous control over the behaviour of students, and made recalcitrance or public disagreement a folly which could lead to what in effect amounted to banishment.

Industrial relocation

One of the key parts of the First Five Year Plan was to establish industrial plants inland, to break the dominance of the coastal areas over China's industry, and to allow the interior to benefit from industry. The state financed the construction of new plants, and transferred others, with their workers, to the interior. This policy promised not only greater equity across China in modernity, which was equated directly with degree of industrialization, but it was also to be a triumph over earlier development, which had been so often been initiated by imperialists.

Zhengzhou in Henan province was a chief beneficiary of diversification into the interior. From 1953 to 1957, it was given major investment from the national government to build factories and create its own working class. Skilled workers, especially in the new textile plants, were moved in from Shanghai. Though they were supposed to be the backbone of Henan's proletariat, they tended to remain apart, complaining and petitioning to be sent back to Shanghai (Domenach 1995:8, 21 and 73).

Lanzhou in Gansu province became a petrochemical centre through state investment under the First Five Year Plan. The population of Lanzhou went up from 400,000 in 1953 to 1.2 million in 1959, most of this increase due to immigration. A telling illustration of the impact of immigration is the fact that in the new plants the language spoken was not Lanzhou dialect, but Mandarin (Su 1988:158).

In Inner Mongolia the decision in 1953 to establish the Baotou Iron and Steel Plant brought in every type of migrant, from technical experts to workers, many sent from iron and steel plants in Manchuria (Anshan, Benxi). Baotou, like other new industrial centres, was also given advanced educational institutions to train the next generation of scientists and technicians (Song 1987:170–2).

These vast schemes worked, even if many of the transferred workers and technicians were unhappy. Heavy industry was established in many cities which had had no industry before. It was only after the reforms started in the

39

late 1970s that the artificial nature of the development became apparent. Since then, industrial development, often with foreign investment, over-whelmingly concentrated in the coastal areas of China. These often were the same areas that earlier had been the first to develop in the late Qing.

In the mid-1960s a new policy for moving industrial plants to the interior emerged, this time based not on the principle of equitable distribution, but of providing a strategic reserve in the event of war. In the paranoia which accompanied the Cultural Revolution, fear of foreign (i.e. Soviet or American) invasion spread through the leadership like wildfire. From 1964 until 1971, a huge proportion (in some years over fifty per cent) of national investment budget went into investment on the so-called "Third Front" (*San Xian*) (Naughton 1988:365). Hundreds of thousands, possibly millions, of labourers were moved into the interior provinces of the Southwest and Northwest, some to work on capital construction, others to work in factories which were moved lock, stock and barrel from coastal regions. Yet the Third Front turned out to be largely a waste of time and money (Naughton 1988). It seems to have become an embarrassment to those who authorized or took part in it, and has remained a murky, largely undiscussed chapter in the history of the PRC. The exact numbers of migrants is unknown; the best one can do is piece together a few figures (Shen and Tong 1992:161–5).

Organized Labour Migration

Since the early 1950s, the Ministry of Labour has played a major role in organizing the supply of labour for engineering and construction projects within China, and occasionally abroad. These labourers were not permanent migrants and did not change hukou, though they were often away for long periods. Other labour migrants were people assigned to work in new industrial cities such as Lanzhou.

Recruitment of labourers was concentrated in North China, especially Shandong, the best source of strong, pliant and uncomplaining young men. In this province, the communist government followed a long tradition, going back to the late Qing, when men were sent to Manchuria, Siberia and South Africa. Later Shandong labourers dug trenches in France for the First World War, in a movement organized by Canadian missionaries (Summerskill 1982). In the 1920s and 1930s, millions of people were recruited commercially for Manchuria by Japanese and Chinese firms. Many more moved through the initiative of small scale labour contractors. During the Anti-Japanese War (1937–1945), Japanese occupying forces took millions of Chinese labourers (*huagong*), essentially as slaves, to Manchuria, Korea and Japan.

There was almost no labour migration during the Civil War (1946–1949). In the 1950s, organized labour migration resumed. Over two million people were recruited in Shandong for industrial, mining and transport projects under the First and Second Five Year Plans (1953–1957 and 1958–1962), over four times more than from any other province (Shen and Tong 1992:178).

The chaos of the Cultural Revolution which put paid to many organized activities did not prevent organized migration; millions of workers were moved to the interior under the Third Front policy. From the end of the Third Front in 1971 to the early 1980s there was a lull in the movement of organized labour within China, but then it resumed with full force. This time, the labour migrations were often initiated by provincial and local authorities who saw the new migrations as commercial ventures. Increasingly, supply of labour organized by the authorities has given way or combined with supply organized by private labour contractors – a return to the pre-Communist system (Yuan, this volume).

International export of workers did not flourish after 1949. In the 1950s and early 1960s, there was some recruitment of labour to work in Soviet Bloc countries, but the Sino-Soviet split put an end to these programmes. After the split there was little further overseas movement until the early 1980s. Since then there have been large organized flows; by 1994 there were 174,000 workers abroad organized by the Labour Export Department of the Ministry of Foreign Economic Relations and Trade, generating revenue of 2.050 thousand million US dollars. There are much larger numbers of organized and unorganized labourers working in Far Eastern Russia, mainly from the Northeast (Washington Post 18 May 1994; Agence France Press, 5 June 1994; De Tinguy 1998).

Punishment Migration

The communist state had an unpublicized agenda for migration: punishment by banishing people or by sentencing them to prison camps. The remote border regions were chosen as the ideal destinations for those being so punished.

The practice of banishment as a means of dealing with individuals considered undesirable by the state goes far back in Chinese history. The Qing dynasty Qianlong Emperor (reign 1736–1795) brought the system to a hideous kind of perfection, transporting criminals and disgraced officials with their families to remote regions, principally to Xinjiang (Waley-Cohen 1991). After 1949, the system of banishment, which had scarcely been used under the Republic (possibly because the then government did not have sufficient control to do so), was reintroduced, on a more complex and articulated level than even Qianlong had managed. The system of reform through labour (*Laogai*) continues to move millions of people around China, a large proportion to the border regions. It is described in great detail by Bao Ruo-Wang and Chelminski (1975) and more recently Harry

Wu (1992). Even when prisoners were released from their incarceration, they were often forced to stay in the borderlands as "free labourers", refused permission to leave the area in which they had been prisoners.

Official figures on migration sometimes include mention of this system, expressed in terms of transformation, or finding a new life (*xinsheng*). In Xinjiang this was done under the slogan of "combining the transformation of criminals with the opening up and construction of Xinjiang" (*ba gaizao fanzui he kaifa Xinjiang jianshe Xinjiang jieheqilai*). Between 1951 and 1973, 102,000 people were sent to Xinjiang, mainly to military farms. By the end of the period, most had found "new lives" through this process (Zhou Chongjing 1990:142).

These laogai migrations do not include the vast army of people moved to remote areas for political reasons, which fell short of formal punishment but were seen by many of the participants as punishment. One of the largest such movements involved the rustication of young people, from the early 1960s to the middle 1970s. An estimated seventeen million young people were sent "up to the mountains and down to the countryside" between 1965 and 1979, five million of them between 1968 and 1970 (Scharping 1981:473; Peng 1992:401, 422; Sausmikat, this volume, footnote 4). Most of them were Red Guards. Once they had fulfilled their political roles in launching the Cultural Revolution, they became a nuisance to Beijing. Sending them to the countryside in the name of spreading socialism, and distributing them in small groups throughout the rural areas, neutralized them as trouble makers. Though many of them went down in the spirit of serving socialism, their enthusiasms seldom lasted, and being sent down came to be equated with banishment (Sausmikat, this volume).

The young people's fate was paralleled by that of millions of older cadres and intellectuals, sent to the countryside in the latter stages of the Cultural Revolution. They lived not with the peasants but in "May 7th cadre schools" (*Wu Qi ganxiao*) – closer to prison camps than schools. Though most of them ended up staying only for a few years, those living there believed at the time that they had been sent down permanently, one of the most distressing aspects of their experience (Thurston 1987; Schoenhals 1996).

The politically motivated migrations of the 1960s and early 1970s did not lead to much permanent settlement. Most people came back as soon as they could. Neither they nor their reluctant hosts wanted them to stay (prisoners of course had no choice of return). In retrospect, these vast forced migrations seem fantastic and improbable. It is hard to imagine how the state was actually able to move such huge numbers, and how officials convinced themselves that such movements would work. Perhaps not surprisingly the people best able to describe what happened are novelists.

Famine Migration[5]

The largest temporary movements of people before the Cultural Revolution were dismally traditional: escapes from famine. Sometimes these were organized by local authorities in hard hit areas. In 1956, for example, Henan was hit by a combination of natural disasters and government dislocations, and famine threatened. The provincial government reacted by sending 160,000 people to Gansu, Qinghai and Heilongjiang (Domenach 1995:45).

The Henan problem in 1956 was a localized problem, and organized migration could at least partially resolve it. There was no such hope when famine gripped entire China, and especially the North, in the early 1960s. At least twenty million people died (Kane 1988). As the famine took hold, people fled without government organization. Many moved along lines of personal connections. Urban residents with relatives in the countryside fled from the cities when the food supply dried up, hoping to find food. At the same time, peasants in severely affected areas moved to relatives in what they hoped would be less affected areas. Government authorities seemed incapable of coordinating the migrations. In many cases, local and provincial authorities encouraged people to go away, but this was a useless response since every province which was hard hit was doing the same thing at the same time; the people who went away from one place were replaced by people whom other provinces had urged to leave. In 1961, for example, a quarter of a million people left Gansu. Some peasants fled to Xinjiang and Shaanxi, others were workers who returned to their original homes in Eastern China to look for work that would at least feed them *(yigong jiushi)*. But in the same year, over seventy thousand people moved into Gansu, the province fled by so many looking for relief (Su 1988:163).

The famine hit Shandong especially hard. The population declined by 2.5 million, nearly five percent, two million of those were outmigrants, five hundred thousand were dead. In the worst year, 1960, 1.63 million people left Shandong (Wu Yulin 1989:189). The migrants went to join relatives and connections from their villages *(laoxiang)* already living in the Northeast, where the famine hit less savagely. These networks, dating from earlier migrations of the 1920s and 1930s, spared many Shandong people the full horrors of the famine experienced in other parts of China, where there were no networks of personal connections beyond the home base.

Spontaneous Migrations (zifa, ziliu)

The tough controls of the hukou system did not prevent peasants from moving. The controls were directed against people who wanted to move into the cities, or to move up the city hierarchy (say from Lianyungang in northern Jiangsu to Shanghai); they were not directed against horizontal (between rural areas) or downward (from a higher to a lower level city) movement. Millions of peasants in these categories simply moved, for work or marriage, or to escape bad situations, without asking for permission. Officials, unable to stop the movement, did the next best thing and failed to report it, thus producing migrations which were official non-events.

Where they were reported, these unsanctioned migrations were referred to as spontaneous (*zifa*) or drifting (*ziliu*).[6] The permanent zifa movement was large. One source (Zhou Xingquan 1988:252) estimates that, from 1949 to the middle 1980s, at least ten million zifa migrants moved permanently within China. Some moved to join relatives and friends, others squatted on empty land. One example was the settlement of an area in the Daxing'anling Mountains in Heilongjiang province. Seven thousand people from various provinces squatted there. They reportedly lived quite well, cultivating the land in the brief summer, and gathering mushrooms for the rest of the year (Zhou Xingquan 1988:253-4).

Peasants could move fairly easily from one rural area to another, where they could work for their keep without needing official ration coupons. Moving to the cities, however, depended on the presence of friendly relatives willing to share food rations, and on the cooperation of neighbours who could be trusted not to report illegal migrants. In remote rural areas authorities were cooperative; zifa migration was a good way to fill their need for settlers. Between 1955 and 1960, over 600,000 people, who had arrived under their own steam in Heilongjiang and had come to the attention of the authorities, were moved on even further to the border areas of this already remote province to settle there (Shen and Tong 1992:194). In the same period, the Inner Mongolian authorities helped to settle 872,000 people, mainly from Hebei and Shandong, who had arrived under their own steam. The authorities welcomed them; their previous experience with organized migrants had not been positive, and return rates had been high. The zifa migrants actually wanted to come, and they had relatives and friends to help them settle (Song 1987:174).

The zifa movements were concentrated in particular periods, the Cultural Revolution and its attendant chaos being one (Wu Yulin 1989:95). Chaos and confusion made movement easy, because so many other people were moving in China to exchange revolutionary experiences.

Escape Migration

Since 1949, large numbers of people have escaped from China, usually to Hong Kong and Macao, the country's only immediate neighbours not under communist rule. Between the beginning of 1949 and the end of 1950, for example, the population of Shanghai fell by half a million, one of the main causes being the departure of people for Hong Kong, Taiwan, or abroad (Zhang 1989:34). Hong Kong's population leapt up, with a influx of refugees of over 700,000 refugees from the Mainland in the first six months of 1950 alone (Young 1994:131–2).

The Hong Kong government at first did not prevent the entry of refugees; formal barriers only went up in the 1960s, more to prevent the political overflow of the Cultural Revolution into Hong Kong than the arrival of refugees escaping from it. After the barriers had gone up, the only option for would-be escapers was to swim across Deep Bay, or, more recently, to be smuggled into Hong Kong by "snakeheads" (*shetou*), the evocative Chinese name for traffickers in people (Giese, this volume).

People in North, Central and West China had few opportunities to leave the country, given the distance from international borders, while few people in the border regions would see any tangible advantage in escaping into the Soviet Union.[7] For some people there were possibilities of escape within China. The old traditions of eremitism and of outlawry did not completely disappear under communist political control. There are tantalizing anecdotal accounts of people living in caves in the hills of Hebei, or in the deep mountains of Hunan (Gu 1985). These people must have lived lives of extreme simplicity, subsisting on almost nothing, and keeping themselves well out of sight of the authorities. Evidence for the continued survival of outlaws comes from the sporadic discovery of "bandits", secret society members and religious sectarians by Communist authorities (Domenach 1995:59–60).

Conclusion

Recent migration within China has attracted enormous attention, both for its scale and for some of its particular features, the return of old patterns of labour recruitment, the reemergence of China as a low wage exporter, and the internal instability which seems to be a byproduct of such massive migration. The present migration is contrasted with the "static" first three decades of Communist rule, and is seen as an example of the "natural" economic forces unleashed by the removal of government restrictions.

The danger in accepting migration simply as a product of economic growth is that it ignores the forms of migration which preceded it. Though these migrations were often non-economic in inspiration, they still involved the movement of vast numbers of people, and give the lie to the idea that China has suddenly been transformed from a static society into a mobile one. Any other interpretation would assume the absence of memory in most people, the inability to base present actions on past experience. In fact, the essentially unhappy experiences of migration in the first three decades of Communist rule have given a strong stimulus to the present migration, and may explain in part why so many people move. People with any inclination towards moving must move while they can; the political system has not changed, and the current policies of allowing movement may be changed arbitrarily and without warning. Foreign governments and investors may reassure themselves that the reforms are here to stay, but people within the Chinese system have learned from their own and their parents' experiences that in China it is essential to seize opportunities. They may not last.

References

Bao Ruo-Wang (Jean Pasqualini) and Rudolph Chelminski. 1975. *Prisoner of Mao*. London: Andre Deutsch.

Chan, Kam Wing. 1989. "Rural-urban Migration and Development in China 1950–1982." In Leung Chi-Keung, Jim Chi-Yung and Zuo Dakang eds, *Resources, Environment and Regional Development*. Hong Kong: Centre of Asian Studies, University of Hong Kong, pp. 353–74.

Dangdai Zhongguo Congshu Bianji Bu. 1989. *Dangdai Zhongguode Shandong* [Contemporary Shandong]. Beijing: Zhongguo Shehui Kexue Chubanshe.

De Tinguy, Anne. 1998. "Chinese Immigration to Russia: A Variation on an Old Theme." In Gregor Benton and Frank N. Pieke, eds, *The Chinese in Europe*. Basingstoke: Macmillan, pp. 301–19.

Domenach, Jean-Luc. 1995. *The Origins of the Great Leap Forward: The Case of One Chinese Province*. Boulder: Westview.

Fei Xiaotong. 1946. *Neidi Nongcun* [Interior Rural Areas]. Shanghai: Shenghuo Shudian.

Gu Hua. 1985. *Pagoda Ridge and Other Stories*. Beijing: Chinese Literature Press.

Heberer, Thomas. 1989. *China and Its National Minorities: Autonomy or Assimilation?* Armonk, N.Y.: M.E. Sharpe.

Kane, Penny. 1988. *Famine in China 1959–61: Demographic and Social Implications*. London: St. Martin's Press.

Lary, Diana. 1996. "Hidden Migrations: Movement of Shandong People 1949–1978." In Kam-Wing Chan ed. Internal Migration in China. *Chinese Environment and Development* 7, nos. 1 and 2, pp. 56–72.

Lary, Diana. 1997. "Recycled Labour Systems: Personal Connections in the Recruitment of Labour in China." In Timothy Brook and Hy Van Luong eds, *Culture and Economy: The Shaping of Capitalism in East Asia*. Ann Arbor: University of Michigan Press, pp. 235–52.

Li, Rose Maria. 1989. "Migration to China's Northern Frontier 1953–82." *Population and Development Review* 15, no. 3, pp. 503–38.

Naughton, Barry. 1988. "The Third Front: Defence Industrialisation in the Chinese Interior." *The China Quarterly* 115, pp. 351–86.

Pan Zhifu. 1988. *Zhongguo Renkou: Guizhou Fence* [China's population: Guizhou]. Beijing: Zhongguo Caizheng Jingji Chubanshe.

Peng Xun. 1992. *Renkou Qianyi yu Shehui Fazhan* [Population migration and social development]. Jinan: Shandong Daxue Chubanshe.

Scharping, Thomas. 1981. *Umsiedlungsprobleme für Chinas Jugend 1955–1980*. Hamburg: Mitteilungen des Instituts für Asienkunde.

Schoenhals, Michael. 1996. *China's Cultural Revolution, 1966–1969: Not a Dinner Party*. Armonk, N.Y.: M.E. Sharpe.

Shen Yimin and Tong Chengzhu. 1992. *Zhongguo Renkou Qianyi* [China's population migration]. Beijing: Zhongguo Tongji Chubanshe.

Song Naigong. 1987. *Zhongguo Renkou: Neimenggu Fence* [China's population: Inner Mongolia]. Beijing: Zhongguo Caizheng Jingji Chubanshe.

Su Runyu. 1988. *Zhongguo Renkou: Gansu Fence* [China's population: Gansu]. Beijing: Zhongguo Caizheng Jingji Chubanshe.

Summerskill, Michael. 1982. *China on the Western Front: Britain's Chinese Work Force in the First World War.* London: Michael Summerskill.

Thurston, Anne F. 1987. *Enemies of the People: The Ordeal of the Intellectuals in China's Great Cultural Revolution.* New York: Knopf.

Tian Fang and Zhang Dongliang eds. 1989. *Zhongguo Renkou Qianyi Xintan* [A new exploration of China's migrations]. Beijing: Zhongguo Tongji Chubanshe.

Waley-Cohen, Joanna. 1991. *Exile in Mid-Qing China: Banishment to Xinjiang, 1758–1820.* New Haven: Yale University Press.

Wei Jinsheng. 1988. "Internal Migration." In Zhongguo Caizheng Jingji Chubanshe/Chinese Financial and Economic Publishing House, ed. *New China's Population.* New York: MacMillan, pp. 57–70.

Wu, Harry Hongda. 1992. *Laogai: The Chinese Gulag.* Boulder: Westview.

Wu Yulin. 1989. *Zhongguo Renkou: Shandong Fence* [China's population: Shandong]. Beijing: Zhongguo Caizheng Jingji Chubanshe.

Xiong Yingwu. 1989. *Zhongguo Renkou: Heilongjiang Fence* [China's population: Heilongjiang]. Beijing: Zhongguo Caizheng Jingji Chubanshe.

Young, John. 1994. "The Building Years: Maintaining a China-Hong Kong-Britian Equilibrium 1950–71." In Ming K. Chan, ed. *Precarious Balance: Hong Kong between China and Britian.* Armonk, N.Y.: M.E. Sharpe.

Zhang Kaimin. 1989. *Shanghai Renkou Qianyi Yanjiu.* [Migration of Shanghai's population]. Shanghai: Shanghai Shehui Kexue Yuan Chubanshe.

Zhou Chongjing. 1990. *Zhongguo Renkou: Xinjiang Fence* [China's population: Xinjiang]. Beijing: Zhongguo Caizheng Jingji Chubanshe.

Zhou Xingquan et. al. 1988. *Dangdai Zhongguo Renkou* [The population of Contemporary China]. Beijing: Zhongguo Shehui Kexue Chubanshe.

Zhu Yuncheng. 1988. *Zhongguo Renkou: Guangdong Fence* [China's population: Guangdong]. Beijing: Zhongguo Caizheng Jingji Chubanshe.

Zou Junyu et. al. 1990. *Zhongguo Renkou: Yunnan Fence* [China's population: Yunnan]. Beijing: Zhongguo Caizheng Jingji Chubanshe.

Notes

1 I prefer "Manchuria" over the term "the Northeast" used elsewhere in this book, because the former was the term used at the time to describe the great migration from North China.

2 Shandong has supplied a disproportionate number of migrants in almost every movement of people within China since the early Qing. The province's major role in supplying migrants stems in part from its location on the North China coast, and its ease of access to Manchuria and to overseas destinations, but movement has also been stimulated by the province's reputation for producing strong, tough men – i.e. the kind of people whom recruiters looked for, whether for labour or for the army. The greatest migration out of Shandong, in the 1920s and 1930s, was to Manchuria. (see Thomas Gottschang and Diana Lary, *Swallows and Settlers: The Great Migration to Manchuria.* Ann Arbor: University of Michigan Press, forthcoming). This migration paved the way for later migrations to Manchuria, by creating personal chains and networks.

3 This article assumes migration to mean a departure from home for a prolonged period, and one which crosses provincial boundaries. This translates the term *qianyi*, the term used in People's Republic of China (PRC) statistics, the major source of statistics quoted in this article (for a further discussion of this term,

see Chan, this volume). The more comprehensive term *yidong* is also used to mean migration. It does not cover local or explicitly temporary or short-term movement, normally called *liudong*. (Wei: 1988. 57; Chan, this volume). These terms do not correspond smoothly to Western typologies of migration, but the nature of the source material dictates the use, to some extent, of the statistical categories used in the PRC.

4 See Thomas Gottschang and Diana Lary, *Swallows and Settlers*, in progress.

5 These migrations are usually termed in Chinese "blind floods" [flows] (*mangliu*).

6 The difference between the two terms is that the first (*zifa*) is more purposeful than the second (*ziliu*), which suggests people moving almost without will power. Since many of these migrations were purposeful, I prefer the first term.

7 One exception is escape migration of Xinjiang minority people to their fellows across the border in the Soviet Union to escape persecution during the Cultural Revolution.

Chapter Three _____

Internal migration in China: A dualistic approach*

Kam Wing Chan

Introduction

One of the major consequences of the economic reforms in China has been a dramatic rise in population mobility, especially to urban centres. This is most obvious in major cities, such as Guangzhou and Beijing, and coastal export processing centres like Dongguan, where large numbers of "floating population" (*liudong renkou*) from the countryside congregate. Estimates have placed the aggregate size of this group of "non-registered" transients in the range of eighty to one hundred million. This speaks clearly to an ongoing relatively radical economic and social transformation in China and the importance of migration in the reform era. The scale of the latest migratory flows of peasants have been likened to irresistible "waves of rural workers" (*mingong chao*). Migrants are not only becoming more numerous but are also crossing longer distances. Some Chinese writers compare the importance of the mobility burst to that of the momentous rural decollectivization programmes in the early years of post-Mao reform (Gong 1994), as the recent rise in mobility has significantly altered the configuration of Chinese society and economy, whose many consequences have yet to be fully studied and understood (Kelliher 1992; Smith 1996; Zhou 1996).

The rapid structural shifts of the post-Mao economy and its transition from plan to markets have eroded many of the barriers erected by the former policy of rural-urban segregation. The recent mass population shifts

_____

* This chapter draws on empirical material gathered for a report to the Asian Development Bank in 1996. I would like to thank the Institute of Population Research, Chinese Academy of Social Sciences, Yunyan Yang, Ta Liu, Alana Boland, and Huang Jianxue for their assistance. Versions of this chapter were presented at different meetings in 1996 and 1997. I also want to thank Cindy Fan, Graeme Hugo, Scott Rozelle, Mark Selden and Dorothy Solinger for their comments and suggestions.

can be broadly attributed to the following factors: (1) rural decollectivization, which has set free surplus labourers previously tied to the place of residence in the countryside; (2) rapid expansion of the urban economy, especially in the labour intensive sectors, creating ten of millions of low-skilled jobs; (3) continuing large gaps in living standards between cities and the countryside in many regions, especially since the mid-1980s; (4) concurrent relaxation of migratory controls and development of urban food and labour markets; (5) increasing regional specialization of skills, partly based on different traditions; and (6) the development and expansion of migrant networks (see Mallee 1988; A. Liu 1991; Chan 1994; Nolan 1993; Zhao 1994).

The mobility change has not only spatially redistributed the work force, but has also seriously disrupted the command economy on which China's social and economic system used to be based. A perhaps even more fundamental impact of the "peasant invasion" of cities has been that it challenged established attitudes and norms, changed the previous structure of opportunities and constraints, and imposed upon the urban population and the state an unprecedented social change and a more diverse, open and plural society. To students of China's development, the mobility spurt has also posed many intellectual challenges, especially considering all the obstacles posed by the many complexities of definitions and measurement (Goldstein and Goldstein 1987; Chan 1994) and a lack of a ready analytical framework. Nor is there a clear picture to allow us to study the patterns of internal migration. This chapter is written to fill part of the information void. And in doing so, I propose and apply a framework that addresses explicitly the *hukou* (household registration) system, one of the China's core socio-economic institutions, in the analysis.

This chapter first reviews the hukou system and the relevant migration statistics. Two types of migrants defined by the hukou system are compared and contrasted, pointing to the importance of this state designed institution in shaping migration patterns. The final section discusses the implications for future studies. Information for this chapter was drawn mainly from the 1990 Population Census (Guowuyuan and Guojia Tongji Ju 1993, especially vols. 2 and 4), supplemented by findings of other surveys made available to me, which include the following:

1 The 1987 one per cent national population sample survey (Guojia Renkou Tongji Si 1988);
2 The national study of floating population in eight large cities conducted in 1988 and 1989 by the Ministry of Construction (*Jianshe Bu*, hereafter referred to as the MOC study) (Li and Hu 1991);
3 The national study of rural migrant labour in 442 counties conducted in 1993 by the Chinese Academy of Social Sciences (*Zhongguo Shehui Kexue Yuan*, or CASS) and the Agricultural Bank of China (*Zhongguo*

Nongye Yinhang, or ABC), hereafter referred to as the CASS and ABC study (Li and Han 1994; Li 1994);

4 The national study of rural labour in 318 villages in 1993 by the Ministry of Agriculture (*Nongye Bu*, or MOA) hereafter the MOA study (Zhang et al. 1995);

5 The study of rural labour migration in twenty-eight counties in 1993 conducted jointly by the Chinese People's Political Consultative Conference (*Zhongguo Renmin Zhengzhi Xieshang Huiyi*, or CPPCC), the Development Research Centre of the State Council (*Guowuyuan Fazhan Yanjiu Zhongxin*), and the Chinese Association of Research on Development of Rural Labour Resources (*Zhongguo Nongcun Laodongli Zhiyuan Kafa Yanjiuhui*), hereafter, the CPPCC study (Nongcun Xingyu 1995) and

6 The study of rural migrant labour in Jinan City, Shandong, in 1995 by the Population Institute (*Renkou Yanjiusuo*) of Chinese Academy of Social Sciences, hereafter the Jinan study (Liu Qiming 1995).

The Hukou System and Migration[1]

The most significant aspect of migration that has struck many Western scholars studying Chinese migration is the "non-voluntary" nature of the process, as noted by Poston and Yaukey (1992:615). While the significance of the institutional/administrative aspect of Chinese migration has been well underscored, it has not been adequately understood. I would argue that any meaningful analysis of Chinese migration must start by making reference to the hukou system, which affects migration in many important ways. In China migration is heavily regulated and controlled by the state. Those wanting to change residence are supposed to seek approval from the public security authorities. A change in residence is deemed official and approved only when it is accompanied by a transfer of one's hukou to the destination. The transfer confers legal residency rights and, most importantly, eligibility for many urban jobs and accompanying subsidized welfare benefits (Cheng and Selden 1994; Mallee 1995). Such a change is granted only when there are good reasons, especially when the move serves, or at least is not at odds with, the state's interests defined in various policies, such as controlling the growth of large cities.

In essence, the hukou system, especially in the pre-reform era, functions as a *de facto* internal passport mechanism. While approvals for migration because of marriage or for seeking support from a family member within the rural areas or within the same level of urban centres are often granted, rural to urban migration was strictly regulated and suppressed in the 1960s and 1970s. In those days, most of this type of migration was reserved for bringing in the necessary labour force in support of state-initiated programmes. An approval for self-initiated relocation to a city from the countryside was only a dream for ordinary peasants. Today, peasants can move to many places, but getting a formal approval to register in a medium-sized or large city is still largely beyond their reach.

State-initiated and directed migrations, such as the cadres *xiafang* and youth rustication movements in the late 1960s, were, in large part, involuntary moves, a feature common to pre-reform China and other centrally planned economies (Chan 1994; Sausmikat, this volume). In the reform era, especially in recent years, by contrast, almost all migratory flows, even including state-initiated migrations within the plan, are voluntary.

Population analysts recognize that migration is arguably the most complex demographic variable (Skeldon 1990). Migrants by nature are harder to track than non-migrants because their mobility involves at least two locations (United Nations 1970). The major difficulties lie in determining what constitutes a move (usually defined by crossing some administrative boundary) and sorting out short term visitors and commuters from permanent movers (usually based on the length of stay, intention of stay, a change of "regular residence", or a combination of some or all of the above). The hukou system and the lack of systematic attention in China to migration that occurs outside the hukou system further complicate the question of defining the concept of "migrant" in China as we understand it internationally.

Taking into account the importance of the hukou, population flows in China can be grouped into three major categories:

1 Migration with residency rights (hereafter, hukou migration);
2 Migration without hukou residency rights (non-hukou migration); and
3 Short term movements (visiting, circulation, and commuting).

In China officially only hukou migration is considered as *qianyi* ("migration"). Other types of mobility (i.e. 2 and 3 above) are merely labelled *renkou liudong* (population movement or "floating"); the population involved in the latter are called *liudong renkou* ("floating population"). The term implies a low degree of expected permanence: the transients are not supposed to (and are legally not entitled to) stay at the destination permanently, and they are often termed, perhaps not appropriately considering the actual length of stay of many of them, "temporary" migrants. They are not the *de jure* residents, despite the fact that many of them may have been at the destination for years.

Hukou migration, on the other hand, is endowed with state resources and, in socialist parlance, is called "planned" migration (*jihua qianyi*). Floaters are a "self-flowing population" (*ziliu renkou*) whose mobility takes place outside the state plans. In the eyes of many central planners, these types of movement are "anarchical" and "chaotic", which is why the official media in China often use the derogatory term *mangliu* (blind flow) in connection with non-plan mobility.

The "floating population" thus refers to those staying in places where they do not have a permanent hukou status. This is a relatively diverse bundle that includes tourists, people on business trips, traders, sojourners, peasant workers contracted from other places, beggars and other unemployed people. Two different groups of floaters, however, are most prevalent. One are rural migrant "workers" (*mingong*), who accounted for about half of the floating population in large cities in the late 1980s according to the MOC study. The Chinese Academy of Social Sciences (Zhongguo Shehui Kexue Yuan 1996) estimates that eighty to ninety per cent of mingong are unskilled labourers. The remaining mingong are skilled craftsmen and traders, often self-employed. The other major group, who accounted for about one third of the floating population, consists primarily of short term visitors using urban facilities, according to the MOC study. They include overnight tourists and business travellers, from both the rural areas and other urban centres (Li and Hu 1991). These two major groups put pressures on the city, but mingong have had far more important consequences as they are both longer term residents and workers in the economy. This is the group which we will give more attention to in this chapter.

A good portion of mobility is short term and seasonal circulation. Seasonal rural migrant labour follows the work rhythms of the farm. Within any given year, the size tends to be larger in the winter season when the demand for work on the farm is low, and usually reaches its peak in February or March immediately after the Spring Festival (Chinese New Year). The MOC study estimates that about half of the floating population stayed longer than six months and about one third stayed longer than one year.

Recent Mobility Trends and International Comparisons

Measuring mobility is no easy task; it has been a particular challenge in the Chinese case for some time, given its enormous complexity (Goldstein and Goldstein 1987). Table 3.1 presents the main available migration statistics and estimates. The number of annual hukou migrants per year based on registration statistics has been kept slightly under twenty million, and the floating population is estimated at about eighty to one hundred million. The hukou-migration figures are directly drawn from registration statistics published by the Ministry of Public Security. They represent the total number of officially approved residence changes within a particular year, excluding those occurring within hukou administration districts in cities and towns and within townships (Zhang 1994). The hukou-migration is

Table 3.1 Major migration figures, 1982–95 (in millions)

1a. Annual Figures

	Hukou Migration (Flows)	Estimates of Stock of Floating Population	
		Total	*Rural Migrant Labour*
1982	17.30	20(?)	
1985	19.69	50	
1988	19.92	70	
1989	18.81	70	
1990	19.24	50	
1992	18.70	60–70	
1993	18.19		50
1994	19.49	80	64
1995	18.46	80–100	

1.b Five year period

	Hukou Migration	Non-hukou Migration	Total
1982–87	20.5	10.0	30.5
%	67.3	32.7	100
1985–90	18.27	15.82	34.09
%	53.6	46.3	100

Notes and Sources:

For (a): Hukou migration figures are official registration statistics, drawn mainly from Shen and Tong 1992 and Gong'an Bu 1993, 1994 and 1995; estimates of floating population are based on a variety of sources cited in the Introduction of the text.

For (b): Figures for 1982–87 are from the 1987 national 1% population survey (Guojia Tongji Ju 1988; Yang 1994). Migrants were defined as those crossing village, town or city boundaries staying at least for six months at the destination. Those for 1985–90 are from the 1990 Population Census (Guowuyuan and Guojia Tongji Ju 1993, volume 4). Migrants were defined as those crossing county or city boundaries staying at least one year at the destination.

slightly overcounted as it is known that births outside the allowable quotas in certain locales have been entered as hukou migrants (Yang and Chen 1993). In any case, the level of hukou migration has remained quite stable between seventeen and twenty million per year since the early 1980s. This reflects strong government intervention, most likely through the operation of a quota system.

The 1987 one per cent population sample survey and the 1990 census also counted the number of permanent migrants (i.e. migrants of types 1 and 2 as defined before) aged five and above for the periods 1982–87 and 1985–90, respectively. The definitions of non-hukou migrants used in those two sources are much narrower than what is commonly known as "floating population." In particular, the 1990 census covers only migration crossing county or city boundaries; measurement of non-hukou migration is primarily based on a one year residence criterion. In other words, both short distance migration within individual cities or counties and short term circulation were excluded.

More significant in policy terms is the rapid rise in the size of the floating population. Floating population figures presented in Table 3.1(a) are stock data and should be taken as broad indicators of the order of magnitude only, as they are estimates based on various regional and sample studies using differing definitions. Most Chinese observers agree that the size of the floating population has been rising steadily since the early 1980s (see for example the CPPCC study). This is also consistent with the general rise of non-hukou migration in the 1980s as shown in Table 3.1(b). Estimates in Table 3.1(a) indicate that the number grew from about twenty million in 1982 to about seventy million in the late 1980s, then dropped somewhat in 1990 due to the economic austerity programme, but swung back in 1991 and has risen quite rapidly since. The estimates for 1995 ranged from eighty to one hundred million. As a major component of the floating population, rural migrant labour increased from about fifty million in 1993 to sixty-four million in 1994.

If we accept the approximate size of the floating population at ninety million in 1995 and fifty million in 1990, this implies an increase of forty million in the first half of the 1990s, or an average of eight million a year. If we assume that about forty per cent of them stayed more than one year,[2] and follow the common convention of counting only those who stay one year or more at the destination as "migrants", then we would have to add another three million non-hukou migrants to the nineteen million hukou migrants each year. This adds up to twenty-two million migrants per year in the first half of the 1990s, or an annual migration rate of about 2.2 per cent. This average annual rate naturally does not include large numbers of shorter distance migrants as stated before and therefore its coverage is narrower than the "one year rate of residential mobility" used in many Western countries. If these differences are taken into account, the annual mobility rate for China would have to be adjusted upward, most likely to three per cent.

Even if we assume generously that China's rate is at the four per cent level, it appears that the it is still quite low, about two-thirds of the rate in low mobility Western countries (typically six to seven per cent in countries such as Ireland, Belgium, or the Netherlands, see Long 1991).[3] China's rate is also lower than that of Taiwan in 1970–1 (ten per cent), but is similar to that of the USSR in the 1980s (Long 1988 and 1991). But China's four per cent rate is higher than the 1.5 per cent of India (based on 1981 Census, see Skeldon 1986), whose population is known to have low geographic mobility. Naturally, there is no straightforward way of comparing geographic mobility across nations. In the Chinese case, the existence of especially large numbers of shorter term seasonal sojourners and migratory workers, an outcome created partly by the hukou mechanism, is not well captured by statistics based on the conventional criterion of one year residence.

Reasons for Migration

As in many other developing countries, job change and family reasons are the two most important causes of migration. The significant disparities in wages and living standards between the urban and rural sectors and between the coastal and inland regions underlie most of the migratory flows in the reform era (Solinger 1997). In other words, economic factors have prevailed in most of the moves.

Migration is selective in many ways. The socio-demographic and economic characteristics of migrants are significantly shaped by their motivations and opportunities for migration. As stated before, hukou and non-hukou migrants face starkly different opportunities and constraints. This duality is clear from the tabulations based on the 1990 census. Table 3.2 shows that non-hukou, self-initiated migration, like most rural-urban migration in other developing countries, is mainly related to work (Skeldon 1990). Male non-hukou migrants of working age in particular were close to full participation in work, compared to only fifty-seven per cent in the same age group of hukou migrants (Yang 1994). While hukou work migrants were almost all in the "work transfers" and "assignments" categories (i.e. within-plan or approved labour transfers between enterprises), non-hukou migrant workers were almost exclusively in the *wugong jingshang* ("employment in industry and business") category. This refers to self sought employment and self-employment totally outside of the state plans. A 1991 Hubei sample survey has also found that three quarters of non-hukou

Table 3.2 Reasons for migration

	1982–87	1985–90		
	All	*All*	*Hukou Migrants*	*Non-hukou*
Work Reasons				
Job transfer	20.6	14.5	18.0	4.6
Job assignment	5.1	4.7	10.4	2.7
Employment in industry and business	8.2	29.7	1.8	50.3
Family Reasons				
Migration with family	19.8	10.8	13.7	7.9
Marriage	15.8	14.2	15.6	11.3
Living with relatives and friends	13.3	10.6	6.6	13.2
Other Reasons				
Study or training	8.7	7.8	21.4	2.8
Retirement or resignation	2.6	1.5	2.1	1.0
Other	6.0	6.5	10.4	6.3
Total	100%	100%	100%	100%

Note and Sources: For 1982–7: Guojia Tongji Ju 1988; For 1985–90: the total figures are from Guowuyuan and Guojia Tongji Ju 1993, volume 4. The hukou and non-hukou migration figures are from the 1% migrant sample of the 1990 census tabulated by the author.

migrant workers surveyed worked in private enterprises (they were in fact largely self employed), compared to only one quarter for hukou migrant workers (see Table 3.6).

Conversely, about seventy per cent of all the hukou migrants in the 1985–90 period moved for reasons other than directly starting a job (Table 3.2). Half of hukou migration was for family reasons (marriage, migration with family, and living with relatives or friends): marriage migration includes a significant number rural-to-rural migrants. Another thirty per cent was related to study or training. Among the non-hukou migrants, family reasons were also the second largest set of reasons (about one third of all the non-hukou migrants). Marriage migration in the hukou migrants category occurred mostly within the countryside.

Socio-economic Duality

Socio-demographic characteristics of migrants

One of the major types of migration selectivity is by age. This is mainly related to life cycle events that generate adjustments in the place of residence. Starting a job, changing jobs until one settles on a career, getting married and going away to college are all closely connected with migration and moreover concentrated in the age of young adulthood. The age structure of Chinese migrants as shown in Table 3.3 is typical of a migrant population. Rural migrant labour, as expected, tends to be concentrated in the most economically active age group, particularly between the age of fifteen to thirty-four.

Table 3.3 also shows that labour migration at the national aggregate level is dominated by males. This is especially pronounced in the rural migrant labour population (including short term floaters), where male

Table 3.3 Age structure of migrants (%)

Age	1990 census		Rural migrant labour	
	Hukou migrants	*Non-hukou migrants*	*Jinan study 1995*	*MOA study 1994*
5–14	7.7	8.6	0.0	4.5 (below 17)
15–24	49.7	43.3	62.0	71.4 (18–35)
25–34	24.7	26.4	26.4	
35–44	9.5	10.6	9.6	23.3 (36–59)
45–44	4.8	4.7	2.0	
55+	3.5	6.4		0.8 (60+)
100	100	100	100	
Sex ratio	124	134	248	303

Notes and sources: The 1990 census figures are from the 1% migrant sample of the 1990 census.

migrants outnumber females by 3 to 1. This, however, masks some notable regional exceptions such as Guangdong, where migrants from the countryside are predominantly female (see Scharping, this volume). Excluding the short term floaters and including other non-work related migrants, the 1990 census figures show that male migrants slightly outnumbered the female ones. Marriage migration, however, was almost exclusively a female affair.

Overall, migrants and rural migrant workers are better educated than the average population (Table 3.4). This is partly an effect of the age structure of the migrants (young adults tend to be better educated than old adults). Despite the general similarity of the age structure between hukou and non-hukou migrants, there is a clear polarization of the two groups in educational attainment. Table 3.4 shows that hukou migrants are disproportionally highly educated (senior middle school level and up), while non-hukou migrants and rural migrant labour are heavily concentrated in the educational levels of junior middle and primary school. The most pronounced disparity – and this clearly attests to the highly selective nature on skills of the hukou migration – is seen in the college educated cohort: while only less than two per cent of the nation's population aged six and above had a college level education in 1990, close to one quarter of the hukou migrants were college graduates!

Despite the lower educational level of rural migrant workers compared to hukou migrants, the former are nevertheless likely to be better educated than the average rural population. More than half of the rural migrant workers has at least junior middle education. Those who are better educated and have special vocational skills also tend to have a higher propensity to leave (Table 3.5), a situation closely related to the nature of the demand for labour in the cities and towns. By contrast, those with no or little formal education have a very low outmigration rate.

Table 3.4 Migrants by educational attainment (%)

Educational level	National	1990 census		Rural migrant labour	
	pop. 1990 (Age 6+)	Hukou migrants	Non-hukou migrants	Jinan study 1995	MOA study 1994
College	1.6	22.2	2.2	12.1	9.8
Technical middle	1.7	11.3	1.9		
Senior middle	7.3	13.6	9.6		
Junior middle	26.5	26.3	43.2	71.0	54.1
Primary	42.3	20.5	30.8	16.0	31.6
No or little education	20.6	5.6	11.2	0.9	3.8

Notes and Sources: Figures for the nation are from Guowuyuan and Guojia Tongji Ju 1993, volume 2; The 1990 census figures are from the 1% migrant sample of the 1990 census.

Table 3.5 Outmigration rate of rural migrant labour by education, 1994

Educational level	%
Vocation training	22.3
Senior middle	19.5
Junior middle	17.7
Primary	10.2
No or little education	3.0
All	14.4

Source: MOA study.

Employment characteristics of migrant labour

Table 3.6 reveals the occupational and sectoral similarities and contrasts between hukou and non-hukou migrants. It is clear that the composition of occupations of hukou migrants (predominantly with urban destinations except marriage migration) broadly resembles that of the urban population as a whole; actually, they are significantly over-represented in professional and technical positions. In contrast, ninety-five per cent of the non-hukou migrants had employment at clerical level or lower. Common jobs were manufacturing frontline workers, construction workers, nannies, and sales

Table 3.6 Migrant workers by occupation and sector

	All Urban	**Hukou Migrants**	**Non-hukou Migrants**
	Population 1990	*1985–90*	
		National	
Occupation			
Professional and technical	14.0	21.0	3.3
Administrative and managerial	4.9	3.6	1.2
Clerical	5.6	7.8	1.5
Sales	8.1	4.2	10.3
Service	6.9	4.6	9.6
Industrial workers	38.1	31.9	18.3
Farm workers	22.5	26.8	55.7
Unclassifiable	0.2	—	—
	100	100	100
Sector by ownership			
	National, 1990	**Hubei Sample Survey, 1991**	
State-owned	70.0	18.8	5.6
Collectives	25.1	55.0	19.6
Private and self-employed	4.8	25.1	73.6
Others	1.1	1.1	1.2
	100	100	100

Sources: The urban population figures are from the 1990 census (Guowuyuan and Guojia Tongji Ju, 1993a). The 1985–90 national figures are from the 1% migrant sample of the 1990 census. The Hubei migrant figures are from Xu and Gu 1994.

and service workers, largely working in the mostly unregulated self-employed sector (Yang 1994; Chan 1996a). A sample survey carried out in Hubei also shows that the fast-growing non-state sector absorbed most rural-urban migrants – both those with hukou and those without, whereas the urban population as a whole were mostly employed in the protected state sector. Non-hukou migrants in Hubei were concentrated in the self-employed sector (seventy-four per cent), while hukou migrants were absorbed mostly by collectives (fifty-five per cent; see table 3.6). The significant number of farm workers among hukou migrants largely reflects rural-rural marriage migration of women.

Among the urban migrants without hukou, a handful might have been able to move upward via connections or entrepreneurship, but the great majority is marginalized. The non-hukou urban migrants are often shut out of more desired urban positions and have to take up the dangerous and dirty jobs, a situation commonly faced by immigrant labour (especially illegal, undocumented workers) in many other societies. In the Chinese case, the situation is worse as these unregistered transients are also legally denied urban citizenship no matter how long they stay at the urban destination.

In sum, a dual urban social structure has emerged: on the one side those for whom jobs, housing, education, subsidized food, and medical care are an entitlement, and side on the other those who must scramble for those goods or even do without them (Solinger 1995; Chan 1996a; Xiang, this volume). Table 3.7 sums up the polarities in their social and economic status. It is clear that hukou status remains an important divide in social and economic terms among the migrants.[4] In many ways, this dualism is parallel to the formal/informal sectoral dualism elsewhere in the developing world and the local/foreign labour dichotomy in many developed countries. Non-hukou migrants in China face many averse conditions that are similar to those encountered by workers in the "informal" sector or illegal alien workers in other countries.

Geography of Migration

According to the 1990 Census, a total of thirty-four million domestic migrants crossing county-level units were recorded over the previous five-year period (1985–90), twenty-three million or two-thirds of whom stayed within their respective provinces (Table 3.8). Guangdong and Sichuan were the two provinces with both the largest intra-provincial migration and the largest inter-provincial migration, except that these two provinces were at the opposite ends of internal migration flows: Guangdong was the largest recipient while Sichuan was the biggest sender. This is further illustrated in Figure 3.1, which maps the largest thirty inter-provincial migration flows.

Generally, in net migration terms, most of the coastal, eastern provinces and municipalities (such as Guangdong, Beijing, Shanghai and Jiangsu) gained from provinces like Sichuan and Guangxi in the central

Table 3.7 Hukou and non-hukou rural-urban migrants

Characteristics	Hukou Migrants	Non-hukou Migrants
Household registration status	Non-agricultural and local	Agricultural and non-local
Entitlement to state-supplied social benefits and opportunities	full	from nil to temporary entitlements
Legal urban resident status	full status	illegal or temporary
The socio-economic sector the migrants move to	state sector and non-state sector	mostly to non-state sector also as temporary workers in state enterprises
Mechanism of effecting migration	transfers determined by bureaucratic decisions within plan limits	"spontaneous" based on personal contacts and market information
Stability of moves	permanent	seasonal or semi-permanent
Labour characteristics of principal migrants		
Skill level	skilled and low-skilled workers	mostly unskilled or low-skilled labor
Employment type	mostly permanent jobs	temporary or semi-permanent jobs in non-state enterprises; or self-employment.
Housing	same as other urban residents	low-cost shelters or homeless

Source: Chan 1996a.

and western regions (see Table 3.9 for definitions). This indicates that the inter-provincial flows were primarily toward the coast, generally reflecting the differences in the level of economic development. A further disaggregation of the long-distance flows based on hukou, shown in Figures 3.2 and 3.3, reveals that non-hukou inter-provincial migration followed economic disparities, while hukou migration did not. The non-hukou flows, mostly for jobs or marriages, are predominantly from the interior to the coast, converging at major economic hubs like the Pearl River Delta and metropolises like Shanghai and Beijing. This type of largely market driven flows strongly reflect the economic forces at work. These forces were so powerful that migrants were willing to cross hundreds, if not thousands, of kilometres taking them to very different places. These migrants expected to benefit from large wage differentials, often in the range of 1 to 3 or 4, between an urban unskilled job in a coastal city and a farm job in an inland province (see CPPCC study and Jinan study). However, for most hukou migrants, such economic gains did not exist. It is therefore not surprising that even out-of-province hukou migrants were still quite "conservative", moving over shorter distances than the non-hukou migrants in that same category. They generally preferred nearby provinces in which culture, language and environment were similar, and therefore, easier to adapt to (see also Ding 1994).

Table 3.8 Inter-provincial migration in the 1980s (in 1000s) age 5 and above

Province	1982–87				1985–90			
	In	Out	Gross	Net	In	Out	Gross	Net
Beijing	321.3	98.6	419.9	222.7	672.7	132.1	804.8	540.5
Tianjin	131.9	46.8	178.7	85.1	244.6	72.2	316.8	172.4
Hebei	593.5	372.8	966.3	220.7	520.4	645.7	1166.1	−125.3
Shanxi	164.5	181.2	345.7	−16.7	307.0	218.5	525.5	88.6
Neimenggu	167.5	204.5	372.0	−37.0	254.3	303.1	557.4	−48.8
Liaoning	313.4	230.6	544.0	82.8	541.4	295.0	836.4	246.4
Jilin	168.8	239.0	407.8	−70.2	237.3	355.5	592.8	−118.2
Heilongjiang	191.3	449.9	641.2	−258.6	367.4	607.5	974.9	−240.1
Shanghai	371.9	81.9	453.8	290.0	665.5	132.6	798.1	533.0
Jiangsu	474.5	320.6	795.1	153.9	791.1	620.5	1411.6	170.6
Zhejiang	122.1	237.1	359.2	−115.0	335.9	632.3	968.2	−296.4
Anhui	164.5	250.8	415.3	−86.3	337.8	533.4	871.2	−195.6
Fujian	87.8	107.8	195.6	−20.0	251.0	238.4	489.4	12.7
Jiangxi	101.3	144.4	245.7	−43.1	224.9	293.8	518.6	−68.9
Shandong	544.2	339.0	883.2	205.2	609.4	534.8	1144.3	74.6
Henan	263.4	315.3	578.7	−51.9	477.8	589.6	1067.5	−111.8
Hubei	273.9	223.3	497.2	50.6	431.1	346.3	777.4	84.8
Hunan	216.4	377.1	593.5	−160.7	271.8	528.6	800.4	−256.8
Guangdong	297.2	153.7	450.9	143.5	1257.5	250.5	1508.0	1007.0
Guangxi	58.4	213.1	271.5	−154.7	142.5	588.9	731.4	−446.4
Hainan					150.1	106.0	256.1	44.1
Sichuan	386.7	471.8	858.5	−85.1	469.9	1316.0	1785.9	−846.2
Guizhou	114.4	122.5	236.9	−8.1	190.4	312.8	503.2	−122.4
Yunnan	95.1	183.0	278.1	−87.9	250.3	277.4	527.7	−27.2
Tibet		35.0	35.0	−35.0		54.6	54.6	−54.6
Shaanxi	224.7	284.0	508.7	−59.3	314.6	362.3	676.9	−47.8
Gansu	93.3	189.9	283.2	−96.6	199.2	280.7	479.9	−81.5
Qinghai	28.5	101.0	129.5	−72.5	115.8	102.1	218	13.7
Ningxia	91.0	50.0	141.0	41.0	91.9	56.6	148.5	35.3
Xinjiang	202.0	238.8	440.8	−36.8	341.7	277.4	619.1	64.3
Total	6263.5	6263.5	12527	0	11065.4	11065.4	22130.7	0

Notes: Gross = In + Out
No information on in-migration was collected for Tibet. Hainan was not a province before 1988.
Sources: Guojia Tongji Ju 1988 and Guowuyuan and Guojia Tongji Ju 1993.

The geography of non-hukou flows shown above is confirmed by studies of the "rural migrant labour" (*mingong*). This is a more sizeable group because it covers all the labour migrants from the countryside, regardless of their length of stay at the destination. According to the CASS and ABC study, rural migrant labour (those who participated in "outside" work (*waichu dagong*), which includes seasonal labour),[5] accounted for about one eighth (12.5 per cent) of the rural labour force in 1993 (Table 3.9). The central region was the largest source of rural migrant labour, having the highest labour outmigration rate (15.9 per cent) and volume (22.8 million), followed by the western region (13.5 per cent and 15.4 million). The eastern region had the lowest rate (only slightly more than half of that of the Central region) and the smallest volume. This pattern is broadly consistent with the

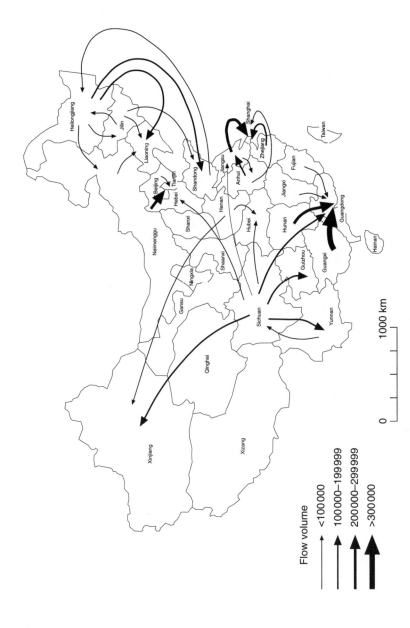

Figure 3.1 The 30 Largest Inter-Provincial Flows, 1985–90
Source: Chan, J. (1996) based on 1990 Census.

Flow volume

<100000
100000–199999
200000–299999
>300000

1000 km

0

63

Table 3.9 Composition of rural migrant labour, 1993

Region centres	Total rural labour (1000)	Out migration rate (%)	No. of migrants (1000)	Share (%)			
				%	Within counties	Within provinces	Toward urban
Eastern	154505.9	8.5	13133	25.6	28.4	66.3	82.0
Central	143295.6	15.9	22784	44.4	40.6	70.4	83.3
Western	113755.6	13.5	15357	30.0	37.0	76.4	66.5
Total	411557.0	12.5	51274	100	36.4	71.1	77.9

East = Heilongjiang, Jinin, Liaoning, Beijing, Tianjin, Hebei, Shandong, Jiangsu, Shanghai, Zhejiang, Fujian, Guangdong, Guangxi and Hainan.
Central = Neimenggu, Shanxi, Henan, Anhui, Hubei, Hunan and Jiangxi.
West = Xinjiang, Qinghai, Gansu, Ningxia, Shaanxi, Sichuan, Guizhou, Yunnan and Tibet.
Source: CASS and ABC study.

findings of the other studies (such as the CPPCC study; Rozelle et al. 1997) in the early and mid-1990s. Because of the large size of the labour force (population) in the central provinces, this region accounted for forty-four per cent of the estimated total outflows. The low rate of outmigration in the eastern region is attributed to the high level of development of rural enterprises in many villages and townships, which absorbed local rural labour. This is not the case for the central or the western regions. Most of the flows in the inland region were within the migrants' own provinces (seventy per cent), but overall, the out-of-province flows appear to be gaining popularity in the last two or three years.[6] Estimates suggest that the volume of the latter rose from about fifteen million in 1993 (Table 3.9) to twenty-five million in 1994 and thirty million in 1995.[7]

Theoretical Implications

This chapter has reviewed the central components that define the Chinese migration systems and statistics. On the basis of migration data, I have argued and demonstrated that there is a clear duality in the migrant population. At the macro-societal level, two different migration streams from different socio-economic strata operate within distinct "circuits", which are defined by social and economic institutions that are based on the hukou system. While they share some similar general demographic characteristics, such as age, they exhibit dissimilar socio-economic characteristics and patterns of flow, because of the different opportunities and constraints faced.

In spite of all the publicity about rural migrant workers, hukou migration continues to be a major and stable component in Chinese migration, although it admittedly decreases in *relative* importance compared to non-hukou migration. The hukou system, an internal quasi-passport or "green card" system, defines the special nature of Chinese migration that should be explicitly addressed in Chinese migration

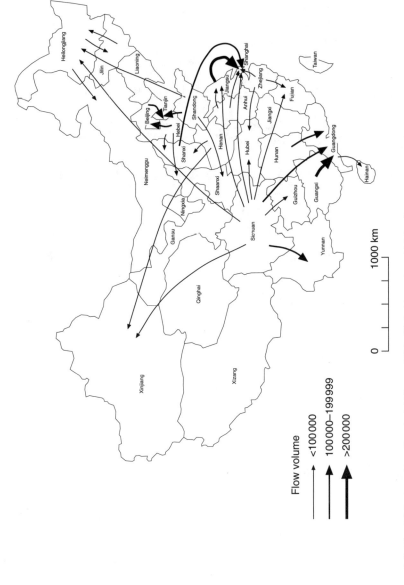

Figure 3.2 The 30 Largest Inter-Provincial Flows, 1985–90 (without Local Hukou)

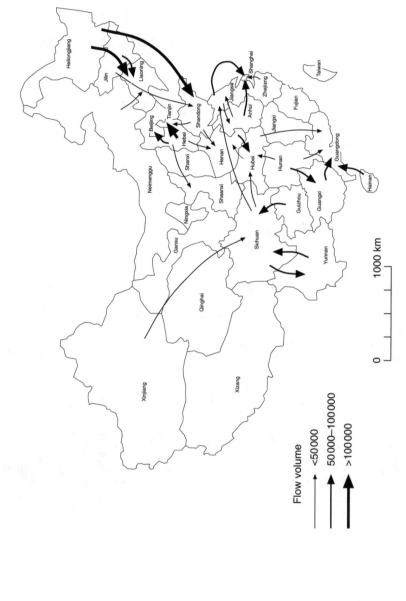

Figure 3.3 The 30 Largest Inter-Provincial Flows, 1985–90 (with Local Hukou)

Flow volume

<50000

50000–100000

>100000

0   1000 km

studies. Its broad outcomes and character are similar to the structural segmentation, especially of the labour market, which has long been observed in the international migration of low-skilled workers elsewhere in the world. A bifurcated labour market has emerged that is made up of a "primary" segment that produces relatively stable, skill oriented jobs with higher pay and benefits, and a "secondary" segment of unskilled, "temporary" and lowly paid jobs, with significant mobility barriers between the segments (e.g. Piore 1979; Taubman and Wachter 1986; Lagos 1995). While in other countries these barriers are attributable to historical/ethnic, social and economic factors, in China one has to add that they are also legal and have deeper institutional roots (Chan 1994). They are related to the social control mechanisms and dualistic social structure created by the state in the pre-reform era. The state therefore continues to be central in the patterning and control of migration in China.

It is clear from the above that contemporary China does not fit neatly into any of the existing internal migration models developed for market oriented economies. At a disaggregated level, as done in this chapter, Chinese migration reveals certain characteristics that are postulated by mainstream internal and international migration theories (notably the neoclassical economics models and a small body of literature on socialist countries, e.g. Brown and Neuberger 1977; Demko and Fuchs 1977; Forbes and Thrift 1987; Ronnas and Sjoberg 1993). Within each labour market segment, for example, the general principles of neoclassical economic theories may apply, if one accepts the, quite reasonable, assumption that most of migration in the post-Mao era is "voluntary" migration. It is true that hukou labour migration is mostly initiated by the state in accordance with national and regional economic and labour force plans, and, in extreme cases, people are treated merely as a production factor freely at the disposal of the planner (Chen 1990; Ma 1995). In practice in the post-Mao era, however, there is a high degree of concurrence of wishes between the individual and the state. Some of the moves are initiated by the state; many more however by the individuals concerned, although their flow continues to be regulated by government's labour plans of various kinds. Migration of this kind appears to be compatible with micro-economic models of personal choice (e.g. Sjaastad 1962; Todaro 1969 and 1976), where actors decide to migrate because a cost-benefit calculation leads them to expect a positive net return from movement, both pecuniary and non-pecuniary.

Even clearer are the patterns of non-hukou migration, especially that of rural workers. In many ways, they operate like "free" migrants do in market economies, subject to only certain (obviously, more in the Chinese case) administrative and economic constraints. As shown before, the geography of migration of non-hukou migration is consistent with neo-classical predictions. In any analytical work of the processes, one will, however, have to adjust the rather mechanistic neoclassical models to take account of the much more complex context and process of decision making in migration.[8]

Finally, while the duality and segmentation of Chinese migration systems has been emphasized, there has been more fluidity across the hukou divide in the post-Mao era, especially since the late 1980s. This happened as hukou became for sale for those who could afford it,[9] and as the accessibility of jobs and state resources is increasingly defined by other factors such as personal *guanxi* (networks). Research on these changes are needed to further our understanding of this important dimension of Chinese society.

References

Bilsborrow, Richard and United Nations Secretariat. 1993. "Internal Female Migration and Development: An Overview." In *Internal Migration of Women in Developing Countries*, New York: United Nations, pp. 1–17.

Brown, Alan A. and Neuberger, Egon, eds. 1977. *Internal Migration: A Comparative Perspective*. New York: Academic Press.

Chan, June S.H. 1996. Population Mobility and Government Policies in Post-Mao China. Unpublished M.Phil thesis, University of Hong Kong, Hong Kong.

Chan, Kam Wing. 1994. *Cities with Invisible Walls: Reinterpreting Urbanization in Post-1949 China*. Hong Kong: Oxford University Press.

Chan, Kam Wing. 1996a. "Post-Mao China: A Two-class Urban Society in the Making." *International Journal of Urban and Regional Research* 20, no. 1, pp. 134–50.

Chan, Kam Wing. 1996b. "Internal Migration in China: An Introductory Overview." *Chinese Environment and Development* 7, nos. 1 and 2, pp. 3–13.

Chant, S., and S. A. Radcliffe. 1992. "Migration and Development: The Importance of Gender." In S. Chant, ed. *Gender and Migration in Developing Countries*. London: Belhaven Press, pp. 1–29.

Chen Jinyong [Kam Wing Chan]. 1990. "Shi Fenxi Shehuizhuyi Guojia Cheng Shihuade Tedian" [An analysis of the features of urbanization in socialist countries]. *Zhongguo Renkou Kexue* no. 21, pp. 6–12 and 53.

Cheng, Tiejun and Mark Selden. 1994. "The Origins and Social Consequences of China's Hukou System." *The China Quarterly* 139, pp. 644–68.

Demko, George J. and Roland J. Fuchs. 1977. "Commuting in the USSR and Eastern Europe: Causes, Characteristics and Consequences." *East European Quarterly* no. 9, pp. 463–75.

Ding Jinhong. 1994. "Zhongguo Renkou Shengji Qingyide Yuanyin Bieliuchang Tezheng Tanxi" [An analysis of inter-provincial migratory streams in China by reason]. *Renkou Yanjiu* 18, no. 1, pp. 14–21.

Forbes, Dean and Nigel Thrift. 1987. "Introduction." In Dean Forbes and Nigel Thrift, eds, *The Socialist Third World*, Oxford: Basil Blackwell, pp. 1–26.

Georges, Eugenia. 1990. *The Making of a Transnational Community: Migration, Development and Cultural Change in the Dominican Republic*, New York: Oxford University Press.

Goldstein, Sidney and Alice Goldstein. 1987. "Migration in China: Methodological and Policy Challenges." *Social Science History* 11, no. 1, pp.85–104.

Gong'an Bu. 1993, 1994 and 1994. *Quanguo Fenxianshi Renkou Tongji Ziliao* [Population Statistical Materials of the Nation by County and City]. Beijing: Qunzhong Chubanshe.

Guojia Tongji Ju. 1995. *Zhongguo Tongji Nianjian 1995* [Statistical yearbook of China 1995]. Beijing: Zhongguo Tongji Chubanshe.

Guojia Tongji Ju Renkou Tongjisi. 1988. *Zhongguo 1987 Nian 1% Renkou Chouyan Diaocha Ziliao* [Tabulation of China's 1987 1% population sample survey]. Beijing: Zhongguo Tongji Chubanshe.

Guowuyuan and Guojia Tongji Ju. 1993. *Zhongguo 1990 Mian Renkou Pucha Ziliao* [Tabulation on the 1990 population census of the People's Republic of China]. Multiple volumes. Beijing: Zhongguo Tongji Chubanshe.

Gurak, Douglas and Fe Caces. 1992. "Migration Networks and the Shaping of Migration Systems." In Mary Kritz, Lin Lean Lim and Hania Zlotnick, eds, *International Migration Systems: A Global Approach*. Oxford: Clarendon Press, pp. 150–76.

Hukou Dengji Tiaoli [Household Registration Regulations] [1958]. Reprinted in Chinese Academy of Social Sciences ed. 1986. *Zhongguo Renkou Nianjian 1985* [Population Yearbook of China 1985]. Beijing: Zhongguo Shehui Kexue Chubanshe, pp. 83–5.

Kelliher, Daniel. 1992. *Peasant Power in China: The Era of Rural Reform, 1979–1989*. New Haven: Yale University Press.

Lagos, Ricardo A. 1995. "Formalizing the Informal Sector: Barriers and Costs." *Development and Change* 26, pp. 111–31.

Li Fan. 1994. "Waichu Dagong Renyuande Guimo, Liudong Fanwei ji Qita" [The size, geographical distribution and other characteristics of outgoing workers]. *Zhongguo Nongcun Jingji* 9, pp. 31–5.

Li Fan and Han Xiaoyun. 1994. "Waichu Dagong Renyuande Nianling Jiegou he Wenhua Goucheng" [The educational composition and age structure of outgoing workers]. *Zhongguo Nongcun Jingji* 8, pp. 10–4.

Li Mengbai and Hu Yin. 1991. *Liudong Renkou dui Dachengshi Fazhande Yingxiang ji Duice* [Impact of the floating population on the development of large cities and recommended policy]. Beijing: Jingji Ribao Chubanshe.

Liu, Alan. 1991. "Economic Reform, Mobility Strategies, and National Integration in China." *Asian Survey* 31, no. 5, pp. 393–408.

Liu, Qiming. 1995. Rural-Urban Migration Sample Survey in Jinan Municipality of China: Sample Design and Preliminary Results. Working Paper, Australian National University.

Long, Larry. 1988. *Migration and Residential Mobility in the USA*. New York: Russell Sage Foundation.

Long, Larry. 1991. "Residential Mobility Differences Among Developed Countries." *International Regional Science Review* 14, no. 2, pp. 133–47.

Ma, Laurence J.C. 1995. "Socialist Migration: The Case of Mainland China." *Proceedings of the International Conference on the Population of Mainland China and Taiwan*. Taipei: Population Research Center, National Taiwan University, pp. 111–26.

Mallee, Hein. 1988. "Rural-urban Migration Control in the People's Republic of China: Effects of the Recent Reform." *China Information* 2, no. 4, pp. 12–22.

Mallee, Hein. 1995. "China's Household Registration System under Reform." *Development and Change* 26, no. 1, pp. 1–29.

Nolan, Peter. 1993. "Economic Reform, Poverty and Migration in China." *Economic and Political Weekly*, 26 June 1993, pp. 1369–77.

"Nongcun Xingyu Laodongli Zhuangyi yu Laodongli Shichang" Keti Zu ["Rural surplus labour transfer and labour market" project group], 1995. "28 Ge Xian(shi) Nongcun Laodongli Kuaquyu Liudong de Diaocha Yanjiu" [A study of inter-regional rural labour flows in 28 counties (cities)]." *Zhongguo Nongcun Jingji* 4, pp. 19–28.

Oi, Jean C. 1993. "Reform and Urban Bias in China." *Journal of Development Studies* 29, no. 4, pp. 129–48.

Piore, M.J. 1979. *Birds of Passage: Migrant Labor and Industrial Societies.* New York: Cambridge University Press.

Poston, Dudley L. Jr. and David Yaukey, eds, 1992. *The Population of Modern China,* New York: Plenum Press.

Ronnas, Per and Orjan Sjoberg. 1993. "Urbanization, Central Planning and Tolley's Model of Urban Growth: A Critical Review." *Geoforum* 24, no. 2, pp. 193–204.

Rozelle, Scott et al. 1997. "Poverty, Networks, Institutions, or Education: Testing among Competing Hypotheses on the Determinants of Migration in China." Paper presented at the Annual Meetings of the Association of Asian Studies, Chicago, 13–16 March 1997.

Shen Yimin and Tong Chengzhu. 1992. Zhongguo Renkou Qianyi [Population migration in China]. Beijing: Zhongguo Tongji Chubanshe.

Sjaastad, L.A. 1962. "The Costs and Returns of Human Migration." *The Journal of Political Economy* 70, pp. 7080–93.

Skeldon, Ronald. 1986. "On Migration Patterns in India During the 1970s." *Population and Development Review* 12, no. 4, pp. 759–79.

Skeldon, Ronald. 1990. *Population Mobility in Developing Countries.* London: Belhaven Press.

Solinger, Dorothy. 1995. "The Floating Population in the Cities: Chances for Assimilation?" in Deborah Davis et al. eds, *Urban Spaces: Autonomy and Community in Contemporary China.* Cambridge: Woodrow Wilson Center Press and Cambridge University Press, pp. 113–39.

Solinger, Dorothy. 1997. "The Floating Population Leaves Its Rural Origins." Paper presented at the Workshop on Rural Labor and Migration in 1990's China, University of California at Irvine, Irvine, CA, USA, 26 April 1997.

Smith, Christopher. 1996. "Migration as an Agent of Change in Contemporary China." *China Environment and Development* 7, no. 1 and 2, pp. 14–55.

Taubman, P. and M.L. Wachter. 1986. "Segmented Labour Markets." In O. Ashenfelter and R. Layard, eds, *Handbook of Labour Economics,* Vol. 2. Amsterdam: Elsevier.

Todaro, Michael P. 1969. "A Model of Labor Migration and Urban Unemployment in Less Developed Countries." *The American Economic Review* 59, no. 1, pp. 138–148.

Todaro, Michael P. 1976. *Internal Migration in Developing Countries.* Geneva: International Labour Office.

United Nations. 1970. *Methods of Measuring Internal Migration.* New York: United Nations.

Wang Jianmin and Hu Qi. 1996. *Zhongguo Liudong Renkou* [The floating population in China]. Shanghai: Shanghai Caijing Daxue Chubanshe.

Xu Yunpeng and Gu Shengzhu. 1994. Dangdai Renkou Qianyi yu Chengzhenhua [Contemporary population migration and urbanization]. Wuhan: Wuhan Daxue Chubanshe.

Yang Yunyan. 1994. Zhongguo Renkou Qianyi yu Fazhande Changqi Zhanlüe [Internal migration and long term development strategy of China]. Wuhan: Wuhan Chubanshe.

Yang Yunyan, and Chen Jinyong [Kam Wing Chan]. 1993. "Zhongguo Renkou Shengji Qianyide Ziliao yu Cesuan" [Inter-provincial migration in China: Statistics and estimates]. *Zhongguo Renkou Kexue* 2, pp. 37–41.

Zelinsky, Wilbur. 1971. "The Hypothesis of Mobility Transition." *Geographical Review* 61, pp. 219–49.

Zhang Qingwu. 1994. "Renkou Qianyi yu Renkou Liudong Gaishu" [An Overview of Population Migration and Population Movements]. In *Hukou Qianyi yu*

Liudong Renkou Luncong [A collection of articles on hukou migration and floating population]. Beijing: Gong'an Daxue Chubanshe, pp. 103–25.

Zhang Xiaohui, et al. 1995. "1994: Nongcun Laodongli Kuaquyude Shezheng Miaoshu" [1994: An empirical description of the inter-regional flows of rural labour]. *Zhanlüe yu Guanli* 6, pp. 26–34.

Zhao Renwei. 1994. "Zhongguo Zhuanxingqi zhong Shouru Fenpaide Yixie Teshu Xianxiang" [Some special phenomena in income distribution in the transitional era in China]. In Zhao Renwei, et al. eds, *Zhongguo Jumin Shouru Fenpai Yanjiu* [A study of income distribution of the Chinese population]. Beijing: Zhongguo Shehui Kexue Chubanshe, pp. 93–113.

Zhongguo Shehui Kexue Yuan. 1996. "Jingji Zhuanggui Shiqi Zhongguo Nongcun Laodongli Liudong Yanjiu" [Rural Labour Migration during the Economic Transitional Era in China]. Unpublished report.

Zhou, Kate Xiao. 1996. *How the Farmers Changed China*. Boulder: Westview Press.

Notes

1 This section is based on Chan (1996b).

2 Li and Hu (1991) estimate that in the late 1980s one third of the floating population stayed one year or more. A study of the floating population in Beijing in 1994 revealed a proportion of forty per cent (Wang and Hu 1996).

3 The rate for high mobility Western countries, such as the US and Canada, is around eighteen to nineteen per cent per year.

4 While the contrasts are clear, it does not imply that hukou and non-hukou migration are totally separate. Indeed, hukou migrants can act as springboards for non-hukou migrant relatives and friends; hukou migrant labour can also be substituted by inexpensive non-hukou migrant labour, as economic pressures on state owned enterprises increase.

5 This most likely refers to work outside the home village. In this study, some migrant workers commute daily to participate in work outside.

6 Rozelle et al. (1997) report that in 1995 about one third of rural migrant workers in their national sample moved to jobs in other provinces.

7 Interviews with researchers at the Chinese Academy of Social Sciences in 1994 and 1995.

8 The other chapters in this book amply address this issue. Most significantly, migration decisions are made more commonly at the household level than at the individual level (Chant and Radcliffe 1992; Bilsborrow and UN Secretariat 1993); information for making decisions often comes from informal channels based on social ties, mainly through family and village networks (e.g. Gurak and Caces 1992). Furthermore, migration is also "cumulative", mainly due to prior migration experience, impact of migration on rural incomes, wealth distribution and agricultural production (Piore 1979; Georges 1990). These features necessitate an explicit recognition of the household and network, or information components in analyzing the perpetuation of migration streams, if not the onset of them. Research using the household approach emphasizes the importance of the family as a decision making unit, the gender role and division of labour on migration.

9 One report cites that by early 1994 altogether three million urban hukou books had been sold to peasants, generating a total revenue of twenty-five thousand million yuan (Xingdao Ribao [Sing Tao Daily], 8 February 1994, p. A5). It would be interesting to analyze the profile of this special "hukou migrant" group when data are available.

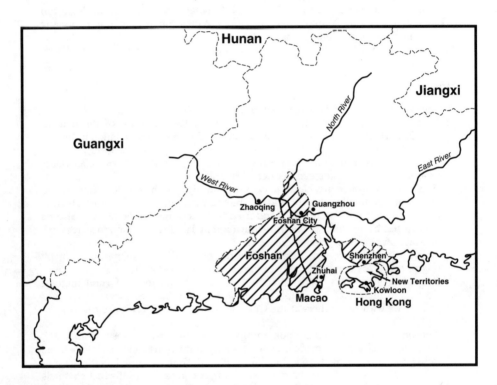

Guangdong Province

Chapter Four

Selectivity, migration reasons and backward linkages of rural-urban migrants: A sample survey of migrants to Foshan and Shenzhen in comparative perspective*

Thomas Scharping

Introduction

Current debates on Chinese migration resonate with a long standing controversy on the question of whether migration is transferring capital to backward or, conversely, to advanced regions. Back in 1958, Hirschman stressed the neoclassical argument. Whereas labour would migrate from low to high wage regions, capital would continue its incessant search for profitable investment opportunities and flow in the opposite direction. This would lead to a new equilibrium in which backward regions gain from the transfer of capital, while growth areas absorb unemployed labour (Hirschman 1958). Hirschman's reasoning was contradicted by Gunnar Myrdal who posited a selective outmigration of capital and labour from poor to advanced regions, with net gains for the growth centres producing ever-widening regional disparities (Myrdal 1957). His arguments were later taken up in the work of Samir Amin and Michael Lipton. They argued that a rural skill drain and remittances to the countryside, which either stay marginal or

*The data presented in this chapter were gathered in the course of a collaborative survey between Modern China Studies at Cologne University, Germany, and the State Statistical Bureau of China. I wish to acknowledge the valuable help of my collaborators from the State Statistical Bureau in Beijing, the Provincial Statistical Bureau of Guangdong and the city statistical bureaus of Foshan and Shenzhen in carrying out this survey. On the German side, Walter Schulze participated in survey work. Last but not least, I am grateful to the Volkswagen Foundation for generously supporting this research.

favour the better-off, led to a net negative balance for rural areas (Amin 1974; Lipton 1982). The empirical foundation for such sweeping generalizations, however, has remained patchy. Fieldwork in a number of developing nations has revealed large discrepancies in the remittance situation. Both substantial transfers and marginal sums, regular and intermittent payments have been documented (Findley 1977:49–51; Standing 1984:264–280; Tirasawat 1985; Chaney 1986; Chaudhuri 1993).

Contemporary debates in the People's Republic of China (PRC) mirror these problems. In the era of economic reforms, the reallocation of redundant labour from agriculture to industry and the tertiary sector has become a major concern. Similarly, the widening of regional gaps in the standard of living has developed into a problem that is said to threaten the inner coherence of the country. Usually, the consequences of migration for urban areas of destination have received most public attention. But just as important is the question whether outmigration from rural areas removes or augments capital there. The ageing, feminization and reduction of the work force in areas of heavy male outmigration is by now well documented (Christiansen 1992:72–93; Mallee 1995). In contrast, reports on large scale remittances from migrants to their places of origin have struck a happier chord (Gu and Jian 1994:359). Both positive and negative effects seem to be present. But as of today, we have barely begun to measure the various flows taking place, and we are as yet in no position to draw up a balance sheet of gains and losses. Do the poor or the prosperous, the better educated or the illiterate leave? Does migration create a measurable increase in disposable income? What kind of information channels connect the rural areas with urban areas of inmigration? To what extent do they structure a slowly emerging labour market? Are rural-urban migrants circulating or intending to stay in their areas of destination? To what extent do they induce comigration or deferred mobility of family members temporarily staying back home?

Migration is an extremely diverse phenomenon, leading to widespread dissolution of families in the Latin American case, and symbiotic relationships between areas of outmigration and inmigration which characterizes the African migration model. While many migrants in Africa spend their working life in the cities, they keep their families in the villages, regularly remitting funds for their wife and children. Their investments back home establish a base for their eventual return home (Du Toit and Safa 1975:56, 67). This is the model the Chinese government also prefers. Whether it will succeed will depend on both policy and autonomous social developments.

The Foshan-Shenzhen Survey and Other Data

By virtue of its proximity to Hong Kong and economic success during the reform period, Guangdong province in southeastern China has attracted migrants from all over the country. According to the census of 1990, seventeen per cent of the "floating population" (see Chan, this volume) were living in Guangdong, the overwhelming majority of them hailing from villages (Giese 1993; Guangdong Sheng Renkou Pucha Bangongshi 1992). Within Guangdong, the Pearl River Delta between Hong Kong and Guangzhou has been the most attractive area for inmigration, which is why it was chosen for the in-depth migration survey reported on here. Choosing the Special Economic Zone of Shenzhen ("SZ" in the tables and figures that follow) and the more traditional regional centre of Foshan City ("FS") in the northern Pearl River Delta as our survey places, we focused on the population above the age of fourteen, irrespective of registration status. We kept the five year residency cut-off point usually applied in Chinese statistics in our definition of migrants, but also included migrants who had arrived just recently with the intension to stay. Commuters and short term visitors were excluded though. In conformity with census procedures, only migration over city or county lines was covered (Scharping and Sun 1997; Scharping and Schulze 1997).

The analysis presented in this chapter reports some results of the survey for a subgroup of rural-urban migrants. Twelve per cent (Foshan) and seventeen per cent (Shenzhen) of this subgroup had transferred their permanent residence. Roughly forty-nine and fifty-six per cent had been staying for more than one year, but kept their rural registration. The rest had arrived more recently and had only obtained provisional registration. Altogether, these are rather long durations of stay, if they are compared to similar tabulations. Also, the sample composition is different from other official data with their usual preponderance of migrants with a transfer of household registration.

The lack of sufficiently detailed breakdowns in nation-wide counts, the paucity of census questions related to migration issues and the different handling of definitions and target groups in other local samples make it hard to obtain suitable other materials to compare with our findings. Great efforts have been made to arrive at compatible figures by appropriate filtering of data from the 1990 census (Guowuyuan Renkou Pucha Bangongshi 1993), the 1987 microcensus (Guojia Tongji Ju 1988; Guojia Tongji Ju, Zhongguo Renkou Tongji Nianjian 1989:571–573; Guangdong Sheng Tongji Ju 1988), and the 1986 survey of migration to seventy-four cities and towns of the Chinese Academy of Social Sciences (CASS) (Zhongguo Shehui Kexueyuan Renkou Yanjiusuo 1988, original database). This exercise entailed the separation of rural-urban migrants from the larger migration totals, the exclusion of dependents below the age of fifteen and the screening of CASS figures for migrants moving across city or county lines between 1981 and 1986.

Despite these efforts, a number of differences in legal, temporal and spatial definitions, as well as in coverage and methodology, remain between the resulting data sets (Scharping 1997). Most 1990 census materials cannot be used, because they only distinguish migration streams by places of origin and thus include rural-rural movement. Similar problems exist in various local studies, investigations by the Ministry of Agriculture (*Nongye Bu*) and the annual rural household survey (Research Group of Annual Analysis of Rural Economy 1994; Nongye Bu 1996; Guangdong Tongji Nianjian 1985 and later years; Guojia Tongji Ju 1993). It therefore has to be stressed that the comparative data presented in the following analysis do not constitute a coherent time series. Figures contain national and Guangdong province data from the 1986 CASS survey (designated "CASS 86" and "GD 86"), as well as data from the 1987 microcensus (designated "China 87" and "GD 87"). Both data sets refer to migrations in the preceding five year period. While the microcensus is clearly the more representative data set, it suffers from partial inclusion of intra-county migration. The CASS survey has more migration items, but is biased in favour of official migration with a transfer of household registration. Moreover, it only covers the cities of Guangzhou, Zhaoqing, Zhuhai and the town of Decheng within Guangdong province.

The analysis below involves first of all a discussion of selectivity criteria of personal attributes and figures for former income. Also considered are geographical patterns and macro-indicators for regions of origin. The following section of this chapter studies trends in migration reasons, comparing regional and gender specific characteristics. An attempt is made to separate pull from push factors. Analysis then proceeds to urban-rural linkages in relation to information flows, job-searching avenues, comigration and home visits. The emphasis here is on the interplay of informal networks, old channels of labour allocation and new mechanisms of an emerging labour market. The last section examines sources, uses and frequency of remittances as well as their volume in absolute and relative terms.

Migrant selectivity

A look at figure 4.1 reveals that young people have always been the dominant group in rural-urban migration. In all samples, rural-urban migrants are younger than other types of migrants and the non-migrant population at large. In particular, the percentage of very young people between fifteen and nineteen years of age is unusually large among rural-urban migrants. In the late 1980s and early 1990s, the share of young migrants seems to have increased further. This is connected both to the increase of rural underemployment and to the selection criteria of urban employers, who favour younger migrants in order to economize on welfare payments. In Foshan and Shenzhen, growth has been mostly due to the larger numbers of migrants with provisional household registration.

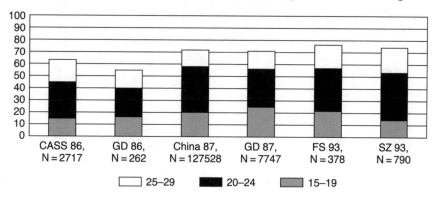

Figure 4.1 Rural-urban migrants by age (%)
Calculated from: database of the CASS 1986 migration survey in 74 cities and towns; Guojia Tongji Ju 1988; Guangdong Sheng Tongji Ju 1988; database of the 1993 migration survey in Foshan and Shenzhen.

Figure 4.1 confirms commonly held notions about migrant selectivity, but does not support the cruder assumption of "the younger the age-group, the higher its mobility". Clearly, people in the age bracket of twenty to twenty-four years are more involved in migration than the younger cohort of fifteen to nineteen years. The finding can be linked to the demands of the urban labour market, which often favours better educated youngsters. As shown by the Foshan and Shenzhen figures, this trend has become even more pronounced over time. In the case of Shenzhen, the demand for better educated migrants effectively raises the average age of migrants. This tallies well with the results of the CASS survey, which shows a correlation between migrant age and city size. Larger cities evidently pick better educated migrants. Another important correlation associates migrant age with household registration status. Both the Foshan-Shenzhen materials and the CASS data on persons with provisional registration show that rural-urban migrants with permanent registration in the cities are noticeably older than peasant migrants with provisional registration, who are employed in less qualified positions.

Table 4.1 compares other basic indicators for the social composition of migrants. A widely held assumption in migration studies is that mobility rises with household size. This has been the historical experience of the growth of Western cities, which attracted the offspring of large peasant families. Above-average household sizes for outmigrants are also found in Chinese village surveys (Nongye Bu 1996:30). Data from the Foshan-Shenzhen survey do not yield comparative information on rural non-migrant households. But the data can be used for assessing developments in time and offer indirect clues on some household factors involved. Viewing the sample as a whole, the data show that more than sixty per cent

77

Table 4.1: Demographic Indicators for Rural-Urban Migrants

	Former median household size	% Female	% Unmarried, female and male
CASS 1986 (N=2,717)		53.0	43.0
GD 1986 (N=262)		63.0	40.8
Microcensus 1987 (N=127,528)		56.5	
GD microcensus 1987 (N=7,747)		58.3	49.6
National Census 1990		45.2	
GD census 1990		48.6	
Shenzhen 1993 (N=790)	6.0	56.8	57.7
Foshan 1993 (N=378)	6.0	58.5	57.1

Calculated from: database of the 1993 migration survey in Foshan and Shenzhen; Guowuyuan Renkou Pucha Bangongshi 1993, volume 4; Guojia Tongji Ju 1988 Volume 1 and 2; Guangdong Sheng Tongji Ju 1988; database of the CASS 1986 migration survey in 74 cities and towns.

of rural-urban migrants mostly are from medium sized families with four to seven members.

The average household size of 6.0 that we found for Foshan and Shenzhen migrants looks large when compared to averages for rural household size obtained from national census data. The Guangdong average was 5.1 persons in the third census in 1982, falling to 4.7 persons in the census of 1990. The annual rural household survey yields a slightly higher Guangdong average of 5.4 in 1993 (Guowuyuan Renkou Pucha Bangongshi 1985; Guojia Tongji Ju, Zhongguo Renkou Tongji Nianjian 1988 1992; Guangdong Tongji Nianjian 1994). This may create the impression that among rural migrants members of large families are overrepresented. It has to be borne in mind, however, that migrants covered in the Foshan-Shenzhen sample were born before the advent of the one-child policy. They mostly belong to the large cohorts of people who were born between 1962 and 1972, when the average number of children born in rural households of Guangdong stood at roughly 6.0 (Coale and Chen 1987). With the enforcement of the two-child policy during 1973 to 1978, the total fertility rate in rural Guangdong dropped to 4.3. Only among people born in this latter period do migrants come from households that are on average larger. Data for Foshan show that the rural household size of migrants born between 1974 and 1978 decreased only slightly from 6.9 for those born in 1974 to 6.4 born in 1978. In the case of Shenzhen the average even went up from 6.0 to 6.7.

Documentation for the gender distribution of rural-urban migrants is better than that for household size as there exist a number of comparative data sets. The figures collected in table 4.1 suggest a rather varied picture of gender roles; they necessitate a revision of the general notion of male dominance in rural-urban migration. The Foshan-Shenzhen figures closely resemble the percentages for female migrants in the microcensus and in the

CASS survey. They also come close to the results of a 1987 Sino-Canadian survey in towns of Guangdong and other coastal provinces (Liu et al. 1990:151; Zhongguo Yanhai Diqu 1989:374). All numbers demonstrate that female migrants predominate in Guangdong, where they make up a bigger share of rural-urban migrants than in the national average.

The general rule is that the percentages for females peak in the age group of fifteen to nineteen year olds (around seventy-five per cent in Foshan and Shenzhen), gradually decreasing for older cohorts. This prevalence has manifold causes. First, it is connected to the fact that the peak of the construction boom in Foshan and Shenzhen is already over: (male) construction workers have only a small share of post-migration occupations in our survey. Perhaps even more important are the recruitment criteria of urban employers in the textile, garment and electronic industries, who clearly favour young women workers. There are also persistent complaints that many employers terminate the contracts of women on reaching the age of twenty-five, the usual time for marriage and child-bearing (China Labour Bulletin 11 (February 1995), pp. 5 and 7). Our data do not confirm that this has become a general rule: roughly thirty-five per cent of women who migrated in search of work were above the age of twenty-five.

A different pattern of gender roles seems to prevail in the interior of China, which slants the national averages in the census results away from our own findings in Guangdong. Apart from some areas traditionally supplying nannies for urban households (Xu 1991), males, many of them construction workers, dominate in migration in the interior. This is most pronounced in provinces of heavy rural outmigration such as Sichuan and Anhui where the percentage of female migrants can be as low as between thirty and thirty-five per cent (Li and Han 1994:3; Zhang Qingwu 1995; Nongye Bu 1996:6). Some rural investigations end up with still lower shares of fifteen to twenty-five per cent (Zhang Chunyuan 1991:14; Far Eastern Economic Review, 4 April 1996).

Percentages for female migrants also seem to be sensitive to the time criteria adopted in empirical research. Typically, they are lower whenever surveys on the floating population also include short term visitors to the cities. With the exception of family-related travel, most other types of short term mobility are dominated by men (Zhang Kaimin 1989:142; Li and Hu 1991:13; Zou 1996:356–59 and 364–70).

The marital status of rural-urban migrants is closely related to age and gender. The young age of migrants in Foshan and Shenzhen and the predominance of work-related migration reasons in both cities effectively raise the percentage of unmarried migrants there to about fifty-eight per cent. This is higher than the usual forty to fifty per cent in many other urban-based surveys. Because the cohort of migrants aged fifteen to nineteen is larger among women than men, the percentage of unmarried women (around sixty per cent) is higher than that of unmarried men (around fifty-five per cent). In village-based surveys of Sichuan and Anhui the trend is even more pronounced: unmarried persons make up almost seventy per cent of the female, but less than fifty per cent of the male migrants (Xu 1991:60; Nongye Bu 1996:8). Until the mid-1980s this was different. Migrants were older, labour migration from the villages was restricted and most women migrated for family reasons. The CASS migration survey therefore produces only a minority of thirty-nine per cent unmarried women among the female migrants of the 1981–86 period.

Figure 4.2 with data on the educational level of rural-urban migrants also reveals the influence of changing times. In the CASS survey of the mid-1980s, percentages for people with college or senior high school education are the highest of all the comparative data sets. At the same time, the share of undereducated migrants is also rather high. The subsequent liberalization of labour migration and the huge increase of migrants with provisional registration depress educational levels thereafter. However, the educational level of rural-urban migrants in most surveys is far higher than that of the rural population at large. This can also be gleaned from migrant surveys in villages in the hinterland, where educational levels generally are lower and decrease as one travels from east to west (Zhang Chunyuan 1991:15; Xu 1991:60; Li and Han 1994:10–14; Nongye Bu 1996:9).

In the Foshan and Shenzhen cases the 1990 census results for Guangdong yield a good yardstick for comparison: more than sixty-five per cent of the rural census population above age fourteen in the group of people with a low educational level (only elementary school or less) contrast with only fourteen per cent (Shenzhen) to thirty-one per cent (Foshan) among

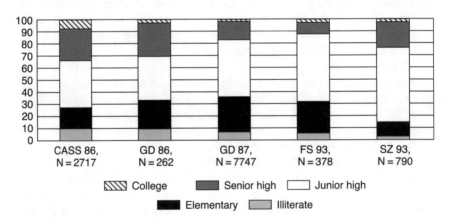

Figure 4.2 Educational level of rural-urban migrants (%)
Calculated from: database of the 1993 migration survey in Foshan and Shenzhen; database of the CASS 1986 migration survey in 74 cities and towns; Guangdong Sheng Tongji Ju 1988.

rural-urban migrants with the same educational level. For persons with higher education (senior high school, technical school or college) these figures are to seven, twenty-four and thirteen per cent (Guangdong Sheng Renkou Pucha Bangongshi 1994). The positive selection of rural-urban migrants is such that in some instances the percentages for people with a modest education are smaller than those for the urban non-migrant population. Undoubtedly, this phenomenon is also caused by the age composition of migrants, which largely excludes elderly people with little formal education. While Foshan seems to be a fairly typical case for the present educational attainment of migrants in coastal cities, Shenzhen with its strong emphasis on education sticks out as a case of strong positive selection.

The conclusion that can be drawn from the figures on former occupation of rural-urban migrants in figure 4.3a is the same as for education. In general, CASS figures on rural-urban migrants mirror official migration with a transfer of household registration and the strong selection

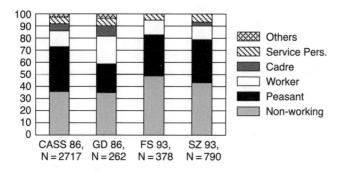

Figure 4.3a Former occupation of rural-urban migrants (%)

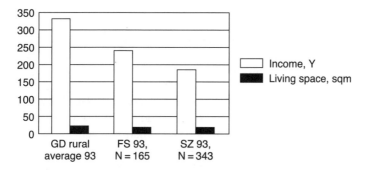

Figure 4.3b Pre-migration monthly income and living space of rural-urban migrants
Note: Income in figure 4.3b is the per capita figure for earning migrants and rural labourers respectively; living space is the per capita figure for all migrants and for the total rural population.
Calculated from: database of the 1993 migration survey in Foshan and Shenzhen; database of the CASS 1986 migration survey in 74 cities and towns; Guangdong Tongji Nianjian 1994.

that change entails. Obviously favoured groups are people with work experience, in particular those having worked outside agriculture. This is reflected in unusually high shares for workers and cadres (including specialists, technicians and administrative personnel). Seven years later, population dynamics, the diminishing age of migrants and the changing migration patterns of the reform period have pushed up the figures for former peasants and rural-urban migrants who had not worked before. Conversely, percentages for former holders of industrial and white collar positions have fallen. But even now they continue to be higher compared to most rural migrants elsewhere or the rural population of Guangdong at large (eighteen and twenty-one per cent in Foshan and Shenzhen and fourteen per cent for rural Guangdong). This also holds true for persons not having worked before migration: at forty-nine per cent (Shenzhen) and forty-four per cent (Foshan) of the total number of migrants in the sample, they make up only twenty-one per cent of the total rural population of Guangdong above age fourteen. Among rural-urban migrants working before migration, a clear achievement orientation seems to be operating in the selection process: There are more people who worked overtime, i.e. more than eight hours per day, before moving (thirty-six per cent of the Foshan and fifty-four per cent of the Shenzhen migrants) than there were people who had been underemployed before migration (twenty-one per cent and ten per cent of the respective total of migrants). In other respects, though, patterns of the past are persisting: rural-urban migrants of Foshan and Shenzhen, who occupied tenured positions in the state sector, still find it easier to acquire urban household registration.

Analysis of pre-migration income figures in the Foshan-Shenzhen sample shows positive associations with former occupation, employment status, working hours and educational levels. A drawback of the sample is the fact that only the former gross personal, rather than the former household income is available.

Although these figures do not fully reflect the economic situation of rural families as the basic production and consumption units, they can be compared to the annual survey figures on gross rural incomes. Such a comparison highlights the point that averages for pre-migration monthly income of earning migrants have been lower than the Guangdong average of monthly income per rural labourer by thirty per cent to forty per cent. Precise figures for Foshan, Shenzhen and rural Guangdong in 1993 amount to 239 yuan, 187 yuan and 330 yuan respectively (annual rural household survey figures from Guangdong Tongji Nianjian 1994). Because cases from the two cities contain accumulated numbers of migrants for the whole period from 1988 to 1993, these figures may be biased. But restricting comparison to those persons who migrated in the twelve months preceding the Foshan-Shenzhen survey and eliminating the glaringly anomalous case of a Guangdong building contractor reduce average former income figures of migrants even more (184 yuan for Foshan 171 yuan for Shenzhen). Furthermore, average numbers are distorted by a few atypically rich rural entrepreneurs and well-to-do workers in village industries. Median figures for the former income of earners, who migrated in the twelve months preceding the survey, are therefore considerably lower (150 yuan for Foshan and 100 yuan for Shenzhen).

How can we interpret such findings? Since there is no significant correlation between age and income in the data, and since figures on education and occupation suggest a predominantly positive selection of migrants, the data point to local poverty as the main push factor. This is further corroborated by the gap between average rural Guangdong and the migrants' pre-migration average income and living standards. The per capita living space that migrants enjoyed before their move to Foshan (15.9 square meters) or Shenzhen (16.1 square meters) is twenty-three per cent lower than the average for rural Guangdong households in 1993 (20.6 square meters). Similarly, the average per capita responsibility farmland in Guangdong (0.06 hectares) is higher than the pre-migration per capita responsibility farmland of the households of migrants to Foshan and Shenzhen (both 0.04 hectares; annual rural household survey figures from Guangdong Tongji Nianjian 1994). It is interesting to note that fourteen per cent of rural-urban migrants to Foshan and twenty-two per cent of those to Shenzhen indicated that their original household did not longer possess any responsibility farmland. These seem to be both people with non-agricultural employment and youths who recently moved out of their natal families without having had land allocated to them yet. In either case, ties to the countryside are certainly much weaker than for migrants who have land.

The information condensed in table 4.2 supports the hypothesis that local rather than personal poverty is an important push factor in migration. The table combines survey data on places of migrant origin with economic and social macro-indicators for these locations. Migration distances were calculated on the basis of questions about the area of origin; the other indicators were taken from the provincial volumes of 1990 census results and from the regular extract from statistical reports of county level units. As a last step, all individual data were divided by case numbers in order to obtain average values. It must be stressed that despite an attempt to arrive at disaggregated data for the local level, these are still approximations only. In a number of cases, migrants only indicated the municipality (prefecture) of origin without specifying the county. For these cases, aggregate data on municipal regions had to replace specific information on rural areas.

The message conveyed by the figures is nevertheless clear. The agricultural performance of Foshan and Shenzhen is about twice as high as of areas of outmigration, but this is dwarfed by the difference in the gross value of non-agricultural output.[1] Industry, construction, transportation and commerce are the main focus of attraction for migrants. Their

Table 4.2 Averages of macro indicators for regions of rural outmigration (1990)

	Rural areas, national average	Rural areas of outmigration to Foshan	Foshan city	Rural areas of outmigration to Shenzhen	Shenzhen city (SEZ)
Distance to destination	—	261 km	—	527 km	—
Private household size	4.2	4.3	3.5	4.3	3.3
Man-land-ratio	0.11 ha	0.06 ha	0.02 ha	0.06 ha	0.01 ha
Agricult. GVO p.c.	918 Y	1,117 Y	2,104 Y	1,004 Y	2,491 Y
Non-agricult. GVO p.c.	1,074 Y	1,369 Y	22,321 Y	1,069 Y	26,319 Y
% Illiterate	26.2%	13.2%	8.0%	14.5%	3.1%
% Senior high	5.9%	6.5%	15.7%	6.2%	25.3%

Note: Rural areas: man-land-ratio for cultivated area, agricultural and non-agricultural gross values of output (GVO) per capita of the rural population; educational levels for rural population aged 6–99, illiteracy rate for rural population aged 15–99, household size for total population aged 0–99. Foshan and Shenzhen cities: man-land-ratio and agricultural GVO per capita for the rural population of the city, all other data for total city population. Non-agricultural GVO is derived by subtracting agricultural GVO (*nongye zongchanzhi*) from social GVO (*shehui zongchanzhi*).

Sources: Places of origin calculated from the database of the 1993 migration survey in Foshan and Shenzhen; average indicators calculated from population census data for these municipal regions, cities and counties in: Guowuyuan Renkou Pucha Bangongshi 1993; from computer tabulations of the Fourth Census in Foshan and Shenzhen cities; from county and city data for the rural economy in Guojia Tongji Ju 1992; and from economic data for Foshan and Shenzhen in Guangdong tongji nianjian 1991 and Guojia Tongji Ju 1991a.

performance is about sixteen (Foshan) to twenty-five (Shenzhen) times as high as in rural areas of outmigration. Clearly, in Shenzhen the gap between urban and rural standards is much more pronounced than in the Foshan case. This is also indicated by the figures for educational levels. Economic and educational indicators for areas of outmigration are lower than the averages of Guangdong counties. Agricultural gross value of output in 1990 was 1512 yuan per capita of the rural population for all Guangdong counties combined, while non-agricultural gross value of output per capita of the rural population stood at 1770 yuan (comparable figures for the areas of outmigration are found in table 4.3 below). It deserves to be stressed, though, that these figures are generally better than the national averages for all rural areas (calculations are based on data in Guojia Tongji Ju, Zhongguo Tongji Nianjian 1991 and 1992; Guowuyuan Renkou Pucha Bangongshi 1993, volume 1–3; Guojia Tongji Ju 1991a and 1991b). This suggests that relative deprivation rather than absolute poverty furthers migration.

Table 4.2 reveals an unsurprising but nevertheless important point. The better endowment of Shenzhen has increased the pull of this place: the average distance between the Special Economic Zone and rural places of outmigration is exactly twice as large as in the case of Foshan. Whereas one third of the Foshan migrants come from places within 100 km from the city, less than six per cent have travelled more than 1,000 km. Strong parochial ties and traditional central-place linkages link Foshan to its hinterland and to areas in the Northwest and North of the province. Two

Table 4.3 Backward remittances to relatives by rural-urban migrants

	Average (yuan)			Average % of income		
	Male	*Female*	*Total*	*Male*	*Female*	*Total*
Foshan (N=193)						
Monthly remittances	179.7	125.0	157.8	35.4	32.8	34.4
Half-yearly remittances	441.2	314.7	372.2	15.8	17.1	16.5
Annual remittances	430.6	310.0	387.5	6.9	7.8	7.2
All regular remittances per month	101.5	66.9	85.0	20.6	19.8	20.2
Shenzhen (N=365)						
Monthly remittances	234.8	172.9	207.1	39.2	33.9	36.8
Half-yearly remittances	549.4	371.6	441.2	11.7	12.6	12.2
Annual remittances	519.7	457.4	486.8	8.1	6.5	7.3
All regular remittances per month	118.8	76.0	94.9	17.4	14.8	16.1

Calculated from: database of the 1993 Foshan and Shenzhen survey

thirds of all rural-urban migrants originate from within Guangdong province, more than twenty per cent hail from Guangxi, the rest come from Sichuan, Henan, Jiangxi, Hunan, or Zhejiang. Shenzhen's pattern is entirely different. The percentage of short distance migrants (less than 100 km) is only nine per cent, while long distance movement over more than 1,000 km is twenty-one per cent. With a share of roughly sixty per cent, migrants from within Guangdong also predominate in Shenzhen. Places of outmigration within the province, though, are more dispersed and tend to be situated in the Northeast and East. In interregional migration, Sichuan and Hunan dominate. As a telling indicator of its attractiveness, Shenzhen shelters a sprinkling of rural-urban migrants from faraway regions such as Jiangsu, or provinces in the North and Northeast of China. The contribution of these places to Foshan-orientated migration is practically nil.

Comparing this geographical pattern with other surveys on rural-urban migration, two tendencies should be noted. The first is the fact that the share of interregional migration increases with the growing size and economic importance of destination cities. In this regard, the Foshan and Shenzhen results closely resemble the Shanghai pattern where a 1988 survey found that nearly thirty-six per cent of all rural-urban migrants originated from provinces other than Jiangsu or Zhejiang. These are high percentages if they are juxtaposed to rural migration directed at small towns, where less than twenty per cent of the newcomers move farther away than 100 km (Zhang Kaimin 1989:146; Liu et al. 1990:133). The second point concerning the geographical pattern of migration is that the share of interregional migration seems to increase in time. In Guangdong it made up roughly five per cent in both the CASS survey of 1986 and the microcensus of 1987, jumping to twenty-nine per cent in the census of 1990. A similar rise can be observed in the national data, where the respective figure stood at thirty per cent for the period 1985–1990.

Migration Reasons

A glance at figure 4.4 confirms the conclusion that economic motives have begun to play the major role in rural-urban migration. The pre-eminence of that motive may be even greater than conveyed by the figure, as any attempt at comparative analysis struggles with a number of definitional problems.[2]

The Foshan-Shenzhen survey has tried to evade these complications by separating questions about job search from reasons for inmigration. "Looking for work" was the only work-related item in the usual list of reasons for inmigration. The figure aptly shows how this motive has grown to be the overwhelming driving-force for rural-urban migration to the Pearl River delta. Before 1981, the causal structure of migration was intimately linked to the history of migration controls and political campaigns (Scharping 1981). The CASS figures for the 1981–86 period still partially reflect these circumstances, as the high shares for "other" migration reasons reflect various remedial policies. Since the mid-1980s, liberalization of movement and phenomenal economic growth, especially in the South, play a major role. Work-related migration increases and family-related migration decreases in the reform period. Once again, this is reflected only imperfectly in figure 4.4. Data from the 1987 microcensus also contain dependents under age fifteen, while 1990 census figures are not included, since they do not allow a strict separating out of rural-to-urban migration. But the available census figures on all types of migration from villages indicate that Guangdong has developed into the most prominent case of economically motivated inmigration in the whole of China. No other

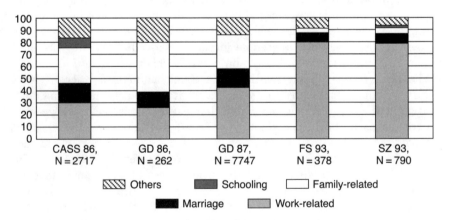

Figure 4.4 Migration reasons of rural-urban migrants (%)

Calculated from: database of the 1993 migration survey in Foshan and Shenzhen; Guangdong Sheng Tongji Ju 1988; database of the CASS 1986 migration survey in 74 cities and towns.

region exceeds the high share of seventy-two per cent of all migrant cases in the "work-related" category. Even in prosperous coastal regions such as Jiangsu, Zhejiang or Fujian, work-related inmigration from the countryside makes up only forty per cent to forty-five per cent of all cases. In the Beijing and Shanghai municipal regions, which are long standing magnets for migrants, this percentage climbs to sixty-five per cent – still lower than in Guangdong. At the other end of the spectrum, work-related inmigration in the backward hinterland provinces of the Northeast, Southwest and Northwest shrinks to less than one third of all cases.

In a further attempt to enhance the understanding of motivational structure, we have tried to separate pull from push factors by also asking why migrants left their original employment in their place of origin. The results for Foshan and Shenzhen, which covered only migrants who had been employed before, were quite similar. Of all respondents, forty-seven and fifty per cent indicated that their former income was too low; fifteen per cent gave redundancy as their primary motive for leaving their job; ten and thirteen per cent left because they were accompanying a spouse; eight and nine per cent were dissatisfied with their type of work.

These figures corroborate the finding that economic motives predominate in rural-urban migration in Guangdong province. As indicated by the figure for labour redundancy and the high percentage of forty-four and forty-nine per cent of rural-urban migrants not working before, rural underemployment has become manifest. It is certainly also an important cause for depressed rural incomes, which are the second major motive for leaving the countryside.

While percentages for work-related rural-urban migration reasons in both cities do not show conspicuously high gender differences, strong sex specifics can be discerned in family-related items. Marriage and staying with relatives are inmigration reasons which almost invariably apply to women (around ninety-five and eighty per cent of all cases in these categories). Comigration, which in this context denotes the permission for transferred cadres, workers and staff to take their family members along with them, is another item which predominantly concerns women (around seventy-eight per cent of all cases within this category). For family-related migration reasons, these are quite ordinary figures and indicators of strong patrilocal traditions in society. Since 1949, the share of women in marriage-related rural-urban migration has consistently exceeded ninety per cent nationally. If marriage migration is calculated as a percentage of all female rural-urban migrations since 1949, it would amount to roughly twenty-six per cent.

As further evidence for the rise of economic forces in migration, the percentage of female marriage related migration has been decreasing in recent years. Conversely, the percentages for women in work-related migration have been rising. Guangdong province is at the forefront of this development: roughly fifty-three per in all work-related rural-urban migrants in the Foshan-Shenzhen survey were women, surpassing the already high Guangdong census figure of forty-seven per cent for the period 1985–1990 and the CASS result of thirty-eight per cent for Guangdong in the period 1949–1986. The number of women in work-related rural-urban migration in the Pearl River Delta was thirty per cent in 1985–1990 and twenty-three per cent in 1949–1986 (calculated from the database of the 1986 CASS migration survey and from microcensus and census figures in Guangdong Sheng Tongji Ju 1988 and Guowuyuan Renkou Pucha Bangongshi 1993).

Information flow and job-searching avenues

Access to information and assistance is a crucial factor for successfully establishing a foothold in the city. In the academic debate on such links, the results of the Foshan-Shenzhen survey come down on the side of those who maintain that most migrants do not act as isolated individuals in hostile and unknown urban surroundings, but rather move within networks. For this reason, the spread of information in the villages of origin must be considered a most important backward linkage. This is the main message of figure 4.5a.

Of all rural-urban migrants to Foshan, no less than seventy-two per cent have acquaintances at their place of destination; in Shenzhen this percentage even climbs to ninety-four per cent. Most important among these acquaintances are relatives. Friends follow closely in second position, other types of acquaintances are less important. The data show that all these people were earlier migrants themselves: the majority had arrived five to seven years before, sizeable percentages were also recorded for those who had arrived between two and four years before.

Acquaintances who acted on behalf of the few rural-urban migrants with a change of household registration had arrived the earliest, on the average eight years before the arrival of the respondent himself or herself.

According to the figures in figure 4.5b, which largely resemble 1995 survey results from villages in Sichuan and Anhui provinces (Nongye Bu 1996:37), relatives and friends were also the most important sources of information on work and life in Foshan and Shenzhen (eighty and eighty-five per cent). The low shares for information through the media (two and four per cent) and state agencies (one and four per cent) reveal the importance of personal connections. They are particularly important for less privileged groups, such as women, dependents, or those with a modest education. The few respondents who gave state agencies as their main sources of information were almost exclusively men and holders of tenured jobs. But even among the group of rural-urban migrants who moved by way of an organized work-transfer one quarter to one third mainly relied on relatives for information.

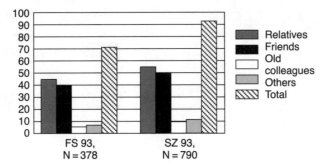

Figure 4.5a Acquaintances at destination of rural-urban migrants (%)

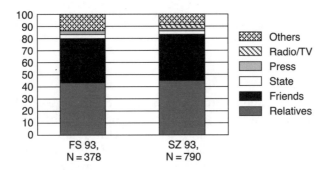

Figure 4.5b Information source for destination of rural-urban migrants (%)
Note: Checking more than one type of acquaintance was permitted. The percentages in figure 4.6a therefore do not add up to 100. Total indicates the percentage of migrants with any type of acquaintance.
Calculated from: database of the 1993 migration survey in Foshan and Shenzhen.

Relatives and friends are not only useful in securing information, but also assist in finding work and accommodation. The 1987 migrant survey in thirty-six coastal towns established these services as the main economic and social functions of urban relatives for their migrating rural kin. Interesting enough, the provision of credit was unimportant (only 1.6 per cent of all cases), while more than forty-two per cent of the respondents in that survey indicated that relatives did not extend any help (Liu et al. 1990:144).

In the Foshan-Shenzhen survey, we tested the importance of personal connections for finding work only. The results plus comparative figures from other surveys are shown in figure 4.6.[3] The CASS data in this figure reveal the characteristics of the early reform period. After its almost total disappearance during 1958–78, self-employment starts to regain an important position. Simultaneously, as a result of large scale army demobilization and increase of transfers and remedial policies for banished

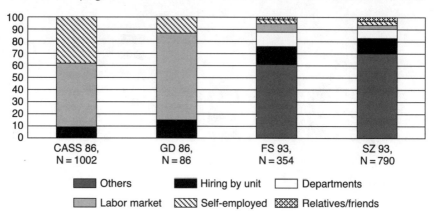

Figure 4.6 Job searching avenues of rural-urban migrants (%)

Note: Data from the CASS survey have been recategorized.

Calculated from: database of the 1993 migration survey in Foshan and Shenzhen; database of the 1986 CASS migration survey in 74 cities and towns.

people, work allocation through departments also rises, while work-replacement of younger family members of retiring members of work units (*dingti*) has slowly receded from the high level it occupied ever since the Great Leap Forward (1958–1961). The figure furthermore demonstrates that, in the early 1980s, Guangdong already showed notable differences from the national picture.

In the Foshan-Shenzhen study, introductions by friends and relatives have become the most important way to find employment (sixty-one per cent in Foshan and seventy-one per cent in Shenzhen), far surpassing self-employment (fifteen and twelve per cent). In twelve (Foshan) and eight per cent (Shenzhen) of the cases, third place is occupied by different forms of job searching under labour market conditions, such as job advertisements, labour exchanges, own applications, or through work team leaders. The various forms of labour allocation by government departments have diminished to seven per cent in Foshan and four per cent in Shenzhen; hiring by units has decreased to a minuscule three per cent in both cities.

These percentages approach the levels of some village surveys, where the proportion of people seeking work through relatives and friends can vary from one quarter to more than eighty per cent (Henan Sheng Nongcun Shehui Jingji Jiaochadui 1991:44–45; Mallee 1995:14; Nongye Bu 1996:14). Generally, the role of personal acquaintances seems to rise with migration distance. Data from Foshan and Shenzhen further indicate that it is mainly rural workers, who respond to job advertisements, or are hired by self-recruiting urban companies, whereas the more numerous former peasants and non-working villagers to a larger degree prefer to work through personal networks. It therefore comes as no surprise that thirty-three (Shenzhen) and thirty-eight per cent (Foshan) of rural-urban migrants indicate that they have relatives in their present work unit.

Comigration and home visits

Because only categories of persons could be checked and no precise numbers were asked, Foshan and Shenzhen data on the comigration of both relatives and non-relatives are inconclusive. They do not allow to test the association between former household size and the volume of outmigration. Moreover, comparative data from larger cities or a nation-wide sample are lacking. Nevertheless, some general trends can be discerned from figure 4.7 and further data analysis. One of these trends is that comigration in both cities under investigation was quite extensive; only forty (Foshan) and twelve per cent (Shenzhen) of migrants moved alone. Not unexpected is the finding that percentages for comigrating members of nuclear families are higher once an official change of household registration is granted. Figures for parents, siblings, spouses and children moving along with migrants with a permanent registration at the destination are more than twice as large as for migrants with only provisional registration. Higher age, smaller family size, longer stay, greater income and better education correlate positively with permanent registration status and comigration of parents, spouses or children. In contrast, siblings tend to come from larger families and comigrate with younger persons holding provisional registration. One group which displays a significantly higher propensity to take relatives along are self-

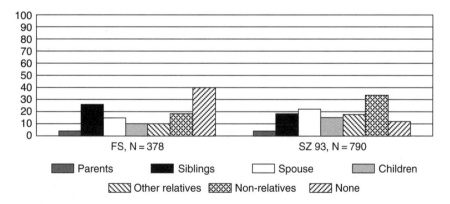

Figure 4.7 Comigrants of rural-urban migrants (%)

Note: Checking more than one type of comigrant was permitted. Figures therefore refer to categories checked and not to numbers of cases within categories. Calculated from the database of the 1993 migration survey in Foshan and Shenzhen.

employed people, whose businesses are mostly organized along family lines. In the majority of cases, these are migrants from areas nearby.

Of particular importance for the evaluation of long term trends is the behaviour of married migrants. Here, the Foshan survey shows that about one third of all married rural-urban migrants took their spouse along; in Shenzhen, on third of the married men and two thirds of the married women migrated with their spouse. Similarly, about one third of migrants took their children along.

Most Foshan and Shenzhen migrants do not take up work seasonally. Their pattern of home visits is different from seasonal migrants, who tend to go back in February/March and October/November. Because of the higher share of long distance migration, in the Shenzhen sample the percentage of regular visitors to the place of origin is lower than in Foshan: twenty-five compared to thirty-eight per cent for half-yearly visitors, and fifty-six compared to seventy-eight per cent for those visiting home at least once a year.

Eighty-four per cent of all rural-urban migrants in both Foshan and Shenzhen have assets in their home villages. These include responsibility land, houses and personal valuables. It is noteworthy that more than one half of rural-urban migrants with permanent registration in the two cities own property at the place of origin. Within the group of those who travel home twice a year there is a pronounced link to pre-migration household size: for large households with more than eight members, the percentage of migrants travelling home twice a year is roughly forty and fifty per cent; thirty and forty per cent from a medium sized household (five to eight members), and ten and twenty per cent from small households (one to four members) return home at least twice a year. Migrants in Shenzhen with provisional registration status are clearly more prone to travel home twice a year: twenty-nine per cent keep up this kind of regular connection, while only ten per cent of migrants with permanent registration do so. The comparatively strongest association, though, can be observed between the frequency of home visits and the distance to places of origin (r = −0.46 for Foshan, r = −0.39 for Shenzhen). Quite obviously, long distances reduce the number of home visits.

Forward and backward remittances

In some recent Chinese discussions remittances are often singled out as the most important positive aspect of rural-urban mobility.[4] Generally, the study of remittances is confined to backward flows to the countryside. For a fuller treatment of the subject forward remittances from the villages to the cities also have to be considered. Forward remittances are needed to cover the cost of travel and the initial period in the city before the migrant starts earning money. Among the expenses incurred are also mandatory lump sums that have to be paid as "deposits" and "loans" to urban enterprises in order to obtain a job (Oi 1990:31–33). Here, as in other areas, legitimate means for capitalizing newly founded enterprises shade into corruption. While our background interviews point to the widespread existence of the practice, in the survey less than five per cent of rural-urban migrants admitted having paid money for a job. Forward remittances include money saved prior to migration, support from relatives and friends, and money raised through membership of credit associations. In view of the fact that acquaintances at places of destination are also migrants, their financial help should also be considered a type of forward remittances.

The data from Foshan and Shenzhen reveal extremely low levels of financial support. Overall, less than five per cent of all migrants used savings or received financial assistance. The savings used averaged 27 yuan in Foshan and 66 yuan in Shenzhen; the average support from relatives at home was only 12 and 33 yuan. In contrast to the situation in Foshan, Shenzhen migrants enjoyed more help from relatives on the spot (29 yuan).[5]

Apart from actual levels of support, the survey question about help in case of need serves as an important indicator of risk spreading. Here, sixty-two (Foshan) and fifty-seven per cent (Shenzhen) of all rural-urban migrants indicated that relatives and friends in home villages remained their primary sources of potential aid. Twenty and thirty-one per cent said they would turn to relatives and friends at the places of origin, the rest of the respondents could not think of any source of help, or was uncertain about it.

Much more substantial figures can be documented for backward remittances, which in the case of the two cities under investigation are almost exclusively earmarked for family assistance. Remittance frequency for Foshan and Shenzhen is basically similar. Half-yearly remittances are the most prevalent form of payment (thirty-two and thirty-six per cent), followed by monthly remittances (sixteen and thirteen per cent) and annual payments (eight and twelve per cent). Payments over a period longer than one year are rather unimportant (three and six per cent). The percentage of non-remitting earning migrants diminishes with the length of stay. In Foshan, it is forty-eight per cent after one year and thirty-eight per cent after five years of stay; in Shenzhen these figures are forty-four and twenty-two per cent.

Table 4.3 presents the findings as to the backward remittances by rural-urban migrants. First, average sums of monthly, half-yearly and annual remittances were calculated; these were then consolidated into an average of all regular remittances per month. Payments over irregular periods of less than one year were not taken into consideration. Finally, the figures were compared to total personal income per month at the time of the survey. Just as in the case of pre-migration income figures, the data on average remittances and present income levels are skewed by a small number of highly affluent individuals. Comparing the absolute amounts highlights the fact that money transfers from Foshan are ten per cent lower than those from Shenzhen. This is certainly due to the higher income levels in Shenzhen. But when one compares remittance level to migrant income, Foshan is ahead of Shenzhen.

Overall, the average percentage of income remitted by our Foshan and Shenzhen respondents approaches levels in other developing countries, but clearly is lower than the thirty-five to forty-nine per cent found in a 1994 rural survey of Anhui and Sichuan migrants. Still higher amounts of up to 165 yuan per month and remittances of fifty to seventy per cent of migrant income were recorded by rural surveys that covered more intraregional and short distance mobility than our own survey (Gu and Jian 1994:4–5, 359; Banyuetan, 25 February 1994; Nongye Bu 1996:45; Henan Sheng Nongcun Shehui Jingji Diaochadui 1991:45; Research Group of the Annual Analysis of Rural Economy 1994:111; Far Eastern Economic Review, 4 April 1996).

The discrepancy between remittances by men and women in our survey is great. Women tend to remit thirty (Foshan) and thirty-five (Shenzhen) per cent less than men. The gap is particularly pronounced for large amounts of more than 2,000 yuan annually. As the relative levels of transfers are largely the same for men and women, this again is caused mainly by differences in present income. Mean incomes of female migrants in Foshan and Shenzhen are twenty-five and thirty per cent lower than those of men. Further analysis of the larger Shenzhen sample reveals an obvious link between comigration and remittance levels. Remitters who took their spouse or children along with them transferred less than those moving without dependents. While fifty per cent of the latter group sent amounts of more than 1,000 yuan per year to relatives back home, this percentage diminished to ten to twenty per cent in the case of remitters moving with spouse or children. Provisional registration status and work related migration reasons were further factors raising remittances, while change of permanent registration and family-related migration reasons tended to lower money transfers. Other variables, such as age and former household size, educational level, employment status and length of stay, only showed weak associations with remittance levels.

Besides backward remittances to relatives, we also asked about money transfers to former work units. It turned out that only two (Foshan) or three per cent (Shenzhen) of all earning rural-urban migrants in both cities made such payments, ranging from 30 yuan per year to 300 yuan per month.

Figure 4.8 is an attempt to sum up the situation by calculating average figures for income and forward and backward remittances by including non-remitters in the balance sheet. It demonstrates that backward remittances greatly exceed forward transfers, leaving migrants with a disposable income comparable to the first (lowest) quintile of non-migrant earners in the city (Scharping and Sun 1997; Scharping and Schulze 1997).

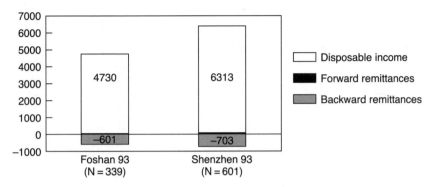

Figure 4.8 Balance of annual income and remittances: Per capita total earnings of rural-urban migrants (yuan)

Note: The average numbers in this table also include earnings of non-remitting migrants. Backward remittances with intervals of less than one year are counted as biannual transfers. The balance does not cover figures for earning migrants with unclear or missing answers as to their present income. Inclusion of these persons and of non-earning migrants lowers annual per capita remittances for the migrant totals to 555 yuan (Foshan) and 532 yuan (Shenzhen). *Calculated from*: database of the 1993 migration survey in Foshan and Shenzhen.

Yet an essentially ambivalent situation remains. Migrant income is large enough to support a large number of villagers. Combining survey data and census materials with information from household registers and background interviews, we estimate that there were a total of 120,000 rural-urban migrants in Foshan and 450,000 migrants in Shenzhen in 1993. Their backward remittances are estimated to be about sixty-seven million and 239 million yuan respectively.

In relation to rural incomes, the Foshan and Shenzhen level of transfers per earning migrant was twenty-seven (Foshan) and thirty-one (Shenzhen) per cent of the per capita income for rural household members in Guangdong (Guangdong tongji nianjian 1994). This level is slightly higher than in a rural survey conducted one year later in villages of Sichuan and Anhui with heavy seasonal outmigration. In these villages remittances received from seasonal outmigrants on average made up twenty to twenty-five per cent of per capita income in migrant households. This percentage was highest among poor households (Nongye Bu 1996:46). For the whole peasant population of China including non-migrant households, though, the share of remittances in per capita income is definitely smaller and may even be declining: The national totals in the annual rural household survey are 3.2 per cent in 1978, decreasing to 0.7 per cent in 1991 (Guojia Tongji Ju 1993:7). Such wide differences in the contribution of remittances to the peasant economy seem to be mainly caused by different income levels and the availability of work outside the villages.

Conclusions

This chapter has tried to establish benchmarks for evaluating temporal and regional variation in Chinese migration patterns. The comparison of a sample survey in Foshan and Shenzhen with other data on rural-urban migration confirms some general trends in the economic and demographic dynamics of China. Work related migration from villages to the cities is rising due to the decollectivization of agricultural production that brought to the fore rural underemployment, depressed peasant incomes and growing urban affluence. Our survey from the Pearl River Delta shows that nearly one half of the migrants are young peasants, who do not have any work experience and prefer to look for a job in the city. Many of them hail from rural households of above average size. A rising number is moving because of labour redundancy. Demographic pressures and the effects of the increased efficiency of village enterprises seem to act as major push factors. These factors are strengthened by the pull of the rural-urban income gap.

Typically, migrants originate from the poorer regions of the country: the northern districts of Guangdong and the largely agrarian hinterland provinces in southwest, central and south China. Nevertheless, macro indicators reveal that economic and social conditions in outmigration areas for Foshan and Shenzhen are still above the national average. This confirms findings from other studies which show that mobility in poverty areas is low. Market access and the availability of non-agricultural employment can be assumed to be the major factors involved.

While traditional central place linkages continue to play an important role in intraregional movement, there is a general trend for an increase in long distance migration. This is most pronounced in Shenzhen, where the income gap with areas of outmigration is particularly large. Within places of origin, the majority of rural-urban migrants seems to be positively selected. Surveys show an ever-rising share of the younger age groups, a predominance of better educated villagers and a disproportionate number of persons from non-agricultural pursuits. This is the general trend for the coastal region. Migration patterns of the hinterland are characterised by the greater role played by undereducated peasants.

In comparison to the earlier period of highly restricted movement from the villages, however, educational levels and former occupational status of rural-urban migrants are falling everywhere. This is connected to the provisional admittance of large numbers of villagers into the cities, where they provide cheap labour without enjoying the benefits of permanent registration. Under the policies of economic reform, the revitalized private sector is the major beneficiary of this development. Its employment share among rural-urban migrants is markedly higher than for the non-migrant population. In the two cities under investigation the ownership of work units of earning rural-urban migrants was as follows (percentages for the non-migrant population in parentheses): Foshan – private enterprises 8.6 per cent (1.7), self-employed 26.1 per cent (9.6), foreign enterprises 3.7 per cent (0.9), enterprises in Hong Kong, Macao, Taiwan or Overseas Chinese ownership 4.3 per cent (0.8); Shenzhen – private enterprises 8.1 per cent (2.1), self-employed 22.1 per cent (10.2), foreign enterprises 3.6 per cent (9.7), enterprises in Hong Kong, Macao, Taiwan or Overseas Chinese ownership 30.0 per cent (8.1).

A further trend worth noting is the rising number of young, unmarried women joining the migration stream from the villages. With its predominance of female migrants, Guangdong is at the forefront of a development which is also found in other coastal regions. The work-related nature of female mobility is a novel element still largely alien to the hinterland, where male outmigration leaves most of the women in the villages. Despite much public attention for a growing number of long distance migrations within the framework of a rural-urban marriage market, marriage migration seems to decrease, at least in relative terms. With a share of less than eight per cent of total migration in the Foshan-Shenzhen sample and ten to fifteen per cent in the other surveys on rural-urban migration, it is much below the level of approximately thirty per cent recorded in many other developing countries. Among the married migrants, one third is taking their spouse along. Other types of comigration mostly involve siblings or non-relatives. They add up to sixty and ninety per cent of migrants moving together with other villagers. This forms the basis for chain migration backed up by regular home visits.

Job searching by way of personal connections has replaced the former channels of labour allocation through administrative departments. With more than eighty per cent of migrants obtaining information on the place of destination from relatives and friends, two thirds relying on kin for obtaining work and more than one third having relatives in their present work unit, the survey documents the extraordinary extent of this substitution. In Foshan and Shenzhen, family-based networks relegate both remaining conduits for labour allocation and new institutions for the matching of employers and job searchers to a minor role. Similar trends can be observed for rural migrant workers with provisional registration in other parts of the country. This makes it necessary to qualify the notion of an emerging labour market in China. Opportunities and information seem to be unequally distributed. This is not only documented by the overwhelming influence of traditional primary groups, but also by state policies in favour of worker recruitment from the same region. The interplay of such regulations with rudimentary market institutions and the all-pervasive personal connections suggest that labour market segmentation along social networks coupled with bureaucratic protectionism at the regional and local level may be the better model for analyzing the mechanics of the new labour relations. For the two survey places in the period 1988–1993, this provided work for most of the inmigrants almost instantaneously upon arrival.

The success of Foshan and Shenzhen migrants sampled is also attested by the balance of forward and backward remittances: personal savings and financial assistance from relatives to support the migrants in their new environment are extremely limited; they are dwarfed by backward transfers to the areas of outmigration. In this respect, the findings confirm other reports about large scale migrant remittances. With annual averages for all earning migrants of roughly 600–700 yuan, equalling some ten per cent of migrant income, the level of remittances in Foshan and Shenzhen is similar to many other developing countries, though it is somewhat lower than the very high figures reported for some other parts of China. Variation in remittances seems to be rather large and to depend on the distance and periodicity of the migration.

But in any case these transfers seem to be large enough to question the arguments of those who lead to a general drain of resources from the countryside. Quite the opposite, in many parts of China remittances seem to have developed into a sizeable part of rural income. Our data do not allow to examine remittance usage, nor do they permit to analyse their effects for income and stratification, investment, production and consumption trends in the countryside. In a similar vein, the data point to a predominantly positive selection of migrants, but they do not lend themselves to generalizing about a skill drain. Exploring the long term consequences of migration for China's villages thus defines the agenda for future studies.

And there are other questions awaiting future research: It is a fair guess that transfer levels are intimately tied to the future expectations and plans of the remitters. Most village surveys demonstrate that up to now the vast majority of migrants return home after several stints of work outside. But although seasonal or cyclic migration seems still to prevail, pressure to stay in the cities is building up. Some eighty per cent of our respondents in Foshan and Shenzhen wanted to keep up their present work. And only one per cent of those desiring to change their work unit wanted to return to their native village. Does this constitute a long range orientation or is it just a short term variation? What will be the chances for permanent settlement in view of enduring state policies for controlling urban population growth? Will migrants continue to define themselves primarily as a rural elite or gradually become urban underdogs? And what would this creation of a new and volatile urban stratum mean for the future social, economic and political structure of China? These are core questions for Chinese migration in the coming years.

Bibliography

Amin, Samir, ed. 1974. *Modern Migrations in Western Africa*. London: Oxford University Press.

Chaney, Rick. 1986. *Regional Emigration and Remittances in Developing Countries: The Portuguese Experience*. New York: Praeger.

Chaudhuri, Jayasri Ray. 1993. *Migration and Remittances: Inter-Urban and Rural-Urban Linkages*. New Delhi: Sage.

Christiansen, Flemming. 1992. "Market Transition in China, The Case of the Jiangsu Labor Market 1978–1990." *Modern China* 18, no. 1, pp. 72–93.

Coale, Ansley J., and Chen Shengli. 1987. *Basic Data on Fertility in the Provinces of China 1940–82*. Honolulu: East-West Center.

Du Toit, Brian M. and Helen I. Safa, eds. 1975. *Migration and Urbanization: Models and Adaptive Strategies*. The Hague: Mouton.

Findley, Sally. 1977. *Planning for Internal Migration: A Review of Issues and Policies in Developing Countries*. Washington: Department of Commerce.

Giese, Karsten. 1993. *Landflucht und interprovinzielle Migration in der VR China, "Mangliu" 1989 – eine Fallstudie*. Hamburg: Institut für Asienkunde.

Gu Shengzu and Jian Xinhua (1994*),* *Dangdai Zhongguo Renkou Liudong yu Chengzhenhua* [Population mobility and urbanization in contemporary China]. Wuhan: Wuhan Daxue Chubanshe.

Guangdong Sheng Renkou Pucha Bangongshi, ed. 1992. *Guangdong Sheng Disi Ci Renkou Pucha Liudong Renkou Ziliao* [Data on floating population from the 1990 population census in Guangdong]. Guangzhou: n.p.

Guangdong Sheng Renkou Pucha Bangongshi, ed. 1994. *Guangdong Sheng 1990 Nian Renkou Pucha Ziliao* [Materials from the 1990 population census of Guangdong province]. Volume 2. Beijing: Zhongguo Tongji Chubanshe.

Guangdong Sheng Tongji Ju, ed. 1988. *Zhongguo 1987 Nian 1% Renkou Chouyang Diaochao Ziliao: Guangdong Fence 1988* [Materials of the 1 per cent sample survey on the national population: Guangdong]. Guangzhou: n.p.

n.a. Various years. *Guangdong Tongji Nianjian* [Statistical yearbook of Guangdong]. Beijing: Zhongguo Tongji Chubanshe.

Guojia Tongji Ju, ed. 1988. *1987 Nian Quanguo 1% Renkou Chouyang Diaocha Zziliao* [Materials of the 1 per cent sample survey on the national population]. 3 volumes. Beijing: Zhongguo Tongji Chubanshe.

Guojia Tongji Ju, ed. 1991a. *Zhongguo Chengshi Tongji Nianjian* [Statistical yearbook of Chinese cities]. Beijing: Zhongguo Tongji Chubanshe.

Guojia Tongji Ju, ed. 1991b. *Zhongguo Nongcun Tongji Nianjian* [Yearbook of Chinese rural statistics]. Beijing: Zhongguo Tongji Chubanshe.

Guojia Tongji Ju, ed. 1992. *Zhongguo Fenxian Nongcun Jingji Tongji Gaiyao 1990* [Statistical compendium of the Chinese rural economy by counties 1990]. Beijing: Zhongguo Tongji Chubanshe.

Guojia Tongji Ju, ed. Multiple years. *Zhongguo Renkou Tongji Nianjian* [Population yearbook of China]. Beijing: Zhongguo Tongji Chubanshe.

Guojia Tongji Ju, ed. Multiple years. *Zhongguo Tongji Nianjian* [China statistical yearbook]. Beijing: Zhongguo Tongji Chubanshe.

Guojia Tongji Ju, ed. 1993. *Zhongguo Nongcun Zhuhu Diaocha Nianjian* [Yearbook of the Chinese rural household survey]. Beijing: Zhongguo Tongji Chubanshe.

Guowuyuan Renkou Pucha Bangongshi, ed. 1985. *Zhongguo 1982 Nian Renkou Pucha Ziliao* [Data from the 1982 population census of China]. Beijing: Zhongguo Tongji Chubanshe.

Guowuyuan Renkou Pucha Bangongshi, ed. 1993. *Zhongguo 1990 Nian Renkou Pucha Ziliao* [Data from the 1990 population census of China]. Volume 4. Beijing: Zhongguo Tongji Chubanshe.

Henan Sheng Nongcun Shehui Jingji Diaochadui. 1991. "Guanyu Nongcun Renkou Waichu Liudong Qingkuangde Diaocha" [A Survey on rural out-migrants]. *Renkou yu jingji* 1991, no. 3, pp. 42–6.

Hirschman, A.O. 1958. *The Strategy of Economic Development*. New Haven: Yale University Press.

Li Fan and Han Xiaoyun. 1994. "Waichu Dagong Renyuande Nianling Jiegou he Wenhua Goucheng" [Age structure and educational composition of migrant workers]. *Zhongguo Nongcun Jingji* 1994, no. 8, pp. 10–4.

Li Mengbai and Hu Xin, eds. 1991. *Liudong Renkou dui Dachengshi Fazhande Yingxiang ji Duice* [The influence of floating population on the big cities and remedial measures]. Beijing: Jingji Ribao Chubanshe.

Lipton, Michael. 1982. "Migration From Rural Areas of Poor Countries: The Impact on Rural Productivity and Income Distribution." In Richard H. Sabot, ed. *Migration and the Labor Market in Developing Countries*. Boulder: Westview, pp. 191–228.

Liu Zheng et al. 1990, *Woguo Yanhai Diqu Xiao Chengzhen Jingji Fazhan he Renkou Qianyi* [Economic development and migration in small towns of Chinese coastal areas]. Beijing: Zhongguo Zhanwang Chubanshe.

Mallee, Hein. 1995. "Rural Population Mobility in Seven Chinese Provinces." Paper presented at the Fourth European Conference on Agriculture and Rural Development in China, Manchester, 10–12 November 1995.

Myrdal, Gunnar. 1957. *Economic Theory and Under-Developed Regions*. London: Gerald Duckworth.

Nongye Bu, ed. 1996. *Zhongguo Nongcun Laodongli Liudong Yanjiu: Waichuzhe yu Shuchudi* [A study of labour mobility in Chinese villages: Outmigrants and labour exporting regions]. Beijing: n.p.

Oi, Jean. 1990. "The Fate of the Collective After the Commune." In Deborah Davis and Ezra Vogel, eds, *Chinese Society on the Eve of Tiananmen: The Impact of Reform*. Cambridge, Mass.: Council on East Asian Studies, Harvard University, pp. 15–36.

Research Group of the Annual Analysis of Rural Economy, ed. 1994. *Green Report: Annual Report on Economic Development of Rural China in 1993 and the Development Trends in 1994*. Beijing: China Social Sciences Publishing House.

Scharping, Thomas. 1981. *Umsiedlungsprogramme für Chinas Jugend 1955–1980: Probleme der Stadt-Land-Beziehungen in der chinesischen Entwicklungspolitik*. Hamburg: Institut für Asienkunde.

Scharping, Thomas. 1997. "Studying Migration in Contemporary China: Models and Methods, Issues and Evidence." In Thomas Scharping, ed. *Migration and Floating Population in China: The Impact of Economic Reforms*. Hamburg: Institut für Asienkunde, pp. 9–53.

Scharping, Thomas, and Walter Schulze. 1997. "Labour and Income Develop-ments in the Pearl River Delta: A Migration Survey of Foshan and Shenzhen." In Thomas Scharping, ed. *Migration and Floating Population in China: The Impact of Economic Reforms*. Hamburg: Institut für Asienkunde, pp. 160–92.

Scharping, Thomas and Sun Huaiyang, eds. 1997. *Migration in China's Guangdong Province: Major Results of a 1993 Sample Survey in Shenzhen and Foshan*. Hamburg: Institut für Asienkunde.

Skeldon, Ronald. 1990. *Population Mobility in Developing Countries: A Reinterpreta-tion*. London: Belhaven Press.

Standing, Guy. 1984. "Income Transfers and Remittances." In Richard E. Bilsborrow, A.S. Oberai and Guy Standing, *Migration Surveys in Low Income Countries: Guidelines for Survey and Questionnaire Design*. London: Croom Helm, pp. 264–316.

Tirasawat, Penporn. 1985. "The Impact of Migration on Conditions at the Origin: A Study on Selected Villages in Thailand." In Philip M. Hauser, Daniel B. Suits and Ogawa Naohiro, eds, *Urbanization and Migration in Asean Development*. Tokyo: National Institute for Research Advancement, pp. 475–95.

Xu Zhong. 1991. "Anhui Sheng Wuwei Xian 12 ge Xiang Liuchu Renkou Diaocha Baogao" [Survey report on outmigration in 12 townships of Wuwei county in Anhui province]. *Renkou Kexue Yanjiu* 1991, no. 6, pp. 58–62, 34.

Zhang Chunyuan. 1991. "Nongcun Renkou Liudong yu Jingji Shourude Zengzhang" [Rural population mobility and income increases]. *Renkou Kexue Yanjiu* 1991, no.5, pp. 13–9.

Zhang Kaimin, ed. 1989. *Shanghai Liudong Renkou* [Shanghai's floating population]. Beijing: Zhongguo Tongji Chubanshe.

Zhang Qingwu. 1995. "Zhongguo 50 Xiangzhen Liudong Renkou Diaocha" [A survey of floating population in 50 Chinese townships and towns]. *Zhongguo Renkou Kexue* 1, no. 1, pp. 25–32.

Zhongguo Shehui Kexueyuan Renkou Yanjiusuo, ed. 1988. *Zhongguo 1986 Nian 74 Chengzhen Renkou Qianyi Chouyang Diaocha Ziliao* [China migration of 74 cities and towns sampling survey data]. Beijing: Zhongguo Renkou Kexue.

Zhongguo Yanhai Diqu Xiao Chengzhen Fazhan yu Renkou Qianyi Diaocha Yanjiuzu, ed. 1989. *Zhongguo Yanhai Diqu Xiao Chengzhen Fazhan yu Renkou Qianyi* [Development and migration in small towns of coastal China]. Beijing: Zhongguo Caizheng Jingji Chubanshe.

Zou Lanchun, ed. 1996. *Beijingde Liudong Renkou* [The floating population of Beijing]. Beijing: Zhongguo Renkou Chubanshe.

Notes

1 "Non-agricultural output" is an indicator derived from the material balances system of socialist economics. It does not include all value created in the tertiary sector, and is inflated by the double counting of inputs. Yet it is the best comprehensive indicator at hand for assessing the rural-urban divide as far as economic modernization, the productivity of non-agricultural sectors and the social product available for distribution are concerned.

2 One of them is the fact that schemes for the categorization of migration reasons adopted in various surveys are not strictly compatible. It is a flaw of the 1986 CASS survey and the 1987 microcensus procedures that subjective motives for migration are lumped together with a list of administrative migration channels under the heading "migration reasons." This makes it hard to distinguish personal from organizational factors, or causes from forms of migration (compare Skeldon 1990:126–131).

   In order to simplify matters and to isolate major causes of migration, several categories in the CASS and microcensus questionnaires are collectively designated "work-related" migration reasons in the figure. This applies to the items "work transfer", "job assignment", "demobilization", "work replacement", as well as "work and business". A similar procedure is adopted with regard to the items "comigration" and "staying with relatives", which are bracketed under the heading "family-related" migration reasons. It must be admitted, though, that the latter categories in reality often serve to disguise a search for work in the city. This also holds true for the residual category of "other" migration reasons which includes such items as "retirement," "special policies" and "return to the city" after the end of political banishment or forced settlement in the countryside.

3 Again, it was necessary to select and recategorize other data on migration reasons in order to reach some rough comparability. Because census and microcensus questionnaires offer a too limited list of work-related migration channels to choose from, they do not lend themselves to this exercise. The range of work-related items in the CASS survey is larger, but, unfortunately, they do not contain entries like "labour market" and "job searching through the assistance of relatives and friends". Nevertheless, CASS data are included for reference. The items "work transfer," "job assignment," "demobilization," "return of sent down youth" and "migration for political cases" were bracketed under the heading "departments", as they usually involve work allocation by labour departments or other state agencies. Work replacement was interpreted as equalling independent hiring by work units.

4 A number of definitional questions had to addressed before the volume of remittances could be assessed. An intractable problem is the kind of monetary transfers that should be included. The Foshan-Shenzhen survey asked for the average sum of money that was sent home by way of regular payment. We were not able to inquire into the methods of remittance. Possible methods include sending back money orders and cash delivered in person by lorry drivers, acquaintances, or fellow migrants travelling back home. It is not clear if all occasional cash deliveries were covered. Also, the scope of the survey did not permit to inquire into non-monetary transfers of goods and services to the countryside. The survey figures are thus limited to regular monetary remittances. The five year period used for the definition of migrants requires to consider the effects of inflation. The survey, though, did not allow us to specify the period in which payments were made. Naturally, remittances are effected well beyond the five year cut-off point. Out of definitional considerations, however, we did not cover transfers beyond the five year period. Finally, as far as statistical treatment of numbers is concerned, the question arises whether averages are to be calculated for all migrants or for remitters only.

5 This surprising result is partially the result of the fact that roughly ninety per cent of all respondents found work immediately upon arrival in the city. These figures either indicate an extraordinary degree of success on the labour market, or reflect the bias of the sample, which did not cover unsuccessful migrants who returned to their place of origin. In the annual rural household survey per capita forward remittances are approximately one third of backward remittances (Guojia Tongji Ju 1993:7 and 11). Distortion in the Foshan-Shenzhen survey by sample bias and small case numbers therefore seems likely. But its degree remains hard to determine, since regional breakdowns of national data or other clues are lacking.

Chapter Five ——————————————

Migrant Construction Teams in Beijing

*Victor Yuan and Wong Xin**

Introduction

On 13 May 1994, a rural youth called Zhang from Quyang County in Hebei Province was chatting with a researcher from Horizon Research Group. The light is poor in the high-rise building at the construction site. "I have been a plasterer for six years now, and have been fed up with it for a long time. Ah, it's hard and tiring. I now work here fourteen to fifteen hours a day and still only get 700 to 800 yuan per month. The contractors and group heads earn more than we do, and they don't do physical labour, they just supervise our work." Zhang sighed deeply while he spoke.

Zhang is twenty-one, married, and has finished lower middle school. "The food in the construction team is ordered by the contractor. In the morning we get porridge, and lunch and dinner are the same: three steamed rolls to go with white cabbage, boiled in plain water with hardly any oil. Sometimes they change it and we eat noodles. When I get too hungry, I go and buy some deep-fried bread sticks or a few stuffed rolls to eat." Zhang's ideal is to become a group head in the construction team or a driver. But he acknowledges "thinking about it and doing it are different things, there is no opportunity, and the thinking is all in vain."

Zhang epitomizes the situation of the large group of rural migrant workers in construction teams (*baogongdui*) in Beijing and in other large Chinese cities similar to Beijing. The majority of them are between

* The authors are researchers of Horizon Research Group in Beijing. A research project with the title *Self-organization among Migrants in Beijing* was undertaken with financial support of the Ford Foundation in 1994–5. The project included fieldwork concerning migrant construction teams, the migrant community from Anhui, self-organized commercial groups among Zhejiang migrants, as well as other types of informal organization among migrants in the Beijing region. This chapter is part of the original report and was translated by Hein Mallee.

eighteen and thirty years old. Among all the groups of labourers who enter the cities from the countryside, the life of workers of the construction teams is probably the hardest and most tiring. Among all migrant construction workers interviewed by researchers of Horizon Research, group leaders and skilled workers were fairly satisfied. Part of the new workers make a basically favourable appraisal of their present situation after comparing it with the poor life in their home villages; dissatisfaction is greatest among workers who have been at their job for some time; they grumble about bad pay and not eating a proper meal.

Construction teams: Mobile peasants within the establishment

According to Zhao Lianping, director of the Urban Construction Management Committee of Chaoyang district in Beijing, there are 500,000 migrant construction workers in Beijing. But if workers who refurbish houses or work as occasional workers in free contracting teams are taken into consideration, the total number would exceed 600,000. Such workers can be found working under all kinds of arrangements in all kinds of contracting teams.

The contracting teams emerged in the early 1980s. In contrast with the construction teams of traditional construction companies, they are a type of economic organization that is involved in spatial mobility. After a labour contractor (*baogongtou*) has arranged construction work in one place, he goes back to his home area or another place in the countryside and organizes a team of experienced and unskilled workers (The latter are called *xiaogong*, which literally means "minor workers"). When the project is completed, the team is disbanded, unless a subsequent new project is found.

Many rural township and town governments supervise construction stations (*jianzhuzhan*), which are collective in nature. In the past, these construction stations mainly undertook construction work in the township itself. In the early 1980s, most construction stations were contracted out to individuals. In order to increase profits, the contracted construction stations became one or more construction teams. Several workers of the construction stations organized their own contracting teams, while continuing to be employed by the stations without salary (*tingshui liuzhi*). These teams undertake work under the name of the construction station, and pay a yearly management fee to the station.

Soon after the rural construction teams emerged, they began to challenge the operations of the established urban construction companies. The contracting teams are in fact a kind of small scale private construction companies, whose flexible assets, high efficiency and low prices made them very competitive once they entered the urban construction market. Naturally, charges and criticisms of contracting teams bribing their customers, cheating on labour and materials, and of contractors tyrannizing workers, embezzling wages, and lining their pockets with public funds are also heard from time to time. Therefore, the social image of contracting teams and contractors currently is not very favourable. In addition, the reform of the management system of medium sized and large construction projects inside the economic plan is slow. In practice, this soon made it very hard for rural construction teams directly to find large and profitable projects in the cities. They therefore mainly contract smaller projects outside the plan, or subcontract work on larger projects.

In the mid-1980s, real estate development in China entered a high tide. As a large number of construction projects got under way, the demand for construction services peaked. Under these circumstances, relying on the original urban construction teams proved grossly insufficient. Moreover, the enthusiasm of the young urban unemployed in the original urban construction teams for such dirty, tiring and heavy work was low and the wages they demanded were high. A large demand grew for low cost construction teams in which rural labour formed the core.

To this end, a national "movement of incorporation of contracting teams" (*baogongdui shoubian yundong*) was formed. This entailed either the inclusion of rural construction teams into construction companies established by the government, or the formation of construction companies of a larger scale and greater competitive power through joint operations of several contracting teams. These companies only took care of arranging projects, and allocated the actual work to its contracting teams.

A considerable part of the construction companies was invested with certain administrative functions by the governments of their place of origin. They acted as temporary agencies of the administrative departments in charge of construction work (mainly the urban construction committee or the urban construction bureau of the government of the place of origin), coordinating and managing construction teams from the area of origin in the area of destination. In Beijing, the construction management departments at the municipal and district levels of Beijing city initiated a system of official permits in cooperation with the governments of the areas of origin of the construction teams; only those construction teams who were subject to team management of the government of the area of origin were to be issued permits to enter the capital and work there. In this way, private rural contracting teams were incorporated into the existing system and could legally enter the Beijing market.

Free contracting teams (*ziyou baogongdui*) do not enter the Beijing market in this fashion, are therefore formally illegal. But such teams have a considerable competitive edge especially for smaller projects, as they do not pay the many "management fees" (*guanlifei*, see below) levied by administrative departments and furthermore can be established even more freely. Skilled workers and managers of the original, legal contracting teams therefore often put together their own free contracting teams. According to estimates of the Beijing Municipal Urban Construction Management Department, about fifteen per cent of the migrant construction teams in the Beijing construction market are free contracting teams.

The construction teams from Jiangsu province, which have a reputation in Beijing for high quality and high prices, are mainly rural contracting teams from the northern part of the province. In order to secure a share of the Beijing construction market, Jiangsu province has used a number of ways to organize construction teams. The province and its municipalities have established specialized construction labour companies (*jianzhu laowu gongsi*), whose subordinate teams follow the principle of establishing a separate team for each project. When a municipality has a project, it informs a county, which in turn informs a township or town. This township or town is then the basic unit for the formation of a contracting team: if the available workers of one township are insufficient, it can recruit workers from other townships, and if one county is insufficient, it can recruit in other counties; however, recruitment in other provinces is not allowed.

Once an assignment reaches the township or town, it is normally put in the hands of the construction station of that township or town. To the original personnel of the construction station are added personnel who have previously participated in contracting teams of the station, and if this is still insufficient, open recruitment in the villages takes place. Some are also introduced by skilled master workers of the station. In some specialized types of work, skilled masters can also take on apprentices. Some private contracting teams have personnel ready, and when they have the right connections, they can use the name of the township or even the county and participate in the provincial and municipal construction companies, as long a they pay a modest management fee to the government department lending its name. In 1994, there were 65,000 migrant construction workers from Jiangsu in Beijing. Of these workers, only about 5,000 work for a contracted project itself, while the majority work under subcontracting arrangements.

Like other migrant workers, the contracting teams face the problem of fees levied by the local government in Beijing. The number of items for which fees are charged are fairly numerous, including a public order fee by the Public Security departments, a work permit for the construction sector, and a work permit of the Labour departments. In contrast with migrant workers who enter the city on their own, these costs are usually paid directly by the contracting teams and formal procedures are also handled in a unified way by the teams. In addition, the construction company of every province or municipality also levies a certain management fee on the individual teams (in the case of Jiangsu, the management fee equals twelve to eighteen per cent of the project funds).

The Municipal Construction Company of Linzhou city in Henan province controls over 10,000 migrant workers, and except for supervision and management of safety and quality, it also provides guidance and assistance with regard to the hygiene of the contracting team's food (previously, collective food poisoning of migrant workers had occurred) and with collecting project funds in arrears. This company also serves as the representative office in Beijing of the Linzhou municipal government, and is also managing the affairs of Linzhou migrants working in other sectors in Beijing.

The number of contracting teams is large and the pressure of competition is great. Under such circumstances, quality becomes an important concern. Large construction enterprises such as the China General Construction Company often use certain teams from the south of the country, who may be more expensive, but whose quality is definitely higher. Gradually, the construction company of which these teams are part obtained a share in the market of principal contracts (*zongbao*) of construction projects. Teams from the north are comparatively speaking cheaper, yet quality problems are also relatively more common. Quality problems also cause the local Beijing construction teams to see their share in the market shrink year after year. In fact, even when it is usually a so-called local construction team who contracts a project, most of the actual work is done by subcontracting to outside contracting teams.

The use of governmental forms to incorporate contracting teams is connected to relevant regulations of the Beijing construction sector management departments. The Urban and Rural Construction Committee of Beijing municipality has established an office for the management of outside construction teams, and it employs a "labour service base area name list system" (*laowu jidi mingdan zhi*) to limit the number of areas of origin of outside construction teams. In 1994, there were over forty prefectures and municipalities (such as Yangzhou in Jiangsu, Dingzhou in Hebei, Luzhou in Sichuan), which had been listed by Beijing as construction labour service base areas, which means that only construction teams from these areas could legally operate in Beijing. Apart from looking at the track record of teams from these areas, Beijing Municipality also demands that the areas of origin adopt acceptable methods with regard to management and the training of experienced workers. Currently, eighty-five per cent of all construction projects in Beijing are undertaken by construction teams that are part of the system. The construction committees of the districts and counties of Beijing investigate and punish free contracting teams in order to force them to enter the system, and each year several of them do indeed link up (*guakao*) with the system.[1]

Generally speaking, Beijing Municipality has effectively controlled the mobility of migrant workers in the construction sector by means of such formal cooperative relations between the governments at origin and destination. Up to now, construction is the only sector that has been able effectively to influence the volume of export of migrant workers and guarantee that the majority of migrant workers is incorporated into the system. The autonomy of contracting teams his hardly jeopardized by the arrangement, and all they have to do is pay a considerable management fee. There are also positive aspects. Formerly, the contracting team was a very temporary organizational form, which was disbanded when there were no projects, but now, because of the continuity of the work, the increased prestige after forming the association, and because a company name plate can be used, it has developed into a relatively stable organizational form. This has clearly led to improvement in the accumulation of technical skills and human resources in the teams, and many teams are now able to take on independent projects of a considerable scale. A further aspect is standardization of operations. We discovered that, no matter whether a team was private, collective or state run, the construction workers, including unskilled workers, all indicated that training to improve safety on the job was taken very seriously. Prior to 1994, about one hundred migrant workers died in Beijing due to construction accidents every year, but in 1994 this dropped to only about forty people.

A concrete case reveals the management situation of the contracting teams under the organized system. Dingzhou Municipality in Hebei is a construction labour base area of Beijing. Seventy per cent of the rural labourers in this municipality have construction as their main occupation, and this is the largest area exporting construction labour in the north of China. The Dingzhou Second Vocational School, the Training Department of the Municipal Construction Commission, and the Training Section of the Labour Bureau all organize technical training for construction. Most of the students come from contracting teams, but some study at their own expense.

The Dingzhou Fifth Construction Company is one of the main construction units from that municipality working in the capital. It came to the capital in 1982. In 1992, the Beijing Municipal Construction Team Management Office designated it a double contracting enterprise, meaning that it could be either principal contractor of a project, or subcontractor of part of the work (*fenbao*). The organizational structure of this company is company → large team → project team (contracting team) → group → individual migrant workers. The company practices internal contracting: the company arranges projects, which it contracts to the large teams, which in turn contract them to the contracting teams. The ten contracting teams under the Dingzhou Fifth Construction Company are divided according to their specialization: there are five building teams, four fitting teams, and one plumbing and electricity team.

Altogether, the Fifth Construction Company has 8,800 employees. Mr Shang, the company's manager, distinguishes between project teams that are "unified management teams" (*zongguandui*) and "associated teams" (*guakaodui*). The former consist of rural construction workers recruited directly by the company from Dingzhou Municipality. Although these teams are independent accounting units, their assets, quality control, and allocation of projects are unified. The latter are teams that were established by individuals in association with Fifth Construction. These contracting teams have "relaxed management relations" with the company. They hand over a certain amount in management fees to the company every year, but in general they "find their own way, are responsible for their own profits and losses, shoulder their own risks, and keep their own benefits." The profits after taxes are all left to the contractor to distribute. In Fifth Construction, the majority of the contracting teams are unified management teams.

The migrant workers in contracting teams

The distinction between unified management and associated teams is common among the construction companies in the organized system in Beijing. However, such distinctions have no decisive impact on the internal organization of the teams or the treatment of the migrant workers.

The majority of construction contracting teams are divided into work units called groups (*banzu* or *gongzhang*). Even in the unified management teams, the appointment of the group heads is decided by the team leader, although in some construction companies a formal appointment by the unified management level is required. Those becoming group heads are mainly key technicians. Even in private contracting teams, examples of nepotistic appointment of incapable relatives and friends as group heads are rare. As the group head is the first responsible person for the quality of work, and since the great majority of contracting teams cannot treat contracts as simple one-off transactions, a bad group head will influence the business of the entire team. Therefore, the person in charge of first line technical issues must be someone with high skills. However, when skill levels are equal, the chance of relatives and friends becoming group head is much greater.

In most situations, the position of group head is taken on by experienced masters or specially engaged skilled workers. The experienced masters form an especially influential layer in the contracting teams, and they constitute the core of a contracting team. The majority of contracting teams have personnel turnover rate of forty to fifty per cent. This occurs mainly among unskilled labourers. The turnover of skilled workers is only about ten per cent, a considerable number of whom are poached by other teams. The influence of master workers concentrates on their own direct apprentices that they brought into the team. From the point of view of the entire team, the experienced masters bear the main responsibility for technical quality control. In Xiqiao Construction Company (which is equivalent to a contracting team) under the Municipal Construction

Company of Taixing, Jiangsu, the ranks are expanded by relying on recruitment of apprentices by experienced masters themselves. But the main source of workers of Guxi and Huangqiao Construction companies from the same area are workers who come to find work by themselves or who are enlisted through open recruitment by the company. Still, these are only unskilled labourers: workers engaging in technical work are brought in by masters appointed by the team.

Non-formal organization inside the teams mainly exists in the closer native place ties, such as village ties or kinship relations, and special recommendations on the basis of reciprocity. The influence of this type of non-formal organization is especially expressed in individual contacts, in mutual assistance and bargaining at work. In in-depth interviews with migrant workers one can discover that the majority of the migrant workers separate work and personal affairs: "For personal problems you ask your fellow villagers and friends and for work problems you ask the leaders in the team." Only when personal problems are so serious that friends cannot solve them are labour contractors or experienced masters asked for assistance.

However, in certain contracting teams, the influence of the masters is relatively small. Sometimes the team leader himself does not like to strengthen the influence of the masters by recruiting apprentices through them (but uses, for example, external training). Alternatively, the work is either very common or very uncommon, and all workers are young without a group of especially influential experienced masters.

Obtaining opportunities for training is very important to the migrant workers. Naturally, the scope of training provided is different; generally speaking, the unified management teams under state owned construction companies provide much more training than associated private contracting teams or collective contracting teams of townships and towns. For instance, all skilled workers in Beijing of the Huangqiao Construction Team of Taixing municipality received one week of training, which included the principles of construction, on-site guidance, and so forth. All workers participating in the training course had to pass an examination, and the certificate issued after this examination is commonly accepted throughout the construction sector. The Guxi Construction Team from the same municipality engaged Tongji University in Shanghai and Yangzhou Light Industrial Machinery College to train project accountants and managers. Training courses for Fifth Construction from Dingzhou, Hebei, were mainly undertaken by technical vocational schools in that municipality.

Of fifty interviewed skilled workers, only three had not received training. It must be pointed out that a considerable part of the workers receiving training had been unskilled workers or technical trainees and the provision of training in itself can be considered a kind of remuneration.

Among the 180 employees of Guxi Construction Team, forty electricians, thirty welders, and twenty-five piping workers had received training. The training fees were all paid by the construction team. Training determined whether one would be able to obtain opportunities to distinguish oneselves in the future.

Different from more open types of migrant worker groups, the non-formal organizations of the migrant workers in the contracting teams are small in scale and scope. Regular interaction with people outside the team is rare. At the same time, because of the strictness of the rules inside the contracting team and because free time is too scarce (as working hours are excessively long), non-formal organizations are rather inactive, and moreover, cannot act as a resistance against the organizational framework of the contracting team. On the whole, informal organizations are very similar to certain types of native palace groups and groups of individual friends in army camps.

The majority of contracting teams have a clear internal management system, mainly involving the times of work and rest, activities after work (in general, workers have to report at a fixed time and when they do not return at the time indicated, the team or group leader may check the number of people and even mete out criticism or deduct wages), regulations on leaving during working time (permission is only granted in cases of great necessity), cleaning and sanitation regulations (in most cases sweeping and cleaning in the morning), a system of checking work attendance, a system of allocation (obtaining work outfits, queuing for food). Some contracting teams rule that with the exception of the weekend, workers can usually not go out. Of 130 interviewed migrant workers in contracting teams, only five regularly used the time after work to go out for recreation, thirty-two occasionally went out together with some friends, and the rest spent their time after work with friends playing chess and cards, chatting, reading, or watching television. Most group leaders report that they use the time after work to think and consider their work.

Adjusting wages and benefits is the most powerful lever over the workers' behaviour. Plasterer Zhang, member of a contracting team from Hebei, under the Beijing Beihai Construction Company, says:

My relation with the team head is simply one between boss and worker; he gives me money and I work for him. If he does not give me money, I don't work. I don't think that he is particularly good at anything; his capabilities are not greater than mine. It's simply that he had the opportunity, and once he became the boss and was able to have us work for him, he did not need to work anymore.

Of all migrant workers, workers in contracting teams are least similar to the residents of the cities in which they stay; their degree of urbanization is even lower than that of migrant garbage collectors. From social relations and interaction, patterns of behaviour, appearance, to mental conceptions, the contracting teams basically exist in an environment cut off from the city. It is hardly possible for the workers in the contracting teams to become city people.

Case studies

Old Hu's free contracting team from Wuwei

This free contracting team is mainly composed of people from Wuwei County in Anhui. The team office is set up in a residential courtyard in Liuliqiao and also serves as a dormitory for the team workers. The team's main way of finding work is to send the workers out in the evening or weekend to post advertisements on the electricity poles in residential districts or along the main streets.

The team includes twenty-six people. The team head is a man who everybody calls "Old Hu" or simply "boss." He does not often go out to arrange work, but only decides which group head will take people to do the work once a job has been found. After the job has been completed, the head reports back to Old Hu and settles the accounts. The workers of the contracting team receive their wages at the end of the month and Old Hu considers whom to give a little extra and whom to give less. The regular workers on average receive only 350–380 yuan per month.

Old Hu used to work as a refurbisher in someone else's contracting team, which worked for a large construction company. When he came to Beijing in 1988, the discovered that a craze of interior decoration was starting among the Beijingese, and he then left the team with some friends to set up their own business. In the beginning, they still needed to learn the tricks of the trade and simply stood at streetcorners waiting for work, but slowly they earned some money and built up a reputation. Then they rented the courtyard that is the present team office. That was in 1992. Little Hu, Old Hu's nephew, who is one of the group leaders in the team, was called in to help from home at that time. Old Hu does not have a business licence, but is well acquainted with the people in the ward office and rarely do people make things difficult for him.

Little Hu is the youngest of the team, but he is one of the five group leaders. All group leaders are Old Hu's relatives or are those who started the team together with him. There is only one woman in the team, Old Hu's wife, who takes care of everybody's food. The team is just like a family; when they eat everybody recounts rumours heard on the streets, and when Old Hu is present no-one feels constrained. Often, Old Hu discusses serious matters during meals, like: "The team has paid a fee of 150 yuan for the maintenance of public order for everybody" or "Tomorrow there is some kind of meeting in Beijing, so everybody should stay home and play poker." Little Cheng, who is with Little Hu's group, told our investigator that sometimes all had gone to sleep when Old Hu suddenly remembered something and would go knocking on windows and doors to tell them.

One day, two fellow villagers were introduced to Old Hu and wanted to join the team. Old Hu talked with them at length and told them there was no work and that he did not need more people. Actually, he did have work, and later Old Hu told Little Hu: "We can't take on these two, they used to sell clothes for the Zhejiangese and have become glib. If we take them now, there is no telling whether they might take over our turf." The right to decide on entry into the team was something Old Hu exercised absolutely.

Hebei First Construction, Lin Da contracting team

The Lin Da contracting team is basically composed of peasants from Qingyuan County in Hebei. They all live in rooms of ten square meters. The ordinary workers, in particular the unskilled workers, sleep on straw, while the group leaders and skilled masters sleep on beds of wooden boards laid out on bricks. The five to six people in a room share the same profession: bricklayers with bricklayers and carpenters with carpenters.

The food in this contracting team is very bad and this seems to be what everybody is most dissatisfied with. Normal meals consist of steamed rolls with vegetables, often salted rather than fresh. "There is hardly ever meat to eat."

There are altogether over ninety people in the Lin Da contracting team. Except for a tiny minority, most workers have come through introductions of friends. Most of the unskilled workers in this team come from the same village or township, and some people have known each other since they were small, so the relations among the youths are very close. Everybody indicated that they were together with people they knew well. In their spare time, they play cards together, tell coarse jokes, or go and watch videos together.

The young workers in this team do not form any clear "gangs" (*bang*), and only to outsiders does their informal socializing appear as "gang" behaviour. Yet there is there is a division between different groups. All those from Anhui live in one room. According to one informant "We from Anhui are together and the Hebeinese are together." In this team, the Anhuinese basically do the heaviest and hardest work. Although the work is tiring, they are still enthusiastic about working in this team. This is because the income is stable and the wages are paid once every quarter. In many other contracting teams wages are always paid once or twice a year.

In this team, the relations between the experienced masters and the ordinary unskilled workers are quite good. No matter whether they are from Hebei or Anhui, the unskilled workers all say the relations with the masters are not bad at all. In particular, everybody admires the experience and skills of the masters. "But young people still want to amuse themselves with young people." Gu, the leader of the bricklaying group, thinks that the direct function of the masters is their influence on their apprentices and their indirect function that of taking the lead in working, as the young people are embarrassed to be thought of as lazy.

Master Zheng Xinsuo began working in the contracting team in 1985. He was asked to come to the team after he retired from another unit. He is now of advanced age and only minds the meals of the team. His monthly wage is 900 yuan, and except for 140 yuan for food expenses, he can save all of it. He is completely satisfied with his job, as with the team the income is stable and the wage is guaranteed. He thinks that many problems in the team are decided by the older people, which is to say that the influence of the masters on the team head's decision making is rather large.

The power of the group leaders is quite large in the Lin Da contracting team. For example, the group leader approves requests for days off and workers always first go to the group head when there is a problem. Moreover, the group head is always an old hand, like the head of the bricklaying group who started to work in this team in 1978. With regard to practical operations, the group heads and masters form the decision making group and they often gather together after work to discuss the next day's tasks.

The closeness of the masters and group heads to the team leader is also reflected in a number of other aspects. For instance, the evaluation of the team head by the masters and group heads is generally more positive than by the ordinary workers. The masters and group heads indicate that they ordinarily talk about work with the team leader: "When there is a problem we go to the team leadership." This shows that they can talk relatively well with the team leader, whereas the ordinary workers mainly interact with the group heads.

The strict control of the contracting team over the external contacts of the workers to a large extent reduces the management costs of the team, because solving problems always involves many twists and turns and expenses. In addition to rules about safety at the workplace, the internal management regulations of Lin Da contracting team also stipulate that workers "cannot leave their work posts on their own account; when necessary they can ask for leave;" "they must return to their dormitories before 9.30 in the evening; the main gate closes at 10." When going out, the workers cannot go too far. Fortunately, there is a television set in the big courtyard (this is the only contracting team visited by our investigators that had a television).

Just like Old Hu of the free contracting team, the main work of the head of Lin Da contracting team is wining and dining. The affairs on the building site are mainly decided through discussion in meetings with the group leaders. This contracting team falls under the First Construction Company of Hebei Province (First Construction) and First Construction exerts control over the team in many ways. The demands of the local government in Beijing are transferred down to the teams through First Construction. The team head often has to go to such meetings, as another of his tasks is to rope in business. First Construction cannot make sure that all its teams get sufficient work, and a considerable part of the work has thus to be found by the team head, using the name of First Construction.

Generally speaking, most of the middle aged and older members of Lin Da contracting team, no matter whether they are group leader or master, still have land in their home villages. Therefore, in autumn basically all of them ask for leave for the wheat harvest. But in comparison, hardly any of the young people under twenty-five still worry about cultivating land. They think about what other team to go to if things don't work out well in this team, while the middle aged and older people tend to think that, when things really go wrong, they can still go back home and till the land. Almost all people, with the exception of Zheng the cook, expressed that they could not be sure whether they work in this team for a long period.

Most members of Lin Da contracting team have no relatives in Beijing to visit and thus the construction site has become their living space; they mainly interact with fellow workers, including fellow workers from the same area of origin. Some people (like Zheng the cook) have relatives in Beijing, but they hardly go and visit them. On the contrary, relatives from their home area sometimes come and visit them to ask for help in finding work.

Yazhu contracting team

Yazhu contracting team is a team from Hebei, which at the moment is building the dormitory building of the Shouzhou Guesthouse, at a construction site to the left side of the Zuo'an Gate wholesale market. The mainstay of the Yazhu team are Hebeinese, but there are also people from Henan. Moreover, among the Henanese there are some who hold a position as group leader or experienced master. There are two types of situation in which a small group of people from a different origin can gain a foothold in a contracting team with a majority people from a certain region. First, workers with an absolute mastery of skills and an ability to take on the work. Second, the occurrence of an urgent need for workers in the project, which temporarily cannot be fulfilled by calling in people from the main area of origin so that resort has to be taken to recruiting people already present. Although the ties between these small groups of strangers and fellow workers from a different area in the same team are more numerous than the communication between migrant workers from different origins working in different occupations, it is still noticeable that these people form relatively tightly knit "gangs" based on the idea of "home area." Many things, in particular those related to changing jobs and to family affairs, are only discussed among fellow villagers. Moreover, people with a high position in the team naturally occupy a certain leadership position in the circle of fellow villagers. T., who came to the team from a position as group leader in Linzhou, Henan, is more or less such a person.

T. is a real master craftsman, who already started working as a construction worker in Zhengzhou in 1966. However, at present he does not earn much: just over 600 yuan a month. In his career, he has received training twice. T. says that usually when he has no work to do, he talks about work with the team head and the accountant, or inspects quality at the construction site. "Grasping management work well" is what T. thinks of as the thing he is most concerned with.

T.'s seniority is also apparent from the fact that he does not at all regard the team head as an extraordinary leader. T. says that both he and the team head are just the management personnel of the team and that the difference is no big deal. Still, he confirms that the team head's work style is not bad at all, that he shows concern for the workers' livelihood. "I've been with him for over ten years and he's quite all right and capable, otherwise I would not have stayed with him." Old T. is satisfied with his own work and position. Old T. says: "I count as the eldest in the team; I'm not interested in running up and down just to make a bit more money."

In comparison, the leader of the electricians earns 1,000 yuan a month, but he still feels that "the money is not enough." Not earning enough is a common perception among the workers in this team. S. is a conspicuous exception, as he earns almost the most of the entire team. He was formally recruited by the team in 1985 and, after a foreman training course of the Beijing Construction Committee, obtained a high vocational diploma. Although he does not have holidays, S. only works eight hours a day; "After work I go home and take care of my child." S. thinks that the fact that he achieved such a position is due to his training and learning a skill and therefore he hopes "to have another opportunity for training that is beneficial to my own development and my wage might become a bit higher."

Yazhu Contracting Team is somewhat different from ordinary contracting teams; although its personnel mainly comprise migrant workers, it is state owned: its formal name is the Sixth Construction Team of Dingzhou Tenth Construction Company from Hebei. This is why in this team management is comparatively strict, training is relatively standardized, with many older workers, low mobility, but also relatively low wages. Generally speaking, the work is also somewhat less hard and strenuous. In terms of mode of recruitment, in comparison to other teams, introduction by friends and recruitment through recommendation are rarely used. The workers in this team are mainly recruited from designated places in

Dingshou. The workers also seem quite satisfied with the team leadership, in the first place because the latter know their business, but also because they show considerable concern for the workers' lives.

Teams such as Yazhu contracting team are state owned, but contracted out to the team head: the team head has complete autonomy in management of personnel and operations; only with regard to on site safety and quality is he subject to supervision by the higher levels of the construction company. Yet the team still retains some of the formal structure of state work units, for instance in political study and in the organization of work. Team head Z. looks more like a cadre than like a business man, and he is quite good to the workers.

Conclusions

In Beijing, except for the free contracting teams, the construction teams exist inside the formal system as legalized migrant groups with native place ties as their main link. This kind of organizational mode is most acceptable to the governments of the receiving areas because it facilitates control and management and it has even become a kind of ideal model that the urban management authorities attempt to employ in standardizing other groups of outside population.

The labourers in the contracting teams are placed under a strict kind of militarized management. Because of the existence of severe regulations that restrict behaviour and an unbecoming appearance caused by hard work and relatively bad labour conditions, the workers in the contracting teams not only have little time and energy for contacts with the outside world, but are also much more fearful of external contacts than other groups of migrants in the city. For these reasons, they form the least urbanized group among the outside population. Except for a minority of people who leave the teams, the migrant population in the contracting teams hardly develops personal motives for remaining in Beijing on a long term basis.

Although the contracting team appears to be an organization with a fairly high degree of organization, generally no non-economic means for maintaining membership exist. At the same time, because of the relatively abundant supply of unskilled labour, a team is composed of a core of a small number of technical and management cadres and a larger numbers of unskilled workers that are more loosely connected to the team. However, the main direction of mobility is still among teams.

The social life of the workers on the teams is limited, and in their work and collective life they are extremely passive. Not only is it out of the question that they make use of public facilities that are earmarked for the residents of the city, but even inside their work unit they have virtually no right to express their opinion and they lack the power to resist unfair treatment.

Note

1 On 20 June 1994, the government of Beijing revised the "Provisional regulations of Beijing municipality concerning construction work of outside construction enterprises in Beijing," originally issued on 1 June 1988. These regulations demand that outside construction enterprises register with the Municipal Construction Sector Management Office, and details the fines imposed for hiring non-organized migrant workers or for contracting projects to teams who are not part of the system.

Chapter Six _____

The floating population and the integration of the city community: A survey on the attitudes of Shanghai residents to recent migrants*

Jinhong Ding and Norman Stockman

Introduction

The term "floating population" refers to a special kind of migrants defined by the *hukou* system in China, who stay[1] in a place without a permanent residence registration. The places of destination usually are city areas, especially metropolises such as Shanghai, Guangzhou and Beijing, while the sending areas cover the countryside broadly, especially the provinces of Sichuan, Hunan, Anhui and Henan. Most of the floaters return to their home village at least once a year and eventually return permanently after a sojourn of several years, so this kind of mobility technically should be classified as circulation rather than (semi-)permanent migration proper (Mallee 1995).

There has been much discussion of the causes, nature and extent of various types of population mobility in China and of their impact on urban economy and society (for example Blecher 1983, Wakabyashi 1990, Li et al. 1991, Shi et al. 1991, Ding et al. 1994). But there has hitherto been relatively little research into the relationships which may be developing between migrants and the established residents of the cities. This relationship between the "established" and the "outsiders" (Elias and Scotson 1965) is fraught with potential difficulties the world over. The established population have their own social structures, hierarchies,

* The authors gratefully acknowledge the assistance of Tan Youlin, Yu Jia, Wang Biwei and Zhang Yonghui, students of the Geography Department, East China Normal University, who were engaged in the site survey.

expectations, living standards and modes of interaction, which they may well believe to be threatened by the intrusion of "strangers" who do not share their assumptions and ways of life. They may also believe, rightly or wrongly, that the incomers pose a threat to some of their privileges, such as employment or the quality of their physical surroundings.

We might expect all this to be the case in relationships between migrants and city residents in China as well, and the floating population have indeed been presented as a social problem in many Chinese cities. The image of migrants presented in the Chinese media has been almost wholly negative (Davin 1996). This has also been true of much of the discussion in Chinese academia on the consequences of migration, although there are signs that this is now beginning to change (Mallee 1995/96). Because of differences in values, lifestyles and customs, it is often claimed, it is difficult for the city dwellers and the floating people to adjust to each other. So the relationship between the floating population and the residents tends to be characterized by mutual suspicion, vigilance and isolation. This is supposed to lead to new forms of social stratification and social malintegration. In the areas at the edge of the city, where the floating population cluster, it may seem to the resident population as if their huts and cottages grow like a mass of hair that has not been trimmed or combed properly and which grows back on again as soon as it has been cut. All this, residents assume, has a serious impact on city planning and management, and on the economic development and social order of the suburban areas.

The floating population coming to the city is a new form of urbanization which will exist for a long time to come, considering that at this time the proportion of urban residents in China is only about thirty per cent of the total population. It is important to understand the nature of relationships between the settled urban populations and the newcomers, and to consider the factors which may condition these relationships. Solinger (1995) has recently sketched out the range of such factors, distinguishing between factors relating to traits of the migrants themselves and those related to features of the receiving urban society. Among the latter she lists the following: the class structure of the city, the pattern of property ownership, the type of labour market, the political system, patronage networks available to migrants, differences in access to the urban educational system, housing opportunities in the cities, and attitudes of the receiving community. This usefully charts the dimensions of established-outsider relations, and could present a programme for future research into specific urban contexts. The present chapter is taking up a small part of this research programme, by focusing on the last of Solinger's categories, namely the attitudes of the receiving community.

Shanghai has been one of the cities most attractive to national and international investment since 1990, the official start of the national development project on the east bank of the Huangpu river (*Pudong*) that flows through Shanghai. At the same time an influx of floating population converged on the city. In 1993, 2.51 million people classified as floating population lived in the Shanghai metropolitan area, or about one fifth of the registered residents. Of the floaters, 2.14 million are of working age, and are now an important part of the labour force in Shanghai's basic industries and social services.

In order to explore these relationships, the first-named author and his assistants conducted a survey of a sample of Shanghai residents. The questions covered the evaluation by established residents of possible negative influences caused by in-comers to community life, and the degree to which residents accept the floating population. In this chapter, we present some of the findings of the survey, with a view to exploring whether the negative images of migrants presented in the media are generally shared by Shanghai residents. From our analysis of the survey findings, we suggest that there is considerable diversity in residents' attitudes to migrants, including reservoirs of sympathy for their predicament and support for their rights, as well as the negative and disparaging views more common in public discourse. These preliminary findings will require further examination in future research.

Survey design and the characteristics of the interviewees

The survey area was Caoyang Xincun[2] of Putuo District, including most of Caoyang community and some of Cao'an community. The total area of this part of the city is about 1.4 square kilometres, containing nearly seventy thousand people, with a density of about fifty thousand persons per square kilometre. The choice of this area was mainly based on the following considerations: (1) Caoyang Xincun was the first workers' settlement established by the Shanghai government in the early 1950s, and it also took in many people re-housed from the central city area in the 1980s. The composition of the population is therefore quite diverse, and can properly represent the general character of Shanghai residents; (2) Caoyang Xincun, while a part of the main city, is located in an outer ring of the city area, giving the established inhabitants more opportunities for contact with the floating population which tends to concentrate in the fringe areas of the city.

The survey used an equal interval sampling method, taking one household out of every thirty. In total 503 households were selected, which covered eighty-five per cent of the designated survey area, and 501 completed questionnaires were gained. To ensure a high response rate, the subjects were interviewed directly at home. Each household sampled was limited to one person who could answer the questions. Assuming that the heads of household were comparatively more likely to have definite ideas of their own and that they could influence other family members, the first choice was the head of household, unless he or she was absent or could not respond for some reason, in which case another adult was chosen who was willing to answer.

To avoid the whole family being away from home, the survey was carried out in the weekend (19–20 August, 1995) and on a few evenings around those days (18–22 August).

Within the sample, males were slightly over-represented, but the difference is quite small (male/female ratio was 57.1/42.9). This suggests that female heads of household are not uncommon and indicates a degree of equality between husbands and wives. The age distribution shows a predominance of those between thirty and forty-four, with a modal range of forty and forty-four. The age structure shown in Figure 6.1 also reveals that up to the age of forty-five the chance of high status of a man or woman within a family increases, while many quickly give up the role of head of household after forty-five.

The respondents have a high level of education: 21.0 per cent of them have had post-secondary education. This proportion is significantly higher than for city residents as a whole (about ten per cent). This suggests that those with high education are also likely to have high family status (as heads of household). Males have a higher education level than females (Table 6.1).

Of the respondents, 73.7 per cent are third generation migrants or less. The largest category, 39.3 per cent, is second generation, fewer are of the third generation, and first generation migrants are the least. Obviously, this corresponds with the age structure of the respondents, most of them being of middle-age. The majority of the migrants or their ancestors (37.3 per cent of respondents) came originally from Jiangsu province. Zhejiang province was the origin of 23.4 per cent,[4] those leaving the other provinces

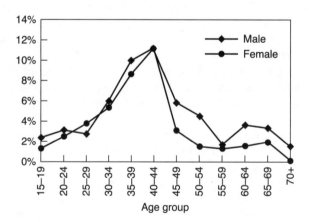

Figure 6.1 Age-sex distribution of the respondents

Table 6.1: Education distribution of the respondents[3]

Education	Male	Female	All
Higher	24.9	15.8	21.0
Upper middle	48.9	50.2	49.5
Lower middle	24.5	30.2	26.9
Primary & below	1.4	3.3	2.2
Unknown	0.4	0.5	0.4
Total	100.0	100.0	100.0
	(57.1)	(42.9)	

all together to provide 13.8 per cent. This shows the important roles of Jiangsu and Zhejiang provinces in the population growth of Shanghai metropolitan city (Table 6.2).

Opportunities for contact and extent of interaction

It appeared that there was little opportunity for contact between residents and floaters (Table 6.3). More than half of the respondents report that their main contact with the floating population was purely casual and occurred by chance in public places. Only about one third of them have their main contact with members of the floating population at work. Although about forty per cent of the floating population are employed by city enterprises and businesses (Wang et al. 1995), the possibility of making contact at work is comparatively reduced because of the uneven concentration of migrant workers in a few sectors, such as construction, textiles and environmental sanitation services.

Personal relationships between migrants and residents were generally not common. The number of floaters personally known to the average resident is about 4.6. Of all respondents, 75.2 per cent knew fewer than

Table 6.2 Migrational generations and the original provinces of the respondents' families

Generations	Original Province				
	Shanghai	Jiangsu	Zhejiang	Other	All
First	—	16.0	13.7	21.7	12.2
Second	—	56.7	48.7	49.3	39.3
Third	—	27.3	36.8	24.6	22.2
N.A.	—	0.0	0.9	4.3	0.8
Native*	100.0	—	—	—	25.5
Total	100.0	100.0	100.0	100.0	100.0
	(25.5)	(37.3)	(23.4)	(13.8)	

*Including those who are more than four generations descendants of migrants, who would find it difficult to remember where their ancestors came from.

Table 6.3 Contacts between floaters and residents

Categories of floating population most frequently interacted with	Number of floating population known to residents						
	0	1–5	6–10	11–15	16+	N.A.	Sum
Met in work units	9.8	45.1	53.2	20.0	61.5	50.0	33.7
Customers	3.6	4.9	12.8	30.0	7.7	0.0	6.0
Servants	0.5	3.3	0.0	0.0	0.0	0.0	1.4
Casually encountered	70.2	43.4	34.0	50.0	29.2	50.0	51.3
Others	15.9	3.3	0.0	0.0	1.5	0.0	7.6
Total	100.0	100.0	100.0	100.0	100.0	100.0	100.0
	(38.9)	(36.3)	(9.4)	(2.0)	(13.0)	(0.4)	

five members of the floating population, including 38.9 per cent who knew none personally but only encountered them as strangers, mostly in the street. Although comparable sociometric data on interaction between city residents is not available, it seems likely that the extent of interaction between floaters and residents is markedly low compared with interaction between residents themselves, who often have wide circles of friends and acquaintances in various districts of the city.

Generally, as Table 6.3 shows, only small percentages of residents personally know more than five floaters. There are however, thirteen per cent of the respondents who know more than sixteen members of the floating population. These respondents are mainly those who have contact with the floating population at work.

Evaluation of the influence of the floating population on the community

Residents were questioned on four aspects of the effect of the floating population on the community's daily life, namely employment, environment, security of property, and traffic and transport. The respondents were asked to evaluate the extent of the perceived influence by choosing from three pre-set levels of influence: serious, somewhat and none. Within the four aspects, the number of aspects perceived as affected (including "serious" and "somewhat") is here referred to as the influence range (R), and the number of aspects identified as seriously influenced as the influence extensiveness (E). Table 6.4 shows that:

1 The floating population are perceived to cause a wide spread of influences on community life. Of the city residents, 97.2 per cent perceived the negative influences at least in one aspect, 74.2 per cent of them perceived at least three aspects, and nearly thirty per cent perceived all four aspects. There are only 2.8 per cent of residents who did not feel any negative influence of the floating population.

Table 6.4 Summary evaluation of the negative influence of floating population upon community

E: Influence extensiveness (number of serious influence aspects)	R: influence range (number of influence aspects)					
	4	*3*	*2*	*1*	*0*	*All*
4	1.4					1.4
3	3.0	1.8				4.8
2	5.8	4.0	0.6			10.4
1	8.2	12.4	5.4	1.2		27.2
0	11.4	26.2	15.8	—	2.8	56.2
Total	29.8	44.4	21.8	1.2	2.8	100.0

2 The extensiveness of the influences is perceived as relatively tolerable. A full 56.2 per cent of the respondents did not indicate serious influences in any of the four aspects, and 27.2 per cent of them perceived some serious influences in only one aspect. Only 16.6 per cent of the residents perceived more than two aspects of serious influence, of which only 1.4 per cent experience the most extreme degree of negative effect, i.e., serious influence on all four aspects.

The respondents have the strongest feelings about the influence of the floating population on transport. 90.8 per cent of them feel these effects, and 30.1 per cent regard this as serious, a markedly higher proportion than for the other three aspects. The second greatest influence identified is on security of property, with 80.8 per cent feeling the effect and 14.0 per cent regarding it as serious. The third most affected aspect is the living environment, which 77.4 per cent of the respondents feel to have been damaged, 17.4 per cent of them seriously. Comparatively speaking, residents feel less worried about the competition for employment created by the floating population. 63.8 per cent of them do not perceive any influence in this respect, 29.8 per cent feel some, and only 6.4 identify this as serious.

If the effects on the four aspects are averaged, then respondents who experience serious influence only add up to 16.9 per cent, further suggesting that, as far as residents are concerned, the influence of the floating population stays within acceptable limits. However, since the proportion of those who feel threatened (either somewhat or seriously) reaches 71.3 per cent, this probably indicates a degree of tension in which the impact of the floating population is approaching a critical point.

Among those who consider the floating population a threat to their property, 42.0 per cent do so because their family have had things stolen in the period since January 1994. Furthermore, two thirds of those who feel that this problem is serious have had this unpleasant experience.

Naturally, not all theft is committed by the floating population.[5] According to Shanghai Municipal Police Bureau, more than seventy per

Table 6.5 Degree of perceived influence of floating population on given aspects of urban life

Aspects	Seriously affected	Somewhat affected	Not affected	Total
Employment	6.4	29.8	63.8	100.0
Living environment	17.4	60.1	22.6	100.0
Property security	14.0	66.9	19.2	100.0
Transport	30.1	60.7	9.2	100.0
Average	16.9	54.4	28.7	100.0

Table 6.6 Residents' reasons for believing that the floating population are a threat to security of property

Reason	Serious threat	Somewhat of a threat	Total
Own family's experience theft since 1994	67.1	36.8	42.0
Neighbour's experience of theft since 1994	12.7	22.4	20.7
Theft frequent in the community recently	17.3	36.4	33.1
Other	2.9	4.5	4.2
Total	100.0	100.0	100.0
	(17.3)	(82.7)	

cent of thefts are carried out by the floating population. Whatever its accuracy, this figure indicates that much theft is at least attributed to migrants. The perception of criminality is the most important reason for mutual wariness and mutual separation in the relationship between the established and the outsiders.

Many residents believe that the floating population damage their living environment through uncontrolled hawking, indiscriminate dumping of litter and uncontrolled construction (Table 6.7). Among the residents who hold such views, 37.4 per cent do so because of the marketing behaviour of members of the floating population, 32.0 per cent because of dumping of litter and 21.6 per cent because of uncontrolled construction. By comparison, belief that they cause pollution through their productive work

Table 6.7 Distribution of residents' reasons for believing that the floating population damage the environment

Reason	Seriously damages	Somewhat damages	Total
Uncontrolled construction	25.4	20.6	21.6
Indiscriminate littering	29.9	32.6	32.0
Uncontrolled hawking	36.6	37.5	37.4
Pollution through productive work	4.5	8.6	7.7
Other	3.6	0.6	1.3
Total	100.0	100.0	100.0
	(22.4)	(77.6)	

is quite limited, which reflects the fact that few of the floating population come into the city as investors. The distribution of reasons is quite similar and shows little variation between those who see this environmental impact as more or less serious.

As shown in table 6.5, only 36.2 per cent of the respondents worry about the threat of unemployment owing to the competition of migrant labour. Of those respondents who do feel that there is such an effect, 14.4 per cent have in the past experienced unemployment (either of the respondent or of family members) which they attribute to the competition of floaters. A further 27.6 per cent are unemployed just now (including currently unemployed members of their family), and one quarter of them feel that the influence of the floating population on employment is serious, and they are the very people actually influenced. 39.8 per cent of those who believe the floaters damage employment chances are just afraid of being unemployed in the future because of the floater competition.

Residents' acceptance of the floating population

Most residents admit the right of the floating population to compete fairly for jobs in the city, but almost half reject their right to equal payment. Of the respondents, 78.2 per cent believe that the floating population have the right to compete for jobs of in the city, which reflects the fact that the floating population are believed to cause relatively slight effects on residents' employment. Even among those who do believe that the floating population have a serious impact, more than half admit their right to seek employment. This may be a positive indication that the city residents are adjusting their attitudes to the new market economy system.

When asked "Do you think that migrant workers should be paid less than residents for the same work?", 45.9 per cent of the respondents answered "yes", of whom 7.4 per cent answered "yes, a lot less", leaving just over half of the sample believing that migrants should be paid the same as residents. Even among those who admit floaters' right to compete fairly for work, 38.2 per cent accepted the idea of differential pay. It seems that Shanghai residents demonstrate some contradictions in their attitudes to migrants' labour. While they confirm their rights in the abstract, they deny them in practice.

Residents show positive attitudes to the schooling of children of the floating population who have been employed in the city (Table 6.8). Primary education is compulsory for children in China. According to a 1993 survey (Wang et al. 1995), within the floating population there are 2.8 per cent, i.e., 70,000, in the primary school age group of seven to twelve years old. Yet few of them are enrolled in city schools. Leaving aside the practical difficulties, we questioned the residents about their attitudes to the right of migrants' children to attend school in the city. A large

Table 6.8 Attitudes towards schooling of children of the employed floating population

Education of respondent	Should city primary schools enroll children of employed floating population?				
	Yes unconditionally	*Yes conditionally*	*No*	*Other*	*All*
Higher	27.3	22.1	11.0	23.5	21.0
Upper middle	45.5	49.3	52.4	52.9	49.5
Lower middle	24.2	26.5	32.9	17.6	26.9
Primary & under	3.0	1.5	3.7	5.9	2.2
N.A.	0.0	0.6	0.0	0.0	0.4
Total	100.0	100.0	100.0	100.0	100.0
	(13.2)	(67.1)	(16.4)	(3.4)	

majority (80.3 per cent) of the respondents believe that the city schools ought to accept those children, of whom 13.2 per cent think the schools should take such children unconditionally. This suggests that the residents take a positive view towards the children of the floating population. Furthermore, respondents who themselves have higher education are more positively disposed towards the schooling of such children than the respondents in general.

There are a large number of people in the floating population, many of them middle aged women without marketable skills, who cannot find formal jobs and do not want to return home unemployed. They live on scavenging from garbage, collecting all kinds of materials (such as plastic, metals or glass) which are recycled. This is often seen as a real job, and the scavengers may well have to pay the work unit or neighbourhood committee for the right to go through their bins. When asked "What is your main feeling when you see a person from out of town scavenging from dustbins", only 9.8 per cent of the respondents reply that they feel "sympathy", while 30.7 per cent report "disgust", and 44.7 per cent share both feelings. Even among those who do not believe that the floating population cause damage to the environment, expressions of disgust outweigh those of sympathy by three to two. It is apparent that the residents reject scavengers not only because of considerations of environment and hygiene. Among those who believe that the floating population are a threat to their property, feelings of disgust at scavengers far outweigh those of sympathy by four to one. Such respondents appear to suspect that scavengers also pick up things from outside the bins.

When asked "What is the personal quality of the floating population that most urgently needs to be improved?", 42.5 per cent of the respondents give first choice to "observance of the law". Clearly, what particularly troubles residents is the threat to property and public order posed by the criminal activities of floaters. The second most important quality mentioned is educational level, which acts as a label for the overall status and reliability of a floater.

Table 6.9 Personal quality of floating population which most urgently needs improvement

Quality	Proportion	Quality	Proportion
Education	28.1	Hygiene	10.6
Morality	17.6	Other	0.2
Observance of the law	42.5		
Work skills	1.0	Total	100.0

Factors influencing residents' attitudes

The main difference in contact with the floating population found within the sample was between the sexes. Male respondents exceeded female in contact with the floating population. Of all men, 33.9 per cent and 45.6 per cent of the women knew none of the floating population. The average number known by men is 5.3 and 3.6 by women.

Although there is no obvious difference between men's and women's evaluations of the influence of the floating population on employment in the city, there is a clear difference in their attitudes towards the right of the floating population to compete fairly for jobs, with men taking a significantly more tolerant attitude towards floaters' labour market rights than women (Table 6.10). This might appear paradoxical, given that the majority of the floating population are men, and therefore presumably more in labour market competition with male residents.

There were also some differences between respondents with different levels of education. Respondents of both the highest and lowest education levels seemed to interact more with members of the floating population than middle levels did (Table 6.11). The greatest contrast appeared among those with the lowest level of education, half of whom claimed to know none of the floating population, while over a quarter knew more than sixteen. This presumably relates to the type of work done by floaters, which may bring them into more contact with less skilled members of the resident population, if at all.

However, the attitudes of these less educated residents towards the employment situation caused by floaters appeared somewhat mixed (Table 6.12). Only a fifth of them felt that the floating population caused harmful

Table 6.10 Sex differences of employment influences and rights of floating population

Sex	Damage influence to employment?				Right to compete fairly for jobs?			
	Yes, seriously	*Yes, somewhat*	*No*	*N.A.*	*Yes*	*No*	*N.A.*	*All*
Male	4.5	31.5	64.0	0.0	82.9	16.8	0.3	100.0
Female	8.8	27.4	63.3	0.5	72.1	27.4	0.5	100.0
Average	6.4	29.7	63.7	0.2	78.2	21.4	0.4	100.0

Table 6.11 Education difference of contacts with floating population

Education	Number of floating population known to residents							Average number*
	None	*1–5*	*6–10*	*11–15*	*16+*	*N.A.*	*All*	
Higher	32.4	41.0	8.6	1.0	16.2	1.0	100.0	4.7
Upper middle	39.5	37.1	8.5	3.6	11.3	0.0	100.0	4.4
Lower middle	41.5	32.6	12.6	0.0	12.6	0.7	100.0	4.4
Primary & below	54.5	18.2	0.0	0.0	27.3	0.0	100.0	5.7
Average	38.9	36.3	9.4	2.0	13.0	0.4	100.0	4.6

*Weighted sum of the mid-value (19 for group 16+) by proportions. The unit is persons.

Table 6.12 Attitudes to floating population's influence on employment and to their labour market rights by respondents' level of education

Education	Damaging influence on employment?				Right to compete fairly for jobs?			All
	Yes, seriously	*Yes, somewhat*	*No*	*n.a.*	*Yes*	*No*	*n.a.*	
Higher	0.0	24.8	75.2	0.0	88.6	11.4	—	100.0
Upper middle	6.9	33.5	59.7	0.0	77.4	21.8	0.8	100.0
Lower middle	10.4	27.4	62.2	0.0	72.6	27.4	—	100.0
Primary & below	9.1	9.1	72.7	9.1	63.6	36.4	—	100.0
Average	6.4	29.7	63.7	0.2	78.2	21.4	0.4	100.0

effects to the employment chances of residents, lower than residents with higher levels of education. Despite this, the least educated residents were most likely to deny floaters the right to compete in the labour market on equal terms with residents. The most highly educated were, unsurprisingly, both least likely to see the floaters as damaging their employment chances and most prepared to accord them equal employment rights.

It seems likely that the degree to which urban residents themselves are "established" in the city's social structure would have an influence on their attitudes towards "outsiders". However, the influence could be argued in either direction. One might argue that the most established residents would feel the least threatened by incomers and take a more neutral and tolerant attitude towards them. Or alternatively, the more recent migrants to the city, and hence perhaps the least settled, might empathize more closely with the floating population and sympathize with their predicament. It is possible to cast a little light on this question from the survey evidence, by distinguishing residents according to the number of generations over which their family had settled in Shanghai.

Table 6.13 shows the attitudes of residents of different generations of settlement towards the employment of the floating population. The differences between the generations are relatively slight, but it appears that the first generation, i.e. those who are themselves permanently

Table 6.13 Attitudes to floating population's influence on employment and to their labour market rights by respondents of different generations in Shanghai

Generations in Shanghai	Damage influence to employment?			Right to compete fairly for jobs?		All
	Yes, seriously	Yes, somewhat	No	Yes	No	
First	11.7	31.7	56.7	73.8	26.2	100.0
Second & over	5.7	29.1	64.3	79.0	21.0	100.0
Second	4.1	27.9	68.0	80.6	19.4	100.0
Third	6.3	35.1	58.6	75.5	24.5	100.0
Natives	7.8	26.6	65.6	79.7	20.3	100.0
Average	6.4	29.8	63.7	78.6	21.4	100.0

registered migrants, hold more negative attitudes towards floaters than the descendants of earlier migrants. This difference holds both in relation to beliefs about the influence of the floating population on city employment, and in relation to opinions concerning the right of floaters to compete fairly for city jobs.

A similar situation appears in regard to the opinions of residents towards the right of children of the floating population to attend city schools, with a higher proportion (21.3 per cent) of the first generation believing that those children have no right to be enrolled in city schools, while only 15.6 per cent of the second generations and over think so (Table 6.14).

This evidence points in the direction of the former of the two arguments presented above, and suggests that the most recent permanent settlers in the city feel the most threatened by the floating population and are thus the least likely to be tolerant towards them and accord them rights in the urban society. But the evidence is slender and, as is the case for many of the findings reported in this paper, requires support from further research.

Table 6.14 Attitudes to the right of employed floating population's children to be enrolled in school by respondents of different generations in Shanghai

Generations in Shanghai	Should city primary schools enroll children of employed floating population?				
	Yes unconditionally	Yes conditionally	No	Other	All
First	8.2	65.6	21.3	4.9	100.0
Second & over	13.9	67.2	15.6	3.2	100.0
Second	15.2	67.0	14.2	3.6	100.0
Third	12.6	69.4	14.4	3.6	100.0
Native	13.3	65.6	18.8	2.3	100.0
Average	13.2	67.1	16.4	3.3	100.0

Conclusion

The question of the relationship between the established residents of the city and the most recent and least settled outsiders is a complex one, and the research reported on here can only begin to tackle a few aspects of it. As we pointed out earlier with reference to the recent article of Solinger (1995), the attitudes of the resident population are only one of many factors which must bear on the nature and quality of these relationships. For example, earlier research on the integration into city life of village migrants in Taiwan (Gallin and Gallin 1974) highlighted the factor of social class in differentiating the experience of migrants, an aspect which is undoubtedly crucial but which could only be touched on indirectly in this chapter through the indicator of education.

However, by concentrating on the attitudes of Shanghai residents towards the floating population, this chapter has been able to show that the almost entirely negative image of migrants presented in the Chinese media has not completely been accepted by the people of Shanghai, and in particular by the residents of Caoyang Xincun, an area notably influenced by a large number of incomers. While many of the sample respondents do indeed believe that the floating population are the cause of many of the economic, social and environmental problems which residents face, these attitudes are by no means universal. And while many respondents react to the perceived threat of the outsiders by denying them equal citizenship in urban society, the majority of the sample is prepared to accord them rights to compete for jobs and to allow their children to enroll in city schools, even though under less than equal conditions.

Migration often raises acute political questions of social integration and the distribution of scarce resources, and the movement of large numbers of "outsiders" into Shanghai is clearly no exception (see also White 1994). The evidence of this modest survey suggests, however, that even a relatively exposed section of the city residents are prepared to take complex and even tolerant views of their new neighbours, partially but not entirely directed by negative stereotypes. We can look forward to a long period of adjustment to the urban social conditions brought about by the relaxation of controls on population mobility, and to future research projects to inquire further into its course and consequences.

References

Blecher, Marc. 1983. "Peasant Labour for Urban Industry: Temporary Contract Labour, Urban-rural Balance and Class Relations in a Chinese County." *World Development* 11, no. 8, pp. 731–45.

Davin, Delia 1996. "Images of the Migrant in the Chinese Media." Paper presented at the Workshop on European Chinese and Chinese Domestic Migrants: Common Themes in International and Internal Migration. Oxford, 3–5 July 1996.

Ding Jinhong et al. 1994. *Shilun Mingongchaode Xingcheng Jizhi yu Zhili Duice* [On the formation mechanism of influx of migrant labourers and policy of control]. *Keji Daobao* 7, pp. 21–3.

Elias, Norbert and Scotson, John L. 1965. *The Established and the Outsiders.* London: Frank Cass.

Gallin, Bernard and Gallin, Rita S. 1974. "The Integration of Village Migrants in Taipei." In Mark Elvin and G. William Skinner, eds, *The Chinese City between Two Worlds.* Stanford: Stanford University Press, pp. 331–58.

Li Mengbai et al. 1991. *Liudong Renkou dui Dachengshi Fazhande Yingxiang ji Duice* [The floating population in metropolitan cities: Impact and policy measures]. Beijing: Jingji Ribao Chubanshe.

Mallee, Hein. 1995. "Rural Population Mobility in Seven Chinese Provinces." Paper presented at the Fourth European Conference on Agriculture and Rural Development in China, Manchester, 10–12 November 1995.

Mallee Hein. 1995/96. "In Defence of Migration: Recent Chinese Studies of Rural Population Mobility." *China Information* 10, no. 3/4, pp. 108–40.

Shi Songjiu et al. 1991. *Liudong Renkou Guanli* [Management of the floating population]. Shanghai: *Shanghai Kepu Chubanshe.*

Solinger, Dorothy J. 1995. "The Floating Population in the Cities: Chances for Assimilation?." In Deborah S. Davis, Richard Kraus, Barry Naughton and Elizabeth Perry eds, *Urban Spaces in Contemporary China,* Cambridge: Woodrow Wilson International Center for Scholars and Cambridge University Press, pp. 113–39.

Wakabayashi, Keiko. 1990. "Migration from Rural to Urban Areas in China." *Developing Economies* 28, no. 4, pp. 503–23.

Wang Wuding et al. 1995. *Jiushi Niandai Shanghai Liudong Renkou* [The floating population in Shanghai in the 1990s]. Shanghai: Huadong Shifan Daxue Chubanshe.

White, Lynn T. III. 1994. "Migration and Politics on the Shanghai Delta." *Issues & Studies* 30, no. 9, pp. 63–94.

Notes

1 Some definitions emphasize that members of the floating population should take part in some activity (Li et al. 1991, Shi et al. 1991), but we see little merit in excluding reportedly "inactive" migrants.

2 In Chinese Xincun means "new village". The new settlement of Caoyang "new village" was built adjacent to Shanghai city proper in the early 1950s.

3 All figures in the tables are percentages except where noted.

4 The difference between Jiangsu and Zhejiang is due to the location of the survey area at the northern side of central Shanghai. It traditionally absorbed migrants from Jiangsu province.

5 To emphasize floater-related theft, we noted in the questionnaire that thefts proved to be committed by native residents should be excluded. This is likely to have strengthened the association between theft and the floating population in the minds of respondents.

Chapter Seven

Issues in the fertility of temporary migrants in Beijing

Caroline Hoy

Introduction

The household registration system in China has mediated population mobility since the 1950s. Economic activity, education and social mobility opportunities have been largely determined by the household registration system that bound an individual to birth place, ensuring that they could only rarely initiate a change of residence. In contrast, government sponsored migration was promoted during the decades that followed (Bernstein 1977; Li 1989; Cheng 1991) and semi-organized migration was tolerated (Shen 1996).

Significant changes in the level of individually initiated mobility took place at the end of the 1970s. However, the creation of a vast mobile "floating" population did not occur until pro-market policies had been established (Solinger 1993) and rural reform instigated (Goldstein, Goldstein and Guo 1991; Gui 1992; Woon 1992; Chan 1994; Wu 1994; Mallee 1995).

In response to this new mobility, first provincial and then national legislation was established. In 1985, the Ministry of Public Security published national regulations under which migrants could register at destination and thus gain legitimacy for their new residence. Yet many migrants do not register. In 1995, it was thought that of an estimated eighty million migrants, thirty-six million had not registered (Renmin Ribao 1995).

Fertility and family planning in the floating population were of increasing concern as it was believed that mobility could be commensurate with self-determination of fertility when children could be born and how many. Transmission of information on new in-migrants was often delayed and unfamiliarity of family planning personnel with regulations of the migrants' area of origin often meant that problems arose in accounting for births (Hoy 1996). Hence the establishment in 1991 of "Measures for the management of the family planning in the floating population". The migrant population was defined broadly as those for whom "the place of their present residence are not the places where their habitual residence is registered" (China Population Today 1992:2). The target population for family planning was similarly broad. There were no distinctions by sex or marital status, simply "those who are fertile" (China Population Today 1992:2).

Under these measures, legislation implemented in the permanent registration area governed family planning of migrants whatever their current location. Concern that out-migration areas should shoulder the burden for acceptance of family planning methods in their population is emphasized. High fertility rates in the migrant population are blamed on negligent organization of family planning at origin (Gui 1992).

Requirements to carry family planning certificates, previously provincially regulated, became nationally applicable under the terms of the 1991 measures. These certificates act as proof of identity and marital status, and increase the ability of each area to police migrants' fertility behaviour by listing fertility histories and contraception status. Before a residence, business, or work permit can be issued, migrants are theoretically required to show this certificate. The advantage of these cards lies in their mobility, giving personnel in destination areas instant access to fertility histories and guidance on future fertility (Hoy 1996).

This chapter examines the life histories of a sample of temporary registered migrants in Beijing. In particular it examines the relationship between fertility and migration. Firstly, I shall examine the sex ratios of the children of migrants in a survey of migrants, and a new hypothesis of migration opportunities for women is suggested. This is followed by an examination of the length of the first birth interval, that is the length of time between marriage and the birth of the first child for different subpopulations of migrants, identified by the timing of migration in relation to other life history events.

In this chapter the term "migrant" refers to the floating population: temporary migrants who have registered at destination under the terms of the 1985 regulations, and it is this population which form the basis for the research.

Data collection and population background

Information was collected in Beijing in 1994 using a questionnaire survey, referred to below as the 1994 Migrant Survey. The target population were ever married women aged between eighteen and forty-nine years whose household registration was based outside the Beijing city region and had migrated into the Beijing city region at some point during their life history. The majority of the migrants were from rural areas and in most cases had migrated to Beijing in the four and a half years immediately preceding the survey. Most held temporary registration permits.

Interviews took place in two districts of Beijing, Haidian and Mentougou, under the aegis of the China Population and Information Research Centre. The areas in which the survey took place were identified by a process of negotiation and as such the interview areas were "not randomly chosen ... but the opportunity was usually seized when some favourable circumstances made it possible to work in a particular area" (Caldwell 1988:459). A total of 403 interviews, conducted using a quota sampling method, were carried out in both home and work environments during May and June 1994. As the target population were ever married migrant women, the survey was not representative of the general population of migrant women. The average age of the migrants was thirty years.

Some eighty per cent of women had children with an average of 1.5 children per woman. Most women, even those with young children, worked, usually as petty traders, selling fruit and vegetables or clothes. Many travelled everyday between their rented accommodation and their places of work, whether it was a market place or a small shop. Most rented a room through a neighbourhood office in the low rise suburbs of Beijing, sharing it with their husbands and their children, if their children had not been left in the care of their grandparents. Rooms were expensive to rent, costing as much as 400 yuan per month, and many had experienced a reduction in their living space on migration to Beijing.

A discussion of fertility

It is more or less implicitly accepted that in less developed areas rural fertility will differ from urban fertility; compared to urban women, rural women have higher fertility levels (Zeng and Vaupel 1989; Mookherjee 1992), shorter birth intervals, and an earlier onset of fertility. Lower fertility rates in urban areas are presented as the result of a complex of values, situations and processes. These include lower child mortality rates, higher costs of children and greater investment in children, time constraints, more intense materialism, the higher status of women (related to greater proportions of women economically active outside the home), higher education levels, greater control over fertility and weaker traditional mores. The reduction or removal of the familial support structure, both practical and emotional, for a couple as a result of migration should also be considered.

Structural influences and cultural conditions are often considered to be the catalysts in the creation of differences between populations (Heaton et al. 1989). In rural society these can support early marriage and early child bearing. Legislation and governance can serve to reinforce the differences between urban and rural areas. This has taken place to such an extent in China that the divide between rural and urban areas has been described as "one country, two systems" (Lavely et al. 1990:823).

Those crossing the rural-urban divide are assumed to be unable to remain impervious to the transition of geography and status. In fertility terms that transition is expressed through reductions in fertility rates. At some point in time after migration, migrant fertility rates are expected to be equivalent to those of the resident urban population. The assumption is that migrants will not consciously favour retaining behavioural patterns which would lead to high fertility, considered to inhibit their participation in the urban environment. Migration itself can shape the patterns of divide. If sufficient numbers of the population transfer to urban areas then the demographics of a country are reshaped. Such transference is part of the process of "development" and "modernization" leading to improved conditions and economic prosperity.

Female autonomy in the urban and rural context is important as urban residence is conducive to individual and gender emancipation and greater control of women over their fertility. Davies (1994:3) considers that "the re-negotiation of identities [of women] is fundamental to migration". Where migration takes place from a more repressive to a less repressive environment, a reduction in fertility rates in urban society is consistent with female empowerment and is not simply a factor in the process of accustomization to the urban context (Hugo 1993). However, in China we are also faced with a semi-paradox: Women's fertility in rural areas is subject to less rigid restrictions on behalf of the state, but, on the contrary, greater rigidity in terms of the fertility norms of their household and local society. On migration, such local control may lessen only to be replaced by greater control on behalf of the state. If lower fertility goals in urban areas, created or prompted by migration, happen to conform with those of the state, can we still say that women's status has increased or improved?

This bifurcation of fertility by geographical area and implicitly, social degree, has been criticized for being "all too general" (Campbell 1989: 104). Rural areas can encompass a variety of fertility regimes (Campbell 1989) and are not necessarily a plateau of homogeneously high fertility rates. Boundaries between urban and rural worlds and the behaviour and perceptions of their populations are much more likely to be fluid, varying between country and time. Although the rural-urban fertility dichotomy remains a useful tool in fertility analysis, it should not necessarily always be used as an explanatory factor for differences in behaviour and results.

Four theories have been used as the basis of analyses of the creation or dissipation of migrant-migrant and migrant-resident fertility differentials. These models were initially codified by Goldstein and Goldstein (1982) and I shall briefly outline them below.

The selection model

This argues that characteristics inherent in the migrant prior to migration condition both the probability of migration and later behavioural responses. The emphasis is placed on variables such as age, education, occupation, marital status and fertility preferences (Wimberley et al. 1989). Those who wish to have smaller families migrate to urban areas where this preference can be implemented since it is likely to be consistent with the overall urban fertility regime. In addition, those with fewer children will have a greater probability of migrating (Goldstein and Goldstein 1982; White et al. 1990).

The criteria for selection change over time and space. The participants change and the outcome of their migration will change with them. Motivation and social status can operate in the creation of migration streams, selecting those with greater skills and ambition (Sabagh and Sun 1980; Tan 1993). Selection effects have been identified for short term migrants whose goal orientated nature pre-determined a lower level of fertility if they had not migrated (Tan 1993).

The socialization model

Socialization is relevant both before and after migration. The post migration socialization model suggests that it may take up to several generations before the fertility levels of migrants and their descendants will match those of urban residents. The pre-migration model socializes the future migrant into rural norms during childhood, prior to migration ensuring that, despite any modulation of those norms by change of circumstance such as urban migration, behaviour remains a product of that early socialization process (Campbell 1989).

The adaptation model

Adaptation involves behavioural adjustments to the urban environment within the span of an individual's fertility history, having controlled for the effects of selection and disruption (Lee and Farber 1984). The adaptation hypothesis requires an immediate, identifiable impact on fertility levels by exposure to financial hazards and time pressures of urban areas reinforced by personal inhibitions engendered by unfamiliarity with a new location.

The voluntary or involuntary nature of migration or the type of urban economy can influence the degree and speed of adaptation. The warmer the reception at destination, the more positive a migrant will feel about an area and the more receptive she will be to these external influences. Various background factors may influence migrants, depending for example, on the role that the woman plays in the decision making process (Hugo 1993).

The urban environment itself may influence the pace of adaptation, not just adaptation itself. A dynamic environment which fosters integration and participation is likely to have a greater impact than a stagnant one which only tolerates its migrant population.

A linear attitude change from rural to urban modes of thought is not necessarily consistent with a linear geographical journey from rural areas to urban localities (McGee 1975). Migrants can embrace both rural and urban attitudes simultaneously which can affect the degree and direction of fertility behaviour modification. Adaptation patterns of migrants to Mexico city depended on a "propitious conjunction of a migrant's personal characteristics and on the urban environment's structural features" (Kemper 1975:226). Variations in the speed of adaptation may also explain the variations in tempo of fertility falls, between more and less recent migrants, noted above. One model which accounts more directly for the effects of short term residence is the disruption model.

The disruption model

This offers a more specific opportunity for examining the immediate impact of migration and the compound psychological and physiological effects rather than a more general process of accommodation to the urban environment. The physical act of migration, moving across distance, can function as a period of interference in a woman's fertility history, delaying a birth or reducing the total number of children. Migration can also cause both psychological and physiological stress and a concomitant reduction in fertility and fecundability. Partners may be separated for longer or shorter periods of time. Rundquist and Brown (1989) use data from Ecuador to show that differences in the number of children ever born for the four categories of circular migrant, return migrant, permanent migrant and non migrant were explained by the varying degrees of disruption experienced by each type of migrant. It would also be wrong to assume that disruption solely results in diminished levels of fertility. A period of disruption to the "normal" progress of fertility can lead to a "bounce back" in fertility. The pace of child bearing increases after a period of disruption causing higher fertility levels for migrants compared to both stayers and residents. This transitory nature of disruption was described in a sample of Bangkok bound migrants (Goldstein and Goldstein 1981), whose fertility levels recovered after a period of migration related disruption.

Effects of fertility on migration

The first part of this section discusses sex ratios of migrant children and son preference. Son preference is a deeply embedded cultural character-istic, reinforced by pro-natalist economic reforms, the continuing practice of patrilocal marriages and expectations that sons will care for parents in old age.

In China, high sex ratios, that is an excess of males, are not a new phenomenon and existed prior to 1949 (Johanssen and Nygren 1991). Sex ratios fell and were stable during the 1960s and 1970s and then rose through the 1980s to a reported 114 in 1989 (Zeng et al. 1993). The sex of the first child has been identified as an indicator in acceptance of one child certificates; parents with a boy were more likely to sign the certificate than those with a girl (Arnold and Liu 1986). Son preference remains a significant factor across socio-economic conditions, educational level, rural or urban household registration and level of urbanization (Li and Cooney 1993). Higher sex ratios for births outside the plan compared to planned births have been reported (Arnold and Liu 1986; Lavely et al. 1990). Stronger son preference exists in rural areas (Xu and Yu 1991) and in densely populated areas (Arnold and Liu 1986; Hull 1990), and for those with a history of abortion (Hull 1990). Widespread availability of contraception coupled with an expectation of low family size may have supported sex preferences (Li and Cooney 1993). In the search for an explanation for the reported high sex ratios (male surpluses) the following factors have been suggested.

The first is underreporting: births are not registered. It has been suggested that between forty and seventy per cent of the difference in sex ratios can be explained by underreporting of female births (Zeng et al. 1993). The second factor is infanticide. There has been intense debate over the role of infanticide in modern China. Anecdotal reports supporting accusations of female infanticide exist, but prove difficult to confirm. The third factor that has been considered is gender specific abortion. Various authors have suggested that pre-natal sex determination is significant in determining sex ratios at birth (Zeng et al. 1993), although the proportion of the difference in sex ratios explained by abortions is debatable (Zeng et al. 1993; Hull 1990; Johanssen and Nygren 1991; Arnold and Liu 1986). High sex ratios may also indicate differential health care after birth (Johanssen and Nygren 1991). The fourth factor is adoption which takes place both formally and informally. The fifth factor is child abandonment. Numbers of abandoned children are increasing. An estimated 150,000 children are abandoned in China's major cities each year, mainly in public places such as railway stations (China News Analysis 1992).

A total of 589 live births were reported in the 1994 Migrant Survey. Some fifty-two women (thirteen per cent) had no children. Very few women had not given birth to their first child within the first two years of marriage. Women, counted as childless at the time of the survey, included many who were married in the calendar year prior to the survey and who may simply not have had time to get a child. Some forty-two per cent of the population had one child only; a further third of the surveyed women had two children. Women with multiple pregnancies, that is, three or more children, were a minority. This migrant population was characterized by low rather than high fertility. Many women were still at the beginning of their childbearing career and the number of children born to this population of women was expected to rise.

The easiest way to measure sex composition of any population is through the use of the sex ratio. This is the number of males for every one hundred females (Shryock and Siegel 1976). The normal expected sex ratio at birth is approximately 105–106 males for every one hundred females (Henry 1976).

Table 7.1 shows the number of male and female children, up to third parity births, and the resulting sex ratios, born to the population of the 1994 Migrant Survey. A total of 578 births were used in the analysis. A high sex ratio for all births of 139 was recorded. Sex ratios are expected to remain constant or decline with increasing parity (Zeng et al. 1993). However, in Table 7.1 the highest sex ratio occurred in second parity births, the lowest for first.

If a sex ratio of 106 and the same total of 578 children were assumed for the survey population, we would expect 298 male children and 280 female children to be born rather than the actual 336 boys and 242 girls. This amounts to sixteen per cent fewer female births observed than expected.

Sex ratios differ according to whether the first child was born before or after 1 January 1979. That is, the date on which the one child policy was introduced. The pattern of births in relation to this date is shown in Figure 7.1. The figures in circles indicate sex ratios where the numbers involved are sufficient for a meaningful sex ratio to be calculated. Overall sex ratios before and after this date are similar at 138 for the population whose first child was born prior to 1979, and 139 for those whose first child was born after 1979. However, the differences lie in the sex ratios at each parity.

For first children born prior to 1 January 1979 a low sex ratio of eighty-seven was recorded. Nearly all women whose first child was born before 1979 also had a second child. For women with a first male child the sex ratio of their second children was almost even. For women with a first female

Table 7.1 Reported births by sex and parity, 1994 Migrant Survey

Parity	Number of male births	Number of female births	Sex ratio
First	197	154	128
Second	110	69	159
Third	29	19	153
Total	336	242	139

Source: 1994 Migrant survey
Note 1: The questionnaire asked for specific details of the first three pregnancies. The figures above are fewer than the reported total as parities of four and over are not included and parity could not be established for all births.
Note 2: Sex ratio = males per 100 females

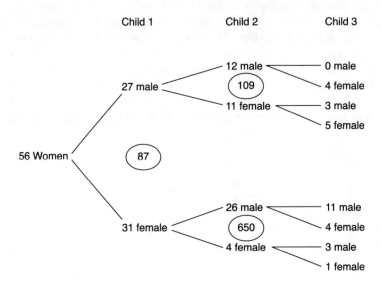

a. Eldest child born before January 1 1979

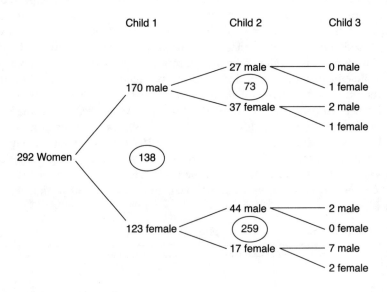

b. Eldest child born on or after 1 January 1979

Figure 7.1 Births by parity, sex and date of birth of eldest child, 1994 Migrant Survey
Source: 1994 Migrant survey

child the sex ratio for second children was very high at 650; twenty-six male children to four female children. Over half of the women who started childbearing before 1979 had a third child. Women with two male children were least likely to have a third child. It appears that in this subpopulation, if the first child was a son, then subsequent sex ratios are within reasonable limits. However, where the first child was a daughter, then later sex ratios were abnormal. It also seems that it was not sufficient for the second child to be male; a third child, preferably a second son, was also important.

In comparison to the low sex ratio for first births prior to January 1979, sex ratios for first births after this date were high at 138. For women whose first child was male the sex ratio for second children fell to seventy-three. Few of the women whose first child was male had given birth to a third child by the survey date. For women whose first child was female sex ratios for second children increased. This also was the case in the pre-1979 population, although not to the same degree. Where the second child was also female, women were more likely to have a third birth.

Sex ratios for this population are higher than those reported elsewhere, although the small size of the data set may affect the pattern to some degree. Some of the variation may simply be due to chance. It appears that some manipulation of sex ratios to achieve at least one son has occurred. In the pre-1979 population the sex of the first child appears to have been left to chance; if there was a bias, it was towards females. Manipulation occurred after the first birth. In this subpopulation nearly ninety-nine per cent had at least one male child by third parity birth. Normally, eighty-nine per cent of a population would have been expected to have had at least one male child by the third birth.

For the population with first births after January 1979 manipulation of sex ratios appeared to start with the first child. If the first child was male then couples either pushed for a daughter, or did not determine the sex of their second child. They appeared content, at the time of the survey, with an older male and a younger female child. If the first child was female then attempts to have a male child increased. Less than one per cent of this post January 1979 population had all female families by the third birth. This contrasts with an expected eleven per cent. These results reflect nation-wide patterns. In Hebei province couples with one son were likely to try for another child, while those with two daughters tried for a third child (Banister 1987; Cleland and Shen 1991). In Shaanxi province the hazard (the likelihood of experiencing an event at a particular time given survival to that time, Norusis 1992) of having a second birth for women whose first child was female was 1.5 times higher than for those with a first male child. The hazard of having a third birth where the first two children were female was 2.9 times higher than that of women with one girl and one boy (Tu 1991).

While it appears that sex ratios were manipulated, the real question is how? It is clear that this process started during the 1970s when techniques currently being blamed for raising sex ratios, such as ultra-sound machines, were unavailable. We also know that, based on information indicating high sex ratios, methods of altering sex ratios were available prior to 1949. Methods left to consider, at present and without proof, are differential health care, infanticide and out-adoption. There are very few clues as to which of these are being used to achieve sex preference. The effect of the one child policy, in addition to consolidating the male child preference, is to shift the timing of this manipulation from second and higher parity births to first parity births, and it remains where the first child is female. It appears that some socially tolerated methods of sex determination exist.

However, there is an alternative explanation for the very high sex ratios in the 1994 Migrant Survey. Migrants are selective by the sex of their children. Women who have given birth to at least one son and who are confident of their position within their marital household may have slightly more freedom than those who have not yet fulfilled this familial obligation, and utilize the opportunity of a relaxation in familial duties to migrate. There is no control population with which to compare this migrant population, but a degree of internal comparison is possible. The sex ratio of children born to women who migrated prior to the onset of childbearing was compared to those who migrated at some point after the birth of their first child.

The sex ratio of children born to women who migrated prior to childbearing was calculated to be 102 (N = 113) and higher for post-fertility migrants at 152 (N = 370). Several factors could explain this pattern. Firstly, migration and duration of residence in urban areas reduces the degree of son preference amongst migrants, which is then expressed in the sex ratios of their children. Secondly, the high sex ratio of the post-fertility migrants is indicative of high sex ratios at origin. Thirdly, migrants who started childbearing before their first mobility event are selective by the sex of their children.

It is difficult to draw a firm conclusion from such small data sets. However, there are indications that a hypothesis for selective migration by sex of children can be suggested for China. Son preference very definitely exists in rural areas. If migration is selective by sex of children then this could result in exaggerated sex ratios in a survey of migrants at destination, as occurred in the 1994 Migrant Survey. Migration itself does not cause higher sex ratios except where urban experience depresses son preference, thereby increasing the urban-rural sex ratio differential. The birth of a male child releases a woman from her obligations. She can then use historical tradition to her advantage by requesting that the older generation take on the responsibility for child care while she seeks new opportunities elsewhere in the name of familial economic advancement. If this tentative conclusion is true, it is indicative of increasing female dependency on male children for valid social status and migration may help to redress this bias.

Fertility and birth intervals

Having discussed sex ratio at birth, this section examines birth intervals in relation to migration experiences. A birth interval is defined as "the time between successive live births" (Newell 1988: 59). The time period between marriage and first birth is not generally defined as a birth interval, but here it will be used as the first birth interval. The interpretation of birth intervals can prove problematic. Whether they should include conceptions which are terminated as discrete intervals or whether live birth to live birth only can be counted as intervals is a point for discussion.

Birth intervals in China were first stressed in the "later, longer, fewer" family planning campaign of the 1970s, although policy did not and has not targeted first births. In preference, emphasis has been laid on later marriage and longer intervals between later births (Feeney and Wang 1993). In contrast, there has been a trend towards decreasing length of the first birth interval (Feeney and Wang 1993; Coale et al. 1988), most pronounced in women who marry at older ages (Qiao and Chen 1991; Tu 1991; Choe and Wu 1991). Increasing first birth interval length is more apparent in some provinces than others (Choe and Wu 1991) and not necessarily positively associated with socio-economic status (Choe and Wu 1991; Tu 1991).

Increased coital frequency in early marriage has been cited as an explanatory factor in the decrease in the length of the first birth interval (Cleland and Shen 1991). Low rates of marital intercourse were encouraged in traditional China to preserve male health, which, together with spousal separation after marriage, kept marriage to first birth intervals long. With a more universal linkage of marriage and cohabitation and "increasingly conjugal" experiences of marriage (Honig and Hershatter 1988:144), first birth intervals have shortened (Coale et al. 1988; Feeney and Wang 1993). The types of contraception available also influence the length of this birth interval. For many women, especially in rural areas, the only contraceptive methods provided are not easily reversible (Intrauterine contraceptive devices or IUDs) or are non-reversible (sterilization). Few women will be willing to use either prior to the birth of their first child, increasing the likelihood of early conception (Cai et al. 1991). Under such circumstances, women will start to use or consider using contraception only after their first child is born.

What is the average length of a birth interval in China? Estimates are fairly tightly clustered. For example, 14.2 months in Shaanxi (Tu 1991), 13.5 months in Shanghai and 15.1 in Hebei (Cleland and Shen 1991). Feeney and Wang (1993) estimate the average length of the first birth interval for women in China to be sixteen months for the period 1981–1987.

The aim of the work reported on here was to try to answer questions about the adjustments made to life histories by women who migrate in

China, and here we focus specifically on the length of this important first birth interval. In an ideal world, attention would be focused on "the comparative fertility of the migrants and non-migrant women in both urban and rural places" (Goldstein and Goldstein 1982:32). While the 1994 Migrant Survey did not include non-migrants, the information obtained makes at least internal comparisons between sample subpopulations possible. To this end, the sample population was divided into five subpopulations based on the relative timing of identified key events in life histories such as marriage and births. The five subpopulations are listed in Appendix 1. The main method of analysis used to identify differences and similarities between subpopulations was the one way analysis of variance or ANOVA. This allows sample subpopulations represented by their means to be compared (Norusis 1983). A discussion of this method is included in Appendix 2.

Analysis was restricted to women who had births within six years prior to marriage, or within six years after marriage. Any earlier births were deemed unreliable, any births more than after six years after were deemed to be connected to fertility problems. Women with no children were excluded from the analysis. Mean length of the first birth interval for each subpopulation by cohort is shown in Table 7.2.

All subpopulations demonstrate relatively short marriage to first birth intervals, characteristic of the general population. First birth intervals range from –0.5 of a year (women who gave birth prior to their marriage) to more than four years in the oldest cohort. On average, women in this sample gave birth to their first child some sixteen months after their

Table 7.2 Mean first birth intervals in years in migrant subpopulations by cohort, 1994 Migrant Survey

Birth Cohort	Migrant subpopulations				Other	Cohort mean
	Migration before marriage	Migration after first birth	Migration in first birth interval	Marriage and migration at the same time		
6/1970–5/1975	1.2	0.9	1.0	1.2	0.5	0.9
6/1965–5/1970	0.9	1.0	1.8	1.3	–0.5	1.0
6/1960–5/1965	1.4	1.6	2.3	2.3	0.9	1.6
6/1955–5/1960	0.0	1.7	2.1	0.0	1.6	1.7
6/1950–5/1955	0.0	1.2	0.0	0.0	0.9	1.1
6/1945–5/1950	0.0	1.7	4.3	0.0	0.8	1.4
Mean	1.2	1.4	2.0	1.2	0.6	1.3
Number of respondents	30	188	29	19	40	306

Source: 1994 Migrant Survey

N = 306. Women with no children and for whom date of first birth could not be established were excluded.

Note: The minus number in the birth cohort June 1965–May 1970 indicates that all births to this subpopulation took place prior to marriage.

marriage. This compares well with the estimates for the general population outlined in the discussion section above.

Analysis of the variance between mean birth intervals for migrant subpopulations, not controlled for birth cohort, results in a relatively high F ratio of 7.1, with a probability of less 0.000 that the same result would be produced if all the population means were equal. This indicates that differences between mean birth intervals for migrant subpopulations may exist and be real. Bonferroni test results indicated that women in the "other" subpopulation had a shorter mean birth interval (0.6 years) compared to the women who migrated after the birth of their first child (1.4 years) and women who migrated between their marriage and the birth of their first child (2.0 years). Women who migrated in the first birth interval had a longer mean birth interval compared to women who migrated before marriage (1.2 years) and women who migrated after the birth of their first child (1.4 years). The extremely short mean first birth interval for the "other" subpopulation is to be expected and should not disguise the patterns in the remaining subpopulations. Migration prior to marriage does not increase the first birth interval. Migration in the first birth interval seems to increase the length of the birth interval, compared with the standard population.

Each cohort was assessed in turn. An F ratio of 0.18 for mean birth intervals in the subpopulations of the birth cohort June 1970–May 1975 meant that the null hypothesis, i.e. all subpopulations have equal birth intervals, could not be rejected. There was no extension of the first birth interval in any subpopulation in this birth cohort.

In contrast, there was a strong probability of differences existing between migrant subpopulations in the cohort born June 1965–May 1970. However, Bonferroni tests indicated that the differences lay between the subpopulation of "other" women migrants who had a very low mean birth interval duration and all other migrant subpopulations. As the "other" subpopulation includes women who gave birth to their first child prior to their marriage, the discovery of significant differences between this subpopulation and the others who gave birth after their marriage, can be easily comprehended. Women whose migration took place before the birth of their first child had a significantly shorter mean first birth interval (1.0 years) compared to women who migrated in the first birth interval (1.8 years).

No significant differences were found in any cohort until the means for women born June 1945–May 1950 were analysed. Bonferroni test procedures identified two sets of differences. Birth intervals for women who migrated in the first birth interval were extended compared with "other" and "post child" migrant subpopulations.

For women born June 1950–May 1975, migration is associated with a longer interval between marriage and first birth on one occasion only.

While differences are identifiable, the statistics cannot prove that migration at any point in the life history prior to the birth of the first child delays the birth of that child.

There are indications that women who migrated more than once between marriage and the birth of their first child waited longer to have their first child than those who moved once. There was a mean of 1.9 years between marriage and first birth for single event migrants and 2.6 years for multiple migrants. These figures are not statistically significant but are unsurprising in their preliminary indications of the impact of multiple upheavals and point the way for future investigation.

Birth intervals summary

Whilst acknowledging the implications of such a restricted sample size in the 1994 Migrant Survey, we can cautiously promote the following conclusions on births intervals, both with respect to length and to timing in life histories. Cultural norms relating to first child birth in the population of married migrant women are currently strong enough to maintain prior behavioural regimes and have been maintained also because they are not targeted by the family planning policy. First births in this migrant population are expected to take place within a defined time limit after marriage. This limit is not exact and has upper and lower values. Within this range behaviour is negotiable. Migration between marriage and first birth results in births towards the upper limit of the range, but the expectation that a first birth should follow marriage without excessive delay is retained and leads to the birth intervals recorded here.

At present we can say for the population in the 1994 Migrant Survey that migration into urban areas has the potential to extend the first birth interval for those who migrate between marriage and the birth of their first child compared to those who migrated after the birth of their first child. Other analysis of the same data set shows that women who migrated prior to marriage saw their first birth intervals compressed slightly by minor postponement in marriage due to migration. Cultural expectations combined with other factors such as the availability of methods of contraception, keep the timing of first births within certain limits. These limits have a certain degree of elasticity but few women will go beyond them.

New regulations and wider contexts

One of the main conclusions to be drawn from this research is the very diversity of behaviour experienced by migrants different forms of marriage, and timing of childbearing even within such a relatively small sample as this. Admittedly, this sample population have shown themselves to be more conformist than other migrant populations by accepting temporary registration, and may thus also be more likely to accept birth control. Yet the low number of children born to women in this survey population is nevertheless a refutation of the popular perception of migrants as a high fertility population.

This perception is enhanced by the introduction of new measures and regulations aimed at increasing state control over migrants' fertility. One example is provided by the initiation of collaborative ventures between out-migration and destination areas. These aimed at improving family planning uptake and conformity with the family planning regulations amongst migrants. One such venture was based in Qianzhuangzi, Ganjiakou in Beijing. This cooperative venture between Wenling county in Zhejiang and Ganjiakou neighbourhood was the first crossprovincial planned fertility association in Beijing and reportedly achieved a significant reduction in out-of-plan births (Beijing Ribao 1994). The family planning personnel in this area were highly motivated towards these migrants. Another example was Putian county in Fujian. Medical and family planning personnel travelled to Beijing to provide family planning services to migrants (Keji Ribao 1994). In July 1996, Fujian province introduced legislation that prevented migrant couples, who had one child and could not present proof of sterilization, from finding employment. Migration may be a way for some women to avoid the birth control regulation in their origin area (Zhou 1996). For many more, however, migration is linked to the uptake of economic opportunities.

For international migrants from China the situation may be very different. Some couples who have had more than one child while outside China have been granted asylum by the United States (Mosher 1993). In Britain there is no blanket policy towards such couples and cases are decided on their individual merit.

Conclusions

Sex ratios in the 1994 Migrant Survey proved unusually high, up to a maximum of 152 in women whose migration was delayed until some point after the birth of their future child. Factors, such as adoption, under-reporting and infanticide, that are normally proposed as explanations of high male to female ratios were examined. None of these can be dismissed casually. Concealment of female births may have occurred and it is a brave woman who would admit to any of the other events. A further explanation was suggested for the recorded high sex ratios: migrants are selective by the sex of their children. The birth of a son enables his mother to make childcare claims on the older generation. The difference in sex ratios of children born to women who migrated prior to the birth of their first child, and those born to women whose migration was delayed until after the birth of their first child supports this hypothesis. There is some evidence to suggest that women who have a first child who is female may have to wait until the birth of a second child before migrating. However, further exploration of this hypothesis is hampered by the small data set. Previous work has suggested that women are selected by marriage (marriage decreases migration possibilities) or children (children negate against migration), but none have suggested that selection factors can be this detailed. Future analyses of age of migrants, take up of migration opportunities and other opportunity costs of children should include an examination of the sexes of migrants' children and the order in which they are born.

Opportunity costs of children, which have not been specifically addressed in this chapter, are complicated by the distinction between male and female children. Sex ratios of migrant children are very high. Manipulation of sex ratios in order to achieve a son is suggested, but its effects may be disguised by the relationship between children and migration. The birth of a male or female child, it is suggested, could dictate how soon migration takes place and is a factor in explaining the low fertility level of this migrant population and suggests that son preference in rural areas is more pervasive and influential than previous studies have indicated.

The implication of these results is that the politics of reproduction are different for a migrant. The pivot for migration is the sex of the first child. If this is true then it is not fertility of migrants which needs to be addressed but the structures in society that support son preference, since this impacts on women's mobility and individuality outside their ability to reproduce.

Analyses of birth intervals in developed countries have shown that the length of the first birth interval influences the overall level of fertility; longer first birth intervals depress fertility levels (Kasarda et al. 1986). This birth interval has proved resistant to change and there has been a trend towards a decrease in length (Cleland and Shen 1991). It has also been unaffected by population planning programmes. The implication is that there are underlying factors in fertility behaviour which have the potential to change fertility should circumstances change. Analysis presented in this chapter related birth intervals to migration and showed that period disruptive events such as migration have a limited impact on first birth interval. Urban residence is associated with longer birth intervals. Subtle, long term factors, such as those associated with urban residence, may have the power to alter behaviour rather than the cruder impacts of period events such as migration. It may be significant that while events like migration may be very disruptive, they can be emotionally and physically planned for, expected and accommodated to. Some of the surveyed women migrated while pregnant. Migration and the changes associated with migration did not prove to be an insurmountable barrier to such women.

One has to be very aware to consciously plan against the quieter impact of attitudinal change.

The impacts of migration in life events such as age at marriage, age at first birth and length of birth intervals are very subtle and must be interpreted with care. However, it appears that migration has a discernible impact on these events, and seem likely to develop further in the future. One of the main impressions gained from these results is the strength of traditional marriage and fertility patterns.

Children remain a high priority for people in China. For women there are few valid alternatives through which their emotional and industrial energy can be absorbed without their security being damaged. Results from the analysis showed that migration was potentially consistent with delays in the onset of child bearing or birth of a first child, but at present cultural norms underlined by more pragmatic issues such as access to contraception counteracted such delays. Where possible, women aimed to have children as soon as possible after marriage irrespective of whether migration occurred in the intervening period. Shocks from disruption associated with migration are absorbed, if not entirely dissipated.

These results show that greater differences can exist between migrant populations or resident populations, rather than between the migrant population and the resident population. Everyone has the potential to become a migrant. Many more people will become migrants in the future. It is likely that changes will start to occur in the construction of life histories. Cultural norms prove adaptable. Migration may prove to be one of the most powerful forces in China's demographic history, replacing the family planning policy as means of change.

Appendix 1: Subpopulations

Subpopulation one targeted women whose first migration event occurred prior to marriage whether or not they gave birth at a later date. Women in this subpopulation may not have any children or have finished childbearing. Subpopulation two consisted of women who migrated after the birth of their first child. Subpopulation three was made up of women who migrated in the first birth interval, that is, after marriage but before the birth of their first child. This subpopulation also included women who migrated after marriage, but had no children at the time of the survey. Subpopulation four consisted of women who had at least one child and whose migration took place at the same time as their marriage. Subpopulation five consisted of women whose life histories fell outside these patterns of behaviour. For example, women who had children prior to marriage.

Six five-year birth cohorts were also distinguished. Each five year cohort runs from June of one year to May of the fifth year, the reference point provided by the date of the survey.

Appendix 2: Analysis procedure

Analysis of variance divides observed variability into variability about means within groups and variability between group means (Norusis 1983). ANOVA produces a statistic called the F ratio, which allows us to determine whether variance is real (Kirkwood 1988). A probability that the F ratio is valid is also produced. Significance levels were set at 95 per cent (0.05) for comparison procedures. The F ratio does not provide an indication of where those differences lie, just an assessment of their existence. Not all means are necessarily unequal. For example, only one pair of means may be significantly different. To identify where the differences lay, a Bonferroni test was employed. This compares the variability of the group means and produces a matrix, indicating the pairs of populations which are significantly different from each other at the 0.05 level (Norusis 1983).

References

Arnold, Fred and Liu Zhaoxiang. 1986. "Sex Preference, Fertility and Family Planning in China." *Population and Development Review* 12, no. 2, pp. 221–46.

Banister, Judith. 1987. *China's Changing Population*. Stanford: Stanford University Press.

Beijing Ribao. 1994. "Ganjiakou yu Wenling Xian Chengli Jisheng Lianhehui" [Ganjiankou and Wenling county form a planned fertility association]. *Beijing Ribao* 15 July 1994, p. 6.

Bernstein, Thomas P. 1977. *Up to the Mountains and Down to the Villages: The Transfer of Youth from Urban to Rural China*. New Haven: Yale University Press.

Cai Wenmei, Yu Sunzheng, Sheng Yezhun, Gao Nansheng, Wang Zhudan and Wang Minhan. 1993. Da Chengshi Zhouwei Nongcun Chuji Weisheng Baojian Gongzuo Mianlinde Xin Tiaozhan [Work of preserving basic hygiene faces up to a new challenge in rural areas around large cities]. Shanghai: Centre for the Preservation of Basic Hygiene, unpublished paper.

Caldwell, John C. 1988. "Micro-approaches: Similarities and Differences, Strengths and Weaknesses." In John C. Caldwell, Alan G. Hill and Valerie J. Hull eds, *Micro-approaches to Demographic Research*. London: Kegan Paul International, pp. 458–70.

Campbell, Eugene K. 1989. "A Note on the Fertility Migration Interrelationship: The Case of Men in the Western Area, Sierra Leone." *Demography India* 18, no. 1–2, pp. 103–13.

Chan, Kam Wing. 1994. "Urbanization and Rural-urban Migration in China since 1982: A New Baseline." *Modern China* 20, no. 3, pp. 243–81.

Cheng, Chaoze. 1991. "Internal Migration in Mainland China: The Impact of Government Policies." *Issues & Studies* 27, no. 8, pp. 47–70.

China News Analysis. 1992. "New Legal Protection for Children." *China News Analysis* 1454.

China Population Today. 1992. "Measures for the Management of Family Planning of the Floating Population." *China Population Today* 9, no. 1, pp. 2–5.

Choe, Minja Kim and Wu Jiaming. 1991. "Analysis of the Trend of First Birth and Its Affecting Factors." In *Proceedings of the International Seminar on China's In-*

depth Fertility Survey, Beijing, 13–17 February 1990. Voorburg: International Statistics Institute, pp. 140–54.

Cleland, John G. and Shen Yimin. 1991. "Later and Fewer but no Longer: Fertility Change in *Hebei, Shaanxi* and *Shanghai* 1965–1985." In *Proceedings of the International Seminar on China's In-depth Fertility Survey, Beijing, 13–17 February 1990*. Voorburg: International Statistics Institute, pp. 273–91.

Coale, Ansley J., Shaomin Li and Jing-Qing Han. 1988. *The Distribution of Inter-birth Intervals in Rural China, 1940s-1970s*. Papers of the East-West Institute 109. Honolulu: East-West Institute.

Davies, Carole Boyce. 1994. *Black Women, Writing and Identity: Migrations of the Subject*. London: Routledge.

Feeney, Griffith and Wang Feng. 1993. "Parity Progression and Birth Intervals in China: The Influence of Policy in Hastening Fertility Decline." *Population and Development Review* 19, no. 1, pp. 61–101.

Goldstein, Sidney and Alice Goldstein. 1981. "The Impact of Migration on Fertility: An 'Own Children' Analysis for Thailand." *Population Studies* 35, pp. 265–84.

Goldstein, Sidney and Alice Goldstein. 1982. "Techniques for the Analysis of the Interrelation between Migration and Fertility." In *Techniques for Analysis of Interrelations between Migration and Fertility in National Migration Surveys, Survey Manual X, Guidelines for Analysis*. New York: UNESCO for Asia and Pacific, United Nations, pp. 132–59.

Goldstein, Sidney, Alice Goldstein and Guo Shenyang. 1991. "Temporary Migrants in Shanghai Households, 1984." *Demography* 28, no. 2, pp. 275–91.

Gui Shixun, ed. 1992. *Zhongguo Liudong Renkou Jihua Shengyu Guanli Yanjiu* [Examination of management of family planning of the floating population]. Shanghai: Huadong Shifan Daxue Chubanshe.

Heaton, Tim B., Daniel T. Lichter and Acheampong Amoateng. 1989. "The Timing of Family Formation: Rural-urban Differentials in First Intercourse, Childbirth and Marriage." *Rural Sociology* 54, no. 1, pp. 1–16.

Henry, Louis, 1976. *Population*. London: Edward Arnold.

Honig, Emily and Gail Hershatter. 1988. *Personal Voices: Chinese Women in the 1980s*. Stanford: Stanford University Press.

Hoy, Caroline. 1996. *Women, Migration and Current Urban Dynamics in China: Fertility and Family Planning*. Working Paper 96/7, School of Geography, University of Leeds, Leeds, LS2 9JT, Britain.

Hugo, Graeme. 1993. "Migrant Women in Developing Countries." In *Internal Migration of Women in Developing Countries: Proceedings of the United Nations Expert Meeting on the Feminization of Internal Migration, Aguascalientes, Mexico, 22–25 Oct. 1991*. New York: United Nations, pp. 47–73.

Hull, Terence H. 1990. "Recent Trends in Sex Ratios in China." *Population and Development Review* 16, no. 1, pp. 63–83.

Johanssen, Sten and Ola Nygren. 1991. "The Missing Girls of China: A New Demographic Account." *Population and Development Review* 17, no. 1, pp. 35–72.

Kasarda, John D., John O.G. Billy and Kirsten West. 1986. *Status Enhancement and Fertility: Reproductive Responses to Social Mobility and Educational Opportunities*. Orlando: Academic Press.

Keji Ribao. 1994. "Putian Xian Guanhao Waichu Renkou Jisheng Gongzuo" [Putian county attends to family planning work of its out-migrants]. *Keji Ribao* 9 June 1994, p. 4.

Kemper, Robert V. 1975. "Social Factors in Migration: The Case of Tzintzuntze-nos in Mexico City." In Brian M. DuToit and Helen I. Safa, eds, *Migration and*

Urbanization: Models and Adaptive Strategies. The Hague: Mouton Publishers. pp. 225–44.

Kirkwood, Betty R. 1988. *Essentials of Medical Statistics*. Oxford: Blackwell.

Lavely, William, James Lee and Wang Feng. 1990. "Chinese Demography: The State of the Field." *The Journal of Asian Studies* 49, no. 4, pp. 807–34.

Lee, B.S. and S.C. Farber. 1984. "Fertility Adaptation by Rural-urban Migrants in Developing Countries: The Case of Korea." *Population Studies* 38, pp. 141–55.

Li, Rose Maria. 1989. "Migration to China's Northern Frontier, 1953–1982." *Population and Development Review*. 15, no. 3, pp. 503–38.

Li Jiali and Rosemary Santana Cooney. 1993. *Son Preference, Government Controls and the One Child Policy in China: 1979–1988*. The Population Council Research Division Working Papers 51. New York: The Population Council.

McGee T.G. 1975. "Malay Migration to Kuala Lumpur City: Individual Adaptation to the City." In Brian M. DuToit and Helen I. Safa, eds, *Migration and Urbanisation: Models and Adaptive Strategies*. The Hague: Mouton, pp. 143–78.

Mallee Hein. 1995. "China's Household Registration System under Reform." *Development and Change* 26, no. 1, pp. 1–29.

Mookherjee, Harsha N. 1992. "Fertility Patterns of Migrant and Non Migrant Populations in Papua New Guinea." *Population Review* 36, nos. 1 and 2, pp. 40–9.

Mosher, Steven W. 1993. *A Mother's Ordeal*. New York: Harper Perennial.

Newell, Colin. 1988. *Methods and Models in Demography*. London: Belhaven Press.

Norusis, Marija J. 1983. *SPSSX Introductory Statistics Guide*. New York: McGraw-Hill.

Norusis, Marija J. 1992. *SPSS for Windows: Advanced Statistics, Release 5*. Chicago: SPSS.

Qiao Xiaochun and Chen Wei. 1991. "Impact of Changes in Marriage Pattern of Fertility in China". In *Proceedings of the International Seminar on China's In-depth Fertility Survey, Beijing, 13–17 February 1990*. Voorburg: International Statistics Institute, pp. 155–66.

Renmin Ribao. 1995. "Tongyi Renshi Qizhua Gongguan Youxu Liudong" [Unify understanding and the joint administration and order of floaters]. *Renmin Ribao*, 9 July 1995. Re-published in *Renkouxue yu Jihua Shengyu* 5, no. 4, pp. 4–7.

Rundquist, Franz-Michael and Lawrence A. Brown. 1989. "Migrant Fertility Differentials in Equador." *Geografiska Annaler* 71B, no. 2, pp. 109–23.

Sabagh, Georges and Sun Bin Yin. 1980. "The Relationship between Migration and Fertility in a Historical Context: The Case of Morocco in the 1960s." *International Migration Review* 14, pp. 525–38.

Shen Jianfa. 1996. *China's Economic Reforms and Their Impacts on Migration Processes*. Migration Unit Research Paper 10. The Migration Unit, Department of Geography, University College Swansea, Singleton Park, Swansea, SA2 8PP, Britain.

Shryock, Henry S., Jacob S. Siegel and associates. 1976. *The Methods and Materials of Demography*. Condensed edition, Edward G. Stockwell, ed. London: Academic Press.

Solinger, Dorothy J. 1993. *China's Transformation from Socialism*. Armonk, N.Y.: M.E. Sharpe.

Tan Xiaoqing. 1993. "Migration and Fertility." In Ma Xia, ed. *Migration and Urbanization in China*. Beijing: New World Press, pp. 26–35.

Tu Ping. 1991. *Birth Spacing Patterns and Correlates in Shaanxi*. Peking University Institute of Population Research Working paper E3. Beijing.

White, Michael J., Lorenzo Moreno and Shenyang Guo. 1990. "The Interrelation of Fertility and Geographical Mobility in Peru: A Hazards Model Analysis." *International Migration Review* 24, pp. 492–514.

Wimberley, Dale W., E. Helen Berry and William L. Flinn. 1989. "Structural Influences in Out-migrant Selectivity: A Panel of Three Colombian Communities." *Rural Sociology* 54, no. 3, pp. 339–64.

Woon, Yuen-fong. 1992. "Circulatory Mobility in Post-Mao China: Temporary Migrants in Kaiping County, Pearl River Delta Region". *International Migration Review* 27, no. 3, pp. 578–604.

Wu, Harry Xiaoyang. 1994. "Rural to Urban Migration in the People's Republic of China." *The China Quarterly* 139, pp. 669–98.

Xu Gang and Yu Jingwei. 1991. "An Analysis of Fertility Preferences of Chinese Women". In *Proceedings of the International Seminar on China's In-depth Fertility Survey, Beijing, 13–17 February 1990.* Voorburg: International Statistics Institute, pp. 177–86.

Zeng Yi and James W. Vaupel. 1989. "The Impact of Urbanization and Delayed Childbearing on Population Growth and Ageing in China." *Population and Development Review* 15, no. 3, pp. 425–45.

Zeng Yi, Tu Ping, Gu Baochang, Xu Yi, Li Bohua and Li Yongping. 1993. "Causes and Implications of the Recent Increase in the Reported Sex Ratio at Birth in China." *Population and Development Review* 19, no. 2, pp. 283–302.

Zhou, Kate Xiao. 1996. *How the Farmers Changed China.* Boulder: Westview.

Zhejiang migrants in Europe and China

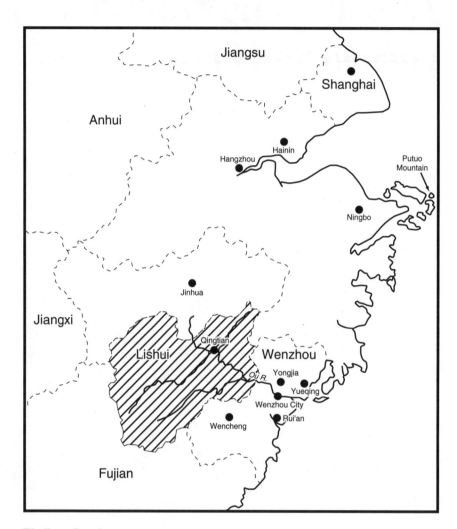

Zhejiang Province

Chapter Eight

Moving Stones from China to Europe: The Dynamics of Emigration from Zhejiang to Europe*

Mette Thunø

Introduction

The twentieth century has seen greatly intensified migration from the Third World to the post-industrial countries. The immense scope of migration is reflected in a flood of publications discussing the causes of these movements of people. Migration researchers have proposed theories at various conceptual levels in order understand migration.[1] The oldest theories, based on neo-classical economics, propose that diversities in wage levels and employment conditions in the sending and receiving countries cause individuals to change residence. Differences in labour market conditions also constitute the framework for neo-classical economic theory at the micro-level. Accordingly, individuals are expected to act economically rational and decide whether to migrate or stay on the basis of personal cost-benefit calculations.

During recent decades, these classical assumptions have been challenged the "new economics of migration". At the micro-level, the role of the individual as the decision-maker has been questioned, and instead, the family or household has been proposed as the location where decisions on migration are taken. These theories also question the value of regarding wage differentials as the only cause of migration. The reduction of risk through diversification of the household's economic activities often serves as a powerful incentive to migrate, despite limited differences in wage levels locally and abroad.

---

* For their comments and suggestions, I wish to thank Arif Dirlik, Ronald Skeldon and Stein Tønnesson.

Analysis of local economic development supplemented by individual statements of migration motives support the above-mentioned approaches. World-systems theory, however, suggests that only macro-level analysis of the capitalist world market structure can explain international migration. The integration of local economies into the world market economy has disrupted local agrarian economies and social stuctures, displacing people and forcing them to migrate to the centres of the world economic system. World-systems theory thus pays much less attention to differences in wage levels and emphasises global capitalism as the primary factor stimulating mobility.

The above-mentioned theories obviously operate at diverse levels of analysis and propose different explanations of international migration. The empirical evidence on which these theories are based suggests that many of these causal explanations may operate simultaneously. Not being mutually contradictory, these theories can advantageously be applied as a broad theoretical approach to single cases of migration. Both Douglas Massey and Ronald Skeldon suggest a dual analytical framework of mobility, considering both the international distribution of resources and power and the specific characteristics of different areas (Massey et al. 1993; Skeldon 1990:132–150).

This framework will be applied here to Chinese emigration from Zhejiang province to Europe in the beginning of the twentieth century. In the course of this analysis, certain shortcomings of this approach will become apparent, and in the final part of this article I will show how Pierre Bourdieu's theory of practice will help us arrive at a fuller understanding of migration (Bourdieu 1977, 1990).

Research on emigration from Zhejiang

Since the beginning of this century, the province of Zhejiang, on the Southeast coast of China, has provided a major share of the Chinese migrants living in Europe. Of the total number of ethnic Chinese in the world, the Chinese in Europe constitute a small minority, approximately one million by the late 1980s.[2] European research of Chinese immigration has been confined primarily to national studies of recent developments in connection with the formulation of immigrant policies (Pieke 1998). Historical aspects of Chinese immigration to Europe have been treated only sporadically and on a national basis.

The increasing interest in Chinese migration to Europe among researchers in Europe and China now allows us to transcend national European borders and investigate the history of the population movements from China to Europe. Regrettably, the quality of Chinese sources for such a research undertaking is mediocre, since emigration from Zhejiang in the beginning of this century was of no interest to officials and hence rarely recorded in local histories or gazetteers (Zhou Wangsen 1991c). Only oral history sources are available today, and since the main areas of emigration in Zhejiang still are off limits to non-Chinese researchers, Chinese surveys have been the main source of information for this article.[3]

Zhejiang Province

Zhejiang Province can be divided into two zones: the fertile plains around Huzhou, Hangzhou and Ningbo in the north, and the larger mountainous and hilly areas stretching from Jinhua in the central part of the province to the south. The north's rich arable land, hills and waterways have for centuries facilitated agriculture, the main products being salt, silk, tea, cotton and jute. Moreover, the southern part of the Grand Canal has linked this area directly to the Chinese inland and since late Ming and early Qing (seventeenth and eighteenth centuries) contributed to the development of urban centres and commercialization (Chen Xuewen 1993). Industrial diversification went hand in hand with overseas trading, and by the nineteenth century Ningbo merchants were present in distant places such as Singapore, Sumatra, and Sri Lanka. Ningbo was also among the first five Chinese ports to be forced open to European traders in the Nanjing Treaty of 1842. In 1895, with the Treaty of Shimonoseki, Hangzhou also became a treaty port (Shiba 1977:391–392, 437; Wei 1995).

In contrast, the larger, southern part of the province, with its inaccessible mountain chains, has for centuries been disassociated from the north and interior of China. The south-eastern port city of Wenzhou was made a treaty port under the Treaty of Chefoo in 1876, yet never experienced the same commercial development as Ningbo and Hangzhou. Connected with the interior only by the shallow Ou River, Wenzhou could not serve as a major centre of trade. Moreover, the production of agricultural goods was severely restrained by limitations of arable land, preventing the southern part of the province from developing along the path of the prosperous north.[4]

It is from the southern, more impoverished part of Zhejiang that migration to Europe originated during the late Imperial and Republican era. Emigration initially began out of Qingtian County, but subsequent migration also took place from neighbouring counties.

The origin of emigration from Qingtian County

Qingtian County is located in the mountainous zone west of Wenzhou and criss-crossed by the Ou River and its tributaries. In the local gazetteer from the late nineteenth century, the geographical situation was described as follows:

> Mountains and rivers everywhere make this an impassable and dangerous area. It has neither plateaus nor fields, and the forests at the foot of the mountains contain all the moisture. In the middle of all of this, the people are living, scaling the mountains to make terrace fields. Potatoes make up their whole diet, for which they work hard all their lives, but they are always hungry. What a bitter life! (Qingtian xianzhi, 1935:31).

Eighty-nine per cent of the county's area indeed consists of mountains, making it difficult for the approximately 220,000 inhabitants in 1912 (rising to 230,000 in 1949) to sustain a livelihood. Although eighty-six per cent of the population in 1941 were engaged in agriculture, grain was still insufficient and had to be imported from other places. As a result, traders were needed, but the low level of income in the county did not allow for more than five per cent of the total population to engage in such business activities (Chen Murong 1990:155, 177, 173).

One alternative vocation or sideline occupation for a minority of Qingtian inhabitants was to undertake stone carving of the pale-green soapstone available in the southeastern part of the county – particularly in the townships of Shankou and Fangshan. This stone material, with its greenish colour and soft quality, is ideally suited for the craft of carving. Since the thirteenth century, carving techniques for the production of jewellery and writing utensils have been developed and refined in this part of the county.

By the late Qing period (nineteenth century) some of the stone carvers established shops outside the county, particularly in the treaty ports (Wenzhou, Shanghai, Wuhan, Tianjin, Nanjing, Beijing) and Putuo Mountain (Dong 1987:11–21).[5] According to one of the last surviving contemporary oral sources on early Qingtian migration, Chen Lite, overseas commercialization of Qingtian soapstones began when Chen Yuanfeng by coincidence sold some stone monkeys to Europeans in Putuo.

Chen Yuanfeng was originally from a poor family, and like many others in Qingtian relied on carving stones for a second income. In 1884, he was engaged as a servant by a local gentry family, whom he later escorted on a pleasure trip to Putuo. Bringing along some of his stone carvings, he laid the stones out for sale in front of the Fayu temple. Visiting Europeans showed great interest in his craftsmanship and purchased his small stone monkeys for very high prices. Subsequently, Chen carved more stones to sell in tourist sites at Putuo and other locations. Following Chen's success, fellow-villagers also started to market their carvings and adapt the objects and shape to the tastes of foreigners (Ye 1986:66).

In 1893, convinced of the potential for selling stones to Europeans, Chen Yuanfeng, with a small group of other stone carvers and traders from Youzhu Township, boarded a French steamer in Vietnam, with Marseilles as its final destination. This voyage supposedly constituted the beginning of European migration from Qingtian, but no information is available about the journey or motives of the group for leaving on such an uncertain voyage (Chen Lite 1995a).

More research on the Chinese-Russian connection may reveal that emigration to Europe commenced over land via Russia and not by the maritime route via the Mediterranean. After the 1842 Treaty of Nanjing forced the Chinese imperial government to approve emigration, Qingtian Chinese began to emigrate to larger Russian cities as far as St. Petersburg to work as miners and to sell stone carvings. According to Ji Meikai (1885–1975), who in 1908 sold his land to travel to Russia via Siberia and trade in stones, he was among the latecomers to Moscow. The Russian market for stone carvings from Qingtian had been saturated, and like other Qingtian Chinese before him, Ji Meikai continued on to Berlin by train (Ye 1986).

Chen Yuanfeng might possibly have been among the first Chinese from Qingtian to reach Europe via France. Furthermore, a single written source indicates that Chen was not the only person who during the 1880s discovered that foreigners showed an interest in Qingtian stone carvings. One of the only written sources available on early emigration from Qingtian is in the form of a gravestone set in 1916 for Lin Maoxiang from Shankou. The epitaph reads:

> Mr. Lin Maoxiang ... was a grown-up man when he had the great aspiration to go abroad to sell his work of art ... [I]n the fourteenth year of Guangxu (1888) he went as far away as America and in San Francisco met the honourable Chinese envoy Mr. Fu Yunlong ... [A]fter a few years, he and his two good sons gradually travelled to all five continents, and all his plans were fulfilled (Zhou Wangsen 1991c:120–21).

This appears to be the earliest verifiable statement concerning emigration from Qingtian, which implies that emigration with the goal of selling carved stones abroad had already been initiated some years before Chen Yuanfeng decided to leave Qingtian. Oral sources also confirm that several stone carvers had left for continents other than Europe prior to 1893. After years of travelling, Zhou Liuxian reached South America in 1890; and in 1892, the merchant Ji Zhaojun went with six other persons to Southeast Asia and India to sell stone carvings (Chen Murong 1990:641; Dong 1987:110–113).

The travels of these pioneers were connected especially to Qingtian carvers' participation in various international exhibitions – such as the World Exhibition in Paris in 1899 – where they obtained several medals for their workmanship (Dong 1987:16–17; Ye 1986). After America sealed itself off from Chinese immigration with the passing of the Chinese Exclusion Act of 1882, Europe became the major destination for Qingtian traders. European colonialism in Asia connected China and Hong Kong with Europe via numerous shipping and rail connections (the Trans-Siberian railway was built 1891–1904) and was an obvious destination given Europeans' preference for Qingtian stone carvings.

Chen Yuanfeng thus boarded a French ship in Vietnam. Allegedly, he had no notion of Europe as a geographical place, but since nothing but a ticket was needed to go, he simply boarded and left (Chen Lite 1995a:4). Other persons followed Chen to Europe. In 1897, Liu Ganmu went to England and Holland to trade; in 1898, Ji Fudian went to Russia to sell carved stones (Chen Murong 1990:641). Chen Bin from Qingtian, who currently lives in Holland, has knowledge of two Qingtian Chinese, who by the turn of the century resided in Paris and were engaged in a successful import-export business. Another Qingtian Chinese was at the same time in Marseilles, having opened a hotel catering to Chinese arriving in France. He also had a representative office for a European shipping company for hiring Chinese sailors and helped to provide other services associated with the Chinese (Chen Bin 1995:8). In 1900, yet another stone carver named Zhu from Shankou was employed by English merchants. After some time he succeeded in opening a Chinese handicraft shop in London (Chen Murong 1990:641).

The number and distribution of Qingtian Chinese in Europe during the early twentieth century

Having established their main foothold in France – especially Paris and Marseilles – increasing numbers of Qingtian traders ventured to Europe. This development, however, was not only caused by trading possibilities in Qingtian soapstones. In 1917, the Nationalist government in Beijing announced its participation in the First World War. Subsequently, England and France, viewing the Chinese as quasi-colonial subjects, drafted 100,000 (Summerskill 1982:1) to 175,000–200,000 (Chen Sanjing 1986:34–35) Chinese labourers, primarily from Shandong, to serve in the war (Chen Hansheng 1984:293–327). In the winter of 1917, the Qingtian county government, too, recruited more than 2,000 contract workers, who after the war were supposed to be repatriated. Having the opportunity to trade in stone carvings and the possibility to utilise networks of former Qingtian traders, 1,000 of those Qingtian Chinese stayed behind in France or went to other countries in Europe (Chen Murong 1990:642).

As Europe started to recover from the war, the many formerly indentured Qingtian Chinese settled down, providing support for relatives and friends wanting to emigrate to Europe. As a result, the 1920s and 1930s became a period of major emigration from Qingtian and approximately 25,000 Chinese from Qingtian county were living in Europe during this period (Chen Lite 1995a).

Table 8.1 Qingtian Chinese living overseas, 1905–1935.

Year	Qingtian people overseas
1905	800
1910	1,550
1915	6,100
1920	16,000
1925	25,500
1930	25,000
1935	18,000

Source: Chen Lite 1995a:5.

This estimate of the development of emigration to Europe from Qingtian corresponds to a survey in 1982 among 1816 returned Chinese originating from the largest emigrant towns and townships in Qingtian county.[6] Sixty-one persons had left in the late Qing period (1888–1911), 130 persons in the early years of the Republic (1912–1918) and 1568 persons in the period after World War I and before the outbreak of the War of Resistance against Japan in 1937. During the Japanese occupation and civil war until 1949, only fifty-seven persons left the county to go abroad. This survey data thus confirms Chen's assumption of a heavy outflow of Qingtian Chinese after World War I and until the early 1930s (Chen Murong 1990:642–643).

A lower estimate of emigration for the same period is in the range of some 10,000 Qingtian Chinese in Europe (France: 3,000, Germany: 2,000, Holland: 1,000, Austria: 1,000, Italy: 1,000, Belgium: 3000, Spain: 300, Portugal: 200, and a few in Scandinavia, Switzerland and Eastern Europe) (Chen Bin 1995:6). A realistic estimate of the scope of emigration from Qingtian to Europe during the 1930s was in the range of 10,000–25,000, but, unfortunately, census data is neither available from the European countries where the Chinese often stayed illegally, nor from reliable local Chinese censuses.

The institutionalization of emigration from Qingtian during the early twentieth century

The exact number of Qingtian Chinese who left to go to Europe, the scope of those who actually stayed permanently and the exact beginning of this process will remain uncertain. Yet the number of 10–20,000 Qingtian Chinese migrants in Europe during the 1920s and 1930 leaves no doubt about the relative magnitude of emigration. Qingtian County had a total population of 226,000 in 1925, so that the overseas entrepreneurs in Europe alone constituted 5–10 per cent of the entire population (Chen Murong 1990:642–643). Migration in Qingtian was thus not just a matter of a few people simply leaving the county for opportunities of greater income abroad, but the course of migration from Qingtian over the decades came to have a profound impact on the county and itself became the cause of the subsequent perpetuated emigration.

Compared to emigration from Qingtian during the late nineteenth and early twentieth centuries, conditions for migration changed during the 1920s and 1930s. The pioneers, who at great costs and risks ventured abroad around the turn of the century, paved the way for the later institutionalization of migration from Qingtian. Professional agents facilitated travel from China to Europe, and networks of experienced migrants supported the new arrivals in Europe with accommodation, credit and work. This reduced the costs and risks of migration and helped perpetuate the flow of migrants from Qingtian to Europe.

As migration to Russia ceased with the collectivization policies of the early 1920s, preventing Chinese migrants from setting up businesses and shops, the majority of Qingtian migrants destined for Europe went overseas by ship, either as stowaways or as regular passengers. By the 1920s, the black market for providing illegal emigrant services had become well established, and for 200 taels[7] any emigrant could acquire the necessary travel documents to travel to France or Italy. Illegal travel as stowaway was arranged by secret societies in Shanghai who had contacts with Chinese sailors working on ocean-going freighters. Disguised as sailors, the stowaways were helped onboard the freighters and hid in the engine or storage rooms. On arriving at their destination port (usually Marseilles) they were led ashore by the Chinese sailors to local inns run by people from Qingtian (Ye 1986:64–77).

Migrants travelling as legal passengers to Europe were also aided by entrepreneurial banking houses in Wenzhou or Shanghai, where passport applications could be submitted and tickets obtained for a service-fee of 300 taels. Other services were also available to the emigrant, such as loans for the purchase of merchandise to be sold in Europe, parcel service, and contacts with wholesale stone carvers (Ye 1986:64–77).

During the 1920s and 1930s, the black market institutionalization of emigration out of Qingtian apparently developed into a profitable business undertaking, because Qingtian migrants were usually financially weak and therefore forced to take loans from the illegal banking houses to finance their travel expenses, passports and baggage. The sophistication of migrant services is also reflected in the changes in the type of goods that migrants sold in Europe and the branching out in the wholesale trade by clandestine migration agencies. By 1916, stone carvings were no longer attractive sales objects in Europe and were replaced by other kinds of Chinese curios (pearls, porcelain, neckties, carpets, paper flowers, glasses, wallets, and silk). The Chinese hawkers on the roads of Europe could easily place their orders in Chinese wholesale businesses in Berlin, Paris and other major cities, who had contacts with companies in Zhejiang and Shanghai. Upon delivery, the wholesale companies would forward the goods all over Europe to local post offices, where the traders paid for their orders and continued their business (Chen Lite 1995b).

It was only in 1937, with the Japanese occupation which closed down all the Chinese banking houses, that the commercialization and institutionalization of emigration from Zhejiang stopped altogether.

The most striking aspect of emigration from Qingtian is its increasing institutionalization. Emigration started as a spin off of Western imperialism that established relatively smooth transportation and communication between Zhejiang and Europe. European companies specialized in buying Chinese curios for sale in Europe, but the popularity and high prices of Chinese handicrafts in Europe also convinced the Chinese themselves to sell these products abroad. A process began that, despite periodic interruptions, has continued until this day.

Ultimately, emigration from Qingtian is therefore a byproduct of the penetration of global capitalism into the Chinese countryside. Yet Qingtian's local economy witnessed neither large-scale import of Western manufactured products and direct foreign investment, nor were peasants forced off their land. Rather, the cultural links produced by the expansion of the world capitalist market forces created an interest among Europeans in exotic items from the "Far East," which led to a special interest in articles such as the stone carvings from Qingtian. This kind of Orientalism was also manifested in the World Fairs and other exhibitions initiated by European and American powers, in which China primarily was represented through curios and other objects of art, in contrast to the industrial products displayed by Europe and North America (Greenhalgh 1988).

Poverty and the promise of high earnings, however, were not unique to the population of Qingtian County, but were also true of many other areas in Zhejiang and China that did not experience emigration. The factor setting Qingtian apart from other counties was initially the soapstone deposits and traditional stone carving workmanship. Thus, it is not surprising that the majority of emigrants from Qingtian originated from a few villages in the Southeast of the county, in the vicinity of the soapstone formations. An example of this kind of village is Qiushan in Fangshan Township; during the period 1904–1931, 125 persons emigrated out of a total of 123 households, implying that close to all families had at lest one member overseas (Ye 1986:69). As emigration from Qingtian became a well-known phenomenon and institutionalization of the migration process was offering services for anyone willing to emigrate, inhabitants of poor villages in counties to the east of Qingtian could be expected to have made their own cost-benefit analysis and venture abroad. Yet despite structural conditions comparable to Qingtian, emigration was pursued from only a few specific villages. The historical accounts below, from the area in between Wenzhou and Qingtian demonstrates the divergence in local development in relation to migration.

Emigration from villages in the Wenzhou area

Records show that overseas trade from the area around Wenzhou took place since the Song Dynasty (960–1279) when traders from Wenzhou went overseas to sell local handicrafts such as ceramics and lacquerware. During the sixteenth century, pirates infested the Chinese coast. In the following century, wars and maritime bans of the early Qing dynasty severely reduced the trade from Wenzhou. After 1876, when Wenzhou became a treaty port, Wenzhou traders re-commenced sailing overseas to Southeast Asia and travelled to the eastern coast of Africa to trade in handicrafts and other goods. Still, Wenzhou never became as important a port of overseas trading as did Quanzhou in Fujian province to the south or Ningbo in northern Zhejiang. Instead, the local population went abroad as coolie workers to Europe, Africa and America, where cheap labour was in demand. In the period from 1847 to 1866 and again in 1904, several persons from Pingyang county, south of Wenzhou city, worked on the plantations and mines of Cuba and South-Africa (Zhang 1991a:1–3).[8]

In the early twentieth century, Japanese industries developed rapidly, especially after the First World War cut international markets off from European suppliers and customers started to place their orders with Japanese industries. The Japanese economy expanded and attracted labour from China. In the early 1920s, 3,500–4,000 Chinese from the countryside of Wenzhou and Qingtian went to Japan as petty merchants selling paper umbrellas manufactured in Wenzhou or stone carvings from Qingtian. When deliveries of goods from home were lacking, the Chinese migrants found work in Japan's booming iron, steel and mining industries (Zhang 1995).

The development of population mobility from Zhejiang to Japan was abruptly terminated in 1922, however, when the Japanese economy slumped due to a range of factors, including inflation, export reduction and a decline in government military expenditure (Reichschauer and Craig 1989:194–5). This serious economic crisis made unemployment rise. Soon, the Japanese government banned further Chinese immigration and expelled resident Chinese labourers from Japan (Weiner 1994:120–21; Zhang 1995). In this atmosphere of economic recession the devastating Kanto earthquake of 1 September 1923 that killed some 130,000 people in the Tokyo area further added to social unrest. Japanese youth gangs attacked workers of foreign origin. In these attacks, 1,000 Chinese workers were killed, 600 of whom were from Wenzhou and Qingtian. In the aftermath of this bloody massacre, the Japanese police expelled some 3,300 Zhejiang Chinese. With these events, Chinese migration to Japan came to an abrupt halt (Yan 1995).

Following this incident and the subsequent Japanese aggressions in China in the 1930s, migration from Zhejiang across the East China Sea halted. Instead, Europe became a migration destination for the people of Wenzhou. Emigration from Wenzhou to Europe had started already when in the 1870s a Wenzhou Chinese from Yongjia County supposedly went abroad to trade, as did the Qingtian Chinese, and managed to open a shop selling Chinese curios in Berlin (Zhang et al. 1987:13). It was only in 1935–1936 that several hundred emigrants from the townships of Baimen, Li'ao and Zi'ao in the Wenzhou area went abroad as traders to Europe. Emigration from Wenzhou did not last long, coming to halt in 1937 with the Japanese aggressions and the launching of the Chinese War of Resistance against Japan (Zhang 1991a:4).

Estimates of emigration from Wenzhou up to 1937 have not yet been attempted by local Chinese scholars, but the total number of emigrants who travelled to Europe is probably much lower than the number of Qingtian traders. The process of emigration from Wenzhou to Europe from a few specific villages, however, is similar to Qingtian migration. Below we take a further look at the history and dynamics of emigration from Wenzhou by focussing on two different areas: Wencheng county and Rui'an city district.

Wencheng

Bordering Qingtian county in the north, Wencheng county geographically shares many features with its neighbour, although Wencheng county is not endowed with any soapstone deposits. With only ten per cent of arable land, destitution was as common a phenomenon in Wencheng as in Qingtian. Today, Wencheng County, with a population of 370,000, still is one of the poorest counties in the Wenzhou city area.[9]

Given the proximity of the two counties, personal contacts between the local populations have prevailed. In 1905, the first emigrant from Yuhu township in Wencheng county supposedly went with a relative from Qingtian to Europe to sell stone carvings. Having established this initial connection overseas, Wencheng pioneers gradually ventured abroad along the same routes as the Qingtian traders, but never in any great numbers. From 1911 to 1929, emigration from Wencheng encompassed 469 persons, but whereas the majority of Qingtian inhabitants went to Europe, 57 per cent of emigrants from Wencheng went to Japan and only 30 per cent went to Europe (France, Italy, Holland and Germany). Being mostly illiterate peasants and craftsmen, the Wencheng migrants worked as coolies in Japan and as carpenters in Singapore. In Europe, the majority of migrants from Wencheng arrived only in the late 1920s, and it is unclear how they made a living. Most likely they were selling curios, since in their endeavour to go abroad they relied on middlemen in Shanghai who had already been to Europe to trade. The institutionalization of emigration was thus a prime factor in the emigration process from Wencheng (Zhang et al. 1987).

169

As in the Wenzhou area in general, emigration from Wencheng accelerated during the 1930s, when 776 persons left the county to go abroad, primarily to Singapore and Malaysia. Here a base of fellow county migrants had by now been established, but some 250 persons also migrated to Europe. The latter group was primarily dealing in Chinese curios on a small scale (Zhang et al. 1987:16, 23). According to a local investigation conducted by the officials in Yuhu Township in 1985, 196 migrants from Wencheng county were living in Europe by the late 1930s, increasing to 417 by 1949 (Wang 1985).

Despite the inadequacy of sources on Wencheng emigration, it is clear that a different pattern of emigration existed than in Qingtian. First of all, emigration was not undertaken on a large scale prior to the 1920s. Second, emigrants went primarily to Japan and Singapore; large scale migration to Europe occurred only during the 1930s.

It has been shown above that emigration from Qingtian was partly caused by the penetration of capitalism of the Chinese countryside. Wencheng County's agrarian economy was apparently more directly affected by the import of foreign manufactured goods such as cotton, sugar, cigarettes, fertiliser, dyed and rubber products. In 1918, the total value of foreign produced goods in the Wenzhou area totalled 1,506,000 taels, which was double the value of exported local products. In Wencheng, this affected local dyers, whose local dyes could not compete with imports. Local weavers were similarly ousted from the market because of foreign competition (Zhang et al. 1987:12).

More intensive studies are needed to analyse the actual economic influence of foreign capital penetration on the peasants and skilled workers and confirm to what degree these groups were actually uprooted and, following Marxist analysis, transformed into a new proletariat. Chinese localities should not simply be regarded as static societies unable to respond to foreign aggression. Despite the economic difficulties in most of Wencheng county, migration remained limited to a series of villages in the northern part of the county adjacent to emigrant villages in Shankou, Fangshan and Youzhu Townships in Qingtian county. Villages in other parts of Wencheng County were not nearly as affected by emigration, although it must be assumed that opportunities to migrate as coolie or contract workers or as petty merchants to Europe by buying migration assistance in Wenzhou applied equally to all people in the county. Differences in migration behaviour at the village level call attention to the importance of the nature of local societies for population mobility, rather than solely focusing on the decision making of individuals.

Rui'an

Li'ao and Baimen townships, located approximately twenty kilometers south of Wenzhou city in the city district of Rui'an, are another area of marked emigration to Europe. According to an investigation undertaken in Li'ao in 1986, 1,266 persons had emigrated since 1929, 303 of whom had left prior to 1937. Except for one single case, the destination was Europe – primarily France (Zhang 1987).

Compared to early emigration from Qingtian, emigration to Europe in Li'ao and Baimen had a much later start. The Rui'an area is lowland country with arable land and waterways, quite different from mountainous Qingtian or Wencheng and consequently poverty was less prominent than in the mountain counties.[10]

In Li'ao emigration did not commence until 1929, when nine people from a few neighbouring villages left for France, Italy, and Holland. Their immigration had been assisted by professional middlemen from Li'ao and Wenzhou. Some years later, and especially in 1935–36, groups of a few hundred people from the same villages followed these pioneers, also with the aid of professional agents. These groups ended up trading in Chinese curios under very difficult conditions. As explained above, many Qingtian traders had advanced from being pedlars to being shopkeepers, or even owners of leather factories and other businesses in large European cities. The latecomers from Rui'an arrived without capital and were not immediately able to open a permanent shop or business. Instead, they tried to find new markets for their products. Three Chinese men from Li'ao even headed for Algeria, but after half a year the profits were still minimal and they returned to Marseilles. Most of the 300 Li'ao Chinese who had gone abroad during the 1930s found business extremely difficult, and 250 had returned home to their villages already before the outbreak of the war.

The neighbouring town of Baimen is also characterised by comparatively late emigration to Europe. Initial emigration from Baimen to Europe started in 1930, reaching a high of eighty-seven persons in 1934–36, primarily to France, Italy and Holland. Of the total of 122 who left during this period, the majority were also hawking Chinese curios and facing the same difficulties as the migrants from Li'ao. Some even returned to their native villages, unable to pay back their initial travelling debts (Zhang 1987).

The area encompassing Baimen and Li'ao is located to the south of Wenzhou, south-east of Qingtian and directly to the east of Yuhu in Wencheng County. Despite the mountains and the severe infrastructural difficulties, it must be presumed that the communities had knowledge of overseas emigration to Europe and Southeast Asia from Qingtian and Wencheng. In Baimen, we know that the inhabitants directly experienced the influence of overseas migration: during the early twentieth century, returned Qingtian migrants from Japan and Europe bought up land in Baimen (Zhang 1991b:46). Still, it was not until the mid-1930s that emigration began from these localities. Neo-classical economic assumptions of individuals conducting cost-benefit analyses hardly apply to the population in Baimen, who were directly confronted with the economic benefits of overseas trading, but still preferred to remain home, despite the fact that emigration had been well institutionalized.

In 1929, drought and ensuing insect plagues destroyed much of the harvest in Li'ao and Baimen. In fact, one of the nine peasants to leave Li'ao in 1929 had most of his grain eaten up by insects. Yet emigration was by no means a natural choice for most people in this area, and population mobility from Rui'an increased only gradually between 1929 and 1934. Some peasants had political reasons for leaving China, such as those who had joined associations opposing local landlords or were members of the Communist Party. In 1936, some peasants also went overseas to avoid recruitment into the army of the Nationalist government (Zhang 1991b:44–46). Political refugees, however, remained a minority among Chinese emigrants. Similarly, according to Chinese sources on this area, capitalist penetration does not seem to have been the primary factor compelling people to emigrate. Explaining emigration solely by applying world-system theories thus do not seem to clarify why emigration from Rui'an became concentrated to large numbers from specific villages at a very late date compared to other adjoining areas.

Discussion

The case of Rui'an indicate that a broad theoretical approach, at both macro and micro levels, is required to understand the dynamics of emigration. Our knowledge of Chinese emigration from Zhejiang is still limited, and historical research on local developments evidently is needed. The diverse accounts of emigration from various Chinese localities, nevertheless, all point to the importance of analysing local developments to understand the reasons why local Chinese emigrated abroad. In interviews with local Chinese researchers, migrants reveal their personal motivations for migrating and repeatedly affirm that they went overseas to improve their economic or social situation: either simply to earn higher wages or, alternatively, to diversify economic risks of their household.

Using interviews or surveys with individual migrants as the primary research method to elucidate the causes of mobility invariably highlights economic or social factors.[11] This method of understanding mobility based on migrants' own perceptions of their actions (being problematic in itself) tends not only to produce trivial responses, but also raises questions about the main assumptions behind these surveys; namely, that human conduct is economically rational and can be primarily explained in terms of economic parameters. Accepting only economic and social factors as causes of population mobility reduces the potential for understanding all the forces at work in international migration movements. Below, I will attempt to supplement the theories mentioned above with Bourdieu's theory of social practice.

The world-systems model focuses our attention on the effects of European imperialism and capitalist market forces on local economies in Qingtian and Wenzhou. Hence, as local products were ousted from the market, peasants and craftsmen became unemployed and were forced to accept the new alternative of migrating abroad to earn a living. Following neo-classical economic theory, individuals calculate the costs and benefits of going abroad, which for most of the population in these areas would have been economically beneficial, considering the difference in wage-levels abroad and in China. After 1876, villages and towns in the restricted area of Qingtian and Wenzhou were all affected by the penetration of capitalism, some places more than others, yet despite differences in socio-economic developments in these localities, it is unlikely that incomes were anywhere comparable to those in Europe.[12] This implies that all localities in the area of Qingtian and Wenzhou should have been affected by overseas emigration. Although the account above does not include all emigrant areas, the fact is that a few villages were affected intensively by emigration and as a consequence have become identified as *qiaoxiang* (areas of overseas migration). Hence, applied to this case study, strictly economic theories appear inadequate in explaining the dynamics of migration.

In the theories of new economics of migration, wage-differences between sending and receiving countries are not considered important because emigrants are believed to leave their native areas not only to increase the net-income of the household economy they take part in, but to help diversify household resources so as to minimise economic risks. Wage-differentials in absolute terms thus need not be necessary in order for people to migrate, but the possibility to accumulate savings outside the local economy, which at a later date can contribute to investments in local economic activities, makes migration an attractive option (Massey et al. 1993:436–40).

Despite the fact that these latter theories explain migration even from the relatively prosperous areas of Li'ao and Baimen, the concentration of emigration from but a few villages in these districts is not satisfactorily accounted for. The chief weakness of these theories is that they assume that human conduct is governed only by economic rationality. In contrast, Pierre Bourdieu's studies demonstrate that analysis based on narrow economic rationality tends to neglect the collective history or *habitus* reproduced in human practices.

The population movements out of Qingtian County to Europe did not occur suddenly after the pioneering exploits of a single entrepreneur, as Chen Lite and others imply. Rather, migration had been an integral part of the social and economic development of Qingtian County for centuries. During the Qing period (1644–1911), stone carvings had become more artistic and began to serve as decorative items. Previously, the stones had been used for household purposes. These changes of production caused

Qingtian traders to disperse to Chinese treaty ports such as Wenzhou, Ningbo, Shanghai, Tianjin, and later overseas to Japan and Korea (Zhou Wangsen 1991b). When the opportunity arose to trade with Europeans (and Americans), emigration to Europe became but a continuation of former practices.

In the early twentieth century, the Qingtian migrants' decisions to leave their native places should thus not ignore the history of early trade experiences. Bourdieu also warns that: "narrow economistic conception of the 'rationality' of practices ignores the individual and collective *history* of agents through which the structures of preference that inhabit them are constituted in a complex temporal dialectic with the objective structures that produced them and which they tend to reproduce" (Bourdieu and Wacquant 1992:123). Emigration as practice is better understood by elucidating those economic and social conditions in Qingtian which shaped the habitus of the local population. Habitus is the product of history and an "open *system of dispositions* that is constantly subjected to experiences, and therefore constantly affected by them in a way that either reinforces or modifies its structures." (Bourdieu and Wacquant 1992:133) In villages of Qingtian County where the stone deposits are located, interregional migration within China had created a habitus that in turn produced the economic and cultural capital necessary to perceive and seize the potential opportunities of going overseas.

Using Bourdieu's theory of practice by which humans are first and foremost a product of historical, economic and social conditions, we may conclude that population movements from parts of Qingtian are not caused simply by the deposits of soapstone, but by the historical developments which were in turn shaped by the objective circumstances of stone formations in the area. As the presence and preferences of foreigners allowed for a renewal of the trade in stone carvings, this opportunity was exploited by the inhabitants of Shankou, Youzhu, and Fangshan, where for decades a habitus shaped by the structural circumstances of stone production had developed. Thus, the inhabitants of these particular villages were among the first to emigrate to Europe. By 1933, the local economies in Qingtian had been transformed into handicraft production with eighty stonecarving workshops in Qingtian, the largest having more than forty employees (Dong 1987:11–21).

In other villages, where stone carving had never been part of the local economy and social structure, responding to the stimuli of emigration by selling stone carvings was less appealing, since the prevailing habitus was shaped by an agrarian economy. The peasants in these villages were not disposed to seize the opportunities to trade in stone carvings, although the conjunctures of imperialism, limited arable land, natural calamities and the possibilities of obtaining emigration assistance were alike in the villages of Qingtian and neighbouring counties.

Bourdieu, however, does not rule out strategic choice and conscious economic deliberations as a possible modality of action. In times of crisis, such as the severe drought in 1929 or Japanese aggression, some residents of Baimen and Li'ao suddenly started to emigrate to Europe. In 1935, a returnee from Qingtian went to Zhuxi village in Rui'an and persuaded more than twenty villagers to pay for a passport and passage to Italy in order to trade in Chinese curios (Wei 1994:1028). In these cases, objective circumstances produced strategic economic behaviour of the population in certain villages. However, it is worth noticing that only when all other options of emigration were ruled out – such as Japan – did emigration to Europe commence as a last resort.

Habitus should thus not to be construed as fate; it is durable, but changing, because it is subject to structural change which reinforces or modifies its structures (Bourdieu and Wacquant 1992:132–133). Sudden emigration from areas where population mobility previously was limited can thus be altered by objective circumstances and influence the habitus of later generations. During the early 1970s, the authorities in Wencheng County and in Rui'an municipality decided that it would benefit the local area if emigration to Europe were encouraged. Having made this decision, emigration was officially encouraged and supported by the issuing of thousands of passports to make it easier for the local population to go to Milan (Sun 1995:46).

It is important to analyse emigration as a social practice "propelled" by certain objective circumstances and by certain dispositions inherent to the habitus, instead of exclusively explaining migration as strategic economic action. This approach explains why emigration can persist even when its economic benefits are limited. Emigration from Qingtian by the turn of the century was temporary and not intended as life-time emigration, although in many cases the emigrants never returned to China. Some did return, and invested their capital. Prior to 1932, in Qiushan village in Qingtian county, fourteen new houses were built using money earned abroad; sixteen emigrant households were able to buy additional land in Wenzhou, Pingyang, and Rui'an; and three emigrant households purchased land outside the county and moved away. In 1933, two members of the first group of nine men to leave collectively from villages in Li'ao township opened in partnership a wholesale shop in Marseilles selling German-produced carpets, table cloth, Italian jewellery and French clothing. They quickly earned money and in 1934 returned home. One sold his land in his native village and bought a pawn shop in Wenzhou; the other built himself a big house in his native village and went back to France until the war broke out (Zhang 1987:42).

Building houses, acquiring land outside the county, or subletting fields to other peasants were not only signs of wealth, but in contemporary society a way of increasing the social position of the family; thus, money earned overseas also became "social capital". Since the scarcity of land in Qingtian did not provide the average individual household many possibilities of upward mobility, overseas money became more important. In Shankou a saying went: "When business is successful overseas, fields can be bought in Wenzhou and you can leave the countryside" (Ye 1986:69).[13] In fact, only very few returned emigrants earned enough money to purchase houses or fields, and today Qingtian still belongs to the emigration counties receiving the lowest remittances from abroad (Ye 1986; Zhou 1991a:117).

By the late 1920s and 1930s, it must have been evident that profits made from going abroad were low. Simultaneously, hawking in Europe had become extremely difficult, since trade licences or long-term passports were needed to do business. Between 1929 and 1937, more than half of a group of ninety emigrants from one village in Li'ao were sent to prison for three months or longer while sojourning in Europe (Zhang 1987:42). Still, Chinese villagers continued to proceed towards Europe in increasing numbers, implying that strategic choices and conscious deliberations were less important aspects in decision-making, and that human action can in this case be explained as a product of interplay between objective circumstances, habitus and the importance of gaining "social capital".

Conclusion

By 1995, 60,000 Qingtian Chinese lived in fifty different countries, eighty per cent of them in Europe. Additionally, 80,000 persons have ventured overseas and returned (*guiqiao*) (Qianyan 1995:1). These massive population movements took place from only a small number of villages primarily in the southeastern part of a county that itself had a mere 480,000 people in 1987 (Chen Murong 1990:159). By comparison, the number of emigrants from neighbouring Wencheng county, with a population of 370,000 in 1994, was only 5,577 in 1984, who migrated from a few villages and spread to twenty-seven different countries (Zhang et al. 1987:11). Although this number has undoubtedly increased during the last decade, it is unlikely to reach 60,000. In addition, the historical accounts have included the villages of Li'ao and Baimen, under the jurisdiction of Rui'an city in Wenzhou municipality. In explaining the causes of the origin of these population developments from the first part of the twentieth century, I have attempted to apply different theories of migration operating at diverse levels and emphasising various causal explanations. The different cases presented from a confined area of Zhejiang province, however, show diversities with regard to orgin, time, scope and countries of destination that cannot be explained adequately by conventional migration theories.

To account for the origin and development of migration, I have proposed to apply Bourdieu's theory of practice, which considers the economic and social conditions together with habitus, thus revealing the human responses to stimuli like the opportunity to emigrate. This theory stresses history and the individual as a social actor, and rejects the notion of narrow economic rational choices for human conduct. Specific historical structures, incorporated in the local habitus, are structuring the present by becoming decisive for the conduct of agents. Former practices of selling stone carvings in Qingtian have thus been integrated as past experiences in the system of lasting, transposable dispositions or habitus, which functions as a matrix of perceptions, values and actions (Bourdieu 1977:82–83). In the dialectical relationship with objective events, and presented with the opportunity of selling stone carvings in Europe, only those disposed by a certain habitus respond immediately. Hence, the urge to go overseas to Europe was strongest among the inhabitants of the stone carving villages of Shankou, Youzhu, and Fangshan, from where trading in stones had been part of history and society for centuries.

Structural changes affecting the social and economic conditions modify the habitus of people in these areas and as a result, later generations become more disposed to emigration because "the past survives in the present and tends to perpetuate into the future by making itself present in the practices structured according to its principles" (Bourdieu 1977:82). Emigration from Wenzhou thus continues to Europe, at great risk and costs for those involved. Increasing numbers of emigrants have decided to leave their native villages, which are by Chinese standards more prosperous than many villages in inland China, and pursue a life abroad.

References

Bourdieu, Pierre. 1977. *Outline of a Theory of Practice*. Cambridge: Cambridge University Press.

Bourdieu, Pierre. 1990. *The Logic of Practice*. Cambridge: Polity Press.

Bourdieu and Loïc J.D. Wacquant. 1992. *An Invitation to Reflexive Sociology*. Cambridge: Polity Press.

Chen Bin. 1995. "Zuizao Dao Ouzhoude Qingtianren" [The earliest Qingtian people who went to Europe]. *Qingtian Wenshi Ziliao* 6, pp. 6–17.

Chen Hansheng, ed. 1984. *Huagong Chuguo Shiliao Huibian* [A collection of historical materials on Chinese emigrant workers], Part 10. Beijing: Zhonghua Shuju.

Chen Lite. 1995a. "Qingtianren Chuguo Dao Ouzhoude Jingguo" [The process of Qingtian people's emigration to Europe]. *Qingtian Wenshi Ziliao* 6, pp. 3–5.

Chen Lite. 1995b. "Zuo Shang" [Going by way of business]. *Qingtian Wenshi Ziliao* 6, pp. 18–25.

Chen Murong ed. 1990. *Qingtian Xianzhi* [Qingtian county gazetteer]. Hangzhou: Zhejiang Renmin Chubanshe.

Chen Sanjing. 1986. *Huagong yu Ouzhan* [Chinese indentured labour and the First World War]. Taibei: Zhongyang Yanjiuyuan Jindaishi Yanjiusuo.

Chen Xuewen. 1993. *Ming Qing Shiqi Hang Jia Hu Shizhenshi Yanjiu* [Urban historical research of Hangzhou, Jiaxing and Huzhou]. Beijing: Qunyan Chubanshe.

Dong Bingdi, ed. 1987. *Qingtian Shidiao yu Chuanshuo* [Qingtian stone carving and anecdotes]. Beijing: Zhongguo Jianshe Zazhishe.

Greenhalgh, Paul. 1988. *Ephemeral Vistas: The Expositions Universelles, Great Exhibitions and World's Fairs, 1851–1939.* Manchester: Manchester University Press.

Massey, Douglas S., Joaquín Arango, Graeme Hugo, Ali Kouaouci, Adela Pellegrino and J. Edward Taylor. 1993. "Theories of International Migration: A Review and Appraisal." *Population and Development Review* 19, no. 3, pp. 431–66.

Pieke, Frank N. 1998. "Introduction." In Gregor Benton and Frank N. Pieke, eds, *The Chinese in Europe*, pp. 1–17. London: Macmillan Press.

Poston, Dudley L., Jr., Michael Xinxiang Mao and Mei-Yu Yu. 1994. "The Global Distribution of the Overseas Chinese Around 1990." *Population and Development Review* 20, no. 3, pp. 631–45.

Qianyan. 1995. "Qianyan" [Introduction]. *Qingtian Wenshi Ziliao* 6, pp. 1–2.

Qingtian xianzhi. 1935. *Qingtian xianzhi* [Qingtian County gazetteer]. (Reprint of Guangxu edition of 1881), 1. Taibei: Chengwen Chubanshe.

Reichschauer, Edwin O. and Albert M. Craig. 1989. *Japan: Tradition and Transformation.* Revised ed. Sidney: Allen and Unwin.

Schoppa, R. Keith. 1982. *Chinese Elites and Political Change: Zhejiang Province in the Early Twentieth Century.* Cambridge, Massachusetts: Harvard University Press.

Shiba, Yoshinobu. 1977. "Ningpo and Its Hinterland." In G. William Skinner, ed. *The City in Late Imperial China*, pp. 391–440. Stanford: Stanford University Press.

Skeldon, Ronald. 1990. *Population Mobility in Developing Countries: A Reinterpretation.* London: Belhaven Press.

Summerskill, Michael. 1982. *China on the Western Front: Britain's Chinese Work Force in the First World War.* London: Michael Summerskill.

Sun Mingquan. 1995. "LüYi Huaqiao Sanji" [Sketches of overseas Chinese who went to Italy]. *Qingtian Wenshi Ziliao* 6, pp. 41–60.

Thunø, Mette. 1996. "Chinese Emigration to Europe: Combining European and Chinese Sources." *Revue Européenne des Migrations Internationales* 12, no. 2, pp. 275–96.

Wang Zhongming. 1985. *Wencheng Huaqiao Lishi Ziliao 1905–1984* [Historical documents on Wencheng overseas Chinese, 1905–1984] cited in Li Minghuan, "To get Rich Quickly in Europe", this volume.

Wei Qiao, ed. 1995. *Shudu Zhejiang Qiqian Nian* [Becoming familiar with Zhejiang's history of 7,000 years]. Ha'erbin: Ha'erbin Ditu Chubanshe.

Weiner, Michael. 1994. *Race and Migration in Imperial Japan.* London: Routledge.

Yan Xinli [pseudonym for Zhang Zhicheng]. 1995. "Guandong Da Dizhen Shi dui LüRi Huagongde Tusha" [The Kanto earthquake and the massacre of Chinese workers in Japan]. In Wenzhoushi Zhengxie Wenshi Ziliao Weiyuanhui and Zhejiangsheng Zhengxie Wenshi Ziliao Weiyuanhui, eds, *Dongying Chenyuan* [Gross injustice in Japan], pp. 20–30. Hangzhou: Zhejiang Renmin Chubanshe.

Ye Zhongming. 1986. "Qingtian Qiaoxiang Tanyuan" [An exploration into the origin of the emigrant county of Qingtian]. *Qingtian Wenshi Ziliao* 2, pp. 64–77.

Zhang Zhicheng. 1987. "Rui'anshi Li'aozhen Huaqiao Lishi yu Xianzhuang" [The current situation and history of overseas Chinese from Ruian city and Li'ao township]. In *Zhejiang Huaqiao Ziliao*, pp. 31–62.

Zhang Zhicheng. 1991a. "Wenzhou Huaqiao Lishi Gaikuang" [A survey of the history of overseas Chinese from Wenzhou]. *Wenzhou Wenshi Ziliao* 7, pp. 1–12.

Zhang Zhicheng. 1991b. "Baimen Xiang Qiaoshi Diaocha" [A study of the history of emigration from Baimen county]. *Wenzhou Wenshi Ziliao* 7, pp. 43–59.

Zhang Zhicheng. 1995. "Ershi Niandai Wenchu Shannong Dongdu Riben Mousheng Gaikuang" [An overview of how peasants from the mountains of the Wenzhou region went east, crossing the sea to make a living in Japan during the 1920s]. In Wenzhoushi Zhengxie Wenshi Ziliao Weiyuanhui and Zhejiangsheng Zhengxie Wenshi Zilliao Weiyuanhui, eds, *Dongying Chenyuan* [Gross Injustice in Japan], pp. 1–12. Hangzhou: Zhejiang Renmin Chubanshe.

Zhang Zhicheng et al. 1987. "Wencheng Xian Huaqiao Jianshi" [A brief history of the overseas Chinese from Wencheng county]. In *Zhejiang Huaqiao Ziliao*, pp. 11–30.

Zhou Nanjing, ed. 1993. *Shijie Huaqiao Huaren Cidian* [Dictionary of the world's overseas and ethnic Chinese]. Beijing: Beijing Daxue Chubanshe.

Zhou Wangsen. 1991a. "Qingtian Huaqiao Tedian Chutan" [Preliminary exploration of the special character of overseas Chinese from Qingtian]. In Chen Xuewen, ed. *Zhejiangsheng Huaqiao Lishi Yanjiu Luncong* [A collection of research on the history of overseas Chinese from Zhejiang province], pp. 104–19. Zhejiang: n.p.

Zhou Wangsen. 1991b. "Qingtian Shidiao ji Qi Shehuishi Yiyi Tanxi" [Finding out about Qingtian stone carving and its social implications]. In Chen Xuewen, ed. *Zhejiangsheng Huaqiao Lishi Yanjiu Luncong* [A collection of research on the history of overseas Chinese from Zhejiang province], pp. 88–96. Zhejiang: n.p.

Zhou Wangsen. 1991c "Yi jian Zhenguide Huaqiao Ziliao" [A valuable source on overseas Chinese], In Chen Xuewen, ed. *Zhejiangsheng Huaqiao Lishi Yanjiu Luncong* [A collection of research on the history of overseas Chinese from Zhejiang province], pp. 120–4. Zhejiang: n.p.

Notes

1 The review of migration theories draws on Massey et al. (1993).

2 The total number of Chinese overseas defies quantification. Depending on various definitions of the term "Chinese", figures ranging from 20 to 50 millions have been suggested. See Zhou Nanjing 1993:936–7; Pieke 1998; Poston et al. 1994.

3 I have discussed the validity of this material elsewhere Thunø 1996. Moreover, I am familiar with the Chinese researchers concerned and the methods they used. I especially want to thank Zhang Zhicheng, Chen Menglin, Chen Xuewen and Chen Yaodong for their assistance in various practical and academic matters related to this chapter.

4 See also Schoppa's socio-ecological division of Zhejiang province in the early twentieth century into four developmental zones according to population density, postal ranking and number of financial institutions (Schoppa 1982:13–26).

5 Putuo Mountain is a Buddhist holy place located on an island east of Ningbo in northeastern Zhejiang.

6 Fangshan, Youzhu, Fushan and twelve other townships, but excluding the important emigrant town of Shankou.

7 In contemporary prices three taels equalled one *dan* or approximately 150 pounds of millet.

8 The local gazetteer for Wenzhou city is currently being written and will be available at the earliest in 1997. No other local studies on the history of Wenzhou exist and the economic implications of foreign presence in Wenzhou remain undocumented.

9 See the statistical data on the contemporary situation in Li Minghuan's article included in this volume.
10 Li Minghuan's article in this volume describes the differential development of Rui'an and Wencheng counties today.
11 See also the discussion in Skeldon 1990:11–26 and 126–33.
12 Qingtian county is often depicted as extremely poor, but during Republican times Schoppa has not been able to identify Qingtian as an extremely backward region of Zhejiang. The connection to the core area of Wenzhou along the shallow Ou River with bamboo rafts did in fact allow for some trade and economic development (Schoppa 1982:17).
13 See also contemporary idioms in regard to emigration cited in Li Minghuan's article in this volume.

Chapter Nine

"To Get Rich Quickly in Europe!" – Reflections on migration motivation in Wenzhou*

Li Minghuan

Introduction

In the course of my study on the history of Chinese migrants in the Netherlands, I have met many Wenzhou people in western Europe, whose special dialect, regional loyalty, wide-ranging circle of "family and friends" and active associations made a lasting impression on me. Quite often I thought: Why have thousands and thousands of Wenzhou people emigrated to Europe during the last hundred years? Are there any special factors in Wenzhou's cultural tradition which predispose its people for migration? If the "Wenzhou model" (*Wenzhou moshi*, see Tomba, this volume) of development has become an example for other rural communities in China, attracting more than 800,000 people each year from inland areas such as Sichuan, Guizhou and Jiangxi provinces (Li Haoran 1996:227), why are ordinary Wenzhou people still eagerly looking for possibilities to emigrate to Europe?

During fieldwork in Wenzhou in January and February 1996, I selected as my study areas Li'ao *zhen* (town) under the jurisdiction of Rui'an *shi* (municipality) and Yuhu zhen in Wencheng county.[1] Both Rui'an and Wencheng are county level administrative regions that fall directly under Wenzhou, a prefecture level municipality in southern Zhejiang province.[2] The fieldwork in Wenzhou is part of my research project on Chinese migrants in the Netherlands. The informants I selected and the issues I raised during interviews were therefore mainly connected to emigration to the Netherlands.[3]

*I would like to thank T. D. Tjeng and Christianne Borghouts for their constructive comments.

181

In this chapter I shall focus on collective migration motivation of people in regions of large-scale emigration in Wenzhou, usually called *qiaoxiang* (overseas Chinese areas) in Chinese.

Background Information

Located at the midpoint of China's eastern coast, and situated in the southern part of Zhejiang province, the area of Wenzhou municipality is about 11,784 square kilometers, with a population of about 6,924,000 at the end of 1994 (Wenzhoushi tongjiju 1995:21). Under the new policy of "the municipality administering the county" (*shi guan xian*) in 1981, Wenzhou municipality now consists of six *xian* (counties), three *qu* (urban districts) and two *shi* (county level cities). The following tables give some basic information on Wenzhou. In order to compare the background of Li'ao and Yuhu, I have presented the figures of Rui'an city and Wencheng county, both located in Wenzhou municipality, separately.

From the figures in tables 9.1–9.3, we can see that Rui'an is a relatively rich area, while Wencheng is relatively poor. For instance, the population of Rui'an is only 16.7 per cent of the whole of Wenzhou, but of the total gross output value of township and household enterprises in Wenzhou, Rui'an makes up twenty-six per cent, compared to less than one per cent for Wencheng. The annual average product per person in Rui'an is three and a half times as much as in Wencheng; the annual average income of peasants in Rui'an is more than double of Wencheng's. In other words, the economic development level of Rui'an is higher than the average level of Wenzhou, whereas the level of Wencheng is much lower than the average. Taken together, Li'ao in Rui'an and Yuhu in Wencheng should therefore provide a reasonable cross-section of the situation in the Wenzhou qiaoxiang.

Motives for emigration to Europe

According to figures provided by the Wenzhou Office of Local Gazetteers (*Wenzhoushi Difangzhi Bangongshi*), at the end of 1994, 248,000 Wenzhou

Table 9.1 Population and areas (1994)

	Whole Wenzhou	Rui'an	Wencheng
Population (thousand)	6,924	1,157	370
Area (square kilometer)	11,784	1,360	1,294
Population density	588	851	286
Total cultivated land (hectare)	173,000	32,000	10,000
Cultivated land (mu⁴/person)	0.37	0.41	0.41

Source: Wenzhoushi Tongji Ju 1995:21.

- Table 9.2 Economic growth of Wenzhou (1980–1994)

	Years	Whole Wenzhou	Rui'an	Wencheng
Gross output value of industry and	1980	2,570	n.a.	n.a.
agriculture (million yuan)	1994	58,048	11,270	503
Annual output value per person (*nian renjun*	1980	312	248	156
chanzhi)(yuan)	1994	4,286	4,965	1,405
Annual average income of agricultural	1980	165		
population (*nongye renkou*)(yuan)	1994	2,000	2,530	1,084
Township enterprises and household workshops:				
(a) Number of units	1980	10,013	n.a.	n.a.
	1994	58,022	11,880	2,516
(b) gross output value (million yuan)	1980	491	n.a.	n.a.
	1994	32,296	8,496	153
(c) Employees	1980	3,346	n.a.	n.a.
	1994	6,967	1,521	77
Private investment in rural areas (million	1980	196	n.a.	n.a.
yuan)	1994	1,108	194	34

Source: Wenzhoushi Tongji Ju 1995:25, 26, 41.

Table 9.3 Rural labour force in 1994 (unit: one thousand)

	Agriculture	Township enterprises	Village enterprises	Household workshops	Out migration
Whole Wenzhou	1,548.9	112.7	72.8	426.3	506.7
Rui'an	305.7	28.7	16.7	87.6	87.5
Wencheng	87.2	1.0	0.6	3.9	44.0

Source: Wenzhoushi Tongji Ju 1995:52.

emigrants and their descendants were living in sixty-five countries. Of those, more than 165,000 reside in Europe, about ninety-five per cent of them, or 145,000 people, in the four countries of France, the Netherlands, Italy and Spain.[5]

The historical records analyzed in Mette Thunø's article in this volume demonstrate that Wenzhou people have emigrated to Europe from as early as the end of the last century.[6] After 1949, emigration came to a virtual standstill. Only in the early 1970s, and especially after 1976, did migration from Wenzhou to Europe pick up again.[7] For instance, in Li'ao, according to figures calculated in the course of a door-to-door survey by local cadres of overseas Chinese affairs in late 1995, a total of 3,003 Li'ao people are living in Europe now. Among them, eighty-two per cent emigrated to Europe after 1980.[8] In Wencheng, I went to Lishan, a remote and small village in Yuhu township. I was told that the population of that village is about 1,000 now, while 700–800 adult villagers make a living abroad. Most of them have settled down in the Netherlands, France and Italy. More than half of them are "new migrants", i.e. people who have emigrated during the last ten years. Moreover, "all capable teenagers are preparing to find their future in Europe", I was told repeatedly.[9]

Such an emigration wave to Europe has attracted the attention of local scholars, who have conducted research in Wenzhou's rural areas and officially or unofficially published a number of papers on the subject. According to these scholars, the factors pushing people out of Wenzhou's rural areas can be summed up as follows: before 1949, poverty was the key factor which provoked Wenzhou people to emigrate to Europe, in addition to local violence and the ambition to become rich (Wang 1985:3–4; Zhang 1991:2, 4, 13–14, 26, and 44–46). After 1949, the main factor has been the pull of family reunion, which meant helping emigrated family members to establish or expand the family's business in Europe. Since the end of the 1970s, moreover, the relaxation of China's emigration policies has much facilitated emigration (Wang 1985:5–6; Zhang 1991: 36–37 and 53–54).

Important as the above mentioned factors are, they do not provide a full explanation for the current surge of emigration from Wenzhou. For instance, they can neither explain why migration keeps rising at a time when the economic situation in Wenzhou is improving rapidly, nor do they consider why only a few villages have become qiaoxiang, despite natural conditions and cultural environment that are broadly similar throughout the Wenzhou area. However, the main question that remains unanswered is why Europe has become Wenzhou's favourite emigration destination, and not Southeast Asia or the United States – the main destinations of many Guangdong and Fujian migrants. In the remainder of this chapter I will try to provide solutions to these puzzles and paradoxes of Wenzhou migration to Europe.

High expectations and relative deprivation

According to migration theories based on what is often conveniently summarized as "traditional neoclassical economics", international migration is a response to differentials in incomes between countries of origin and destination (Massey et al. 1994:708–711). Undoubtedly, dreams of getting rich, high expectations and fanciful imagination have pushed people to emigrate despite the ethnic and cultural differences that they will encounter. Observing the situation of Wenzhou migrants today, similar phenomena can easily be found. However, the striking point is that the dream of riches of recent Wenzhou migrants did not fully develop until the economic situation in Wenzhou itself had become much better.

Since the end of the 1970s, the reform movement in China has resulted in considerable changes in economic, political and cultural life. Being an experimental zone and home of the now-famous "Wenzhou model" (Fei 1992a; Nolan and Dong 1990), the relevant changes in Wenzhou have been greater than in many other parts of China. Table 9.2

shows that the annual average income of peasants in Wenzhou in 1994 was more than twelve times that of 1980. On numerous occasions, local cadres told me the following story:

> Some years back, a high ranking cadre from Beijing came to Wenzhou for an inspection tour. Being impressed by the high level of development of Wenzhou's rural areas, he composed a poem before returning to Beijing. The poem begins with the following line:
>
>> Going from one village to another village, every village seems like a city.[10]

From how they talked about this event, it is obvious that they were very proud of the achievements of rural urbanization in Wenzhou.

When asked to compare their living standard now with twenty years ago, all people whom I talked with confirmed that they have become much richer. However, when asked why they are still eager to go abroad, their answer remains as simple as before: because we are poor, and we want to be rich there. "We are richer than in the past, but we are much poorer than our fellows in Europe" is the common sentiment among the people of Wenzhou's qiaoxiang. The following quotation from one of my interviews may serve as an further illustration:[11]

> Why do I want to go abroad? Very simple, to earn money, to become rich... Yes, I can earn money here. As a woodworker, I can earn more money than those guys who can only farm the land, but if I go to western Europe, I know I can earn much more. I can become rich very quickly and bring a lot of money back to do anything I want here. I imagine I can build a new and big house for my family, although I have this five-story house now and it is not bad. I will rebuild my family tomb, which will be among the best in this area, if not the best. Of course, if I have a lot of money, I may also donate some money for building a school or an old people's home in my village (laughing) (...) Now I am waiting for my uncle's help. I have two uncles living in the Netherlands with their families. My eldest uncle has agreed to arrange the relevant immigration procedures for me. I know it is not easy, but I am tired of waiting. You see, my passport has been in my pocket for more than five years now."[12]

In Wenzhou qiaoxiang, whenever asked about their personal knowledge of Europe, the interviewees would without exception immediately talk about how high the wages are that people can earn there. Many interviewees know very well that the average wage of a cook in a Chinese restaurant in the Netherlands is about 2,500 guilders (about 830 pound sterling) a month. Without relating this wage to the Dutch cost of living, and without comparing it with the average income in the Netherlands, this salary seems astonishingly high in Wenzhou. In 1994, it was seventy-five times the average income of a peasant in Wenzhou, or about sixty times that of a peasant in Rui'an and nearly 140 times that of a peasant in Wencheng.[13] Yet the difference is so great that the pull of this income is about equal for all people in Wenzhou, regardless of whether they live in relatively rich Rui'an or poor Wencheng.

Moreover, in the eyes of Wenzhou migrants, you can expect a high income in any European Chinese restaurant without possessing any special skills,[14] investment, or even knowledge of the host society. All that is required is to be a hardworking person. When talking about which kind of job he may expect to find in the Netherlands, the interviewee I quoted earlier told me:

> I know that I may not be able to find a job as a carpenter in the Netherlands! But I don't care about that. I am a young man of great strength. I can work in any Chinese restaurant. I believe I can earn Dutch guilders simply by exerting my utmost effort (. . .) Yes, recently, I have seen someone who became rich in China very quickly. But to accomplish that, you need capital, you need special knowledge and you have to have very good *guanxi*.[15] I have none of those. Therefore, I have no prospects if I stay here and be a carpenter all my life, but I do believe that I may become a restaurant boss in the Netherlands in a few years, just like my uncles and other fellow villagers. Maybe I am not wiser than they are, but at least I am as clever as any of them. What I need is a good chance. This chance is in Europe.

Such a future is especially attractive for unskilled peasants. I still remember vividly the teenage girls in distant villages, who replied very clearly to me that they wanted to earn money in Europe. Yet they could only speak their own dialect, while many were illiterate.

Expectations outrun the facts, and disappointment is worsened by the anger about unequal opportunities. Villagers reason that since we have become richer than before, we should be even richer soon! Since their family members, friends and neighbours earn such large amounts of money in Europe, why should they themselves not be able to do that as well?

Wenzhou villagers' expectations and envy are thus the result of what Merton and Kitt (1950) call "relative deprivation." In the words of Robin Williams:

> [R]aising the incomes of all does not increase the happiness of all (. . .) Individuals assess their material well-being, not in terms of the absolute amount of goods they have, but relative to a social norm of what goods they ought to have (. . .) [W]hen levels of real

income received are rising for a majority of a population over a substantial period, there will be increases in expected levels, in aspirations, and in feelings that the achieved levels are appropriate and deserved (that is, an increase in levels of normative claim). (Williams 1976:360–1)

Taking migration to the United States from Mexico as an example, Douglas Massey and his co-authors have argued that households migrate not only to improve their absolute income, but also to increase their incomes relative to others in the community. In other words, through international migration, people try to improve their relative social position in the home community. Moreover, Massey et al. find that people in places with an unequal income distribution are more likely to migrate than people located in areas where income is relatively equally distributed (Massey et al. 1994:714).

This also applies to Wenzhou qiaoxiang. When poverty is a common phenomenon in people's direct environment, it is easier to accept a low living standard. However, when some households, especially close neighbours, become rich in a very short period, while others benefit from remittances from their family-members or relatives in Europe, people raise their expectations and become more and more dissatisfied, even when their standard of living already has significantly improved.

In Wenzhou today, one result of the economic reforms has been that the expectations and value orientation of many people have changed. The pursuit of material wealth is no longer taboo, and often seems to override all other concerns.

Against this background it is likely that the emigration wave from Wenzhou will continue as long as there is some hope (however faint) of getting out. But why go to Europe?

Why Europe?

A first answer to this question should be sought in the history of Wenzhou's relations with Europe. During the first decades of the twentieth century, Wenzhou emigrants went mainly to three destinations: Japan, Southeast Asia and western Europe. Among these three areas, Japan was the destination of choice for most Wenzhou migrants (Thunø, this volume).

Japan is close to China (making travel cheaper and shorter) and its cultural tradition is not too alien to Chinese people.[16] According to Zhang Zhicheng, between 1914 and 1922, more than 5,000 Wenzhou people went to make a living in Japan (Zhang 1995:1). During the 1910s and early 1920s, 303 persons went to Japan from Wencheng alone (Wang 1985:2). Japan received more Wenzhou immigrants than either France, the Netherlands, or Italy. However, in the wake of the Kanto earthquake of 1 September 1923, Japanese militarists and anti-foreign extremists massacred an estimated 700 Chinese workers in Japan (Renmufumeizi 1995:1; Yan Xinli 1995:24–30). Almost all of the surviving 3,000 Chinese tried to rush back to their hometown, putting a virtual halt to Wenzhou emigration to Japan. The trickle of emigration that continued after 1923 was cut short in 1931 when hostilities broke out between Japan and China.

When Wenzhou people began to emigrate to southeast Asia, millions of Guangdong and Fujian migrants had already settled there. It was not easy for Wenzhou migrants, as newcomers who spoke an incomprehensible dialect, to create a profitable space in an economy dominated by the established Guangdong and Fujian migrant communities and native peoples. As a result, the number of Wenzhou migrants to Southeast Asia remained limited.

However, in Europe, Wenzhou migrants found virtual virgin territory. Mette Thunø's paper in this book discusses the origins of emigration from the Wenzhou area, and I will therefore only briefly recapitulate her argument here.

Many studies have shown that "each new immigrant creates a large pool of potential immigrants" (Massey et al. 1994:732). In Wenzhou, the situation is similar. Once begun, the emigration from Wenzhou to Europe has snowballed and developed as part of a specific habitus and life course. Chain-migration is of great significance here. Some examples illustrate this point:

> Mr. Hu Yundi, born in 1915, emigrated to Europe in 1934. Having tried to make a living in several European countries, he established his business in Italy in the early 1950s. Since then, he first had his wife and children come over, followed by other relatives. Up till now, there are forty-three such relatives living in Italy. Besides, he has helped nearly sixty *qinpeng haoyou* (literally "relatives and good friends") to emigrate to Italy, some of whom now live in other European countries. He is very proud of his special contribution to his family, or, more to the point, his clan and home community to which he continues to feel very much attached.[17]

Mr. Cai Zhengshen emigrated to France in 1963 and in 1992 resettled in his hometown Rui'an. During the 1970s and 1980s, he had arranged immigration procedures for more than ninety qinpeng haoyou.[18]

Mr. Cai Zexuan emigrated to the Netherlands in 1930 and has since helped more than forty fellow villagers emigrate to this country. One of his cousins in turn sponsored the emigration of about twenty qinpeng haoyou to Europe soon after he himself had settled down.

It should be noted that, before leaving China, most migrants look to "Europe" rather than to any specific European country as their destination. After arriving in Europe, it is quite common for them to transfer from one country to another, and then to a third or fourth, especially just after their arrival (Li Minghuan 1998).

A second cluster of causes for Wenzhou's choice of Europe are found at the western European side. In addition to the above mentioned point that high income in Western Europe has formed an important pull factor for Wenzhou migrants, lenient immigrant policies of some West European countries have significantly lowered the entrance barrier. First, almost all West European countries have kept doors open for migration through "family reunion". However, for Chinese, "family" (*jia*) is a broad concept, of which the boundary is not clearly defined (Fei 1992b, chapters 4 and 6). For instance, all brothers and sisters, either married or not yet married, belong to one family. Besides, their children also belong to the family. Sometimes even only sharing the same family name will be taken as sufficient evidence for the descent from a common ancestor and membership of one great family. It is not rare for an immigrant to adopt an underage child from a family with no connections abroad. This child can then immigrate using the "family reunion" procedure, and, upon reaching adulthood, sponsor the immigration of his or her original family members.

Second, in the 1960s and 1970s, guest workers were recruited by many western European countries, and lenient immigration policies were generally speaking in place. The same period was also the golden time for Chinese restaurants in Europe, which desperately needed large numbers of cheap workers. Wenzhou people remember distinctly that up to the first years of the 1980s, if you could "prove" to be a certified Chinese cook, you could easily get a work permit and visa for European countries such as the Netherlands or France.

Since the second part of the 1980s, several European countries have tightened their immigration policies. However, from then on illegal migration from Wenzhou to Europe has become a major issue. There are several factors behind illegal migration, but it cannot be ignored that one crucial factor is that the policies of western European countries offer illegal migrants some hope. For instance, potential migrants in Wenzhou are told by "black migration brokers" that regardless of whether you are legally or illegally in a western European country, you can expect a residence permit from the government simply if you can prove that you are a victim either of the family planning policy or political movements in China.

Illegal migrants are also hopeful of the occasional regularization that allows illegal immigrants in a country to legalize their stay. As soon as I settled down in Wenzhou to begin my research there, I found that a hot topic of conversation among my interviewees was the most recent regularization law in Italy. Having already put two earlier such laws into effect which directly involved the Chinese (in 1986 and 1990, see Tomba, this volume; Carchedi and Ferri 1998; Montanari & Cortese 1993:280–281), Italy promulgated its third regularization law at the end of 1995. More or less like the first two laws, this new law gave a chance to illegal immigrants to obtain regular work and residence permits. Although the procedures stipulated by the law will be very costly, many families of illegal migrants throughout Europe were excited when this law became known. western Europe is looked upon as a single entity and the internal borders between most European Union countries are known to be hardly guarded. Illegal migrants are confident that they can easily leave any western European country where they have temporarily settled and go to Italy to apply for a residence permit. Many also believe that what has happened today in Italy, might also happen in some other European countries tomorrow. A question I was asked very often during my interviews was whether regularization laws were in the offing in other European countries, especially in the Netherlands and France. One informant asked me:

> My son (an illegal migrant in the Netherlands) wrote to me that the Dutch people are friendly, but the Dutch government is cold-blooded. It does not want to follow Italy. The Dutch government should do that. Both countries are in one Europe. Why are the immigrant policies so different?[19]

Another villager told me very seriously:

> We have heard that the Netherlands will announce a similar law very soon. Otherwise all Chinese restaurants have to close because the workers will all go to Italy for their residence permits.[20]

The fact that some fellow Wenzhou people in those countries have become legal has brightened the hopes of illegal immigrants in other countries, and has strengthened the attraction of emigration for Wenzhou villagers.

In sum, the Wenzhou pioneer migrants who settled down in Europe before the Second World War have been the first links in migration chains after the Second World War. This chain migration has continued partially because of the pull of the actual and imagined possibilities and advantages of emigrating to western Europe. Chain migration and immigration policies together make western Europe the ideal destination for Wenzhou migrants.

But migration to Europe is more than a matter of convenient access and high expectations. People in Wenzhou's qiaoxiang consider "getting rich in Europe" an opportunity reserved only for them; some even feel it is their common destination or birthright. Such an orientation cannot be easily changed by outsiders.

This strong "qiaoxiang consciousness" was expressed by almost all officials in Wenzhou qiaoxiang whom I interviewed; it also frequently appeared in the local newspapers, expressed in slogans urging that the best possible use should be made of the unique opportunities that the overseas Chinese connections offer, and that everything should be done to strengthen overseas Chinese's love for the fatherland and native place.

However, how to use this opportunity? My interviewees give different answers: some told me about magnificent goals for the whole area; others talked about concrete plans of their own. But in my experience, if you go to the grass-roots level, the responses are simple and remarkably consistent:[21]

> Going to Europe is our special opportunity. If one member of a family goes to Europe, the whole family will profit from it.

> Our predecessors have established excellent opportunities for us to get rich in Europe. If we cannot grasp these opportunities and maintain these links, we are unworthy sons.

Conspicuous consumption in Wenzhou qiaoxiang

In Wenzhou, qiaoxiang is a highly visible and respectable social category. Qiaoxiang people have been labelled a "rich" and "lucky" group, even when there is no economic gap between people with and people without overseas Chinese connections. Conspicuous consumption[22] by returned migrants continually strengthens the rich and lucky image of the European Chinese.

In the published studies on transnational migrants, I found that almost all migrants, regardless of their ethnic background, are expected to display their wealth and success upon return to their native place. The well-known Chinese proverb "to return to one's hometown in silk robes" (Yijin huanxiang) illustrates how important this is for Chinese migrants as well. Another proverb is arguably even more interesting. "Walking at night wearing silk robes" (Jinyi yexing) is a label attached to those who do not want to live up to the standards of behaviour expected from a returned migrant. Study of a society cannot only be based on proverbs, but both yijin huanxiang and jinyi yexing neatly express the behaviour expected from migrants.

I happened to observe the funeral rite for an overseas Chinese dependent (qiaojuan) in Rui'an. The deceased was the seventy year old head of a family. Two of his sons and their families had emigrated to France and set up a restaurant and a leather workshop there. The funeral rites began early in the morning, in the centre of the village. Almost all villagers, around one thousand, had come to pay their last respects. Then hundreds of people accompanied the coffin to the tomb built on a mountain. When I saw the tomb, I almost could not believe my eyes! In order to protect the coffin, a crypt of around 30 square meters had been dug out. Outside the crypt, stones had been removed and a garden laid out. Moreover, around the tomb a wall had been built in the style of the Great Wall. Having enjoyed free cakes, cigarettes and drinks, all villagers followed the family members back to the village. There a big free banquet began of altogether seventy tables (each table for about ten persons). Something even more incredible happened at the middle of the banquet: one of the sons of the deceased walked from table to table distributing 100 yuan notes to all guests. "You should get wages for having dinner here", I was told. Then, some packed food and whole boxes of cigarettes were distributed, regardless of whether you wanted any, and regardless of whether you smoked. "If you don't accept it, the host will be angry", I was warned. Afterwards I calculated the expenditure. I believe such a funeral must have cost at least 200,000 yuan, excluding the construction of the tomb. All the guests admired the ostentatious funeral:[23]

It's a great honour for the dead and his family.

This was not the best one. You know, last year another family had a death. They have five sons in Europe. They had held a funeral banquet with nearly 100 tables. Of course, the more tables offered, the richer the family and the higher the status of this family in the village.

I dare not mention any funeral of mine. I have no son in Europe. I cannot expect my sons to hold such an honourable funeral for me. Such a funeral can only be held by families with rich sons in Europe.

Nowadays in Wenzhou spacious houses and large family tombs can be seen in the suburbs and countryside, many belonging to migrants in Europe. Some huge houses have been closed since they were finished, or used only once every while when the owner comes back for a visit.[24] Tombs have been prepared even for family members born abroad and at present still being children. Migrants and local villagers alike consider large houses and lavishly decorated tombs the attributes of wealth and social status.

However, few have seriously thought about how much those migrants and their families have suffered. One interviewed returned migrant told me his own story:[25]

My sister is in the Netherlands. She went there soon after she married. Her husband's family is there. I wanted to go to Holland and I kept asking my sister for help. At last, in 1984, I was able to go to Holland with a tourist visa. The second day I arrived there, I began to work in a Chinese restaurant, as a cleaner. After three months, my visa expired and I became an illegal worker there. However, I had very clearly decided that I went there just for earning money. So I worked very hard. I was in Holland for eight years, from 1984 to 1992. It was a very hard time! I went to work every day, regardless of how tired or how sick I was. No free weekend. No holiday. In order to save money, I ate and slept in the restaurant,[26] and bought nothing for myself, no new clothes, no new shoes, not even socks. I just wore any used clothes given by my sister and my boss. I didn't see my wife and two sons for eight years (...) Once I heard from a newcomer that my wife was having an affair with a man whom I knew, and I was very angry! Having heard the gossip, my boss brought me to a prostitute. It was the first time that I went to that kind of dirty place. I thought I will take my revenge on my wife. But my heart ached when I paid seventy-five guilders to that prostitute. Seventy-five guilders, in my home village, would be enough money to buy food for a family for one month. I made a rigorous decision that I would never again waste money on such stupid things (...) I had been a crazy hard-working guy in Holland until 1992, when I discovered that the guilders I had saved could be changed to 700,000 yuan. I was very happy and I suddenly felt completely exhausted. The money would be enough for the rest of my life in the village. Meanwhile, I could see no prospects of getting a residence permit in Holland. I decided to return home (...) From that amount of money, I spent 200,000 yuan to buy this five-storey house and moving my family from our village to this town. I have spent another 200,000 yuan to rebuild my family tomb. Yes, I am about fifty years old now, but I have built tombs not only for my parents, who are in their seventies, but for myself and my wife as well. I have deposited the remaining money in several private bank accounts[27] and receive interest every month. Now every day is a holiday for me. I just enjoy life and am doing nothing else. The work I have done in those eight years is more than enough for all my life (...) (Showing me his hands with scars of burns and cuts from working in restaurants) Who here would know how pitiable I was in Holland. Here I am just a lucky and rich man![28]

It is true. What his fellow villagers like to talk about is the visible result: another "rich migrant" has come back, raising the social status of his family overnight.

It is apparent that the influence of conspicuous consumption in qiaoxiang is wide and deep: migrants who engage in conspicuous consumption "not only derive gratification from the direct consumption but also from the heightened status reflected in the attitudes and opinions of others who observe their consumption" (Veblen 1928:32). Local villagers without overseas Chinese ties very openly show resentment of their position as well as eagerness to become like those lucky migrants, who were ordinary villagers until recently.

"He [a migrant who has donated some money to build a school in his hometown] is not an intelligent person, but he is lucky. If I have a chance to go abroad, I can be as rich as him, and maybe even richer."

"If I have a chance to earn money abroad, I will be more generous with my money than any of them [those returned migrants]."

Villagers, especially the younger generation, take migrants as their reference group. To work in their home village or in a township industry is not what they want, although thousands and thousands of people from inland China have come to Wenzhou to grasp the new employment opportunities. In the minds of many people in Wenzhou qiaoxiang, to get rich in Europe is a special opportunity for Wenzhou qiaoxiang people, so the employment possibilities near at hand tend to be disregarded. In well-known qiaoxiang such as Li'ao and Yuhu, a family that sends one more member abroad, either legally or illegally, will receive congratulations from outsiders. If one family has nobody in Europe, its members will be ashamed of themselves for lacking in resourcefulness (*mei benshi*); if someone has a chance but does not want to go abroad, she or he will be derided as "lazy" or "strange." The more qinpeng haoyou migrants have helped emigrate, the higher the respect will be that they get from their home community. Migrants are proud of their contribution to chain migration, although many complain about the heavy financial burden of meeting the requests for assistance from their home community.

Conclusion

According to postmodern theorists, "the circulation of people, goods, and ideas creates a new transnational culture that combines values, behaviour, and attitudes from sending and receiving societies to create a new, largely autonomous social space that transcends national boundaries. This transnationalization of culture changes the context within which migration decisions are made" (Massey et al. 1994:737). In Wenzhou qiaoxiang, a "culture of migration" has emerged that is distinct from the culture of surrounding areas. As qiaoxiang people, they are proud of their close connections with rich Europe. They believe "getting rich in Europe" is their common destination. They ignore how few of their peers in Europe can really be considered successful and how hard life really is for many migrants. People in Wenzhou are impressed by the conspicuous consumption of returned migrants and the remittances that are received by the families of migrants. The belief that every migrant is or can be a millionaire has been created, and migrants in Europe are widely admired and taken as a reference group. In such an environment chain migration cannot completely be stopped soon, despite the many opportunities that the booming Wenzhou economy offers and the tighter control of migration exercised by the European and Chinese governments.

References

Carchedi, Francesco and Marica Ferri. 1998. "The Chinese Presence in Italy: Dimensions and Structural Characteristics". In Gregor Benton and Frank N. Pieke, eds, *The Chinese in Europe*. Basingstoke: Macmillan, pp. 261–77.

Chen Xuewen, ed. 1991. *Zhejiangsheng Huaqiao Lishi Yanjiu Luncong* [Collected essays on the history of the overseas Chinese from Zhejiang]. n.p.

Fei Xiaotong. 1992a. "Wenzhou Xing" [Visit to Wenzhou]. In *Xingxing Chong Xingxing: Xiangzhen Fazhan Lunshu* [Travels: On rural development]. Lanzhou: Gansu Renmin Chubanshe, pp. 274–90 (originally written in 1986).

Fei Xiaotong. 1992b. *From the Soil: The Foundations of Chinese Society.* A Translation of Fei Xiaotong's *Xiangtu Zhongguo.* Translated by Gary G. Hamilton and Wang Zheng. Berkeley: University of California Press.

Kipnis, Andrew B. 1997. *Producing Guanxi: Sentiment, Self, and Subculture in a North China Village.* Durham: Duke University Press.

Li Haoran. 1996. *Wenzhou Xin Yueqian* [New Development of Wenzhou]. Shanghai: Shanghai Shehui Kexue Chubanshe.

Li Minghuan. 1995. *Dangdai Haiwai Huaren Shetuan Yanjiu* [A study on Chinese associations abroad]. Xiamen: Xiamen Daxue Chubanshe.

Li Minghuan. 1998. "Transnational Links among the Chinese in Europe: A Study on European-Wide Chinese Voluntary Associations." In Gregor Benton and Frank N. Pieke, eds, *The Chinese in Europe.* Basingstoke: Macmillan, pp. 21–41.

Massey, Douglas S., Joaquin Arango, Graeme Hugo, Ali Kouaouci, Adela Pellegrino and J. Edward Taylor. 1994. "An Evaluation of International Migration Theory: The North American Case." *Population and Development Review* 20, no. 4, pp. 699–751.

Merton, Robert K. and Alice S. Kitt. 1950. "Contributions to the Theory of Reference Group Behavior." In Robert K. Merton & Paul F. Lazarsfeld, eds. *Continuities in Social Research: Studies in the Scope and Method of "the American Soldier."* Glencoe, Illinios: Free Press, pp. 40–105.

Merton, Robert K. 1968. *Social Theory and Social Structure.* New York: The Free Press; London: Collier-Macmillan.

Montanari, Armando and Antonio Cortese. 1993. "Third World Immigrants in Italy." In Russell King, ed. *Mass Migrations in Europe: The Legacy and the Future.* London: Belhaven Press, pp. 275–91.

Nolan, Peter and Dong Furen, eds. 1990. *Market Forces in China: Competition and Small Business – The Wenzhou Debate.* London: Zed Books.

Renmufumeizi [Niki Fumiko]. 1995. "Xuyan" [Preface]. In Wenzhoushi Zhengxie Wenshi Ziliao Weiyuanhui and Zhejiangsheng Zhengxie Wenshi Ziliao Weiyuan-hui, eds, *Dongying Chenyuan: Riben Guandong Dadizhen Chansha Huagong An* [A gross injustice in Japan: The massacre of Chinese workers after the Kanto earthquake in Japan]. Hangzhou: Zhejiang Renmin Chubanshe, pp. 1–2.

Rex, John & Beatrice Drury. 1994. *Ethnic Mobilisation in a Multi-Cultural Europe.* Aldershot: Avebury.

Stark, Oded. 1991. *The Migration of Labour.* Cambridge: Basil Blackwell.

Thomas, William L. & Florian Znaniecki; edited and abridged by Eli Zaretsky. 1984[1918–1920]. *The Polish Peasant in Europe and America.* Urbana & Chicago: University of Illinois Press.

Thompson, Paul. 1994. "Preface." In Rina Benmayor & Andor Skotnes, eds, *Migration and Identity.* New York: Oxford University Press, pp. v–vi.

Veblen, Thorstein. 1928. *The Theory of the Leisure Class,* New York: Vanguard Press.

Veraart, Jan. 1993. "Young Turks in the Dutch labour market." In Hans Entzinger, Jacques Siegers and Frits Tazelaar, eds, *Immigrant Ethnic Minorities in the Dutch Labour Market: Analyses and Politics.* Amsterdam: Thesis Publishers, pp. 71–92.

Vos, Jan, "Illegal Migrants in the Dutch Labour Market". In Hans Entzinger, Jacques Siegers and Frits Tazelaar, eds, 1993. *Immigrant Ethnic Minorities in the Dutch Labour Market: Analyses and Politics.* Amsterdam: Thesis Publishers, pp. 93–114.

Wang Zhongming, ed. 1985. *Wencheng Huaqiao Lishi Ziliao (1905–1984)* [Historical documents on Wencheng migrants abroad (1905–1984)]. Unofficial publication.

Wenchengxian Tongji Ju, ed. 1995. *Wencheng Tongji Nianjian (1994)* [Statistical yearbook of Wencheng county (1994)]. n.p.

Wenzhoushi Tongji Ju, ed. 1995. *Wenzhou Tongji Nianjian (1995)* [Statistical yearbook of Wenzhou (1995)]. n.p.

Williams, Robin M. 1976. "Relative Deprivation." In Lewis A. Coser, ed. 1976. *The Idea of Social Structure: Papers in Honor of Robert K. Merton.* New York: Harcourt Brace Jovanovich, pp. 355–78.

Yan Xinli. 1995. "Guandong Dadizhen Shi dui LüRi Huagongde Tusha" [Massacre of Chinese workers in Japan at the time of the Kanto earthquake]. In Wenzhoushi Zhengxie Wenshi Ziliao Weiyuanhui and Zhejiangsheng Zhengxie Wenshi Ziliao Weiyuanhui, eds, *Dongying Chenyuan, Riben Guandong Dadizhen Chansha Huagong An* [A gross injustice in Japan, the massacre of Chinese workers after the Kanto earthquake in Japan]. Hangzhou: Zhejiang Renmin Chubanshe, pp. 20–30.

Yan, Yunxiang. 1996. *The Flow of Gifts: Reciprocity and Social Networks in a Chinese Village.* Stanford: Stanford University Press.

Yang, Mayfair May-hui. 1994. *Gifts, Favors & Banquets: The Art of Social Relationships in China.* Ithaca, N.Y.: Cornell University Press.

Zhang Zhicheng. 1987. "Rui'anshi Li'aozhen Huaqiao Lishi yu Xianzhuang" [Historical profile and contemporary situation of Rui'an Li'ao migrants abroad]. In Zhejiangsheng Qiaoshi Yanjiushi, ed. *Zhejiang Huaqiao Shiliao (1987)* [Historical documents on Zhejiang migrants abroad (1987)]. Unofficial publication, pp. 31–61.

Zhang Zhicheng. 1991. "Wenzhou Huaqiao Lishi Jiankuang" [A brief overview of the history of the overseas Chinese from Wenzhou]. In Wenzhoushi Zhengxie Wenshi Ziliao Weiyuanhui, ed. *Wenzhou Wenshi Ziliao* [Historical documents of Wenzhou]. N.p., Zhejiangsheng Xinwen Chubanju.

Zhang Zhicheng. 1995. "Ershi niandai Wenchu Shannong Dongdu Riben Mousheng Gaikuang" [An overview of how peasants from the mountains of Wenzhou region went east, crossing the sea to make a living in Japan during the 1920s]. In Wenzhoushi Zhengxie Wenshi Ziliao Weiyuanhui and Zhejiangsheng Zhengxie Wenshi Ziliao Weiyuanhui, eds. *Dongying Chenyuan, Riben Guandong Dadizhen Chansha Huagong An* [A gross injustice in Japan, the massacre of Chinese workers after the Kanto earthquake in Japan]. Hangzhou: Zhejiang Renmin Chubanshe, pp. 1–12.

Zhang Zhicheng, Wang Zhongming & Shao Muxi. 1987. "Wenchengxian Huaqiao Jianshi." [A brief history of the overseas Chinese from Wencheng county]. In Zhejiangsheng Qiaoshi Yanjiushi, ed. *Zhejiang Huaqiao Shiliao (1987)* [Historical documents on Zhejiang migrants abroad (1987)]. Unofficial publication, pp. 11–30.

Zinn, Dorothy Louise. 1994. "The Senegalese Immigrants in Bari: What Happens When the Africans Peer Back." In Rina Benmayor & Andor Skotnes, eds, *Migration and Identity.* New York: Oxford University Press, pp. 53–68.

Notes

1 Fieldwork was supported by WOTRO (The Netherlands Foundation for the Advancement of Tropical Research) and CASA (Centre for Asian Studies Amsterdam).

2 The Chinese government is organized in five hierarchical levels: country (*guojia*), province (*sheng*), prefecture (*diqu*), county (*xian*, in rural areas) or urban district (*qu*, in urban areas), and lastly township (*xiang*, in rural areas) or street (*jiedao*, in urban areas). What complicates this reasonably straightforward picture is the fact that sufficiently urbanized rural units at each level (except for the national level) are given "city" or "municipal" (*shi*) status. Hence the existence of "county level cities/municipalities" (*xianji shi*) such as Rui'an, which should not be confused with districts (*qu*) which are at the same administrative level, namely the county, but are urban areas located within cities. Confusingly, at the lowest level of the township (xiang), such a city status is indicated by suffixing zhen (town) rather than shi (city) to the place name, i.e. Li'ao zhen rather than Li'ao shi.

3 The interviewees I selected fell mainly into three groups:
26 *Guiqiao*: Returned overseas Chinese. Twenty-three have returned from the Netherlands, two from France and one from Italy. Some of them have permanently settled in their hometown while others are paying a long visit there.
21 *Qiaojuan*: Overseas Chinese dependents, i.e. people with direct family members or close relatives abroad. These relatives of my informants mostly lived in the Netherlands, Italy, or France.
10 *Qiaowu ganbu*: Local officials in charge of overseas Chinese affairs (*Qiaowu*).

4 A *mu* is a unit of land equivalent to one-sixth of a acre or 0.0667 hectares.

5 Interview in Wenzhou on 28 January 1996 with Mr. Zhang Zhicheng, historian and editor of the Wenzhou local gazetteer (*Wenzhou difangzhi*). The figures he gave me were quoted from an unofficial publication.

6 For further details of the history Wenzhou emigration to Europe, please consult Mette Thunø's article in this book.

7 In Li'ao, for instance, only eleven people went abroad between 1950 and 1960, according to figures collected by local cadres in charge of overseas Chinese affairs in the course of a door-to-door survey. In the 1960s, emigration to Europe was less than ten per year. In 1966, there were only two emigrants; in 1967, five; in 1969, only one. Beginning in 1971, the numbers rose somewhat (14 in 1971; 18 in 1972; 8 in 1973; 21 in 1974; 10 in 1975). In 1976, the figure jumped to thirty-eight; in 1979, it increased to forty-four, reaching 144 in 1980 (Zhang 1991:35–37).

8 Interview with a cadre for overseas Chinese affairs in Li'ao, 2 February 1996.

9 Interview with Lishan villagers, 7 February 1996.

10 The whole poem is as follows: "Going from one village to another village, every village seems like a city; Going from one city to another city, every city seems like a village; Going from one mountain to another mountain, every mountain is full of tombs." I was told that the first sentence praised the rural urbanization of Wenzhou, the second one criticized the fact that all cities in Wenzhou are too dirty, while the third one criticized Wenzhou people, who spend too much money and use too much land to build their ancestors' tombs.

11 Interview with Mr. H., around thirty-five years old, a woodworker living in Yuhu, married, having one daughter and one son, 10 February 1996.

12 In China, applying for a passport is the first step to emigration, and one needs to go through many official procedures.

13 See also Table 9.2. Naturally, for illegal migrants wages will be much lower, around 1,500 guilders (500 pound sterling) for a cook and 800 guilders (270 pounds) per month for a waiter or waitress. Still, these wages are incomparable to the incomes in the migrants' hometowns, especially for migrants without a family in Europe, who can live for free in the restaurant where they work.

14 According to my informants, the cooks in European Chinese restaurants will usually be divided into three levels, *Dachu* (the chief cook); *Erchu* (the second

cook) and *Sanchu* (the assistant cook). Neither *Erchu* nor *Sanchu* work demands any special cooking skills, and even *Dachu* work can be learned on the job. I believe this is the normal situation in most small size and some medium size Chinese restaurants in Europe. In big Chinese restaurants, only *Dachu* with proper qualifications will be employed.

15 *Guanxi* is a popular Chinese term which means having special connections (see Kipnis 1997; Yunxiang Yan 1996; Yang 1994)

16 It was said that the travel to Japan would cost only 15.4 silver dollars, whereas several hundred dollars were required for travel to the other two areas (Shen Bao 7 July 1923); interview with Zhang Zhicheng on 27 January 1996 in Wenzhou; interview with Hu Kelin on 28 January 1996 in Rui'an; interview with Yu Xinchou, an eighty year old returned emigrant who holds a Singapore passport with a permanent residence permit for the Netherlands, on 15 February 1996 in Wenzhou; interview with Lin Changnai, also eighty years old and holder of a Chinese passport with a permanent residence permit for the Netherlands, 12 February 1996, in Yuhu.

17 Interview with Hu Yundi, eighty-one years old, 11 February 1996 in Yuhu.

18 Interview with Cai Zhengshen, sixty-five years old, 5 February 1996 in Rui'an.

19 Interview with Lishan villagers, 7 February 1996.

20 Interview with Lishan villagers, 7 February 1996. Although the Netherlands did not adopt a regularization law in the 1990s, Spain and Portugal have done so.

21 Quoted from my fieldwork log.

22 The term "conspicuous consumption" was coined by Thorstein Veblen in *The Theory of the Leisure Class* (1928). The leisure class experiences pride in "wasteful" expenditures since wealth, in turn, is honorific. For them, the consumption of goods is its symbolization of "pecuniary strength and so of gaining or retaining a good name," and "it results in a heightening or reaffirmation of social status" (Merton 1968:123). Migrants' "conspicuous consumption" in their hometown reveals their similarity to Veblen's "leisure class."

23 Quoted from my fieldwork log, 31 January 1996.

24 Usually there are no daily necessities of life, television set, or telephone line in those houses, which remain unused after having been built. Thus, when the owners come back for a short visit, they often feel uncomfortable to live in their own house and some prefer to live in a hotel and only come down to have a look at their houses.

25 Interview with Mr. Zhang Juhao, a returned migrant from the Netherlands of approximately fifty years old, on 1 February 1996 in Rui'an.

26 It is a common custom in Dutch Chinese restaurants to offer free accommodation in the restaurant. Employees who want their own house have to pay for it themselves.

27 In China, all banks are state owned except some branches of foreign banks. However, during my research in Wenzhou, I discovered that private banks (*qianzhuang*) are rather active there. The interest rate paid by qianzhuang on personal savings is higher than that paid by state owned banks (see also Xiang, this volume).

28 I met this interviewee first at the small hotel where I stayed. "How can you accept such a hotel? It's too bad, too simple." Then he suggested that I visit his new house, insisting that we take a rickshaw rather than walk. His house was well decorated and furnished. Sitting in a comfortable sofa chatting with me, he gave "working orders" to his wife in rapid succession. "She once did something wrong to me but I have forgiven her after I came back; now, you see, she is completely under my control," he concluded.

Chapter Ten

Patterns of migration from Zhejiang to Germany

Karsten Giese

Introduction

From the mid-1980s onward, Europe has experienced a strong inflow of Chinese nationals, immigrating either legally or, increasingly, illegally. This upswing in irregular migration is hardly surprising in the light of the increasingly restrictive immigration regimes in most European countries.

In 1987, the German authorities for the first time acknowledged the increase in irregular migration. Especially after the fall of the communist regimes in Eastern Europe in 1989 and 1990, the number of Chinese irregular migrants, travelling to Germany through Eastern Europe, has risen considerably, slightly dropping off again only in the mid-1990s.[1] In addition, Germany is a prime transit country for migrants destined for other western European states or North America (Grenzschutzdirektion 1994:31–5). Further travel from Germany has the great advantage that in case of apprehension illegal immigrants are sent back to Germany, where they can apply for asylum and again try to reach the Golden Mountain (Grenzschutzdirektion 1994:12, 18–9).

Statistical data collected mainly by prosecuting organs since 1992 reveal that on average 370 Chinese smuggled into Germany are apprehended every year. This is small compared to other nationalities, while the number remains relatively steady. But the German authorities believe this does not adequately reflect the extent of actual irregular Chinese immigration. Rather, the small number is a telling comment on the effective reception of Chinese immigrants in firmly established structures and the strict organization of human trafficking between China and Europe (Grenzschutzstelle 1993:14; Grenzschutzdirektion 1994:31–5).[2]

It is known to German authorities that irregular immigration is controlled mostly by Chinese restaurants in Germany and other European countries. New immigrants find employment with those restaurants, whose managers often pay the costs of immigration. It is assumed, therefore, that until the mid 1990s almost all Chinese smuggled into Germany were at least for a certain period employed by Chinese restaurants (Bundeskriminalamt 1991:11–2; Grenzschutzdirektion 1994:24–7; Grenzschutzstelle 1994:6–8). Irregular immigrants in Germany mainly come from the county-level regions of Wencheng, Qingtian or Lishui in Zhejiang province (see Thunø, this volume and Li, this volume).[3]

In this chapter I will discuss the patterns of regular and irregular immigration from these regions in Zhejiang, drawing on a great variety of informal information provided by either immigrants themselves or German prosecuting organs. I shall do this by accompanying a typical migrant on his way from Zhejiang to Germany.

You never know for sure: Questions of sources and methods

Like any study on irregular migration, this chapter faces the almost insuperable difficulty of describing something which exists by virtue of its ability to avoid official detection: not without reason do English language sources often refer to "undocumented migrants"! Equally worrying is the fact that the main providers of information are prosecuting organs and the judiciary. In Bourdieu's words:

> So long as you take it as you find it, as it presents itself, the social world offers ready-made data, statistics, discourses that can easily be recorded, and so on. In a word, when you question it as it asks to be questioned, it has a great deal to say for itself, it tells you whatever you want to know, it gives you figures... (Bourdieu 1991:249–50).

But what if we have to ask different questions? This study will try to find a way out of this dilemma by making use of information given by the parties involved, that is both by those willing to give testimony and those normally not willing to do so. Sources of German prosecuting organs will be combined with the impressions gained from the author's numerous conversations with the otherwise silent immigrants and traffickers themselves.[4]

Let us now accompany the immigrants on their long road to the land of milk and honey.

At home

The decision to emigrate is to a great extent influenced by the information available about migration routes, organization and the conditions in the places of destination. The nature and sources of this information are therefore of paramount importance.

It is only very occasionally that media in China serve as an important source of information for potential migrants, but if they do, the picture drawn is generally very biased, exaggerated and distorted. Much more important is information from other (potential) migrants, their families and *shetou* ("snakeheads," human traffickers). Before departure, several routes and methods of emigration are intensely discussed, sometimes for a couple of weeks, sometimes for as long as several years. This nevertheless is not a completely rational process, and the information gathered, especially from friends or relatives, often gives a very distorted picture of reality. It is, to give just one example, very common for potential migrants to believe that money can solve all the problems one normally faces when trying to obtain visas or residence permits. Rumours are often spread that money given as a gift to officials in foreign embassies and consulates will automatically produce the desired visa. While corruption does indeed exist in embassies and consulates (see below), the "sale" of visas remains exceptional and is by no means normal.

Friends and relatives abroad and at home are – or are believed to be – very well informed about the possibilities of entry, legal residence and life and work at the destination. Migrants already residing in the country of destination play a decisive part here. This information is often very subjective, depicting not reality but these migrants' perceptions.

Opinions and information are exchanged primarily in letters, but long distance telephone calls seem to be very common as well. This flow of information runs in both directions. Irregular migrants abroad, for example, are repeatedly provided with information and suggestions gathered from various sources by their kin in China to help them sort out their residence problems. Here again the possibility to use money to solve all legal problems connected with residence permits is the main subject.

Negative aspects of migration very often seem to be ignored. Returned migrants seldom admit to having failed abroad. Failure abroad generally is taboo and when discussed by potential migrants, is normally assigned to individual shortcomings of those who had failed; possible structural reasons behind individual failures are rarely investigated.

Though general living conditions in the Zhejiang home communities might be low compared to the richest areas in China, migrants are by no means poor. This is actually not surprising, because money is the most important prerequisite for international migration (for further information see below and Li, this volume). There is often no other urgent reason for emigration than a general lack of economic opportunities. In general, neither the privileged top earners nor the underprivileged poor are the first to emigrate. Most emigrants are drawn from a middle group with certain financial possibilities, who are aware of their own limits in China.[5] But potential migrants do not come from a single class, and can include both the son of a peasant and the daughter of a university professor. Chinese officials, too, are not immune either to the temptations of the western world and consider emigration an acceptable strategy for their own offspring.[6]

Certain other restrictions of life in the People's Republic of China (PRC) also induce people to become migrants. One of these reasons, though certainly not the main or only motivation, is the birth control policy pursued by the Chinese government.

When talking to immigrants one fact very quickly becomes clear. If one member of a family emigrates, there will soon be many other candidates for migration, so that the migrant abroad – irrespective of whether he or she is an irregular or a legal one – is under increasing pressure to help bring other members of the family over as well.

The vast majority of Chinese irregular immigrants in Germany are men of between twenty to forty years of age. Most of them originate from rural or suburban areas in Qingtian. Their income back home was normally quite limited, whereas the desire for consumption drastically increased during the reform period. Their level of education is only average, and in most cases they did not obtain any institutionalized vocational training (Grenzschutzdirektion 1994:16).

The organization of migration is managed mainly within networks of kin. Kinsmen who are established migrants in countries of destination are very often asked for assistance. In the case of more distant kin, the relationship may be close enough to have a solid base of confidence, while there is also sufficient distance to make it possible to demand adequate pay for the service offered. In those cases where the organization of irregular migration is not handled by relatives or acquaintances, lack of trust is often prevailing.

Even in cases where human traffickers and migrants know one another or are members of the same extended family, trafficking is not free of charge. To meet the migrant's need to safeguard himself against the loss of the very large sum involved, shetou prepare contracts that give detailed information on the entire operation. These contracts normally list the costs for the migrants at all stages of the migration as well as the services the shetou will offer. Generally, the shetou demands a first instalment of several thousand yuan for preparations (e.g. passports and other documents needed for leaving China). The total sum involved is 60,000 to 120,000 yuan, the first half to be paid before leaving China, the rest upon the migrant's arrival at the destination.

Even if the actual planning and organization of the migration is not taken charge of by the family, they all take an active interest in every single case. Everyone makes a financial contribution to the migration in accordance with their means and the distance of the relationship. Sometimes only a symbolic contribution like a fish or vegetables for the farewell banquet is made; in other cases, loans, not gifts are given. Migrants themselves take these contributions very seriously and generally keep good records of them. The concept of *renqing* (favour; relationship) or *mai renqing* (to buy a favour) is very central; a favour received has to be returned in the future.

Yet contributions alone are often not enough and families very often become heavily indebted to loan sharks in order to finance the emigration of a member. Reports by migrants and information obtained by the investigating authorities in Germany indicate that the local Chinese authorities involved, such as the work unit, are becoming more reluctant to give the permission needed for an application for a passport or exit visa. On the other hand, the issuance of such permits can be a lucrative source of additional earnings for corrupt officials (Grenzschutzdirektion 1994:8).

Migration plans rarely fail because of a lack of cooperation from the Chinese passport authorities, who are only one of the many hurdles that emigrants have to overcome before they can leave the country. Several authorities are involved in the procedure of the application for a passport: the many different statements, certificates of conduct and recommendations needed provide ample opportunity to squeeze money out of the emigrants. Not least the work units, now responsible for their losses and gains under the responsibility system, find facilitating the emigration of their members a lucrative source of income. In view of these many obstructions, emigrants frequently decide to take the risk and simply leave without the required papers.

On the road

A distinction has to be made between legal, semilegal and illegal migrants, since their migration is organized differently and they travel along different routes. Only a few ways to gain legal entry into Germany are left now for citizens of the PRC. In the mid-1980s, extensive use was made of all possibilities of family reunion. As a result, the relevant regulations have now been tightened and investigations in cases of applications are much more thorough. Generally speaking, legal entry is by now only granted to students, members of delegations, tourists, relatives on family visits and, lastly, three-year work permits are issued for Chinese speciality cooks.[7] All these (quasi) legal ways are made use of by individual irregular migrants and professional traffickers alike.

The easiest way to leave the PRC is through relatives in Hong Kong. Migrants will have to overcome several obstacles in the PRC itself, but normally it is easy to get a seven-day visa for visiting relatives in Hong Kong. Chinese tourists in Hong Kong are also given seven days to continue their travels to a third country, for which they must have a ticket and a valid visa when leaving the PRC. This opens the door to legal visits to Vietnam or Kampuchea, which require no visa, and Thailand, North Korea, or South Korea, for which visas visas are easily obtained (Grenzschutzdirektion 1994:24; Grenzschutzstelle 1994:6–7; Conversations with members of the Anti Illegal Immigration Centre of the Royal Hong Kong Police in 1995).

Prague in the Czech Republic also occupies a special position. There is almost no control at its border to Slovakia, making the Czech Republic a natural centre of human trafficking to neighbouring Germany and further afield into western Europe. The Czech Republic moreover issued permanent residence permits to Chinese who established a limited liability company with only an equivalent to 6,400 German marks in common stock. Such firms were often empty shells through which a continuous stream of new "partners" in the business were brought over from China.[8] Estimates are that, in the early 1990s, up to twenty people a day came to Prague alone (Grenzschutzdirektion 1994:29–30).

Other migrants leave the PRC for Hungary, Ukraine, Tadzhikistan, Mongolia, or Russia as traders. Vladivostok usually is the first destination for people who leave by train through northern China. Local border traffic, now flourishing along all of China's borders, moreover offers a wide range of possibilities for quasi-legal exit of potential emigrants.

Migrants with passports often directly fly from Beijing to Moscow or from Kunming to Bangkok. Ninety per cent of Chinese migrants who were asked by the Federal Office for the Assessment of Foreigners Seeking Asylum in Germany admitted that they had come directly to Moscow by train or plane. A great number of direct flights of small groups of Chinese (consisting of two to six persons) from Beijing to Berlin-Schönefeld (and other destinations in Germany) took place in 1992 and 1993. According to the German border authorities, those attempts were the results of either less careful control in Beijing or increasing corruption of the Chinese authorities. After control had been tightened in Berlin and several migrants had been denied entry despite their possession of a visa, the route lost some of its importance (Grenzschutzdirektion 1994:13–6).

Migrants without any valid documents often cross the border with the successor states of the Soviet Union. Everywhere in China, from Manchuria in the Northeast to Xinjiang in the far West, Chinese are illegally crossing the borders. The region in the extreme Northeast seems to be frequented most often. Many irregular migrants go on foot or hide in trucks, presenting forged papers, bribes, or both to the local border officials to get to Vladivostok, whence they take a transsiberian train to Moscow or Ukraine.

Another important alternative is to leave China from Yunnan in the Southwest, going first to Thailand or Mianmar and from there to Ukraine or Moscow. Three ways of illegal exit are known. Small groups travel from Kunming in Yunnan on foot, riding bicycles, or with the help of border officials to northern Thailand. This journey takes about twenty-four days. Far away from the main roads, large groups of up to 200 people are smuggled through the jungle to Mianmar and from there to Thailand. The third alternative is by boat down the Mekong river through Mianmar and from there on to Thailand.

There are two factors that determine the selection of method: the price the migrant can pay and the choice of trafficking organization (currently at least four are known to exist in Southeast Asia). Leaving the country by one of the above routes seems practically unthinkable without involving such an organization (Grenzschutzdirektion 1994:20–2).

Some very few migrants reported to have left China via Tibet for Nepal. It is, however, difficult to ascertain how relevant this route is, all the more since the Chinese security organs closely monitor developments in Tibet.

In general, Moscow is the first important stopover on the way to the West. Migrants often stay in Moscow for several months, living in private flats that have been converted into boarding houses. It is unclear whether this is to await a favourable moment for illegal onward travel, or simply another additional source of income for the shetou.

The main route leads through Ukraine, Slovakia and finally Prague, where the migrants again may have to stay for a longer period. Interrogations of immigrants revealed that eighty per cent travel from Moscow by train, ten per cent by bus, six per cent by private car and only four per cent by plane.

Migrants report that the traffickers who accompany them between Moscow and Prague receive expenses amounting to about 200 US dollars per person as well as a single payment of 4,000 dollars as remuneration (Grenzschutzdirektion 1994:27–9).

If the migrants leave for Thailand, Bangkok will be their first main destination, and local travel agencies will play an important part in organizing their onward travel. Sometimes migrants stay in Bangkok or elsewhere in Southeast Asia for several months. Some migrants reported very long stays, for instance in Singapore, where they were given jobs to finance the remaining part of their journey.

Normally travel will be continued from Bangkok by air. Every migrant is reportedly provided with up to four different passports, for which he or she has to pay 5,000–7,000 dollars. In most cases Prague will be the next destination. After their arrival there the passports are sent back to Asia for use by other migrants. The migrants are subsequently provided with other forged, or sometimes even genuine "borrowed" passports for the border crossing into Germany (Grenzschutzstelle 1994:4–5).

The final main route starts off in Hong Kong. A first alternative sets the migrants off on a fictive tour to Frankfurt and Prague and then back to Hong Kong, or to London, Copenhagen and Riga back to Hong Kong. In most cases, they only have visas for the Czech Republic or Latvia, where the circular tour is cut short and the migrants have their unused flights refunded. In this operation, Hong Kong travel agencies do the main organizational work. From Riga the migrants are smuggled to Germany or Scandinavia either through Poland or the Czech Republic, or directly across the Baltic Sea.

The second alternative from Hong Kong is to leave for a Southeast Asian country using one's real Chinese passport. Upon arrival in Thailand or Singapore, these genuine passports are exchanged for forged Southeast Asian passports that are used to enter Germany on a business trip or a visit of a fair or relatives.

At the beginning of the 1990s, the German Federal Border Police noticed that a great number of visas for visits to relatives had been issued by the German Consulate in Shanghai. Clearly, the Shanghai Consulate handled the procedures in a more generous way than the German Embassy in Beijing, a fact which potential migrants obviously had been quick to catch on to. Especially during checks at airports officials noticed that these Chinese, who ostensibly had come for a three month visit to relatives, had sometimes brought along all their household equipment. Upon investigation it transpired not only that visa for visits to relatives were indeed issued corruptly in Shanghai, but that permits for long term stay in Germany were issued illegally in Hamburg and Berlin as well. Obviously only migrants and traffickers from Zhejiang, for which the Consulate in Shanghai is competent, could use this way to obtain visas.[9]

As from the early 1990s, it also became known that irregular migrants first gained legal stay in an eastern European country, and then came to Germany with visitors' visas where they went underground. The possibility of recruiting qualified cooks from China is used by traffickers as well. Certificates attesting due qualification as speciality cook or pursuit of a cook's vocation can simply be bought in the PRC. Blank certificates and obviously forged documents of that kind were on several occasions confiscated by the German Border Police when searching people in the early 1990s.

Illegal entry to Germany is taking place both by air and land. However, most migrants come by land. Thus far, only one or two cases are known of migrants who came by sea. Illegal immigrants coming by air always use forged documents. Those coming overland either cross the border at certain checkpoints with forged documents, or secretly cross the border without any papers.

Migrants who travel with papers often use genuine passports issued by other Asian states that were acquired on the black market or stolen from tourists in Asia. After changing the photograph, those passports are ready for use. Japanese passports are especially popular, since they allow for visa free entry to a great number of foreign countries. Passports from Singapore, Macao, Hong Kong, South Korea, Taiwan, Malaysia, Thailand and Indonesia are also frequently used, as are passports from Latin American countries with a relatively large Asian population, such as Peru. In general, migrants prefer to use passports with old visas for several countries to reduce suspicion. In case the passport does not have any old visas, these are forged as well. After making the appropriate changes, the passports are then used for visa applications with a German mission abroad, and the visas are often granted.

Migrants without real or forged visas or passports with residence permits for eastern European states normally cross the Czech-German border on foot. They are usually driven to a destination near the border, accompanied by guides familiar with the area (often taxi drivers or former border guards), smuggled into Germany by night and then picked up by a car (often with the help of Vietnamese). The same method is used by irregular Chinese immigrants entering from Poland, although their number is much less significant (Grenzschutzstelle 1994:7–8).[10]

The land of milk and honey

Detailed information on the life of immigrants in Germany is hard to obtain. German prosecuting organs are usually not interested in socio-logically relevant data, while the migrants themselves are unwilling to talk. This is mainly due to their fear of punishment by the traffickers, who undoubtedly would be able to get hold of the migrant or his family back in China. The German border police know about detailed interrogations carried out by traffickers of repatriated migrants, especially those who were denied entry by the German border police.

Given the general lack of information, I can only give a bare outline of the migrants' life and work in Germany. Once they arrive in Germany, migrants are first and foremost concerned with making money. Beyond that, life abroad is strange and often difficult.

> I came to Germany with my wife in early June. It is the first time that we are in western Europe. Everything is strange and I do not understand the language. It is rather difficult to handle certain things, and this is even more true if one has no legal residence permit. Thus, many things cannot be attended to at all (Letter from Y.Q. in Germany to Z. in the PRC, 28 July 1992).

The main motivation for migrating to Germany were the very lucrative jobs in the kitchens of Chinese restaurants, where they also get board and lodging. It used to be rather easy to find such a job between 1989 and the early 1990s, but with the saturation of the restaurant market, especially in former East Germany, it has become more and more difficult to find (illegal) employment in this sector.

This leads us to the crucial and often very ambivalent role of one specific person in the life of the migrants: the employer or _laoban_ (boss).

The relationship between migrant and laoban is often problematic, because it is in many cases a kinship relationship, even if only a distant one. The migrants consider themselves indebted to their laoban: thanks to him they have been able to leave China. Yet, facing often severe exploitation by their benefactors, the migrants normally hold very mixed feelings toward their employers. The migrants, without the legal right of abode and normally without any knowledge of the German language, know very well that only the owners of Chinese restaurants are in the position to provide an opportunity for earning a salary.

Even under these marginal conditions, many people are willing to migrate and take a job in a restaurant, providing an inexhaustible supply of cheap and highly motivated labour. Though in many cases it is not the owners of Chinese restaurants who take the first steps to recruit cheap labour in their home country, they, nevertheless, act as facilitators of migration and, as a result of their own success, moreover promote migration.[11] In most cases Chinese who are well-established in Germany or other countries are requested to help in obtaining an exit visa and getting a job for a family member or relative.

People asking the laoban for help in connection with visas or jobs normally moderate their demands from the very beginning, since their own job has two functions. On the one hand, the income is of paramount importance, but on the other hand performance at the job is a return favour for the laoban's act of friendship. Migrants are thus under great moral stress, since they have to repay for the help received by due performance and obedience, even though the work and living conditions entail considerable hardship.

Some privileged migrants seem to be in a better position as they have made written agreements on the conditions of their emigration and employment, such as the following example.

Conditions for X.Y's coming to Germany

1 The residence permit for Germany for Y.X. will be arranged for by X.A. or has already has been obtained. After his arrival in Germany, Y.X. has to work in the restaurant of X. for five years. During this five year period he has to follow all orders of the restaurant owner without contradiction. Q.L. and Y.Z. will vouch for him and furnish a security to the amount of DM 20,000.

2 In case Y.X. arbitrarily leaves the restaurant of X. during the five-year period, or is dismissed by the boss on grounds of disobedience, the amount of DM 20,000 will be considered the pay for the residence permit and not be refunded.

3 At the end of the fifth year, it is up to Y.X. what he does, and X. will help in getting a long term residence permit. In case

> Y.X. is disobedient during the coming five years, X. can withdraw the residence permit at any time.
>
> 4 (...)
> 5 The wage will be DM 500 a month during the first year. In case the government demands that Y.X. goes to school, he gets DM 300 a month. He will get DM 800 in the second year, DM 1,000 in the third, DM 1,500 in the fourth and finally DM 2,000 a month in the fifth year. (Anonymous, PRC, to Y.X., Germany, not dated).

The above example is, no doubt, an exception. This very young migrant is brought over from China to Germany on the basis of a close family relationship, and his position is certainly a privileged one. This does not, however, protect him against exploitation, as can be seen very clearly from the conditions quoted.

It seems that mainly migrants known to the families of restaurant owners are brought over to Germany this way. But this does not often happen out of pure kindness. Even those happy regular Chinese migrants who are able to obtain a mid-term legal stay in Germany as so-called speciality cooks in a Chinese restaurant are by no means immune to exploitation. Chinese employers in Germany charge much for their help. A three year contract as a speciality cook can cost up to 80,000 yuan, and the cook's real wages will be far below those stipulated in the employment contract which was signed only for the purpose of the visa application.

> Bilateral Declaration of Consent to the Employment Contract.
>
> In connection with the employment contract of Mrs Q., restaurant owner, (hereinafter called Side A) with H.J., (...) district, Zhejiang province, to be employed as a cook (hereinafter called Side B) the following declaration is made:
>
> The labour legislation in the Federal Republic of Germany stipulates that a cook's remuneration has to amount to at least DM 2,700 a month. Only then can all applications necessary be made in a legal way and the entry formalities be settled. Therefore, Side A has prepared for Side B a written employment contract based upon the laws of the third country [i.e. Germany]. That was mainly done in the interest of smooth settlement of all formalities. The parties agree, however, that the validity of the contract drawn up in Chinese and in German, shall be limited to the application for the visa and the settlement of the formalities. The parties declare herewith that paragraph 3 shall become void after the formalities have been settled (Q.S. and H.J., contract signed 22 March 1994).

209

Living abroad

After arrival in the imagined land of milk and honey, the migrant very often lives a dual life. His workaday life is confined to the microcosm of the restaurant, while his feelings and concerns reach out to his home and family far away back in China.

Only very few aspects of life abroad are discussed in the correspondence between migrants and their families or friends back home. One soon gets the impression, as one does from conversations, that life in Europe is mainly limited to the narrow world of the Chinese restaurant. The exhaustion from work, the dullness of everyday life and loneliness predominate. After a long working day of ten to twelve hours, the workers sit together with colleagues, have supper, and spend the rest of the time on karaoke or gambling. On the rare days off they stay with acquaintances in other restaurants or lose their hard-earned money in casinos.

In Germany today, the lives of the Chinese migrant workers confined to the kitchens of Chinese restaurants, both regular and irregular, take the same rhythm as those of the "Chinese laundrymen", described by Paul Siu in the US in the 1930s and 1940s:

> Whatever contacts the laundryman has with the general public tend to be impersonal and commercial (...) Only to his fellow Chinese is he a person (...) He is a sojourner, an individual who clings to the heritage of his own ethnic group and lives in isolation.
>
> For the Chinese laundryman, to be able to speak English is something extra rather than necessary (...) He has, in fact, no time, no chance and no facility for learning. He has not the incentive to learn English (...) In leisure time and social events, the Chinese have a world of their own (...) Laundrymen from different laundries visit each other when they are free. A social gathering usually takes place in Mr. Laundryman's shop on Saturday afternoon. But the party seldom lasts long. Unless they sit down an play ma-jong (Siu 1988:137–139).

In Germany in the 1990s there is not much to be added to that. Exploring life outside the sphere of the restaurants is impossible because of language and cultural barriers, lack of knowledge with regard to everyday life in Germany and, especially, the insecure position as an illegal foreigner.

The families back home in China are the main concern of the migrants. This is not surprising also in view of the large sums the families of the migrants paid to finance the migration. Most families understand that the migrants initially cannot give financial support, because they are in a difficult situation in the country of destination. Direct requests for money are rare. But in case remittances fail to come without any clear reason, people at home normally do not hesitate to send a polite reminder to the migrant. In return, the migrants themselves often have a say in the use of their remittances.

Successful migrants often invest, in one way or another, in their home towns and villages. Most commonly, they build luxurious houses for themselves, their parents, or other members of the family. But not only the families ask for remittances. Frequently, a public institution, for instance a school or hospital, expects a contribution from fellow villagers regardless of their legal status in the country of destination.

Migrants do in many other ways participate in the problems of daily life in China, either by letter or by phone. The relatives left behind likewise are involved in the migrants' affairs. The death of a close family member sometimes is withheld from the migrant out of consideration for his or her feelings. Conversely, business difficulties of the family in China are often discussed at length. School grades of children who stay with their mothers or grandparents in China are an important issue regularly reported to the fathers abroad. The family left behind in China is, of course, also taking an active interest in the migrant's life abroad. So it can happen that the family decides upon the most auspicious day for the wedding of a migrant, or even interferes in his choice of a marriage partner.

Some final thoughts

Analyzing documents from investigating authorities in Germany, one gets the impression that immigration and employment only involve triad-like criminal organizations, but conversations with the migrants themselves reveal a different situation. Migration and employment take place in the context of a multiplex network of social relations that includes contractual arrangements with hardened criminals and corrupt officials as much as social ties with family, kin and friends. The boundaries between benevolence and profiteering, mutual assistance and exploitation, and chain migration and human trafficking are fluid and often indistinct; it is only rarely possible to tease them apart.

As ever, the truth lies somewhere in between. Many Chinese businessmen in Europe have discovered that immigration and related services (help in getting a tourist visa or a residence permit by way of bribery, human trafficking, illegal employment) can be very lucrative. On the other hand, relatives and acquaintances in the home districts in China do exert quite considerable pressure on these very same businessmen abroad to help kin leave the country. As has been documented in the chapters by Thunø and Li, a tradition of migration has developed in a few districts of origin in southern Zhejiang in which illegal employment and human trafficking develop almost naturally when necessary to continue a way of life in which international migration is the norm rather than the exception. More broadly, this is also illustrated by the life and work conditions of the migrants in the country of destination. There are many parallels between contemporary Zhejiang migrant life in Germany and Paul Siu's Chinese laundrymen in the USA and Ellen Oxfeld's overseas Chinese communities in India (Oxfeld 1993; Siu 1988). This suggests that the strong cultural and structural connections between migration, life in the home communities and life abroad found for the German Zhejiang migrants are part of a pattern that is much larger than just this case.

References

Bundeskriminalamt. 1991. "Schwerpunktthema: Chinesische Triaden in der Bundesrepublik Deutschland" [Main topic: Chinese triads in the Federal Republic of Germany]. In Bundeskriminalamt, ed. *Wöchentlicher Lagebericht 42/ 1991* [Weekly report number 42, 1991].

Bundeskriminalamt. 1995. "Berechnung Präferenzen der Tatverdächtigen" [Estimate of preferences of suspects] and "Berechnung Tatverdächtigenanteile an den Kriminalitätsbereichen" [Estimate of the shares of suspects in the criminal sphere]. In Bundeskriminalamt, ed. *Lagebild organisierte Kriminalität Bundesrepublik Deutschland 1994* [Report on organized crime in the Federal Republic of Germany 1994]. Wiesbaden.

Bourdieu, Pierre. 1991. "'Meanwhile, I Have Come to Know All the Diseases of Sociological Understanding:' An Interview with Pierre Bourdieu, by Beate Krais." In Pierre Bourdieu, Jean-Claude Chamboredon and Jean-Claude Passeron, *The Craft of Sociology: Epistemological Preliminaries*. Berlin: Walter de Gruyter, pp. 246–59.

Grenzschutzdirektion, Zentralstelle zur Bekämpfung der illegalen Einreise von Ausländer. 1994. *Bericht über die illegale Einreise von Chinesen* [Report on illegal entry of Chinese]. Last update January 1994.

Grenzschutzstelle Flughafen Düsseldorf, Ermittlungsdienst. 1994. *Ermittlungsbericht/Zwischenauswertung Ein- und Durchschleusung chinesischer Staatsangehöriger* [Report on the enquiry into the trafficking of Chinese nationals to and through Germany]. Last update 22 April 1993.

International Organization for Migration. 1998. "Chinese immigrants in Central and Eastern Europe: The Cases of the Czech Republic, Hungary, and Romania." In Gregor Benton and Frank N. Pieke, eds, *The Chinese in Europe*. Basingstoke: Macmillan, pp. 320–49.

Nyíri, Pal. 1998. "New Migrants, New Community: The Chinese in Hungary, 1989–95." In Gregor Benton and Frank N. Pieke, eds, *The Chinese in Europe*. Basingstoke: Macmillan, pp. 350–79.

Oxfeld, Ellen. 1993. *Blood, Sweat, and Mahjong: Family and Enterprise in an Overseas Chinese Community*. Ithaca: Cornell University Press.

Siu, Paul C. P. 1988. *The Chinese Laundryman: A Study of Social Isolation*. New York: New York University Press.

Notes

1 There are no statistics made available specifically on the number of illegal entries by Chinese, because in absolute numbers and compared with illegal migrants from other countries the number of Chinese is still small (Grenzschutzstelle 1993:14).

2 Relative to the total number of approximately 30,000 Chinese legal residents in Germany (according to 1996 information from the Representative of the Federal Government for the Interests of Foreigners), the number of illegal entries is not as low as it seems at first sight. According to official statistics, during 1994 Chinese suspects were prosecuted in a total of 131 cases connected to organized crime. This included forty-nine cases of trafficking in Chinese migrants and twenty-one cases of falsifying of official documents such as passports or visas (Bundeskriminalamt 1995). From 1990 to 1993, German prosecuting organs carried out investigations against a total number of approximately 150 suspected traffickers in Chinese migrants. At least one half of them were ethnic Chinese, of whom fifty came from the People's Republic of China (PRC). Thirty were from Zhejiang, five from Guangdong, four from Fujian, while the province of origin of the remaining eleven was not registered. One more statistical clue is provided by asylum statistics. The sixfold increase in the number of asylum applications, from 723 in 1992 to 4,396 in 1993 is very suggestive. It is not possible to clarify whether this increase has in fact been caused by a sudden growth of the illegal Chinese population in Germany, intensified pressure applied by prosecuting organs, or a general deterioration of the Chinese restaurant business where virtually all Chinese illegally staying in Germany find employment. But the fact that in 1993 only three per cent of all asylum applications forwarded by Chinese were handed over at the borders, whereas ninety-seven per cent of those applications were submitted in Germany itself, does at least indicate a generally high success rate of Chinese human traffickers (Gesetzschutzdirektion 1994:13).

3 Smaller numbers of Zhejiang migrants are from the rural areas of Wenzhou city district and Yongkang county in Jinhua prefecture. The small number of people from Fujian or Guangdong involved were transit travellers on their way to the US. (Grenzschutzstelle 1994:4, 12–13 and personal conversations with members of the Directorate of Border Guards East (Grenzschutzdirektion Ost), Berlin, 1992–1996).

4 The author of this study is a long time Chinese language interpreter. As part of his work he had access to a large number of documents originating with the immigrants themselves which were used as evidence in court against individuals suspected of illegal immigration or human trafficking. This material, though possibly of very high value to research, will not be drawn upon in this study because of the impossibility of getting the migrants' permission for using it. This study is therefore, at least as far as the immigrants themselves are concerned, based on information voluntarily provided to the author in personal conversations. All the migrants who provided information to the author knew very well from the beginning that they were in no way obliged to answer any of the author's questions and that they did not have to fear any repercussions. When being asked by the author, all of them knew the purpose of the questions asked. In all cases where written sources are directly quoted, permission has been granted by those who provided the source material.

5 A typical example was a former self-employed blacksmith with three children and a monthly income of 400 to 600 yuan, whom I spoke with on 28 December 1995.

6 Personal conversations with members of the Directorate of Border Guards East (Grenzschutzdirektion Ost), Berlin, 1992–1996.

7 The possibility for foreign restaurants directly to hire cooks from their home countries for a period of only three years was reportedly further restricted in mid-1996; visa extensions are not granted anymore.

213

8 Immigration through nominal firms appears to have been popular throughout Eastern Europe in the early 1990s. See Nyíri 1998 and International Organization for Migration 1998.

9 Personal conversations with members of the Directorate of Border Guards East (Grenzschutzdirektion Ost), Berlin, 1992–1996.

10 Attempts to enter Germany are also made from Austria, France and the Netherlands by Chinese, underlining the great spatial mobility of Zhejiang Chinese in Europe (Grenzschutzstelle 1994:7–8).

11 It seems, therefore, that no active and direct recruitment of people willing to migrate by smuggling organizations is necessary. Potential emigrants themselves actively seek out local traffickers through a network of personal connections.

"Zhejiang Village" in Beijing: Creating a visible non-state space through migration and marketized traditional networks*

Xiang Biao

Introduction

Large scale transregional migration in contemporary China has attracted wide attention both in China and abroad. Migration has become a "structural" fact: an established phenomenon affecting many aspects of China society, whose scope exceeds all earlier estimates.[1] The state seems unable fully to control the migrant populations, worrying both the government and established residents of the destination areas.[2]

The state itself initially made individual rural-urban migration possible by granting certain rights to individuals.[3] But how exactly have these rights unleashed such unprecedented migration? Although much work has been done on Chinese migration at the macro level, its inner rules and mechanisms remain largely a "black box." Furthermore, what are the relationships between this large scale flow and other social changes at the macro level?

Migrants in China whose mobility has not been mandated by the state are usually referred to as the floating population or more politely non-*hukou* (household registration) migrants,[4] which indicates that they are not only undergoing a change of residence and occupation. They are also released from the state control and support system to a degree unparalleled by any other social group in contemporary China, including private

* I would like to express my sincere thanks to Wang Hansheng, Zhou Qiren, Wang Mingming, Sun Liping, Liu Shiding, Shen Yuan and other teachers at Peking University and the Chinese Academy of Social Sciences.

entrepreneurs.[5] Yet they are a thriving social group that is responsible for much of the current vitality of China's urban and rural economy. How does this group, almost completely severed from the state system, survive and even grow?

In this paper, I will argue that the floating population has carved out a new "social space." In this space, they have created their own life styles, values, rules of behaviour and social networks. Yet this space is not well integrated in the established structures. My earlier fieldwork in 1994 and 1995 among *baomu* (nannies or domestic servants) in Beijing provides a good illustration of this point. The predominant influence on their behaviour, moulding the relations between them and society, are neither the families that employ them nor the administrative department that is responsible for baomu, nor even their home communities. The pivot around which their life revolves is the "*baomu bang*," the group of other baomu from their own place of origin. Baomu bang generally gather in a park to chat or go shopping together on Sunday. The interaction within the "bang" shapes the self-identity of baomu, and influences their strategies and ideas about society. What is good and what is bad about urban life? What to do if your employer tries to intimidate you? Advice of the "sisters" is of crucial importance in matters such as these. My study of agricultural migrant workers in Guangdong Province similarly revealed the great social significance of bang (Xiang 1995a:76–80).

Such bang are examples of a type of social entity mediating between society and individuals, which I propose to call "social space." I shall show that this space is different from Western "civil society," despite some superficial similarities.

Then how has this "space" been created? The process of the "marketization of traditional networks" in contemporary China is the fundamental mechanism responsible for the continuous flow of non-hukou migrants and the growth of their social space within and beyond the existing social structure.

Finally, I shall discuss the implications of this space for the change of existing structures. No outright change of the state system occurs, but a specific structure resembling three concentric circles has emerged. This shows that Chinese reform has moved from the stage of readjustments within the state's system to that of conflict between the state and non-state spaces.

Much has been written about the processes and consequences of migration. In my analysis of non-hukou migrant communities in China, I shall draw on both practice theory and what is sometimes referred to as the "articulation model" of migration. The latter argues that migration brings into direct contact what are usually considered opposites: capitalism and pre-capitalism, modernity and tradition, city and countryside (Meillassoux 1981; Kearney 1986:341–356). Breaking through traditional boundaries, migration produces new "space" (Rosaldo 1989:77–87; Rouse 1991), which is, as has been said above, the core concept that I shall develop further in the course of this chapter. Practice theory argues that migrants should be treated as social and political agents, actively creating and changing the social structures, discourses and processes that are the very context of their mobility and settlement (Rouse 1987:28; Goldring 1992:26–30 and 39–66; Thunø, this volume).

Adapting practice theory to contemporary China, I bundle the factors affecting the migratory flows together into three fields: state, market and social networks (see also Pieke 1995). The "state," through its policies, administrative structure, and control of certain resources, constrains people's possible arenas of behaviour. The "market" with its pricing mechanism is likewise a determining factor in population mobility in modern society. The "social networks" are relationships cemented through long periods and are different from administrative or pure market relations. This chapter distinguishes between "traditional networks" (referring chiefly to the relationship based on kinship and native place), "migration networks" (the relationships between migrants established during migration) and the connections between these two. This chapter will argue that the development of spontaneous migration is the result of the interplay of these three arenas, and in turn, that migration has changed the relationships between them through the migrants' daily practices and strategies.

The floating population is far from homogeneous, and includes groups as different as workers, traders, and nannies. This chapter therefore cannot possibly comprehensively cover them all, but will instead provide an ethnographic study of one well-known community of migrants in Beijing that is usually called "Zhejiang Village" (*Zhejiang Cun*). Members of Zhejiang Village are mostly businessmen and businesswomen. Such migrants are often the most independent and, from the point of view of the state, the most difficult to control.[6] Selecting them for a case study therefore seems pertinent to the questions asked here. Since 1992, I have carried out a social anthropological study of the community. The material gathered in the course of this longitudinal study is reported on below.

What is "Zhejiang Village"?

Zhejiang Village is situated in Fengtai district (*qu*) in the south of Beijing municipality. Located where Dahongmen street (*jiedao*) borders on Nanyuan township (*xiang*),[7] Zhejiang Village is at the very edge of the area in Beijing municipality that continues to be administered as a rural rather than an urban area, although the majority of the local residents long ago abandoned agriculture.

Zhejiang Village is the biggest community of non-hukou migrants in Chinese cities. It consists of twenty-six natural villages with altogether

14,000 Beijing rural residents and 96,000 migrants.[8] Among the migrants, I estimate that more than 50,000 are businessmen and women and their family members, seventy-five per cent of whom come from Yueqing city (county) in Wenzhou prefecture, Zhejiang province, twenty per cent from Yongjia County in the same prefecture and the remaining five per cent from other prefectures in Zhejiang. The other 40,000 migrants are mainly from Hubei, Anhui and Hebei provinces, and work for Zhejiang employers.

The community has a brisk economy. It is mainly engaged in garments, achieving a sales value of 1,500 million yuan in 1995 according to official statistics.[9] The community boasts sixteen large marketplaces and is now the supply base for medium and low grade clothes for the whole of northeastern and northern China.

Zhejiang Village has been formed spontaneously; even now, it has no formal administrative structure or community organizations of any kind. Juvenile criminality is serious, and public hygiene, public security and other public facilities continue to be in a sore state. All of this is reminiscent of slums and squatter settlements in other developing countries.[10]

Zhejiang Village has become a special concept and even an important "category" of social life in Beijing. Government organizations at different levels and many people of the municipality are involved in one way or the other in the interaction with this community. I have counted no less than fifteen media articles on Zhejiang Village, including in Newsweek (7 March 1994, pp. 18–9) and The Washington Post and International Herald Tribune (28 November 1995). One internal government report from Fengtai district to Beijing municipality starts by saying "Some of the inhabitants of the capital may not know Nanyuan township, but there is hardly a single person who does not know of Zhejiang Village. The saying goes in government departments 'The key district in migrant administration is Fengtai, and the key area in Fengtai is Zhejiang Village'."

A brief history of Zhejiang Village

Wenzhou has a tradition of migration (Fei 1992:276–7; Lin et al. 1987:10; Wang 1994:57–60), but this tradition was broken off in the late 1950s and especially in the mid-1960s. The household registration system separating rural and urban areas, the work unit system in the cities and the commune system in the countryside, together with the abolition of the market and establishment of a planned economy, brought non-state migration to a virtual halt in the Chinese society.

1970–1980: Covert migration in small groups

Contrary to what is generally assumed, the resumption of spontaneous migration began not with the official start of the reforms in 1978, but already during the Cultural Revolution (officially between 1966 and 1976). In Zhejiang Village over sixty per cent of male employers above the age of thirty had experience with migration to other provinces before coming to Beijing. They mainly went to northwestern China to make furniture and to Hubei and some other provinces in central China as carpenters or cotton fluffers.

Yao Xin'an, now living in Zhejiang Village, told me: "I went far away from home in 1971 at the age of eighteen to Dunhuang in Gansu. We all took advantage of the chaos at the time to leave. We didn't have to pay even for the railway tickets during a certain period of time! Most of us from Wenzhou used to go to Shanghai or thereabouts, but they were still relatively strict with outsiders there these days. So we went to the northwestern cities instead, where no one was really running things though the [political] struggle was raging in earnest."

But the "Cultural Revolution" did less damage to the social order in the countryside. What made it possible for these pioneer migrants to leave? Zhou Niantao, who left his village for the first time in 1975 and arrived in Beijing in 1986, said: "There was no problem leaving the village. Since the days of my ancestors, my family has believed in 'peace bringing in wealth.' When I was young, I experienced political movements of all sorts, but I had never offended anyone. When I left home, the leader of the production team I belonged to was a member of my own lineage. He did nothing to stop me, as that would do him no good and there wasn't much work to do in the production team anyway.[11] The leader of the production brigade pretended not to notice my departure, and the commune leaders were similarly winking at such matters. Of course, I could no longer earn any work points, and had to pay 2.5 yuan to the team each month to help support the *wubao hu* [the aged, the infirm, old widows and orphans, X.B.] in the team. When I returned to the village to get married in 1978, I was elected leader of the team, for two factions in the team were locked in strife and could only be made to agree on a neutral person."

How did people make their final decision to migrate and where did they get the necessary money and information from? The answer is found also in traditional networks.

According to Yao Xin'an: "In the 1950s, groups of young students were sent from Yueqing to support the construction of the border areas in the Northwest, so we knew something from their letters. We also thought we could call upon them for help in case we had difficulties there."

"I didn't take any money with me when I left. Just after Liberation in 1949, a paternal uncle had migrated with his master to make furniture. He had some tools and money. He consulted with my father and asked father to let me go with him as an apprentice. My father agreed. Uncle would take care of my lodging and food, and I would be given one to two hundred yuan at the end of the year."

Migration brought about an underground market. "We dared not go to big cities," said Yao Xin'an, "and generally went to county towns and villages in the suburbs, going from house to house asking whether they would have furniture made. We stayed with whichever family we worked for, buying rice and coal through them. We were better artisans than the locals and had no difficulties in getting work. We were considered typical 'profiteers' (*touji daoba*) in the prevailing political atmosphere. But the common people did not really carry out class struggle everyday, and had to have some cupboards and a bed when their son or daughter got married. We were informed against only when the neighbours were at odds with our landlords, or when people were irritated with the noise we made. It was not at all rare when we had to hide in a pigsty or cowshed in the dead of night. I myself have been detained and sent back to my native place twice by the police. But we did not care. We managed to carry on somehow."

Many other migrants share Yao's attitude towards being detained or sent back. As another informant put it: "We did not care. Relatives and village folk would never look down on anyone who had been sent back home. It's perfectly justified for people to live by the sweat of their brow and seek a fortune outside. One went round carrying one's head high just the same. What people really minded was a lack of ability to make money and live a good life." This difference in values between local communities and the state is a key cause of spontaneous migration and the growth of the market economy in Wenzhou.

But migration relying on an underground market could only develop at a very slow speed. Yao Xin'an: "It was forbidden to individuals to buy timber or to sell furniture. We could only charge for the work we did, and were only slightly better off than when living at home. (. . .) The first time I went out with two others. We usually went in a group of two to five people. We had to rove about and dodge those who tried to get us, and in a large group it would be difficult to do so. In 1973, I became a master myself and took my paternal cousin and my sister's son with me. My master and senior fellow apprentice decided to stay back, unable to put up with the hard life over long periods of time."

According to the recollections of some folk in the villages of Qianjiayang and Heshenqiao in Hongqiao town, Yueqing county and other villages in Yongjia county, about five per cent of the villagers went out, a number that grew only slightly in the course of the 1970s.

1980–1982: Overt migration in small groups

A switch took place in 1980 after the appearance of the open non-state economic sectors. Self-employment was rehabilitated and traditional marketplaces were restored everywhere in 1980. The government criticized the earlier repudiation of the export of labour as the "tail of capitalism" and "profiteering," but made no clear statement on migration itself. Under such circumstances, once again traditional networks would bring about a new stage in migration.

Liu Zebo, pioneer of Zhejiang Village, told me, "Our village (Shanggutou village, Yanfu township, Yueqing city) has more tailors than any other village. We mainly make clothes for people of our township. A young senior high school graduate from my village went to Wuhai city, Ningxia province in 1966 during the campaign to 'support the construction of the border areas,' and later became the head of the supply and marketing cooperative there. When he came back to visit his family during Chinese New Year in 1980, he told us that tailors in his city could make three yuan more than the ones at home on each item of clothes![12] He asked us to have a try and work in his cooperative.

"He did not do this for any financial reason. His father had been a landlord before liberation, and he therefore had, to use the terms of the 1950s and 1960s, a bad background. However, we had never ill-treated them. At that time, his father and brother still stayed in the village and needed looking after. He himself said he was drawn to folk in the village and felt he was one of us. Early in 1978 and 1979, he had asked our village to run factories and supply his cooperative with brooms and ropes. When we worked in Wuhai, we went to see him during festivals from time to time with some rapeseed oil and biscuits. But it was not his purpose to help us in order to receive gifts."

"We went to the township government in Wenzhou to get our credentials, as the director had suggested. When we got to Wuhai, the supply and marketing cooperative allotted a place for us to work, and our charges were also fixed by the cooperative. Later, with the help of this director, I went through the necessary formalities and got transferred to make clothes and sell them in the free market, again run by the cooperative. I bought my cloth from the cooperative and gladly paid the tax and administrative charge each month."

Almost all members of ten families went to Wuhai, each family with 800 to 1,200 yuan saved from tailoring in the home village and loans from fellow villagers. The reason why so many people went and so much money could be risked was that "times were not what they had been in the 1970s any more. We couldn't do wrong: the director was a state official administering the marketplaces."

With more capital and labour and an open market, Liu Zebo naturally made more money than either Yao Xin'an or Zhou Niantao. Liu Zebo made over 10,000 yuan in the first year. The ten families came from several villages close by and their members, although they belonged to two separate groups of relatives, nevertheless knew each other quite well. Yet the families operated independently and looked after each other only in matters of daily life.

221

1982–1984: Completely marketized migration in small groups

Since 1982, the state accelerated the reform of trade and commerce. The national government demanded the "smashing the blockade between regions" (Guowuyuan 1987:266), permitted "communes, production brigades and individual farmers to engage in long distance transportation of goods for sale" (Shangye Bu 1983:483) and decided "to use a unified business licence for individual businesspeople throughout the country." (Geti Si 1987:346). But the activities of Liu Zebo and others took a further step away from the state.

"At Wuhai," Liu Zebo continued, "we came to know that Baotou was a big city nearby. In the course of a chat with the cadres of the cooperative, I gathered that they bought the cloth they sold to us from companies in Beijing at the wholesale price, and that individual producers could do the same. I thought we could make more money in Baotou, and the 20,000 yuan I had at that time would enable me to make a new try."

Liu Zebo and five other families moved to Baotou in 1982, put up in a hotel and sold clothes in a marketplace run by some cooperative in Baotou. Liu's assets rose to almost 100,000 yuan by the end of the year. When he went to Beijing to buy cloth in 1984, he found the market potential in Beijing to be even greater. Six of the original ten families then moved on to Beijing that year. They rented rooms in the rather bleak and desolate Muxiyuan area and thus became the pioneers of Zhejiang Village that was to develop later. Ever since, maximization of economic returns has become the core rule in deciding whether to migrate, and especially where to migrate and how to migrate.

Migration at this stage still proceeded within the fundamental framework designed by the state, but it already produced some tension with it. "In Baotou we basically applied the experience we gained at Wuhai," said Liu Zebo, "But we dared not take any risks in Beijing and asked the Bureau of Industry and Commerce of Xuanwu district beforehand whether we could come or not. We were told that we could come, if a certain document issued in my home town was addressed to Beijing. I went back to Wenzhou especially to obtain the required credentials for each of the six families. The paperwork in order, we managed to get the approval from the district authorities for renting street stalls."

But the marketplaces opened for them by the state could not satisfy people's demands. "At first, I rented a stall in the marketplace in Changchun Street run by the Bureau of Industry and Commerce of Xuanwu district," said Liu Zebo. "Not much business could be had there. So I let my wife and son keep a stall outside the gate of the Xiannongtan Stadium, with goods spread out on the ground (*bai ditanr*, to set up a 'ground stall'). At first the people of the industry and commerce administration and police drove the stallholders away every few days. As nothing came from their efforts, they gradually let up." "Ground stalls" were the first stalls for many "Zhejiang villagers" when they arrived in Beijing in the early 1980s.

In Beijing, the six families were no longer protected from the full impact of the market by a friendly state agency. They could not possibly expect other people to supply them with cloth, stalls and information. The internal relationship between the families then underwent a change. They began to buy their cloth together and shared whatever valuable information they had gathered. A simple division of labour and cooperation began to emerge in production. But each family still kept its own books. "We, the six families, were all alone," said Liu Zebo, "just taking care of one another was not enough. We had to 'go it together' to some extent. That would do everybody good." Traditional networks had started to assume economic functions.

1984–1986: Chain migration

"Chain migration" was introduced in population studies in the 1950s to describe the phenomenon that established migrants help their relatives or friends migrate to the same destination (MacDonald and MacDonald 1964). Chain migration is generally thought to help migrants fit quicker into the destination society. But more is at hand than just convenience and assistance. Why would the earlier migrants want to develop the chains? Whom do they bring over from their native places? What do they provide for them, and what relationship do they establish with the newcomers?

In Zhejiang Village in 1984, the principle of "bringing labourers" prevailed. Zhejiang villagers have made great profits in Beijing. Liu Zebo, for instance, spent about 100,000 yuan on a new house and participation in a mass credit association (*Taihui*[13]) when he went back to his native place in late 1982. He had only 7,000 yuan left when he returned to Zhejiang Village, but had 40,000 yuan to his credit again before the year was out.

Another informant, Lian Aisong, said about this: "We had too much work and too few people to do it these days." Migrants wrote letters home or went back personally to urge their relatives and other girls in the villages to go to Beijing with them. They promised the skilled ones a good pay. "A distant cousin of mine made good clothes. She worked in the factory of the township and received sixty-five yuan a month. I told her that I would give her 200 yuan each month" (Lian Aisong). The employer was responsible for their travel expenses, food and lodging and would pay a part of their wages each month and the remainder at the end of year. This applied even to their own sisters! The migrant chains were in fact invisible labour markets.

About two to three years later, these workers started their own chains. Having learnt the business, these girls left the employment of their relative, brought their family over, and started on their own.

In 1985, the reform of the urban economic system was in full swing,[14] and in Beijing shop counters began to be leased out to individuals.[15] A large number of marketplaces were set up at the same time. Individual traders were no longer confined to street stalls or "ground stalls" in marginal areas.

Xiang Yousheng told me: "I sold goods spread out on the ground for half a year and then rented a counter in a shop in downtown Wangfujing Street. I sold a lot of clothes and made a tidy sum of money. I took clothes from other tailors in addition to my own. But those were not enough; I needed a sure and steady supply. I thought of getting a partner from my native place, someone I hit it off with, capable, with enough capital to employ many workers and make good garments. The tailors in around Yueqing had practically all left, but many girls had begun learning to tailor and there were some courses to train new hands. Bosses don't have to make garments themselves. What they need is a good head on their shoulders and enough capital."

"Later on we had to have partners in renting shop counters too. The shops liked to lease counters to a group of people. That was desirable for us too. Several counters with similar clothes would attract more attention. It's easy to get assistants from home. I persuaded a purchasing agent of a farm tools factory, a distant cousin and two classmates of the primary school at home to come to Beijing with me."

With the expansion of the market, migrants felt that it was no longer enough just to enlarge their own production. "Operation networks" had to be set up to create a system for the division of labour. But a preference for relatives or fellow villagers soon made itself felt again. In Yao Xin'an's words: "We all want good partners. But there are not many people who are both capable and willing to cooperate with you. Zhejiang Village had a lot of people then, and there were some conflicts. I felt my own people would be more reliable after all. By one's 'own people,' we mean close relatives and good friends who stand up for you when events so require. I feel at ease doing business with them. Besides, it's only right and proper to give chances of earning good money to one's own relatives and friends."

Yet these "capable people" and "one's own people" started their own businesses once they got to Beijing. Qian Amu said, "My cousin asked me to come to Beijing. He meant well, for he found my family was not living well enough. Of course, he also had a mind to expand his influence here. I tried to rent a counter when I first came. He told me where I could rent one and how to rent it, but did not mention one particular shop with a good front. We are all in business, and it's only natural that he should keep better counters for himself. I succeeded in getting a good place through my own effort."

But alongside the opening of the market, the state began to put procedures in place that regulate various aspects of migration itself. Stays of longer than three months now needed a "certificate of temporary residence"(*zanzhu zheng*); renting housing required permission from the migrant's original work unit or local government.[16] Individual business-people from outside were normally only allowed to do business after the issuance of a business licence, unless they could produce a duplicate of a licence of a company or other unit. But developments could no longer sufficiently be monitored. Qian Amu: "Most of us did not do as we were required to at the time. Those coming to make clothes usually met only folk from the same county. Who knew you had arrived? Those coming to rent counters had no difficulty getting a duplicate of a factory's business licence. There were so many enterprises back home, and a lot of duplicates were in use in Zhejiang Village. You could borrow or rent a duplicate to show to the shops, and generally no one would trouble himself about you any more after they had leased you the counters. In large markets, such as Baihua and Minzu Dashijie, the business licence issued back home must be replaced by one for Beijing individual entrepreneurs. But you had no problem renting one from the Beijingese!"

When I mentioned the procedure for renting housing, my informant Qian Amu looked surprised. "I didn't know of such a procedure. Only in 1987 and 1989, when police came to drive us away, we were told that we were renting illegally. But once the 'typhoon' passed, all went on without any changes and the only thing you had to do to get a room was pay the rent." Liu Zebo's travel back to Yueqing especially to get the necessary papers for the initial six families some years ago quickly became a distant memory. "Before 1986, we did not have many fellow provincials here and felt uneasy. You met Beijingese and "Big Peaks" (*Dayanmao*, a reference to certain administrative staff who wear a high topped cap as part of their uniform) everywhere. But there are so many of us here now, and no one seems to bother about formalities any more!"

Although Wenzhou inmigration originated in 1984, "Zhejiang Village" became a commonly known feature of Beijing's urban life only in 1986. In that year, the number of migrants reached 12,000, or almost equal to the number of local residents. It was named Zhejiang Village because at the time Beijingese did not know about Wenzhou. The migrants had no choice but to refer to themselves as "Zhejiangese," although they all came from Wenzhou. The name "Zhejiang Village" is thus a product of the interaction between the migrants and receiving society. At the same time, the Beijing authorities conducted a brief investigation and concluded that Zhejiang Village "must not be allowed to exist for a long period." According to an official in the municipality whom I interviewed about this matter, this conclusion was based on the fact that the government's urban plan did not allow for the development of a clothing market in Dahongmen, coupled with the concern that the local government would be paralysed if more migrants were to gather there.

1987–1995: Mass migration

The concept of mass migration was probably first advanced by William Petersen (Petersen 1958). A few people in a place set the precedent of moving to another place, starting a process of semi-autonomous continued migration. Individual decisions to migrate are not made on the basis of a cost-benefit analysis, but result from a social momentum. As Liu Zebo put it, "At first, we felt Beijing was a nice piece of meat and did not want too many people to know of it. But, in 1987, we could not hide the fact any longer, and folk began to pour in."

Qianjiayang village of Hongqiao township under Yueqing city has over 200 households and a population of nearly 1,000. Its villager Wan Guanghong's experiences are similar to those of Liu Zebo. Wan moved to Beijing from Gansu province as the leader of a group of tailors in 1984, knowing that some natives of Yueqing were doing business around Muxiyuan. By 1995, over 600 villagers of Qianjiayang, including the head of the villagers' committee and the secretary of the Communist Party branch, had migrated to Beijing. Eighty per cent of these people came to Beijing, the rest went to cities such as Shijiazhuang or Taiyuan to make garments. The nephew of my landlord when I conducted fieldwork in Qianjiayang failed the entrance examination for secondary middle school in 1991, and came to Beijing with his neighbour to work as a salesman. In 1995, he was trying to lease a counter for himself. He told me that "only capable and skilled people went outside in the past, but now people remain in the village only for special reasons. The first thing my schoolmates and friends think of after finishing school is to find work in the outside world. Muxiyuan is our second native place. We feel perfectly at home here." Migration has become a "culture" in Qianjiayang, and costs very little.

After Deng Xiaoping's tour of southern China that gave the green light for a new round of market liberalization and reform in early 1992, the Bureau of Industry and Commerce of Fengtai district, and soon after that many individuals (mostly wealthy entrepreneurs of Zhejiang Village), invested in the construction of large wholesale marketplaces in the community. Zhejiang Village become a big production base and marketing centre of low and middle grade clothes for the whole of northern and northeastern China. The shift from marketing outside to inside of Zhejiang Village itself promoted mass migration. In 1987–1988 and again from 1990 to 1994, Zhejiang Village witnessed a rapid expansion (a break occurred in 1989 because of the political disturbance in Beijing).

What the mass migration has brought about is not only the increase of the population scale, but also some more important changes. One interviewee told me: "The marketplace is only a few yards from your house, and one call to friends or relatives in other cities saves all the effort to buy material and sell jackets. All business can be done without leaving home." Qian Amu said, "When I first came, I had to rely on my relatives and friends, especially the one who brought me here. I personally had to go back to employ workers, ask friends to buy cloth and seek connections in Beijing to rent counters. Now it's different. There are special channels for everything. You can go to the labour exchanges and cloth marketplace, and there are even people specialized in getting counters. The main thing is whether you have enough capital and a good head on your shoulders" (1993).

Doing business without leaving home and the existence of special channels for everything indicate that there are some stable relations and rules in the business. Zhejiang Village is no longer a community only, but has become a "business space" embedded in a national and even an international network. Important changes have also taken place with regard to the respective role of the three fields of the state, market and social network.

Formation of a "business space"

Undertake international trades

Zhejiang Village turned out its most competitive product, leather jackets, in 1988. In the two years that followed, a large number of traders from Russia and eastern Europe came directly to the community to purchase jackets. Almost all households of Zhejiang Village at the time recall producing leather jackets for days on end without ever going to bed. Another way for Zhejiang villagers to enter the international market is "to open windows" (*she chuangkou*), i.e. to rent a counter and fill it with all kinds of samples to attract foreign buyers, in a big department store or at Yabao Lu, an international exchange marketplace in Beijing. In 1990, Zhao Yongbao, a young man in his early thirties, rented a room in the Ritan Hotel in Yabao Lu and put a notice on the door saying: "All kinds of jackets to be found in this room." He made several million yuan in two months. Zhao broke new ground in international business. Quickly, the Ritan Hotel was almost fully occupied by people from Zhejiang Village. In 1996, Chen Dawu, another businessman successful in trade with foreigners, leased an apartment building in Yabao Lu, renting out individual rooms to people from his native area.

Zhejiang villagers have not only been receiving foreign traders, but have also gone abroad themselves. Since 1989, *bianmao* (border trade) has become a new industry. There are several ways to do it. One is to open a company and register branches in Heihe, Suifenhe or Manzhouli (towns or cities at the border of the Russian Far East with the Chinese provinces of Heilongjiang and Inner Mongolia, see map on p. xii), or even in Russia or some eastern European countries such as Hungary. But much more commonly, people just collect clothes and transport them to the border with rented lorries. An interviewee told me: "The more people participate in an exchange, the less you will get yourself. Why not go to the border to trade with the Russians directly? It's very simple. I asked those who returned from the border and their interpreters about it, and just followed their track to start my own border trade. I make much more profit even after deducting the transportation cost (...) There generally are no contracts between the Russians and me. The kind of jackets that I produce or collect from others in Zhejiang Village is decided by the experience gained on the previous trip. Going abroad? It is not impossible. Just trace them back further, and surely you are in Russia. Some others have gone there to do business. They just have more initial capital than me."

The opportunities provided by foreign traders promoted cooperation within the community. A friend told me: "*Laowai* (foreigners) are all unreasonable. Generally, we must make several hundred jackets for them in three or four days. It can't be done by one family alone. I take the order and divide it up among my relatives or friends, taking a cut of about three per cent of the total sum."

Many Wenzhou communities in Europe, such as France and Italy, specialize in roughly the same products as Zhejiang Village (Tomba, this volume). However, they have no direct connections. Within the same tradition of migration, several separate migration configurations exist in the Wenzhou area. International migrants come from Qingtian county (in adjacent Lishui preference administratively, but culturally part of the Wenzhou area), Wenzhou city, Wencheng county and some parts of Yongjia county; while Yueqing, other parts of Yongjia and other districts specialize in migration to destinations in China itself. Another cause for the separation between Zhejiang Village and its overseas counterpart communities is migration selection: people with relatives abroad usually do not want to migrate within China, they have the options to either emigrate themselves or open a relatively large scale business at home. For example, I met three private entrepreneurs in Wenzhou city who produce lighters and leather shoes. They export their products through their relatives abroad, while an uncle in Holland of one of them had remitted an important part of the initial investment needed.

Zhejiang villagers usually have no tradition of international migration, and they have recently "simply" (as the interviewee above put it) entered the international market as part of the much broader northern Chinese trend of trade and emigration to Russia and eastern Europe. People are constantly reconstructing and even creating tradition. In fact, "Zhejiang Village" itself is created rather than a product of tradition.

Mature market systems

In the stage of mass migration, two new forms of mobility have appeared. The first is the "proliferate flow" of migrants from Beijing or directly from the native places who start producing garments in the cities of north-eastern, northern and northwestern China. Beijing is no longer the predominant place of destination. The second form of mobility is the "itinerant flow" of people who trade in cities throughout China, making use of differences in market prices and the different timing of the seasons. These two types of mobility have transferred the resources of Zhejiang Village across an unprecedentedly vast area. A network of migrants across the whole country has been formed. For example, a large part of the products of Zhejiang Village are sold by Yueqing traders in the Northeast. Zhou Niantao told me a story of his: "Before the Chinese New Year (of 1996), I had about 200 leather jackets that I couldn't sell anymore in Beijing. But I didn't have to be worried. I phoned a cousin in Chongqing. Clothes fashions are like the tides. The wave generally starts in Hong Kong and Guangdong, then it comes to Beijing, Shanghai et cetera. One or two months later, the wave reaches cities like Chongqing [where my cousin lives]. Knowing what kind of jackets I had, my cousin told me that those could be sold at a high price there. I put the phone down and immediately brought the jackets to the airport. Most of the clothes are transported by air, only a layman would be surprised about it. Time is money! Six hours later, I received a phone call from my cousin. He told me the first jacket had already been sold in Chongqing! It is impossible to do any business if you must travel and do everything yourself (laughs). Naturally, previously we had no other option but go everywhere ourselves."

Mass migration also promoted the formation of entire production factor markets. First, the labour market. Certain individuals ran special courses in provinces like Hunan and Jiangxi. They trained young tailors and brought them to the labour exchanges (*laowu jieshao suo*) in Wenzhou. Migrant Wenzhou employers hired these tailors at the exchanges when they visited home during the Chinese New Year. Both employers and employees paid the exchanges, and the exchanges in turn paid the individuals who ran the tailoring courses.

Hongqiao town with a population of only 30,000 had as many as sixty-nine such exchanges during the 1995 New Year.[17] Yet only twenty odd remained when I visited the town again during the 1996 New Year. A master of an exchange, who had talked with me before told me: "Girls from Jiangxi and Hunan now know the way and bring people directly to Zhejiang Village. They rent a few rooms there and wait for the employers to hire workers from them!" The links of the labour market have been further simplified.

A second production factor market was the market for raw materials. Some raw materials come from external markets. Leather, for instance, was mainly directly bought from Wuji and other counties in Hebei province, and Hainin city in Zhejiang province (which culturally does not belong to the same area as Wenzhou). Other materials were provided by the transregional networks of migrants. Cloth is a case in point. The cloth used in Zhejiang Village comes from China's biggest wholesale market of cloth in Keqiao town of Shaoxing city, Zhejiang province. This market is organized by migrants from Yueqing and almost all people in Zhejiang Village have relatives or friends in Keqiao town: "Give them a ring and you have any amount and kind of cloth you need."

The third production factor market was the capital market. Loans were often given by personal relatives and friends, and interest on these loans was paid without fail (the monthly rate varied between two and three per cent in recent years). Another source were the "rural financiers," women of about forty to fifty years of age. They usually borrowed money that they lent out again through their social network, keeping the difference in interest for themselves.[18]

Zhejiang Village has rapidly become a community of long term residents. The first kindergarten of Zhejiang Village appeared in 1988, and the first food marketplace was established in 1989. Since 1990, clinics, barbershops and repair shops have been set up one after another, and each trade has formed a network of its own. The most important new industry however is real estate, that is, building "big compounds" (*dayuan*) of private housing for rent. The rooms the local farmers in Zhejiang Village can spare for the growing numbers of migrants are far from enough. What is more, migrants demand unified services and closer cooperation. Since the end of 1992, rich migrants pool their capital as shares to invest in the building of dayuan, cooperating with the local administrative bodies. There are now forty-six (or forty-eight, according to another source) such compounds that accommodate about 30,000 people from Wenzhou. These compounds have water, electricity, sewerage, postal services and educational and recreational facilities. Public security has been taken care of and effective management has been introduced. In the words of the migrants, these compounds were built by people with "money, influence and prestige."

Side by side with these new trades have come new trade rules and new social resources. Transactions on credit are carried out among, for instance, garment makers, embroiderers and overcasters, who balance their accounts at the end of each month or year. Some medium and big employers have adopted shareholding for major ventures, such as contracts for marketplaces or consigning stations, or the construction of dayuan, strengthening their influence in the community through these public projects.

Changes in government behaviour

The farmers-turned-individual-entrepreneurs can now migrate without requiring the sanction of the state. From 1986 to 1990, the number of migrants in Zhejiang Village shot up from 12,000 to 30,000, after which it continued to rise at a rate of fifty per cent a year until 1995. Yet the number of people registered as out-migrants with the Yueqing Bureau of Industry and Commerce remained 3,000 to 5,000, and only some 30,000 migrants entered their names in the temporary hukou registers of police stations in Beijing. In 1992, the State General Bureau of Industry and Commerce (*Guojia Gongshang Zongju*) published a document announcing that merchants doing business outside their place of residence no longer need to provide certificates issued by the industry and commerce branches in their native places. Migrants attained further freedom from the state.

But large numbers of migrants living in a compact community could not but arouse the attention of the government. Since 1986, the municipal government has taken different approaches to migrants in Zhejiang Village.

The earliest strategy was wholesale ejection. In the words of the migrants, a violent "typhoon" would blow through Zhejiang Village in August or September of each year. But local traders and shops still needed supplies. The migrants divided up into small groups of five to six families, and went into hiding in villages in Hebei province around Beijing. From there they continued to supply goods to Beijing and kept in contact with other small groups. When the storm began to let up, they would speedily return to Muxiyuan.

Shortly before the 1990 Asian Games, the local government sent over 2,000 policemen and security personnel to "clean up" Zhejiang Village. The migrants returned and continued to expand their networks soon after the Asian Games were over.

In 1990, Beijing raised the slogan that it was to "buy from and sell to the whole country" (*mai quanguo mai quanguo)*, and changed the policy toward Zhejiang Village from suppression to the provision of "correct guidance." The local government carries out an investigation and the local bureau of industry and commerce issued some certificates, but ultimately "correct guidance" failed. The migrants had practically nothing to do with the government, and their autonomous networks kept growing at a fast rate. "Correct guidance" in effect boiled down to laissez-faire.

Since 1992, the local government of Beijing tried to intervene and formed relationships of cooperation with individuals in the village for joint public-private funding of the construction of a large marketplace, the Jingwen Garment Wholesale Centre. From 1986 on, a marketplace for agricultural products near Zhejiang Village at this location had step by step been taken over by Zhejiang villagers, and changed into a clothes market. In 1989, the Beijing Bureau of Industry and Commerce, together with its branch of Fengtai district, conducted an investigation into this development and concluded: "[It is necessary] to adhere to the proper direction and manage the marketplace for agricultural products well. Everything that does not conform to this 'direction' should be cleared away."

What was outside the "proper direction" was never made clear, yet those who did not "adhere to" it were nevertheless expelled from the market place. Subsequently, the market place remained unused until 1992. What happens after that merits quoting at some length, as it illustrates the emerging patterns of interaction between the local administration and Zhejiang Village. One of the chief administrators of the Jingwen Centre, a middle level cadre in the Fengtai Bureau of Industry and Commerce who had participated in the project from the beginning, said to me: "Lessons of those years [before 1992, X.B.] told us that it is nearly impossible to expel the Zhejiangese from here. But we dared not put forward new ideas, for the attitude of higher leaders was ambiguous. The question was suspended. After Comrade Xiaoping's southern tour in 1992, from the central government to us the local administration here were all saying that we had 'to liberate thoughts and make rapid strides'. The leader of our bureau grasped this opportunity and proposed to construct a clothes marketplace like Baihua at Xidan [in downtown Beijing, X.B.]. Baihua is now approved by the municipal leaders but originated with Beijing individual entrepreneurs who occupied the site. Using such a marketplace as an example and then doing something more with it were our tactics."

"It is impossible for an administrative department like ours to make such a large investment itself. Learning from other places in the country, we decided to "pool" money (*jizi*). But we had no idea how to pool money with the Zhejiangese, we were not even able to talk to them! We went to the representative office of the Wenzhou government in Beijing and through them we contacted the Wenzhou Bureau of Industry and Commerce. (. . .) We agreed to cooperate, and named the marketplace 'Jingwen', meaning it's the product of the cooperation of us two sides [BeiJING and WENzhou, X.B.]. (. . .) The plan was that the marketplace would have five floors and about 1,600 stalls. Those who now contribute 130 thousand yuan to the project will get a stall in it upon completion."

"We organized a pooling group with the deputy leaders from our bureau and the Wenzhou bureau as directors. Most of the staff are administrators from the Wenzhou bureau, especially from its branches in Yueqing and Yongjia county (. . .) who have quite a few relatives and friends in the community here. (. . .) But the situation was harder than we expected. Zhejiangese are cunning: they 'will never free the hunting hawk unless they see the rabbit,' they will not invest if there are no immediate returns. They didn't trust us the government either, maybe because of the policies and plans during those years. We were all worried about it."

"Then the Wenzhou staff proposed a new idea, to construct a temporary market first, a simple marketplace that could be completed in two or three months, to enable the Zhejiangese who pay into the pool to get a temporary stall at once. This is the Muxiyuan Light Industry Wholesale Marketplace that began business in August. At first, many were waiting and seeing. Only about 800 stalls were issued until October (the number of stalls of Jingwen and of Muxiyuan is approximately the same). In

November, the business in Muxiyuan Marketplace started to thrive; after all, it is the first large scale market in Zhejiang Village. People began to compete to join the pool, and the remaining 800 stalls were taken in only ten days."

This brought a "stall boom" and "marketplace boom" to Zhejiang Village that reached its climax in the middle of 1993. The contract with the Bureau of Industry and Commerce became a valued asset in the community. One day in May 1993, one of my interviewees told me in delight that he had just bought a "stall ticket" at a "low" price: 60,000 yuan. I was surprised at him. But he proved to be right after the Centre opened: a stall on the first floor was sublet for more than six million!

The government always met with failure when it was going against the community, but soon found out that going with it did not always bring the desired result either. First, its actions were immediately interpreted as a sign that it allowed migrant communities to develop. The "stall boom" and "marketplace boom" quickly led to a new migration wave, a rather embarrassing development for the local government.[19] Second, the marketplace has enhanced the cohesion of Zhejiang Village, for the Jingwen project provided it with an explicit "public field" and a common counterpart: the government. Most traders in the Jingwen Centre hold that they should have an equal say in the administration of the marketplace. All activities in Zhejiang Village to promote the public interest *vis-à-vis* the government (see below) are related to the Jingwen marketplace. Third, the market stirred up conflict inside the government. A cadre of the Wenzhou Bureau of Industry and Commerce told me: "The Fengtai Bureau of Industry and Commerce now have all the property and management rights, and the Wenzhou bureau is only paid several million yuan a year during the first four years and will lose all its stakes in the Jingwen project after that. We are angry. Sometimes they ask us to deal with some questions that they cannot handle, such as conflicts between traders, but we refuse to help them."

Another case of government intervention in the community that resulted in conflicts within the administration itself is the joint defence team (*lianfangdui*). Confronted with the virtual absence of police in the community, the of Public Security Bureau of Fengtai district decided to try to form a joint police squad from Wenzhou and Fengtai. The Public Security Bureau of Wenzhou accepted the proposal and the team came into being in October 1993. With the exception of the two team heads, the other ten-odd members of the team were all residents of Zhejiang Village. The Public Security Bureau of Fengtai gave them uniforms, but the team itself had to collect money for their wages and expenses from the community. Soon after its formation, the team was at loggerheads with the Dahongmen Police Station, the branch of the Public Security Bureau of Fengtai in Zhejiang Village. The police station held that the joint defence team was subordinate to it while the team thought itself autonomous, because it "had never taken a penny from you and you Beijingese know nothing about us Wenzhounese," according to a member on the team in 1994. One afternoon in December 1993, the team arrested several Wenzhounese and their Beijingese landlord. The landlord had a relative in Dahongmen police station and called three policemen to the site. The police tried to free the landlord but the team refused to let him go, seeing this as an opportunity to express their dissatisfaction with the police station. Fighting ensued and the policemen were beaten up, an incident that was not resolved until the municipal governments of both Beijing and Wenzhou intervened. The joint defence team was dismissed and the Fengtai and Wenzhou public security bureaus refused to cooperate again.

In July 1995, a national work conference was held by the central government on the administration of the floating population. Earlier, a large meeting on the administration of migrants in Beijing had been convened by the municipal authorities in June. Since these two meetings, Beijing has promulgated eleven laws and regulations in this regard; in November 1995, a large scale campaign was organized to "put the affairs of Zhejiang Village in order" (*qingli zhengdun*). The government has decided to build a "Garment City" in the village. The measures adopted by the government have shown a conspicuous inconsistency and fickleness, indicating that the government lacks resolution and continues to be at odds with the migrants.

Who has the power?

In the spring of 1995, I had a chat with twenty-five year old Deng Busong. "I have come to make a social investigation and market analysis in Beijing," he said, "to find out which pays: to make Western style garments or leather jackets, rent a counter, or go into real estate with a partner, and to make sure whether I can make my way into one of these trades if it is really profitable. I must find out who the bigwigs are here, who are the top people, who listens to whom and whether I would gain anything from coming here. We are not just 'doing business' here! Some time later, I'll go to Shijiazhuang and Harbin to have a look and make some comparisons." His elder brother Deng Bulin came in 1988. His decision to migrate was based on a different consideration: "They [i.e. the people back home, X.B.] all said that it's easy to do business in Beijing, so I left my town-run factory and went with them [i.e. the other migrants, X.B.]. One could make garments or rent counters to sell clothes. But people did not stick doggedly to such a division. It was not unusual that people made clothes in the first half of the year and rented a counter in the second. There was not much difference in our incomes. Things were rather simple. The only problems we ran into were falling ill, quarrelling with Beijingese, getting cheated, or some such thing. We talked it over with some friends, and with their help the difficulties were easily solved."

Deng Busong's decision to migrate will be based chiefly on a cost-benefit calculation of the opportunities that migration offers, rather than the individual persuasion or vague expectations that are typical of an ordinary chain migrant such as his brother. This indicates the formation of business space. But what is more important, he must make clear "who the bigwigs are". Zhejiang Village is something more than a space for business.

Then who are the bigwigs and what kind of power do they have? This is not only a key to reveal the inner structure of the community, but will also provide insights in the relationship between state and this spontaneously formed social space.

Especially after 1992, the development of Zhejiang Village has split its members into three groups: elites, the ordinary people and gang members. According to their power base and residents' opinions on them, I further divide the community elites into four types: silent rich man, elder, broker, and public leader.

Silent rich man

Liu Zebo is thought to be a silent rich man. After a steady development of their business over more than ten years, Liu and his family now have a medium size garment factory, several shops in Beijing and other big cities, and several cars. Liu had even tried to open a commercial branch in Russia in 1994. A good many people in the village have heard about him and call him an "able person" (nengren) though they may not be acquainted with him personally. Yet wealth has not brought power for Liu Zebo. He told me: "I have some economic advantages, but I am not interested in social power (shili) (. . .) I never want to establish a force of my own. My ideal is just to do business peacefully. Once you get power, you face danger. You will never be detached once you become involved in some matters [i.e. the activities of gangs, see below, X.B.]." Liu's sons have intimate connections with many businesspeople in Beijing, and the formalities they have to go through for buying their cars and flats (both require a Beijing hukou) were all conducted by their "friends in the city." But the functions of these connections are limited to mutual benefit and "facilitating business" (banshi fangbian). They have not been used to gain control over community affairs.

Liu is accepted as an elite not only because he succeeds in business. More importantly, Liu's attitude of "developing business but not pursuing power" represents the consensus among the common people in the village. One informant of about the same age as Liu said to me: "If all us Wenzhounese were like old Liu, the world would be much more peaceful!" Even Liu Hefei, a typical example of the second kind of elite, the elders, nodded with a smile, "Yes, Zebo is the best, and he most of all deserves to be envied."

Elder

The second kind of elite, who I call "the elders" (*laoda*), are the most powerful and influential individuals in the community. The aforementioned Liu Hefei is a typical example. Almost all adults in Zhejiang Village know him. His guest room is always full whenever I visit him. With his guests, most of the topics of conversation are about public affairs, such as events in the community or the world outside, or rumours about the municipal or national government (interestingly, Wenzhou itself does not play an important role in their conversation). People seem to like gathering here to chat even when Liu himself is absent. He is a public man and his home is part of the "public space" of the community around him.

When I told him that I would call him the "nongovernmental general judge" in my work, he smiled. *Duan'an* (settling a case) is a very important part of his life. In his role as judge, he not only applies practical logic, but also bases himself on traditional morality. For instance, there is always a "unity dinner" in the end, symbolizing that the issue has formally been settled and that any side who disobeys his ruling will be held responsible.

Liu is mentioned as "manoeuvring both in the black way and the white way" (*heidao baidao dou lai*, using both legal and illegal means). Similarly, the source of Liu's power lies equally in his connection with the mass of the ordinary people and with members of the gangs. He is always generous and warm-hearted to the common people. He offered a *laoxiang* (person from his place of origin) a few thousand yuan for curing his leukaemia, and sponsored a collection in his compound in 1995 to help a tenant suffering from some severe disease.

Yet I found that his power grew to new heights when the gangs emerged in 1994. Just like in the Chinatowns abroad, gang members in Zhejiang Village are young men of fifteen to twenty-five years old. They have three main sources of income: extortion and racketeering, as roughnecks employed by others for a reward, and pocket money given by "*dahu*" (successful person, "big man"). One can gain prestige but no power without contacts with gangs, who are the unique "weapons of the strong" to protect their interests in the community. Shortly after I started fieldwork in Zhejiang Village, someone told me: "There are some 'lads' (*tongzilao* in Wenzhounese, gang members) who are obedient to Liu. He adopts them!" "To adopt" here means that Liu often offers them money. Liu gave three members of a gang 5,000 yuan in delight after a successful business deal. On another occasion when I was present too, Liu offered another gang 3,000 yuan when they asked Liu to "lend" them 2,000. There are always a few youths about him who take him not only as their leader (*laoda*) but also as their master (*shifu*). As far as I know, Liu has never had to use the gangs physically to intimidate others. Many of my informants agree with me on this. One said: "Who dares to offend him?

Gangs for him are just like nuclear weapons for our country. He cannot go without them but needn't employ them." But the gangs must ask him for permission before they undertake an "action" to make sure that their target has no special relations to Liu.

The gangs allow Liu to provide "protection." The compound built by him and his twenty-four fellow shareholders is the largest in Zhejiang Village with a capacity of about 4,000 people. A tenant: "It is impossible for common people to build such a big compound. So many people live in the houses and pay you the rents, you are responsible for them. And both tenants and gangs will trouble you if you don't have enough power. But Liu has no problem. People think they would get some security from him and will obey him." This view was repeated by many people.

With his status in the community further enhanced and attracting more and more attention, especially after the building of the compound, Liu said to me: "Do you think there will be a good future for me? (. . .) With such a visible compound here, I am afraid of getting trouble if I don't establish good relations with the government, especially the bureau of public security." The local police station has in fact tried to use him as an assistant, calling on him to attend certain routine meetings. Some of Liu's suggestions, including how to deal with the gangs, were accepted. During the Mid-Autumn Festival of 1994 and the Chinese New Year of 1995, Liu sent boxes of cigarettes and fruits to the police on duty as "*weiwen*."[20]

Simultaneously, Liu began to institutionalize his connections with the ordinary people, especially the tenants of his compound. He issued a series of regulations and a "public pledge for civilization" and he gradually broke with the gangs.

In 1995, Liu's developing connection with the local administration suddenly collapsed. Liu was listed as a "dangerous man" by some municipal department and his compound torn down. When he tried to develop a "new Zhejiang city" in a town near Beijing, the "typhoon" of government periodic suppression quickly passed and people could return to Dahongmen. Liu's initial investment was a total loss. Liu was very depressed in that period. "The loss of money is not the most serious," he said. "What depresses me is that I lose my fundamental authority. Your country collapses when others want it to, you are expelled once others want to. Who will follow you in the future?" At least according to my observation, Liu's fall has not brought about a better social order in the community at all, and it seemed unwise for the government to sever its connection with somebody like him.

Broker

The third kind of elite, brokers, have the most intimate contact with government officials. Chen Jili, one of my closest friends, when talking about his brother-in-law, Hong Yang, said: "People think him a man of ability, but I don't like him. He is just a broker (*qianke*). When you get in trouble and ask him for a favour, he asks for your money! He knows a lot of the officials in all administrative departments, which is his source of wealth."

Hong is also very successful in business, but his strategy is totally different from Liu Hefei's. His highest profits come from exploiting the "cracks" (*kongzi*, meaning something that is not neither wholly legal, nor directly forbidden). According to Hong, "Several Wenzhounese pooled money to build a clothes marketplace at the northern end of Dahongmen street last year, but could not obtain the necessary approval. With this information, I managed to rent that partially completed marketplace under a temporary contract with the government, which said that I would vacate whenever the government has new plans for that place. The rent is rather low, and, you know, it is impossible for the government to decide on a new plan in a short time. I have acquaintances in all departments. (...) Liu Hefei makes his money from volume, the larger the scale, the more he earns. But that requires investment! I think I have a higher profit rate."

It is a basic rule of the gang heads to try their best to release their gang members upon arrest, otherwise they may lose their leadership position. Hong, with his access to government cadres, thus became a valuable partner for the gang leaders. Hong nevertheless avoids long term and intimate relations with the gangs because he thinks it to be "too dangerous." Common people in the community also frequently ask him for help, although many of them think he is earning "black heart money" in that way (*heixin qian*, money earned in an immoral or evil way). As one informant explained, "It is unavoidable to deal with the government, and it is very difficult or even impossible for us to do that routinely. With no other way, asking people like Hong is the best choice for me."

The power of the gangs and corruption in the administration are among the most severe problems facing the government, but, ironically, one source of these problems are the government's own officials and their friends.

Public leader

Public leaders have emerged since 1990, and especially 1993. This kind of elite has three characteristics. First, they are not the most authoritative leaders in the community: they tend to be leaders of smaller businessmen who have to join forces to make their voice heard. Second, organizations headed by public leaders are always vulnerable. Third, most efforts to promote the public interest turn out to be fruitless.

Zhejiang Village has adopted three strategies to promote the public interest: "ingratiating," "struggling" and "negotiating and harmonizing." Zhejiang Village tried to ingratiate itself with the municipal society by contributing money to the Asian Games held in Beijing in 1990. Chen Jili, who first came up with this suggestion, told me, "I think the government will surely expel us from Beijing for the duration of the Games. Could it change our lot if we offered a donation to the government? I saw on the TV that many small private businesses in Beijing contributed money to the Games and received praise from the government. I discussed this idea with others and many people thought it a good proposal. It is not only in our own interest, but is also an honour. The problem was that we had no idea how to make such a contribution. I asked a secretary in a ministry for help. He asked me how much we could collect. To my disappointment, he indicated that it would be 'meaningless' if the collection were anything less than 100,000 yuan. I hesitated, but at last decided to give it a try! But, unfortunately, the 'typhoon' expelled us just before we could begin executing the plan."

Typical cases illustrating the "struggling" strategy are the following two events, called the "strike disturbance" (*bashi fengbo*) and the "June revolution" by one of the organizers. In February 1993, the administration of the Muxiyuan Light Industry Commodity Market increased the monthly stall rent from sixty to 200–400 yuan. The stallholders refused to pay the higher rents, arguing that the market was built by them and the government together. The cadres, who could not collect any rent for a whole month, in the end declared that those who would not pay up would be forbidden to enter the market. The stallholders persisted. Getting quite alarmed by now, the market administration and police station formed an "emergency coordination group" (*jinji xietiao xiaozu*) to patrol the marketplace. The group arrested nine stallholders and locked them up for a day. A strike was on and seven days later the administration yielded to the strikers' demands.

The "June Revolution," also called the "second revolution," (implying that the strike of 1993 was the first "revolution") was once again the result of dispute on fee payment. The administration of the Jingwen Centre ordered in June 1994 that all stallholders pay 4,000 yuan for "stall redecoration." The traders refused to pay, referring to their contract which says that "stallholders need not pay anything except the initial contribution to the pool and their monthly rent." A "lawsuit committee" of seven people was formed. They collected 20,000 yuan for expenses to go to Hangzhou, the capital of Zhejiang province, to ask the Zhejiang court to support them. At this point, the administration cancelled its decision, and the "second revolution" ended before it got started.

The strategy of "negotiating and harmonizing" is adopted by the Benevolent Group (*Aixin Xiaozu*) of the Jingwen Centre. The Benevolent Association (*Aixin She*) was formed by Peking University students to appeal to citizens' public consciousness and spirit of mutual help; with the support from the government it has won a wide influence in society. Chen Jili learned about the Benevolent Association on television, and it occurred to him that a similar association might build up the good name of both the Centre and Wenzhounese in Beijing in general. With help from outside the community, the Benevolent Group was established at the end of 1994. It organized public works and collected money for disaster-struck districts elsewhere in China, thus gaining the administration's recognition and enhancing the solidarity of the people involved in the Jingwen Centre. The group also carried out a dialogue with the market's administrator, but soon the relationship soured due to two events. First, in March 1995, the administration of the market unilaterally decided to lease unoccupied space out to increase its income. After protests from the Benevolent Group, the administration finally adjusted its decision, but felt rather embarrassed about it.

The other event occurred in May 1995, when a policeman from the local police station beat a stallholder. The Benevolent Group and the victim jointly wrote a letter to the market administration, the police station and the Fengtai Bureau of Public Security, demanding that disciplinary action be taken against the policeman. The protest failed. Instead, the group was warned and gradually excluded from most scheduled activities (Xiang:1995b).

Discussion

Migrant entrepreneurs who have not been accepted by the established administrative system have created a "non-state space." The concept of non-state space comprises two terms that require some clarification: "non-state" and "space". As said earlier in the introductory section, both Rouse and Rosaldo developed the concept of "space" in their studies of transnational migration. Space emphasizes that migrants develop new practices, which are distinct from those of the societies of origin and destination. The idea of space emphasizes the multiple, and not necessarily coherent, combination of social practices and social relationships that develop through migration (Rosaldo 1989:77–87; Rouse 1991). Combining the concept of space with another group of concepts, such as "transnational community" and "migration circuit" (indicating the continuous circulation of people, information, and other materials), makes it possible to understand migration as an aspect of a single community spread across a variety of sites (Rouse 1989:9; Georges 1990:234–52).

The other element in the concept of non-state space is that of the "state". Similarly during the mass migration stage, Zhejiang migrants mobilized resources and established networks all across the nation, even extending abroad and far beyond the planned allocation system of the state. Moreover, Zhejiang Village has not only established such a transregional space of production and management, but also a political space outside the state administrative system.

240

Recently, a prominent debate has raged about civil society in China and its relationship with the state. One side holds that China is developing a civil society, or can potentially develop one (Yang 1989; Ostergaard 1989; Strand 1990; Deng and Jing 1992:59), while others argue that civil society can hardly appear in China in the near future (Xia 1993; Xiao 1993).

In this article I have tried to show that, as far as migrant groups are concerned, the boundary between state and society in contemporary China has become clearer. In Zhejiang Village, people "no longer bother with the formalities" and autonomously manage the affairs of village, to which the state and urban society outside the village are considered immaterial. Individuals and groups pursue their own private interests and simultaneously cater for at least some public interests (cooperation with other stallholders, constructing the village's infrastructure) independently from the state, while the state has difficulty exercising even indirect control. The community elite builds up power within the community in ways that are sanctioned by community structures and norms rather than the state. For example, people like Liu Hefei have found the space to mediate conflicts far removed from the procedures and principles of the state judicial system. Also given the government's rather negative or at best half-hearted attempts at involvement in the community, these elites manage to check any further government penetration.[21]

But separation between state and non-state is not necessarily congruent with the Western experience summarized in the concept of civil society. Civil society has been discussed in a variety of contexts, but in the study of state socialist societies three factors are central: (1) Autonomy of social life from the state; (2) limits to the power of the state; and (3) both autonomy and limits should be institutionalized, for instance in citizens' rights and obligations. As demonstrated repeatedly above, there is no institutionalized interaction between Zhejiang Village and the government. Migrants have developed a plethora of strategies to operate outside the state controlled sphere of society, but have no idea about their legal status or rights *vis-à-vis* state. When it comes to state-society relations, their key strategy is to dodge the attempts of the state to interfere with their life and business.

The term "non-state" and the emphasis on the absence of institutionalized interaction should not lead to the impression that this space has no relations with the state at all. On the contrary, "non-state space" has been produced in the interaction of migrants and government. What is special is that the two sides work at cross-purposes: the state uses the policies, administrative agencies, and system that have been established and refined since 1949, while the migrants have developed many new strategies in their daily life. A member of the administrative staff at the Jingwen Centre complained to me: "Zhejiangese are very difficult to deal with. Their dialect is so monstrous that I can never master a word. I was just looking at them like a doll while they were talking over how to cheat me and play some tricks." I think that the doll is a perfect metaphor for the role of the government in its relations with Zhejiang Village. The migrants are playing hide-and-seek with the state. After the community became a visible "category" of Beijing life in the mid-1980s, only when the government complied with the logic of the community could it get a grip on it. Yet by doing so, the community's logic is promoted and its independence is strengthened, as manifested in the case of the Jingwen Centre.

Zhejiang Village has also brought to the fore the conflicts between the regions, hierarchical levels and departments of the state. Zhejiang Village thus aptly demonstrates a fundamental error of the state-civil society paradigm: it assumes the existence of unitary structures ("state," "society") that are in actual fact composites of corporate and individual actors. Contradictions within the state have received much attention in modern Chinese studies, but the conflicts studied tend to be the outcome of routine bureaucratic strategies. The conflicts surrounding Zhejiang Village, however, are rather different. Their source is located outside the system and proves to be beyond the state's control.

Some studies on China hold that state and party continue to control most of the vital economic and political resources even after the reforms. Groups outside the system thus have to link up with the system in order to develop. Solinger's studies on migrants in contemporary China, which could be seen as representative for this model in the field of migration, argue that migrants have to "develop connections – *guanxi* – with party members and other gatekeepers in order to mediate the acquisition of capital, education, and other essentials necessary for upward mobility" (1995:137). As a result, migrants contribute to, rather than challenge, the state, "performing a whole array of functions" for it (1993:81). These inferences seem unduly functionalist to me. The strong may have their measures, but the weak have their "weapons" too. Their ambiguous legal position has not inevitably made migrants as vulnerable as Solinger would have it (1993:100–1); the same ambiguity is also the migrants' source of strength. If the state ignores migrant communities, members of these same communities do not need the state to survive and can afford to ignore, dodge, or bend the rules and structures of the state. A lack of commitment comes at the price of a lack of control that stops short of blanket repression or expulsion. The weapon of migrants is thus their human agency: their ability to create the structures of a non-state space through their strategies of daily life that for convenience's sake I have referred to as the "marketization of traditional networks."

As You Dashan said, "How can we compare with Beijingese private entrepreneurs? As the saying goes: 'One is as strong as a tiger at home, but as weak as a cat in a strange land'. They have their own shop-fronts (*menlian*)[22] and many connections. Besides, the state supports only resident private entrepreneurs. Though no definite stipulations exist against migrants, we are not given any preferential treatment, to say the least. Even now we are not regarded as 'individual entrepreneurs' (getihu), but are referred to as 'farmers coming from other provinces to do business here'! The urban entrepreneurs can earn enough just by trading (dao) or by leasing out their stalls, because they were in the urban market from the very beginning. We were denied good marketplaces at the earlier stages and had to engage in production."

Outsiders still had problems even in production. Take Liu Zebo for instance. He had to go back to Wenzhou in 1983 to get official documents so that he and his relatives and friends could stay in Beijing. They had difficulty in obtaining materials and information. Not being formally recognized, they could not invest large sums, and their products therefore lacked in quality. Several options were open to the pioneering migrants of Zhejiang Village to remedy this situation. They could cooperate with Beijing private entrepreneurs, or they could "anchor" (guakao) themselves to collective or state owned enterprises, thus gaining an established protective network within the system. But both strategies would require a long period of painstaking effort and trial and error. The alternative method that Liu Zebo and his fellows adopted was to band together. The loose migration network was knit much more closely together, enabling the group to survive outside the system rather than blend with it. In hostile, but potentially profitable Beijing the traditional networks of the Wenzhounese provided trust and understanding on the basis of shared knowledge of each others' background and families in Wenzhou.

Some contradictions still remain. Zhejiang Villagers have shied away from investing their profits in expanding the scale of their production, or entering the main market beyond their original market segment. In You Dashan's words: "I have never thought of running a factory [instead of informal household production] here. Back home, I have my own house, but here I have to pay 600 to 700 yuan each month just to rent a room of acceptable size. I have no ties in Beijing either. Chances are my things get confiscated tomorrow and my family is driven out. How dare I buy any machines? Apart from this, we are mostly small producers with just a little capital and a little education. We can not handle big groups."

With regard to external cooperation, why do Zhejiang villagers continue to work within the nationwide Wenzhou network? Yao Xin'an's words cited above indicate that without formal organizations or legal guarantees, migrants judge the reliability and stability of the network more important than the higher efficiency that might result from cooperation with strangers. By doing so, the migrant community as a whole seized a bigger portion in the market. Under these circumstances, traditional networks expanded rapidly, becoming the basis for the emergence of the new market structures and community elites that define the social space that is Zhejiang Village.

Zhejiang Village survived and developed by "taking a roundabout way" (*raozhe zou*). Not confronting the state system outright, the villagers surreptitiously created a new space outside the state. When the government started to take notice of the village, "raw rice had already been cooked" (*shengmi zhucheng shufan*): a return to the original state of affairs had become impossible. The community had mastered the essence of Taichi martial arts and guerrilla warfare: to escape when the enemy attacks and return as soon as he withdraws. By doing so, the state system and state-society relations remained formally unchanged, without new laws or policies, but the social structure had in fact undergone an important transition.

The development of Zhejiang Village cogently illustrates how migration leads to structural change in and between the social fields of state, market and social networks. A "three-circle structure" has appeared in Chinese cities.[23] The majority of the state owned units, together with the resources they control and the personnel belonging to them, form the first concentric circle. Urban private enterprises and individual businesses, which have won considerable economic autonomy, constitute the second circle. As urban units existing outside the system, they are the products of the state's policies and remain within the framework that the state has designed for them, and maintain intricate ties with the first circle. The third circle is made up of the businesses of migrants. Before 1986, the three circles interacted with one another. But the third circle has gradually separated itself from the other two since 1986.

The relationship between the third and the first circle is fraught with the frictions that have been discussed above. The relationship between the third and the second circle is, if anything, even more complicated. With the marketization of the traditional networks and the formation of a non-state space in Zhejiang Village, some Beijing individual businesses and private enterprises have started to cooperate with the migrants and invest in the community, and many of the community elite have also cooperated with local entrepreneurs in large projects. Through such combinations, the second circle is gradually teased apart from the state system. Typical examples are subsidiary companies of a government department (*chuang-shou*, see Pieke 1995) that have obtained more autonomy and power from the mother work unit through their connections with the new space of migrant business. The development of the interaction between the two outer circles is likely to be a crucial aspect of any future changes in urban China.

References

Ba Dachengshi Diaoyan Jigou Lianhe Ketizu [Joint Research Group of Government Investigation Units of Eight Metropolises]. 1990. *Zhongguo Dachengshi Renkou yu Shehui Fazhan* [Population and social development in Chinese metropolises]. Beijing: Zhongguo Chengshi Shehui Jingji Chubanshe.

Deng Zhenglai and Jin Yuejin. 1992. "Jiangou Zhongguode shimin shehui" [Establishing Civil Society in China]. *Zhongguo Shehui Kexue Jikan* 1, no. 1, pp. 58–68.

Fei Xiaotong. 1992. "Wenzhou Xing" [Visit to Wenzhou]. In *Xingxing chong Xingxing: Xiangzhen Fazhang Lunshu* [Travels: On rural development]. Lanzhou: Gansu Renmin Chubanshe, pp. 274–90 (originally written in 1986).

Fei Xiaotong. 1986. *Jiangcun Jingji: Zhongguo Nongminde Shenghuo* [The economy of Jiang village: The life of Chinese farmers]. Nanjing: Jiangsu Renmin Chubanshe.

Georges, Eugenia, 1990. *The Making of a Transnational Community: Migration, Development and Cultural Change in the Dominican Republic.* New York: Columbia University Press.

Geti Si (Guojia Gongshang Xingzheng Guanliju, Geti Jingji Si) [The Department of the Individual Economy of the National Bureau for Administrative Management of Industry and Commerce]. 1987[1983]. "Guanyu Quanguo Tongyi Geti Gongshangye Yingye Zhizhao Youguan Shixiang Guiding (1983) [Regulations on questions concerning the national unification of business licences for individual industry and commerce (1983)]. In Geti Si, ed. *Geti Gongshangye Zhengce Fagui Huibian* [Collection of laws and regulations on individual industry and commerce]. Volume 2. Beijing: Jingji Kexue Chubanshe, pp. 346–8.

Goldring, Luin Penelope. 1992. Diversity and Community in Transnational Migration: Comparative Study of Two Mexico – U.S. Migrant Circuits. Unpublished Ph.D. dissertation, Cornell University.

Gong'an Bu [Ministry of Public Security]. 1987[1985]. *Guanyu Chengzhen Zanzhu Renkoude Zanxing Guiding* [Provisional rules on temporary resident population in urban areas]. In Getisi, ed. *Geti Gongshangye Zhengce Fagui Huibian* [Collection of laws and regulations on individual industry and commerce]. Volume 2. Beijing: Jingji Kexue Chubanshe, pp. 458–60.

Guowuyuan [State Council]. 1987[1982]. "Guowuyuan guanyu Shutong Chengxiang Shangpin Liutong Qudao, Kuoda Gongyepin Xiaxiangde Jueding (1982)" [The decision of the State Council on opening up the circulation channels of commodities in the urban and rural areas and expanding the sale of industrial goods in the countryside]. In Getisi (Guojia Gongshang Xingzheng Guanli Ju, Geti Jingji Si) [The Department of the Individual Economy of the National Bureau for Administrative Management of Industry and Commerce], ed. *Geti Gongshangye Zhengce Fagui Huibian* [Collection of laws and regulations on individual industry and commerce]. Volume 2. Beijing: Jingji Kexue Chubanshe, pp. 266–8.

Hongqiao Zhen Zhengfu [The People's Government of the Hongqiao Town of Yueqing County]. 1993. *Hongqiao Zhen Zhi* [Gazetteer of Hongqiao town] Beijing: China International Broadcast Publishing House.

Jaffe, A.J. 1962. "Notes on the Population Theory of Eugene M. Kulischer." In *The Milbank Memorial Fund Quarterly* 40, no. 2, pp. 87–206.

Ji Dangsheng et al. 1996. *Beijingshi Liudong Renkou Yanjiu* [Study on floating population in Beijing]. In Zou Lanchun, ed. *Beijingde Liudong Renkou* [The floating population in Beijing], Beijing: Zhongguo Renkou Chubanshe, pp. 95–111

Kearney, Michael. 1986. "From the Invisible Hand to Visible Feet: Anthropological Studies of Migration and Development." *Annual Review of Anthropology* 15, pp. 331–61.

Kuznets, Simon et al., eds. 1957. *Population Redistribution and Economic Growth – United States, 1870–1950.* Volume 1. Philadelphia: American Philosophical Society.

245

Kuznets, Simon et al., eds. 1964. *Population Redistribution and Economic Growth – United States, 1870–1950.* Volume 3. Philadelphia: American Philosophical Society.

Lee, Everett S. 1966. "A Theory of Migration." *Demography* 3, no. 1, pp. 45–57.

Liao Zhenghong. 1986. *Renkou Qianyi* [Population mobility]. Taiwan: Sanmin Shuju.

Li Zongling et al. ed. 1990. *Tansuode Zuji: Beijingshi Jingji Tizhi Gaige Zhongda Shijian Yanjiu* [Tracks of exploration: Studies on important events in the reform of the economic system in Beijing]. Beijing: Jingji Guanli Chubanshe.

Lin Bai et al. 1987. *Wenzhoude Jueqi* [The rise of Wenzhou]. Nanning: Guangxi Renmin Chubanshe.

Liu Qiuhua. 1996. *Beijingshi Liudong Renkoude Zhuyao Tedian* [The major characteristics of the population in Beijing]. In Zou Lanchun, ed. *Beijingde Liudong Renkou* [The floating population in Beijing], Beijing: Zhongguo Renkou Chubanshe, pp. 112–15.

Liu, Yia-ling. 1992. "Reform From Below: The Private Economy and Politics in the Rural Industialization of Wenzhou." *The China Quarterly* 130, pp. 293–316.

MacDonald, John S. and Leatrice D. MacDonald. 1964. "Chain Migration, Ethnic Neighbourhood Formation and Social Networks." *The Milbank Memorial Fund Quarterly*, 42, no. 1, pp. 82–97.

Meillassoux, Claude. 1981. *Maidens, Meal and Money: Capitalism and the Domestic Community.* Cambridge: Cambridge University Press.

Ostergaard, Clemens Stubbe. 1989. "Citizens, Groups, and a Nascent Civil Society in China: Towards an Understanding of the 1989 Student Demonstrations". *China Information* 4, no. 2, pp. 28–41.

Parris, Kristen. 1993. "Local Initiative and National Reform: The Wenzhou Model of Development." *The China Quarterly* 134, pp. 242–63.

Petersen, William. 1958. A General Typology of Migration. *American Sociological Review* 23, no. 3, pp. 256–266.

Pieke, Frank N. 1995. "Bureaucracy, Friends, and Money: The Growth of Capital Socialism in China." *Comparative Studies in Society and History* 37, no. 3, pp. 494–518.

Rosaldo, Renato. 1989. "Ideology, Place, and People Without Culture." *Current Anthropology* 3, no. 1, pp. 77–87.

Rouse, Roger. 1987. Migration and the Politics of Family Life: Divergent Project and Rhetorical Strategies in a Mexican Transnational Migrant Community. La Jolla: Center for US-Mexican Studies, University of California, San Diego. Unpublished manuscript.

Rouse, Roger. 1991. "Mexican Migration and the Social Space of Postmodernism." *Diaspora* 1, no. 1, pp. 8–23.

Sauvy, Alfred. 1966. *General Theory of Population.* New York: Basic Books.

Shangye Bu [Ministry of Trade]. 1987[1983]. *Guanyu Wancheng Liangyou Tonggou Renwu hou Shixing Duoxudao Jingying Ruogan Wentide Shixing Guiding* [Trial regulations on some questions concerning the implementation of multi-channel management after the fulfillment of the task of unified purchase of oil and grain]. In Tigai Ju (Guojia Jingji Weiyuanhui, Tigai Ju) [System Reform Bureau of the State Economic Commission]) ed. *Zhongguo Jingji Guanli Zhengce Faling Xuanbian* [Selection of documents and laws of the Chinese economic administration]. Volume 2. Beijing: Jingji Kexue Chubanshe, pp. 482–5.

Solinger, Dorothy J. 1992. "Urban Entrepreneurs and the State: The Merger of State and Society." In Arthur Lewis Rosenbaum, ed. *State and Society in China: The Consequences of Reform.* Boulder: Westview Press, pp. 121–41.

Solinger, Dorothy J. 1993. "China's Transients and the State: A Form of Civil Society?" *Politics & Society* 21, no. 1, pp. 91–122.

Solinger, Dorothy J. 1995. "The Floating Population in the Cities: Chances for Assimilation?" In Deborah S. Davis, Richard Kraus, Barry Naughton and Elizabeth Perry, eds, *Urban Spaces in Contemporary China: The Potential for Autonomy and Community in Post-Mao China.* Cambridge: University of Cambridge Press and Woodrow Wilson International Center for Scholars, pp. 113–39.

Strand, David. 1990. "Protest in Beijing: Civil Society and Public Sphere in China." *Problems of Communism* 39, no. 3. pp. 1–19.

Wang Chunguang. 1994. Shehui Liudong he Shehui Chonggou: Shoudu Zhejiangcun Yanjiu [Social mobility and social reconstruction: A study of Zhejiang Village in the capital]. Ph.D. dissertation, Chinese Academy of Social Sciences.

Wood, Charles H. 1982. "Equilibrium and Historical-Structural Perspectives on Migration." *International Migration Review* 16, no. 2, pp. 298–319.

Xia Weizhong. 1993. "*Shimin Shehui:* Zhongguo Jinqi Nan Yuande Meng" [Civil society: a dream that will be impossible to realize in the near future]. *Zhongguo Shehui Kexue Jikan* 5, no. 4, pp. 176–82.

Xiang Biao. 1995a. Chengshi Shehui Chengzhang yu Mingong Wenti Yanjiu: Yi Guangdong Dongguan wei Anli [The growth of urban society and the problem of migrant workers: The case of Dongguan City, Guangdong Province]. Department of Sociology, Peking University. Unpublished manuscript.

Xiang Biao. 1995b. "Zhejiangcun zhaji" [Notes on Zhejiang Village]. Nos. 10, 11, 12 and 13. *Zhongguo Nongmin* 1995, no. 5, pp. 57–9; no. 8, pp. 57–9; no. 9, pp. 55–7; no. 10 pp. 42–5.

Xiao Gongqing. 1993. "Shimin Shehui yu Zhongguo Xiandaihuade San Zhong Zhang'ai" [Civil society and three obstacles to China's modernization]. *Zhongguo Shehui Kexue Jikan* 5, no. 4, pp. 183–95.

Yang, Mayfair Mei-hui. 1989. "The Construction of Corporateness in a Chinese Socialist Factory." *The Australian Journal of Chinese Affairs* 20, pp. 31–60.

Yuan Yayu et al. 1994. *Zhongguo Nongminde Shehui Liudong* [Social mobility of Chinese farmers]. Chengdu: Sichuan Daxue Chubanshe.

Zhang Tiejun. 1996. Liuru Renkou LaiJing Qianhou Zhiye Zhuangkuang Qianxi [An preliminary analysis of the occupations of the inflowing population before and after coming to Beijing]. In Zou Lanchun, ed. *Beijingde Liudong Renkou* [The floating population in Beijing]. Beijing: Zhongguo Renkou Chubanshe, pp. 134–36.

Zheng Dajiong. 1992. *Wenzhou Gaige – Lilun Sikao yu Shijian Tansuo* [Reform in Wenzhou – theoretical reflections and practical explorations]. Shanghai: Fudan Daxue Chubanshe.

Notes

1 There were 1.31 million migrants in Beijing in 1989, 1.01 million of whom had registered with the department of public security. Originally, it was planned that the floating population in the urban districts of Beijing municipality would rise to 2.1 million by the year 2000 (all figures above are from Ba Da Chengshi 1990:9). However, this figure has been greatly surpassed. According to the statistics gathered by the Beijing Statistical Bureau and other units in the course of a survey of the floating population on November 10, 1994, the municipality's migrants had already reached the figure of 3.295 million in that year (Ji 1996:95), 2.38 million of whom lived in the urban districts (Liu 1996:112). Only less than fifty per cent of these migrants had registered with the department of the public security (Ji 1996:105).

2 For perceptions of migrants, see Ding and Stockman, this volume. In an interview with a correspondent of the Xinhua News Agency weekly *Outlook*, Meng Xuenong, Vice-Mayor of Beijing Municipality, said that criminal offences committed by migrants constituted fifty-six per cent of the total in Beijing (Liaowang Zhoukan 1995 48:24) This ratio has rapidly increased from 25.5 per cent in 1990 and 37.6 per cent in 1992 to more than fifty per cent in 1994 (Ji 1996:104). My own investigation in Guangdong shows that the rate of solved criminal cases among migrants is one third of the rate of cases involving established residents.

3 Rights connected with decollectivization of agriculture after 1978 include farmers' rights to make decisions in agricultural and side-line production and freely use one's own labour also in non-agricultural production, and the right to trade in certain materials. The right to settle in small towns and open independent accounts in urban banks were won later by farmers rather than being granted by unilateral action of the state.

4 On the differences between hukou and non-hukou migration, see Chan, this volume.

5 I got this idea from discussions with Wang Hansheng, Sun Liping and Shen Yuan.

6 City administrative bodies unanimously are of the opinion that migrants working in factories and living with local residents (like the nannies) are easy to administer. Migrants doing business in marketplaces, keeping stalls along the streets and doing other service work are difficult to manage, and are often accused of involvement with criminals. Individual businessmen and women are the largest single group of migrants in Beijing. In 1994, 34.9 per cent of all migrants, or more than one million were engaged in business (Zhang 1996:134). In October 1995, a cadre in charge of the supervision of private enterprise in Beijing told me that the great majority of these migrant entrepreneurs have no business licence. "Doing business without licence in itself is a breach of the law," he said. "What is worse, many of them have set up workshops to turn out fake and shoddy goods to cheat people. Their illegal activities have seriously affected life in Beijing and created great difficulties for the departments in charge of law enforcement."

7 A "street" (*jiedao*) is the urban equivalent of a "township" (*xiang*) or "town" (*zhen*) in rural areas (for further details on the relevant Chinese administrative terminology, see note 3 in Li Minhuan's chapter in this volume).

8 The term "natural village" (*zirancun*) usually refers to geographically distinct clustered settlements. It should not be confused with the terms "administrative village" (*xingzhengcun*) or "villagers' committee" (*cunmin weiyuanhui*), which are the lowest level of administration in rural areas (directly under a township or town).

9 Zhongguo Funü Bao and Fazhi Ribao 6 November 1995.

10 According to an investigation carried out by Beijing municipality in November 1994, Shi village, located in the central part of Zhejiang Village, had 3,724 employers of whom 3,376, or 90.6 per cent, had no business licence. Only four of the 4,884 women of child-bearing age had signed an agreement to conform to the family planning scheme. Of all married women of child bearing ago, 1,143, or fifty-four per cent, had more than one child. Ninety-one per cent of the criminal offences were committed by migrants (Liaowang Zhoukan 1995 48:24). Even now, there is not a single mailbox. Sewerage and electric power could hardly meet the needs of the place (interviews with cadres of Beijing municipality and Fengtai district).

11 During the collective period (roughly between 1958 and 1982), the countryside was organized in communes (*gongshe*, now townships or towns), production brigades (*shengchan dadui*, now usually administrative villages), and production teams (*shengchan dui*, now largely defunct).

12 The charge for a jacket at Shanggutou village was 0.5 to 1.5 yuan and 2.5 to five yuan in Wuhai. The prices in the city of Wenzhou were only slightly lower than in Wuhai. Other villagers told me later why they did not go to the Wenzhou city instead: "People in the city know from our accent we are country folk and do not like us. When we go to other provinces, we just say we are southerners."

13 This association failed later and Liu lost his share. Credit associations (*Hui* or *Chenghui* in Wenzhou) are a time-honoured folk organization in China (Fei 1986:188–92), witnessing a rapid development in Wenzhou since the early 1980s (Liu Yia-Ling 1992:298; Parris 1993:248; Zheng 1992:238–41). Several forms exist, such as *biaohui, ganhui* or *lunhui*, which mainly differ in their way of collecting money.

Strictly speaking, the taihui that Liu participated in is not a form of chenghui. taihui ("tai" may be translated as "to rise" in English) have rising interest rates. For example, the monthly rate had gone up to ten per cent or even thirty per cent in Yueqing county in the early 1980s (interviews in Yueqing county from 1992 to 1997). Being originally the result of the great demand for investment capital in the private economy, the high rates later became fraudulent. The person who organized the hui (*huizhu*) used the interest rate to persuade people to become members of the hui (*ruhuiren*), only to run off with the money that these members had invested (interviews with a former leader of the Policy Research Department (*Zhengce Yanjiushi*) of the Wenzhou Communist Party Committee in 1996 and 1997).

14 The Third Plenum of the Twelfth Central Committee of the Chinese Communist Party adopted the "Decision on the Reform of the Economic System" in October 1984, making cities become the main arena of further reform.

15 The Beijing Municipal Party Committee decided in January 1983 to try out the responsibility system in state and collective commercial and service enterprises of Qianmen and Xidan street. From May 1984, the reform of "remoulding the enterprise, switching to other industry, and leasing out" (*gai, zhuan, zu*) was carried out in small state commercial enterprises with an annual profit of less than 200,000 yuan. In 1986, the contract system became the central measure in the reform of Beijing's commercial enterprises. With the ensuing delegation of power to lower levels, the practice of leasing out counters to individuals appeared in state and collective shops (Li et al. 1990:153–70).

16 Gong'an Bu 1987:459.

17 This figure was provided by the deputy head of Hongqiao town.

18 These activities are different from *qianzhuang* (private banks). A *qianzhuang* is an open and established institute, while private money lending has been forbidden by the state.

19 I was told later that the Fengtai Bureau of Industry and Commerce was criticized by the municipal government of Beijing and its Fengtai branch because the marketplace project suffered from "the absence of far-sightedness and did not take the situation as a whole into account."

20 Formal expression of gratitude and sympathy. This term usually refers to formal greetings by officials or organized citizens to heroes, labour models, or people in disaster areas, commonly accompanied by gifts.

21 There are cases in which the interaction between the government and the society has had more beneficial results. The textile market in Keqiao Town near

249

Shaoxing in northern Zhejiang is run mainly by about 10,000 people from Yueqing. In Keqiao, the Yueqing administration has set up a Government Representative Office, an Office for Migrant Members of the Yueqing Party Committee and a Shaoxing Branch of the Yueqing Association of Individual Entrepreneurs. There is a "joint meeting" of these three organs; all twenty-eight members, except the director of the government office, are private entrepreneurs. The representative office represents the Yueqing government with the Keqiao government. The joint meeting exchanges information, make important decisions and performs internal government functions. Yueqing gangs at Keqiao are likewise kept in check through the joint meeting. Similarly, at the "spectacle village" in Beijing's Chaoyang District (made up of migrants from Zhejiang and Jiangsu provinces, who are engaged mainly in the making and marketing of spectacles), and in a settlement of Jiangxi migrants in Wuxi City social order is maintained through the active involvement of local government and migrants.

22 Having one's own shop front to attract customers is certainly important in a city. But it is impossible for migrants without a Beijing hukou to buy a shop front. Such an unequal distribution of resources between urban and migrant entrepreneurs was the reason that the latter had to devise alternative strategies to build up their businesses.

23 I got this idea from a discussion with Li Meng. I would like to express my thanks to him here.

Chapter Twelve

Chinese organizations in Hungary 1989–1996: A case study in PRC-oriented community politics overseas

Pál Nyíri

Large-scale Chinese migration to Hungary started in 1989–1990 and peaked in 1991. The migrants came overwhelmingly from the People's Republic of China (PRC). Most of them already had been making money in China's expanding market sector, or else had decided to do so but had their confidence in the security of private business in China shattered by the recession following the repression of the 1989 demonstrations. Hungary offered an attractive business destination with a newly liberalized market, a relatively well-developed business environment, considerable foreign investment, forecasts of rapid economic development, and above all, a newly signed treaty abolishing the visa requirement for PRC citizens. A "Hungary fever" (*Xiongyali re*) developed, and in 1991, the number of Chinese entering Hungary exceeded 27,000 (Nyíri 1994a). Migrants hailing directly from the PRC (mostly Mandarin-speaking Northerners) were joined by a far smaller but influential group of Chinese businessmen from western Europe, America, and Southeast Asia. With few exceptions, these were not "old overseas Chinese" (*lao huaqiao*), but people who had left the People's Republic in the 1980s and 1990s and had kept their PRC citizenship. Most of them were originally from Wenzhou or Qingtian in Zhejiang province.

During the first two years, most Chinese in Hungary shuttled between China and Hungary, bringing goods to be sold in their personal baggage. After a major crackdown by the immigration authorities in 1991, the Chinese population in Hungary declined to about 10,000 and has remained around that number since. Those who stayed were the ones who had managed to consolidate their trade and become established

251

importers, wholesalers, or retailers. Contrary to older overseas Chinese communities, imports remained the main occupation of Chinese in Hungary.

The growth of the Hungarian Chinese community is part of a new wave of Chinese migration, which is dubbed "the new gold digger emigration boom of the nineties" (*jiushi niandai xin rechao chuguo taojin*) in the popular Chinese media (Mao 1992). This new wave of migrants ended up in places as far apart and diverse as Australia and New Zealand, the United States, the Pacific islands, northern Burma and the Russian Far East. The new Chinese migrant wishes to escape neither political persecution nor grinding poverty, but is driven by the desire to find an environment with the best money-earning opportunities and least competition. The migrants, moreover, do not leave one home for another or one society for another; they merely shift base. They continue to travel to China and other countries for business and are always ready to move again – to a third country or back to China – if a better opportunity presents itself.

In this structure, the role of kinship and native-place ties in international organizational and trade links diminishes, and that of connections to mainland Chinese officialdom increases. As Li Minghuan points out, organizations, schools, and the press are often seen as the mainstays of overseas Chinese society (Li Minghuan 1995). A review of organizational development in the Hungarian Chinese community, to which this chapter is devoted, may be useful in understanding the transformation of other overseas Chinese communities as the impact of the "new gold rush migration" becomes more pronounced.

The consolidation of the Hungarian Chinese community in 1991–1992 was marked by the appearance of voluntary associations. After two attempts at creating "centres of crystallization" within the community failed, the Hungarian Chinese Association (HCA; Xiongyali Huaren Lianhehui, Magyarországi Kínaiak Egyesülete) was established in Autumn 1992. HCA claimed to be the representative of all Chinese in Hungary; at the same time, it emphasized loyalty toward Beijing as a number one priority.

HCA established itself in a leading position within the Hungarian Chinese community and has retained that position ever since. Given its non-traditional, politically engaged nature, it is remarkable that it has succeeded in doing so. This is, no doubt, related to the late appearance of native-place organizations, which, in turn, can be accounted for by the fact that the Chinese who came to Hungary were mostly young and drawn from the cities of northern China.

To legitimize themselves as orthodox and respectable organizations, overseas Chinese organizations strive to appear as local conveyers of "Chineseness" in the sense of a moral-ritual system of national and traditional rhetoric and symbolism. Since the mid-1980s, the PRC government has been making efforts to construct an image of the guardian of this "Chineseness" as a "unifying and mobilizatory political myth" (Goodman and Segal 1997). Combining with a more modern pan-Chinese nationalism (reminiscent of that which swept through overseas Chinese communities in the first half of the twentieth century), this is intended as a replacement of Communist ideology in the communication with overseas Chinese.

HCA draws on this moral and cultural rhetoric in its declarations of loyalty to Beijing. It stresses patriotism (*re'ai zuguo*) and "obligations toward the home country", emphasizing the association's goal of "fostering the virtues of the Chinese nation" and calling it "the embodiment of the Chinese nation" and "the representative of the civilization of the Chinese nation" (Huikan 1994a; Ouzhou zhi Sheng 1995h). Trade is portrayed as part of these cultural values: as a former HCA leader said, "trade contacts are cultural contacts" HCA increasingly attempts to assume functions of cultural preservation and charity usually fulfilled by traditional organizations (native place associations, surname associations, etc.). This is reflected in a rhetoric featuring such phrases as "happy to do things for Chinese compatriots", "what can we do for our compatriots?", and "the home of Chinese people" (*huaren zhi jia*). Similarly, patriotism, cultural perservation and charity are played up in the intense publicity surrounding charitable fund-raising and cultural events organized by the association, in the solemn commemoration of holidays, and in the condemnation of offenders against morality (e.g. Hungarian customs) and law.

HCA has indeed been the predominant organizer of charitable and cultural events, and it has played the role of the host at major festival celebrations (Nyíri 1994b). Its fund-raising drives have so far resulted in over US$200,000 in merchandise and cash for the Hungarian poor, handicapped, and children. The HCA also supports the Hungarian section of the International Soong Qingling Children's Foundation (Hu 1995). One of the largest festival events organized by HCA is the annual New Year performance of the Chinese Folk Art Troupe (*Zhongguo Minzu Yishutuan*), a folk and popular music and dance troupe dispatched by the PRC's China Overseas Exchange Commission (*Zhongguo Haiwai Jiaoliu Xiehui*), which attracts over a thousand spectators. Parties of this troupe annually tour Europe, Southeast Asia, and the U.S. Stations of the European tour are usually hosted by Beijing-oriented Chinese organizations and attended by PRC embassy officials. Recently, the Shanghai City Overseas Chinese Affairs Bureau dispatched its own group of entertainers on a similar European tour (Bi-Zhong Qiaosheng 1996). This trend reflects the increasing importance Beijing attaches to cultural policy toward overseas Chinese, as well as of overseas Chinese organizations' increasing role in this policy. Significantly, the role of these organizations as link between their communities and China is formally standardized by their performance of one and the same New Year's ritual (Huikan 1994b; Ouzhou zhi Sheng 1994; Huaren Tongxun 1996).

While the charity events have been accompanied by intense public-relations activities directed at Hungarian authorities and media,[1] HCA itself talks about "extensive propaganda work to make *Chinese living in Hungary* understand that these steps are a result of respecting Hungarian traditions" (Ouzhou zhi Sheng 1995h; my italics). In other words, they are aimed more at legitimacy of their presence in Hungary in the eyes of the Chinese themselves than at closer relations with Hungarian authorities or society, though the latter is also an important purpose. In an interview with *Hua Sheng Bao* – the PRC's mouthpiece for overseas Chinese – HCA's president claimed that the association sends congratulations and gifts to families with newborn children, commemorates the deceased, pays visits of condolences to their families, and tries to aid their families back in China (Hua Sheng Bao 1994). HCA leaders have also "immediately" paid visits to Chinese victims of skinhead attacks (Ouzhou zhi Sheng 1995d). Such activities have obvious moral-ritual significance and are typical of clans and *tongxianghui* (native place associations).

An editorial celebrating the association's third anniversary in its weekly *Ouzhou zhi Sheng* (Voice of Europe) draws a balance of its meritorious deeds grouped into items that reflect the association's programme: charity, patriotism, organization of services and cultural events for Chinese, protection of Chinese interests in Hungary, maintainance of contacts with Hungarian society, support of other Chinese organizations, contact with overseas Chinese organizations abroad, and finally the publication, since August 1994, of *Ouzhou zhi Sheng*, which is distributed across Eastern Europe as well as to PRC government agencies (Ouzhou zhi Sheng 1995h).[2]

Individual connections to PRC authorities and the traditional role of patron of charitable events and guardians of traditional culture are thus equally important sources of legitimation for HCA's leaders. In contrast, lobbying with local authorities and organizing professional activities are far less important for them. Despite their youth and high education, these leaders resemble more traditional overseas Chinese leaders than leaders of professional and community organizations and other interest groups in the United States, the United Kingdom, who depend more on political brokerage and lobbying.

Yet, while "managerial" or lobbying skills and professional reputation have not been decisive criteria in the selection of Hungarian Chinese leaders, neither has wealth. Traditional Chinese community leaders have usually emerged from among the outstandingly wealthy, those whose wealth bought protection for the group around them. In Hungary, this is not the case: HCA leaders are businessmen and businesswomen of some repute, but the wealthiest individuals are not among them. Perceived connections with PRC authorities have supplied these leaders with the legitimacy they were lacking in economic achievement. Economic polarization is weaker than in most overseas Chinese communities thanks to the economic success of the Hungarian Chinese. This has probably increased the weight of connections in determining political success.

The first president of HCA was a thirty-three year old Hong Kong businessman from England. He established good relations with the Chinese embassy, which recognized HCA as the representative of the Hungarian Chinese. After a year, in Autumn 1993, a fifty year old Qingtianese from the Philippines was elected president. There have been no new elections since. Wenzhounese and Qingtianese influence increased within the association, and loyalty toward the Chinese communist government became the top priority. In February 1994, the new president met with government officials in Beijing and several provincial capitals and participated in a conference organized by the Zhejiang provincial government for overseas leaders from Zhejiang (Hai Ming 1994). Such meetings, both in China and Hungary, have since become regular (see e.g. Ouzhou zhi Sheng 1995c). In lobbying for recognition by PRC authorities, HCA leaders used money raised from their enterprises; PRC recognition, in turn, was used to gain business advantages. In 1994, the association's president enjoyed the PRC's National Day parade from the Tian'anmen Square rostrum. In July 1995, he and other leaders were received in Budapest by visiting PRC Chairman Jiang Zemin, and stood on the runway next to embassy personnel during the chairman's arrival and departure ceremony. In early 1996, the HCA chairman became a member of the People's Political Consultative Conference (PPCC) of the PRC. When a new PRC ambassador arrived in Hungary in 1996, he had to reckon with HCA as a force not to be offended, for it might exercise its political connections within China to his detriment.

Since 1993, HCA's leadership, and its president in particular, has often been criticized by local Chinese for creating a personality cult around themselves, entertaining hegemonic ambitions within the community, and using force to achieve that aim (see e.g. Ouzhou zhi Sheng 1995h; Távol-Kelet 1996c; A Dong 1996). Many HCA leaders left the association during the year after the new president took office. Nonetheless, membership, according to the association's own data, grew to around one thousand during the same period. In addition, HCA succeeded in winning over some Chinese, whose intellectual background added respectability to the HCA. Among the smaller Chinese organizations, many of which were formed in late 1994 or early 1995, there are only one or two that do not cooperate with HCA, and none claim to be universally representative of Hungarian Chinese. In the summer of 1995, even HCA's first president joined his successor's supporters. HCA came to be regarded as the only Chinese organization that can do something to protect the interests of the Chinese, even if it rarely does so in actual fact.

The primary reason behind HCA's growth is the legitimation provided by PRC officials. Chairman Jiang's visit boosted the association's influence enormously. On the other hand, HCA showed that it was indeed capable of success as defender of the Chinese. After its strong condemnation of the harassment of Chinese vendors at a Budapest market in May 1994, action was taken against the offenders and a joint management committee was formed. Later, HCA's engagement made the market's owner withdraw his requirement that Chinese vendors purchase their stalls (Polonyi 1995; Ouzhou zhi Sheng 1995h). In March 1997, HCA together with Vietnamese traders represented by the Hungarian Vietnamese Association, staged a strike at the same market to protest a planned twenty-five per cent raise of stall rents. The strike succeeded in driving down the increase to five per cent. In March 1995, HCA initiated talks with customs officials to discuss new customs duties which were severely damaging Chinese business. The talks continue but have failed to produce results. This maybe because a Chinese warned the officials that HCA, which wants to tie the use of any preferential tariffs to its own approval, could not speak for the whole community.[3] Furthermore, to combat crime within the Chinese community, the association established a Chinese Legal Protection Committee, which, however, has been wholly inactive.

Only representatives of companies officially registered as owned by Chinese state enterprises or governments are reluctant to support HCA. First, they have their own connections with the PRC officialdom. Second, they have an abundance of capital available from their mother companies. The economic difficulties HCA fights are therefore these companies' competitive advantage. HCA has tempted them with "honorary advisor" positions, but few have agreed.

The Hungarian Chinese Chamber of Commerce (*Xiongyali Huaren Shanghui*) was established together with HCA and is really the latter's commercial section. Its more prominent activities included the establishment of an HCA market and attempts to reach a binding price control agreement among Chinese retailers. These were short-lived but important as they represented a degree of business cooperation rare among Chinese and indicated HCA's aspirations for universal representativeness, legitimation, and power.[4]

The Hungarian Chinese Federation of Industry and Trade (*Xiongyali Zhonghua Gongshangye Lianhehui*, or *Gongshanglian*) was established in January 1995 (ZhongOu Shangbao 1995a). It is in fact a branch of the PRC's *Gongshanglian*, the "democratic party" supposed to represent the "national bourgeoisie" and elevated to new prominence by its former president, now PRC Vice-President Rong Yiren. The founding of the Gongshanglian in Hungary reminds of the establishment of Kuomintang branches across Southeast Asia and the Pacific in the pre-war period. The Gongshanglian's chairman is the wealthiest Chinese in Hungary, who now divides his time between Hungary and the United States where he has also set up business. The Gongshanglian's honorary president is HCA's president. The Gongshanglian, too, has sent several delegations to the PRC and met with the national Gongshanglian's current secretary-general, Hu Deping, Hu Yaobang's son. In 1996, the Gongshanglian stood behind the launch of the European edition of *Gongshang Bao* (Industry and Trade Journal), a PRC publication and the fifth Chinese periodical in Hungary at the time.[5]

The PRC connection in trade, whether for HCA, the chambers of commerce, or individuals, is necessarily strong because most of the working capital of the Chinese companies comes from state enterprises. Neither the two chambers of commerce nor the Hungarian Chinese Catering Association (*Xiongyali Zhongguo Canyinye Xiehui*, established Summer 1995) have been able to assume the significant role played by their West European and American counterparts: they are yet to show themselves as credible negotiatiors of Chinese economic interests or mediators in intra-community disputes.

Organizational pluralization in the Hungarian Chinese community started in late 1994 and enjoyed a one-year boom before dying down under the pressure of an economic crisis. The first grassroots-type organization, though officially registered only in April 1995, was the Association for the Promotion of Chinese-Hungarian Friendship (APCHF, *Zhong-Xiong Youhao Cujinhui*). The goals of this organization are the promotion of the "entry into mainstream [Hungarian] society" (*rongru zhuliu shehui*) and improvement of the cultural and educational level of the community. The APCHF publishes the weekly *Ouzhou Daobao* (Europe's Way Weekly, see Ouzhou Daobao 1994). There probably stood a confluence of interests behind the birth of APCHF, which stresses loyalty to and relations with Beijing less. Some leaders, however, are primarily motivated by personal ambitions they had not been able to satisfy in HCA. Distrust toward HCA is a uniting factor within the association. Some of its leaders, reflecting the organization's relatively high percentage of members with intellectual backgrounds, are reluctant to accept the leadership of HCA's bosses, most of whom are secondary or just primary school graduates. They also emphasize the need to find a use for Chinese professionals in Hungary, meaning that those coming from the intelligentsia should, for example, offer their knowledge of the Chinese language and market to Hungarian companies or the government.

APCHF has tended to pay more attention to Hungarian than to Chinese politics and sought contacts with a broad range of Hungarian authorities. Though it represents a political alternative to HCA, APCHF does not claim to be a representative of all Hungarian Chinese: it only speaks for its several dozen members. Characteristically, HCA incorporated the new values offered by APCHF into its own moral symbolism: *Ouzhou zhi Sheng* picked up, for example, the phrase "entry into mainstream society".

As to the other source of HCA's legitimation, the PRC government, APCHF obviously is at a disadvantage. Its leaders, too, have contacts with Communist officials – a prerequisite for business success – but the importance of these contacts is limited in commerce and they are not used for organizational legitimation. Officials at the PRC embassy favour HCA and refuse to deal with APCHF.

APCHF's appearance as an alternative to HCA's political leadership without the latter's hegemonic aspirations helped the growth of various organizations, some borrowing from the tradition of native-place and religious organizations, others assuming non-traditional shapes of interest-group formations. Organizationally and rhetorically, HCA had reconstructed the political environment of Communist China, in which a single top-down organization represents the people and the official orthodoxy in its rhetoric. To the average PRC migrant, this was a natural situation. But a few with a broader experience and better education were sympathetic to APCHF's more spontaneous and flexible grassroots model. The APCHF actually encouraged the growth of the fledgling organizations by establishing contacts with them, seeing them certainly as a counterbalance to HCA and perhaps as a step toward a less Beijing-dependent and more integrated Chinese community. The period between December 1994 and Spring 1995 saw the establishment of Fujian, Guangdong, Tianjin, and Shandong tongxianghui, followed in July by the Xinjiang and in August by the Sichuan tongxianghui.[6] They typically number a few dozen members and are, as of now, very limited in both influence and scope of activities. They have been unable or uninterested to wrest, even in rhetoric, the traditional charitable and other functions from HCA. Even when the immigration authorities ordered a vice president of the Fujian Tongxianghui to leave the country in March 1996, the organization chose not to face the authorities. The limited role of tongxianghui is also illustrated by the fact that the leading community of Wenzhounese do not have a tongxianghui. The tongxianghui of another important group, the Qingtianese, was the last one to form on 17 November 1996, although it claims to have a full 2000 members (Távol-Kelet 1996g).

The role of a religious association established in the summer of 1995 is similarly minimal. It was created around a temple established with the help of lay missionaries of the Great Way of Primeval Heaven (*Xiantian Dadao*) from Taiwan. There are an estimated 300 regular visitors at the temple, whose cult is centred around Maitreya Buddha and the Eternal Venerable Mother (*tianshang shengmu*).[7] The Chinese Christian Church, created in 1990 by a Korean Presbyterian missionary who served as minister until

Summer 1995, never played any role in community life during those five years.

Although the tongxianghui nominally follow an organizational tradition well-known to exist in overseas Chinese communities, there is little of that tradition found in their functions and *modus operandi*. Their leaders, in most cases, are farther removed from the type of the traditional community patron and closer to that of the broker who represents his particular group. In addition to seniority and financial status, education played a role in their selection: most are college-educated.

Non-traditional organizations, representing professional and other interest group, appeared concurrently with the tongxianghui. They bring the number of Chinese organizations in Hungary to nearly twenty. Their leaders similarly base themselves on a mixture of authoritative patronage and brokerage, with the latter usually outweighing the former. This happened much sooner than in the history of earlier overseas Chinese communities, where such "new-type" (Wong 1982) or "Western-style" organizations were usually created by the second generation (Weiss 1974). Indeed, equivalents of the Hungarian Chinese Women's Association (*Xiongyali Huaren Funü Lianhehui*), the European Society of Chinese Artists (ESCA, *Ouzhou Zhongguo Yishujia Xiehui*), the National Hungarian Chinese Physical Education and Sports Federation (*Quan-xiong Huaren Tiyu Yundong Zonghui*, or *Tizong*), the Cultural and Educational Association for Chinese-Hungarian Friendship (*Zhong-Xiong Youhao Wenhua Jiaoyu Xiehui*, or *Wenjiaoxie*), the Hungarian Chinese Writers' Association (*Xiongyali Huaren Zuojia Xiehui*), or the Hungarian Chinese Youth Association (*Xiongyali Huaren Qingnian Lianhehui*) exist only in large Chinese communities such as those in France, Britain, or the United States. There, because of the size and stratification of the communities, they tend to be isolated from each other and, even more, from traditional organizations which typically build on a different membership base.

In Hungary, "new-type" and traditional organizations have largely been formed from the same stock, and they are aware of and maintain regular contacts with each other. Some organizations are clearly tied to HCA; in fact, the women's and youth organizations were created by HCA apparently following the CCP's model. The Writer's Association seems to model itself after the PRC Writers' Association in its political "patriotism," distinct from other organizations of Chinese intellectuals in Hungary.[8]

Organizational pluralism contributes to the building of contacts with Hungarian NGOs and Chinese organizations elsewhere in Europe. For example, Tizong's soccer team, the European Dragons, plays in Budapest League IV and has represented Hungary at an international Chinese soccer tournament in the Netherlands; the Wenjiaoxie, whose concerns have included the organization of Chinese-language education, has Hungarians in its leadership; and the Gongshanglian's delegation represented Hungary at the Third World Congress of Chinese Businesses in December 1995 in Bangkok.

The PRC embassy reacted to the pluralization with calls for "unity." Meanwhile, when addressing the problem of residence permits, several Hungarian politicians made it clear that they would only have substantive talks with a group that represented the whole community. These politicians were aware of the proliferation of independent associations that contradicted HCA's claim of being the sole representative of the Chinese (Hajdú 1995).

In June 1995, the four then existing tongxianghui, the Wenjiaoxie, Tizong, ESCA, the Chinese Christian Church, and a committee representing the owners of several dozen Chinese shops joined APCHF to form the Joint Conference of Hungarian Chinese Organizations (*Xiongyali Huaren Shetuan Lianxi Huiyi*). The cooperation appeared to work: in the following months, the Joint Conference organized several meetings and conferences with the participation of Hungarian officials.

HCA sensed a threat to its leading role and again resorted to the use of connections with PRC authorities and moral rhetoric. It called the organizational proliferation a natural phenomenon, supported the traditional values expressed through tongxianghui (native land, cultural heritage, etc.), and emphasized that the tongxianghui reflected the patriotism of their members and their work toward a common goal. Instead of attacking the new groups, HCA chose to co-opt them, stating that "HCA's organizational life represented an inspiration to the native-place associations that have formed in the past year" (Ouzhou zhi Sheng 1995h). It thus toned down its claim to universal representation. In some cases, HCA created equivalents of already formed organizations under its own control, which remain completely inactive (Ouzhou zhi Sheng 1995h).[9] Immediately after their exclusive meeting with Jiang Zemin, HCA used a banquet in his honour (but in his absence) to announce a proposal for the Representative Committee of Hungarian Chinese Organizations (*Xiongyali Huaren Shetuan Daibiao Weiyuanhui*) – its own alternative to the Joint Conference of Hungarian Chinese Organizations. Embassy officials present voiced their support.[10] This pressure caught representatives of all organizations who had come to honour the PRC chairman unprepared and they joined the initiative. Only APCHF, ESCA, and the Guangdong tongxianghui did not sign up for membership in the Representative Committee. "It is the Committee's right and duty to represent all Chinese living in Hungary ... to protect [their] interests and struggle for the improvement of their position in society", *Ouzhou zhi Sheng* wrote in an editorial. The first item in the Committee's statement of purpose is "Spread the fine tradition of patriotism... Promote reunification of the fatherland. Do not tolerate any behaviour not in line with the interests of the fatherland." The sixth item is "Enter the mainstream of the society of the country of residence" (Ouzhou zhi Sheng 1995a).

After the Committee's establishment, HCA attempted to secure the membership of any newly formed Chinese organization. A case in point is that of the Shanghai tongxianghui. One of HCA's defected founders was planning to establish an organization to be called Association of Hungarian Chinese Entrepreneurs from Shanghai (*LüXiong Shanghai Huaren Qiyejia Xiehui*), but refused to have it join the Representative Committee (Ouzhou zhi Sheng 1995b). While some seventy people were holding a meeting to found the association, HCA's president invited a dozen Shanghainese pedlars from a market to dinner and asked them to sign a document establishing a Shanghai tongxianghui. In the end, the Shanghai Entrepreneurs' leader decided to avoid confrontation by ceding the chairmanship to another man close to HCA's president. Several other examples of HCA's influence can be given. Beijing Chinese failed to establish an association after one prospective member signed a document about the organization's admission to the Representative Committee. This proved to be unacceptable to other leaders of the prospective association (see Jingxuan 1995). The Shandong tongxianghui lost its entire membership after its president became vice chairman of the Representative Committee.

In October 1995, the Joint Conference of Hungarian Chinese Associations co-sponsored a conference on the theme of Chinese in Hungary with the city government of Budapest and the Hungarian Association for Migrants, an NGO. Held at the city assembly's building, this was the first meeting on such a scale organized by Chinese in Hungary, and it expanded the Chinese theme from police news and entertainment to political sections of newspapers. Due to poor organization on the Hungarian side, however, attendance was low, and HCA's boycott of the meeting caused most organizations not to attend. The conference took place in a tense atmosphere and showed the split between what the Chinese called the "party of power" (*quanlipai*) and the "party of friendship" (*youhaopai*). APCHF hoped to increase the latter's influence by mustering massive support and spectacular success at the conference. This failed, and APCHF's leaders – who had been labelled "anti-party elements" by HCA's president – faced a precarious situation.[11]

HCA's high-profile display of political muscle has had a little-publicized but widely known side. After the association scored its first success in relieving Chinese vendors' grievances at the Józsefváros market (see Nyíri 1998 for more details), HCA's people tried, "retroactively," to press for protection money from them. The effort was largely unsuccessful. In February 1996, HCA established a commercial company called Great Wall Detective and Protection Ltd. Led by the Representative Committee's vice chairman, this company, in turn, established a foundation which "welcomes [contributions from] Chinese businessmen who are not members of the company's board but are interested in personal and property protection work for Hungarian Chinese" and "is open to all Hungarian Chinese organizations and counts on their support" (Távol-Kelet 1996c).[12] HCA's claims about its relations with PRC security authorities add weight to such invitations. Rumours, confirmed by several sources, that Great Wall was attempting to register passports of Chinese in Hungary to supply the information to Beijing thus sound very credible to the ordinary Hungarian Chinese. Great Wall's chairman found it necessary to deny explicitly that his company is HCA's armed militia and that organizations and individuals are forced to join its supporters (Távol-Kelet 1996e). It appears that the association sees the policing of the community as Beijing's right and duty: it has suggested that Chinese police come to Hungary to participate in criminal investigations. *Ouzhou zhi Sheng*'s assertion that "cadres of the Chinese Ministry for Public Security pay careful attention to the livelihood of Chinese businessmen living in Hungary and will take appropriate, effective measures at the right time" went even further, suggesting that the livelihood of Chinese abroad is ultimately also Beijing's concern.

While HCA may not be the insider it depicts itself to be, its boasting is a reflection of the current trend in the PRC's overseas Chinese policy that manifests itself in PRC-sponsored overseas Chinese organizations, overseas Chinese conventions organized by PRC authorities, or symbolic cultural missions such as the Chinese Folk Art Troupe. Since the mid-1980s, the PRC leadership has embarked on a path of economic, political, and military expansion. It increasingly aims to replace nominal Marxism with an etatism composed largely of elements of traditional morality and early-twentieth-century nationalism. As a result, the PRC has become increasingly interested not only in securing overseas Chinese investment but also in resuscitating the national loyalties of overseas Chinese, much in the same way as the Guomindang government did in the years before the Second World War. Since 1984, a number of political bodies have been revitalized or created for this purpose. These include the National Association of Overseas Chinese, Returned Overseas Chinese and Dependents of Overseas Chinese (*Quanguo Huaqiao Guiqiao Qiaojuan Lianhehui*), the Overseas Chinese Commission (*Huaqiao Weiyuanhui*) of the National People's Congress, the Overseas Chinese Affairs Bureau (*Qiaowu Bangongshi*) of the State Council, the China Overseas Exchange Commission, and the equivalent of these bodies at lower adminstrative levels (Nyíri 1995). If current trends continue, we are likely to see more and better organized links between the PRC and the overseas Chinese.[13]

Hungarian police have repeatedly liaised with Chinese authorities in the fight against Chinese crime in Hungary. HCA has attempted to manipulate its contacts with the latter to influence the outcome of the investigations, stating that "[w]e have contributed to the success of Chinese and Hungarian police authorities in securing the safety and unity of Chinese compatriots" (Ouzhou zhi Sheng 1995h). Indeed, the victims, apart from the police and the PRC Embassy, usually turn to HCA for help, even when they observe that the latter is no more effective than the former two in solving their problem. But contrary to traditional Chinese communities, where organizations took up law-enforcement functions not performed by the host state, HCA leaders clearly consider PRC public security organs, rather than their own organization, as the ultimately legitimate authority in maintaining public order. The scope of Great Wall's activities and the political rhetoric used by HCA's president against rival associations seem to indicate that HCA's attempts to assume government functions are driven neither by the community's need for an agent to perform these functions nor by the government's inability to act as that agent. Rather it is the HCA's own desire to control the community, to represent the orthodox authority of the PRC over the community, and to project that authority to the non-Chinese environment.

In 1995–1997, a series of murders and robberies were commonly attributed to Fujianese, who were partly newcomers and partly concentrated in the lower strata of a Hungarian Chinese community hard hit by a sharp business recession. Many Chinese felt that the inaptness of Hungarian police in dealing with these cases was the number one problem the community was facing. In order to solve these cases, the Hungarian police stepped up cooperation with their PRC counterparts. In March 1997, personnel from the Chinese Ministry of Public Security arrived in Hungary for a two-month fact-finding visit. HCA interpreted this as a victory in its struggle to control the community, and one leader proposed that two HCA delegates work with the PRC policemen to identify evil-doers, possibly including "anti-party elements" and anyone challenging HCA.

In October 1995, HCA forwarded copies of the Chinese dissident journals *Beijing Spring* and *China Spring* issues to the PRC embassy, alleging that APCHF's secretary-general was involved in them. The man, who had belonged to the core of the Democracy Wall movement in Guangzhou in 1978–1979 (see Liu Guokai 1995), had left China in 1990 and had in fact not been close to any of the émigré pro-democracy organizations. He had helped found HCA and had served as the association's secretary-general for one year, but after the ascension of the new leadership he and several other founders left the association (Nyíri 1996). HCA's leadership targeted him, of course, not so much for his past dissidence against the Party but for his resistance to HCA dominance in the community. The APCHF realized it could not make peace with HCA while he continued to occupy a leadership position. On 14 December

1995, he was dismissed from the position of secretary-general (ZhongOu Shangbao 1995b). A month later, he disappeared and has not been heard of since. APCHF's vice-president and the main financier of *Ouzhou Daobao* did likewise. On 16 December, APCHF's members came to the banquet celebrating HCA's third anniversary (Távol-Kelet 1996a).

In February 1996, ESCA – another of the three organizations that had not joined the Representative Committee – announced the suspension of its activities (Távol-Kelet 1996b). Due to HCA's sabotage, the Joint Conference of Hungarian Chinese Associations similarly practically ceased operations. The Hungarian Chinese press, including the APCHF-sponsored *Ouzhou Daobao*, began to write about HCA in a tone that effectively recognized it as the organization representing the Chinese in Hungary. HCA's president, in particular, came to be regarded as a personality who possessed political stature, despite his dishonesty, his lack of concern with the community's interests, and perhaps even his inability to achieve tangible results.

With APCHF's defeat, its alternative strategy of less contact with PRC authorities and more interaction with Hungarian government structures was marginalized before it could come off the ground. To be sure, contacts have increased between Hungarian officials and Chinese individuals and organizations, including HCA. Such contacts are seen as a means to create business opportunities or more favourable treatment of immigration, and are often publicized to raise the prestige of the organization or individual. Several Chinese have targeted officials of smaller towns with little outside investment in the hope to secure construction permits, favourable real estate deals, or, more interestingly, to use them to promote business with China. The Hungarian Chinese and Hungarian press regularly reports sister-city agreements between rural Hungarian towns and obscure Chinese localities, brokered by Chinese.[14]

The Chinese in Hungary seem to have successfully reapplied the PRC practice where officials or government agencies act as nominal partners while actual financing comes from other sources. A brilliantly organized case in point is the trip to Lanzhou city in Gansu province of a ten-person delegation of the Somogy County Assembly, accompanied by the chairman of the Hungarian-Chinese Friendship Association, a Hungarian organization dating back to the times of the Soviet-PRC friendship. According to a Hungarian press report, the delegation and Gansu provincial officials signed an Memorandum of Understanding on the construction of a twenty-five storey trade centre in Lanzhou. Three-quarters of the US$20 million to be invested will come from "the Hungarian side, including Chinese working in Hungary" (g.j.a. 1996). Although the report does not mention that Chinese from Hungary took part in the trip, this investment, as well as indeed the financing of the trip itself, is essentially coming from them. Thus, the astute organizers obliged the Hungarian officials, "gave face" to Gansu officials, created publicity around the deal, and raised their own respectability in China. They rightly chose to export Hungarian construction expertise to an inland Chinese province where foreign competition is less intense and is more likely to be overcome by the advantage of a province-level visit by foreign officials.

For Hungarian Chinese, relations with Hungarian officials are thus often a means to improve relations with PRC officials, whereas legitimation of power within the Chinese community in Hungary itself is usually not the objective of cultivating such relations with Hungarians.

Among Hungarian Chinese leaders, interaction with Hungarian authorities is therefore seen as tactical, rather than strategic, and its business importance is not nearly as great as that of contacts with the PRC. APCHF's October 1995 conference discussed above was the only organizational attempt so far to offer an alternative. In the confrontational atmosphere during the run-up to the conference, APCHF underlined its platform of integration in Hungarian society. It boldly demonstrated the support of Hungarian authorities, who were willing to enter into a dialogue with the Chinese. APCHF's chairman suggested that, as a first step of such integration, Chinese should use their knowledge of China's market and politics for the benefit of Hungarian government and business. Leaders of some minor partners in the Joint Conference went farther, floating the idea of an eventual minority status within Hungarian society. This latter proposal immediately led to controversy both in Hungarian media and within the Chinese community (Távol-Kelet 1995; Cz. G. 1995a and 1995b; Czene 1995; Népszabadság 1995). Many Chinese, even among those sympathetic to APCHF, viewed it as insulting. As one pointed out "Chinese can never be a minority anywhere." Besides anti-assimilationism and a rejection of sovereignty of foreigners over Chinese, this reaction reflects the negative connotation that is often attached to the expression "minority" (*shaoshu minzu*) in the PRC, where it has, in effect, replaced various terms meaning "barbarian" in referring to "backward" ethnies such as Tibetans or Uighurs.[15]

APCHF's defeat showed that relations with Hungarian authorities could not, at this point, serve as a source of legitimation. Furthermore, HCA's statements about its relations with PRC Public Security organs, referred to earlier in this chapter, appear to reflect that Hungarian authority is really seen as limited to arbitration between Hungarians and Chinese, but does not apply to relations between Chinese. For HCA, if problems encountered in Hungary cannot be resolved by negotiations, the next step is to hope for PRC authorities to apply pressure.

The Hungarian Chinese press, especially HCA's *Ouzhou zhi Sheng*, has lately become considerably more sensitive to wrongs suffered by Chinese at the hands of Hungarian authorities and critical of the latter. After the beating of a Chinese merchant by security guards at a Budapest market, *Ouzhou zhi Sheng* devoted its entire front page to this matter. After another skinhead attack and a robbery, the *Ouzhou zhi Sheng* asserted that these demonstrated increased racial discrimination and xenophobic violence and a "serious threat to our living environment." Highlighting the reluctance of the police to deal with them adequately, the newspaper questioned the functioning of law and justice. It implied that Chinese should form a tighter alliance around the Hungarian Chinese Association and the PRC embassy to protect their interests in a hostile environment and in the face of a biased authority (Ouzhou zhi Sheng 1995f and 1995g). In another article, an HCA spokesman pointed out the need for a "united struggle" (*tuanjie zhandou*, Liu Zhixian 1996).

Other quarters of the community took a more moderate stand. *Ouzhou Daobao*'s reporter asked if "the Chinese Ministry of Public Security could work with Hungarian police to find an early solution to crimes against Chinese" (Ouzhou Daobao 1997). Another newspaper, *ZhongOu Shangbao*, emphasized the role of Hungarian authorities:

> The old view, "Sweep in front of your own gate, don't look at the snowflakes on others' shoes," has long been eroded by history (. . .) We therefore repeatedly call on Hungarian police to take strong measures and do all they can to crack one or two evil cases within the shortest time (. . .) At the same time, we also hope that Chinese in Hungary of all walks of life will strengthen their unity (Zheng 1997).

A recent proposal by HCA's president to set up a residential Chinatown – one that has been floated earlier but failed to alter the current scattered pattern of Chinese residences in the city – is another plan intended to strengthen HCA's control at the expense of seriously impeding integration and increasing distrust toward Chinese on the part of Hungarians.

In the past, rising demands for Chinese emancipation in Southeast Asia and America have indicated a rise in integrative trends. Conversely, when attention within the community turns entirely toward China, concern with legal or social status in the country of residence has been low. From this perspective, the exclusive orientation the Hungarian Chinese community's dominant force, the Hungarian Chinese Association, toward the PRC largely reduces the porspects of integration in Hungarian society. At an earlier stage, an interest on the part of Hungarian authorities in the Chinese living under their jurisdiction could have promoted their integration. Now, however, any attempt at a conscious integration strategy will actually have to counter HCA's influence.[16] Meanwhile, attempts at *ad hoc* problem solving continue. In late 1996, the State Secretary in the Prime Minister's Office received an HCA delegation who asked him to lower customs duties and facilitate permanent residency for Chinese who meet the legal requirements. In 1997, the Hungarian Chinese Catering

Association made a gift of 2.5 million forint (US$15,000) to a foundation supporting the work of the homicide unit of the Budapest Police Department in the wake of the death of two Chinese women in an explosion at a Chinese restaurant (Polonyi 1996a and 1996b; k.z.t. 1997). Yet on the whole, in Polonyi's words, "the community behaves as if it were in Hungary on business and could leave it for good at any time." Spokesmen refer to the community at best as a bridge, whose main pillar is in China. The PRC authorities regard the Hungarian and other Chinese communities in Eastern Europe as some kind of branch of the PRC. This situation, while relatively harmless thus far, is hardly a healthy one, and should serve as a warning to other European governments who wish to integrate the Chinese communities in their countries (Polonyi 1996a).

Throughout the history of Chinese migration to Hungary, the Hungarian state has seen the Chinese only as individual aliens, and its contact with them was largely limited to routine administrative procedueres such as the extension of stay permits. In two cases, however, Hungarian immigration and economic policies deeply affected the Chinese. In both cases, however, the effects were inadvertent and remained largely unnoticed by the authorities. The first case was the tightening of immigration rules in 1991 that resulted in a reduction of new migration and a drop in the total number of Chinese living in Hungary. The second time that government policies affected the Chinese community was in 1995. At that time, an oversaturated market and a drastic rise in tariffs for Chinese goods caused a downturn in Chinese business that deepened into a crisis by the end of the year. Yet simultaneously the authorities relaxed immigration restrictions, resulting in an inflow of new migrants. In the prevailing economic climate the newcomers presented a danger to the safety and prosperity of the settled Chinese population. The subsequent bankruptcy or exodus of many leading companies provided an opportunity for HCA to extend its control over business.

The year of 1995 witnessed the formation of two alliances of larger companies that decided to pool their investment capital and issue shares. Several HCA prominents joined one of these, the Chinese Investment Group of Hungary Rt, but HCA's chairman appeared unsatisfied with his degree of control within the body, whose president was his predecessor as HCA Chairman. In March 1996, HCA established the Preparatory Committee of another investment group under its own control, called the Hungarian Chinese Patriotic Enterprises Group, naming one of its leaders as chairman and its president as honorary chairman. Again describing its business activity in moral-ritual terms, it declared that the aim of the new group was "to teach patriotism and love of the country of residence" (Távol-Kelet 1996f).

HCA's strengthening control and the economic crisis are an impediment to the further growth of a plural organizational structure that had just begun to show a potential to fulfil a range of traditional and non-traditional functions and represent a variety of interests.[17] In 1995, for instance, a new influx of Chinese from neighbouring countries, often without stable financial means, threatened to jeopardize the reputation of the community by leaving disorder or unpaid bills in rented apartments. An article in *Ouzhou zhi Sheng* suggested that this could be remedied if each organization act against such behaviour, ostracize offenders, and, if necessary, hand them over to the police (Song 1995). Native-place associations, attempting to gain leverage, were also becoming more high-profile, with PRC embassy officials appearing at their activities celebrating the PRC's official holiday.

Yet despite these developments, HCA has secured a leading role in the Hungarian Chinese community in just three years after its establishment, and its headquarters now occupy a five-storey building. HCA's legitimation strategy of appearing both as Beijing's representative and the carrier of traditional morality thus seems to have worked. Many Chinese in Hungary, however, doubt that the association really is Beijing's representative or bearer of traditional values, and accuse it of being "a fox imitating the tiger's grandeur" (*hu jia hu wei*). Yet few dare to challenge its arguments for legitimation.

In western European Chinese communities, traditional and commercial associations have never exercised the control or power of their counterparts in Southeast Asia or North America[18]. In the mid-1980s a number of Chinese organizations that are oriented toward the PRC and claim to be the representative of all Chinese have appeared in those communities.[19] Their formation or resustication took place at a time of renewed interest in the overseas Chinese on the part of the PRC government, which was now willing to accept their national loyalties without ideological strings attached. These organizations received encouragement, endorsement, or sometimes even direct sponsorship from Beijing. These organizations were able to gain a central role especially in relatively new and small Chinese communities where traditional associations had not fully developed, such as in Spain or Belgium.[20]

Most of HCA's founders had come from western Europe (Spain, the Netherlands, Belgium, Austria), and some had previous experience with organizations of this kind. HCA's contacts with them, including a "sister organization" agreement with the Spanish Overseas Chinese and Chinese Association (*Xibanya Huaqiao Huaren Xiehui*, see Yiwen 1994), were facilitated by the fact that HCA's leadership, just as the leadership of those organizations, has overwhelmingly been in Wenzhounese hands. HCA and its West European counterparts show some key similarities in political phraseology. For example, HCA's statement of purpose – which includes promoting the unity of Chinese people, the welfare of Hungarian Chinese, Chinese-Hungarian friendship and, lately, the reunification of China – is a reflection of official PRC rhetoric and is almost literally identical to the goals stated by the General Chinese Association in the Netherlands (Pieke and Benton 1998). There are also important similarities in the organization of symbolic events tying the community to the PRC, such as the annual ceremony of hosting New Year's performances of entertainment troupes dispatched by the PRC. In Belgium, for example, the hosts are the Belgian Overseas Chinese Association and the Shanghai Friends' Society.

Li Yiyuan has argued that overseas Chinese dialect groups (which indeed structure the overseas Chinese communities of Southeast Asia) apply three models to the construction of their identity and relations with the outside. The first is the "immediate model," which defines the set of cultural characteristics that identify the group itself. The second is the "internal observer model," which positions the community *vis-à-vis* other dialect groups. The third is the "ideological model," which constructs the group's belonging to a pan-Chinese cultural community. When external influence from the host society is limited, the ideological model plays little role; but when external influence is intense, the ideological model is used either in uniting various dialect groups or in attempts by one of them to establish hegemony over the others (Li Yiyuan 1970).[21]

The identity of the Hungarian Chinese as a community within the host society clearly rests on the ideological model. Although this model played a prominent role in overseas Chinese relations with China in the pre-war and wartime years, the immediate model was at least as significant, since direct contacts with the *qiaoxiang* (the home village or region) accounted for the greater part of those relations. Hungarian Chinese indeed belong to one community, rather than to the traditional, national or transnational ethnic (Cantonese, Wenzhounese, etc.) overseas Chinese core communities that have been typical of western Europe. In both trade and the political sphere, they deal with a centralized China, represented by national organizations and commercial enterprises from all around the country; a China that can no longer speak the language of the immediate model but only that of the ideological model. Compared to these modes of interaction – especially to trade – qiaoxiang ties in which the immediate model plays a role are reduced to secondary importance. Accordingly, the ideological model has arisen as the sole informer of the Hungarian Chinese identity discourse. It is being used both to forge a unified community and legitimize HCA's hegemonic position.

In the 1990s, China's growing international stature and the replacement of Marxism with nationalism in the PRC's rhetoric toward the overseas Chinese helped legitimize the new organizations. At the same time, Chinese in Western Europe, who had until then largely abstained from exploiting business opportunities in China, gradually recognized that mainland China was a source of investment capital, something that they, confined to oversaturated economic niches in the catering trade, needed more badly than ever. On the other hand, the spread of Chinese-made garments and other consumer goods in Western markets made West European Chinese interested in investing in industry, especially in their qiaoxiang (Li Minghuan 1995). News of the quick fortunes the "gold-diggers" have made in such places as Hungary spread fast, while "gold-diggers" themselves increasingly flowed to western European countries. It provided an attractive model of how to build and exploit business connections in the PRC and showed how to use organizations for this purpose. A good example is provided by the Shanghai Friends' Society in Belgium (*LüBi Shanghai Lianyihui*), established in 1992 by post-1980 migrants. The Friends' Society's membership count is over 100 family heads, including citizens of the PRC, Hong Kong, Taiwan, Belgium, and other countries, both Chinese-born and overseas-born, and not all Shanghainese by origin. The declared tasks of the Society include community mediation, aid to the poor, organizing cultural events for the community, and promoting integration into Belgian society and legal emancipation. It stresses that the scope of these activities is not limited to members. The Society maintains close ties with the PRC embassy. Its chairman has expanded from catering into exports from Belgium to China and started a thriving business in Shanghai. He boasts of being on good terms with officials, particularly tax officials, in both Shanghai and other big cities. The Shanghai Friends' Society's newsletter largely carries political and economic news from the PRC and Hong Kong taken from the mainland press. It is edited and printed in Shanghai by a former editor of the *Shanghai Qiaobao* (Shanghai Overseas Chinese News) and is distributed both to the PRC Embassy in Belgium and government agencies in the PRC. The bulletin is called *Bi-Zhong Qiaosheng* (Belgian Overseas Chinese Voice), reflecting that its scope extends beyond Shanghai.

It is easy to see the similarities between the Shanghai Friends' Society, which has taken up a role and significance far exceeding that of a tongxianghui, and HCA.[22] Like HCA's president, delegates of four Belgian Chinese organizations – the Shanghai Friends' Society, the Belgian Overseas Chinese Association, the Chinese Chamber of Commerce, and the Qingtian tongxianghui – were present at state ceremonies hosted by Premier Li Peng and Foreign Minister Qian Qichen on the PRC's National Day in 1996. Significantly, the Shanghai Friends' Circle's vice-president referred to their host from the Overseas Chinese Affairs Commission as "comrade Tian Jiyun".

A further example is provided by Spain. Like Belgium, in this country a Shanghai Friends' Circle was being formed in 1996, "with the close attention of government officials from the Chinese Embassy."[23] In the same year, the president of a recently established Beijing tongxianghui in the United States called for the reunification of the fatherland.[24] Such political statements and such close contacts between what in form are traditional overseas Chinese associations and the PRC government are a very recent affair.

Meetings brokered by Chinese communist authorities which lead to business deals in China or political prestige gave impetus to the growth and legitimation of the new organizations. For example, the Zhejiang Provincial Overseas Chinese Affairs Bureau and the provincial Overseas Exchange Commission regularly organize "overseas leaders'" meetings, and not all participants are actually of Zhejiang origin. This shows co-optation of the native-place connection into the dominant, centralized quasi-political network centred around the PRC, robbing its traditional organizational forms of their significance. At the sixth meeting in Hangzhou in September 1995, along with Chinese from Europe, there were participants from Hong Kong, Macao, Southeast Asia, Australia, and North and South America. The provincial governor and a department head from the central Overseas Chinese Affairs Bureau were among the speakers (Ouzhou zhi Sheng 1995c). The 1996 meeting was held in Paris.

There is a broad overlap between participants of these Zhejiang conferences and the leadership of the European Federation of Chinese Organizations (EFCO, *Ouzhou Huaqiao Huaren Shetuan Lianhehui*). HCA became the first East European organization to join EFCO, a group of mostly pro-Beijing bodies which enjoys the PRC's support (Nyíri 1994b). Its joint activities are mostly ceremonial and political, but it also serves as a forum of the economic and political connections of its members. In 1995, HCA hosted an EFCO meeting in Budapest, and HCA's president became vice president of the federation after making an unsuccessful bid for its presidency.[25]

Native-place connections in this network are subordinated to the common quasi-political ground: EFCO leaders include Cantonese, Wenzhounese and Qingtianese. This is all the more significant because Zhejiang garment traders in Hungary – the predominant element of the Chinese economy in Hungary – do *not* rely on the many villages in their home area in Zhejiang that specialize in tailoring. Instead, most traders source their merchandise from their own or contracted factories in Guangdong. When Zhejiang traders do purchase garments in Zhejiang, they buy from state trading companies who often offer clothes at low subsidized prices, rather than from village tailors in their home communities. Native place ties thus neither exclude outsiders nor establish monopolies; they are a political and commercial resource that Zhejiang Chinese tap into only if and when advantageous.

Many business connections are forged at meetings such as the ones organized for "overseas leaders" by Zhejiang authorities, as well as at EFCO meetings around Europe. They extend to both trade between the overseas Chinese and China and among overseas Chinese in different countries; the PRC is the symbolic entrepôt of these new channels of the trade network. It has been argued that local CCP organizations have become something between a club for local notables and a Rotary or Lyons branch to catch up on the latest news and find business partners, and the authorities are opening the doors of this club toward overseas Chinese. While it is clear that the nature of the club has little to do with the CCP's ideology, it would be wrong to disregard its direct connection to the leadership in Beijing and the nationalism it espouses.

Organizations that attempt to represent all Chinese and operate with a mix of traditional and nationalistic rhetoric and allegiance to the PRC will probably grow in relevance and power in western Europe. The second generation and new immigrants become increasingly interested in culturalistic concepts of Chineseness. Economically, older Chinese communities have to look beyond the catering trade, and doing business with the People's Republic of China can be an very attractive option. If current trends in PRC policy continue, we are likely to see broader, more organized, and better controlled relations between the PRC and the overseas Chinese that may turn overseas Chinese organizations and businesses into representatives of PRC interests.

Just as Chinese in Hungary are, to a certain extent, starting to play the role of business intermediaries between West European Chinese oldtimers and the PRC, it is possible that the organizational patterns of European Chinese communities will follow that of HCA's development. In North America large communities that calls themselves "CSS" (Chinese students and scholars) as well as an increasing number of expatriates, working at multinational companies, establish contacts with the older communities of Chinese migrants, ending a period of a rather isolated existence.[26] This process may bring Chinese organizations closer together as well as make them much more politically visible and easier to control from Beijing. In 1996, several CSS organizations persuaded the New York United Federation of Chinese Associations to join a very high-profile campaign protesting an NBC anchorman's comments about Chinese swimmers during the Atlanta Olympics, which implied that they had used doping. Incidentally, the remarks were also one of the main themes in the PRC media campaign to use the olympics to stir up anti-American sentiments (see China News Digest 1996). In Belgium, the Shanghai Friends' Society's bulletin launched a special column devoted to Chinese students in Belgium, and is reprinting news articles from their electronic newsletter. Previously, CSS media and newsletters of local Chinese targeted strictly separate audiences: the two even used different characters – the former the simplified, the latter the traditional type.

Both in the Americas and in Western Europe, post-war immigrants from Taiwan whose roots are on the mainland (*waishengren*) are confronted, with each visit to the island, with an increasingly Taiwanese-speaking culture and a government and people that are no longer very much interested in them. More and more of them are joining not only functions organized by the PRC embassy in their countries of residence but also organizations run by migrants from the mainland. These organizations bring them together with "gold-diggers," who sometimes help them set up business ties with the mainland.[27]

In the Philippines, the unified celebration staged by the otherwise fractious local Chinese community for Jiang Zemin during the latter's visit to the Philippines in 1996 was even attended by prominent members of the pro-Taiwan faction and included Kuomintang members. This visit reminds of Jiang's sojourn to Hungary the year before. Both were first visits of a Chinese head of state. Like in Hungary, local Chinese leaders were delegated by organizations – surname, commercial, and sports associations – reportedly in return for donations. The guest list was finalized by the PRC embassy (Tan-Co, 1996).

Pieke recently wrote that changes currently underway in the established European Chinese communities in Britain, France, and the Netherlands may in time be repeated in eastern Europe at "the periphery of the European Chinese world" (Pieke 1998:15). Yet in the light of the analysis provided in this chapter it seems likely that developments may very well go exactly the other way around. The Hungarian periphery provides valuable insights and lessons that can be applied not only in the European core countries, but equally in the even larger and more firmly established communities on other continents.

References

A Dong. 1996. "Benyomásaim Zhang Manxinről" [My impressions of Zhang Manxin]. *Távol-Kelet* 1, p. 4.

Bi-Zhong Qiaosheng. 1996. "Shanghai Yishujia Chunjie Weiwentuan Fang Ou Yanchu" [Shanghai artists' Spring Festival troupe performs in Europe] *Bi-Zhong Qiaosheng* 5, pp. 8 and 10.

Chen Xiangyong. 1991. *Niuyue Huanghou Qu Xin Huaqiaode Shehui Jiegou* [Social structures of new Chinese immigrants in Queens, New York]. Taipei: Institute of Ethnology, Academia Sinica.

China News Digest (Global News, no. GL96–128). 1996. 31 August 1996.

Cz. G. 1995a. "Kisebbségi jogokra vágynak a kínaiak" [The Chinese wish minority rights]. *Népszabadság*, 12 October 1995.

Cz. G. 1995b. "'Nem időszerű' a kínai önkormányzat megalapítása" [Establishment of Chinese self-government "untimely"]. *Népszabadság*, 20 October 1995.

Czene Gábor. 1995. "Pekingi kacsa" [Peking duck]. *Népszabadság*, 30 October 1995.

g.j.a. 1996. "Kereskedelmi központ Gansu tartományban" [Trade centre in Gansu province]. *Magyar Nemzet*, 7 May 1996.

Goodman, David S. G. and Gerald Segal. 1997. "China without Deng, Part 2." *China News Digest* (Global News, no. GL97 029), 25 February 1997.

Hai Ming. 1994. "Chun Man Huaxia" [Spring fills the Chinese people]. *Huikan* 24 (30 April 1994).

Hajdú János. 1995. "Kihívás kérdőjelekkel" [A challenge with question marks]. *Kelet* 4, p. 2.

Hu Yiren. 1995. Zhengshi Huaren Shequ dui Xiongyalide Zuoyong [Consider the Chinese community's usefulness to Hungary]. Paper presented at the conference of the Budapest City Government Committee for Human Rights, Minorities, and Religious Affairs, Menedék – Hungarian Association for Migrants, and the Joint Conference of Hungarian Chinese Organizations, Budapest, 20–21 October 1995.

Huaren Tongxun (Antwerp). 1996. "Bilishi Bing-zi Shunian Chunjie Wanhui" [Spring Festival evening events for the *bing-zi* Year of the Rat in Belgium]. *Huaren Tongxun* 27 (April 1996), p. 17.

Hua Sheng Bao. 1994. "Zhongguoren Lixiangde Taojindi" [An ideal goldmine for Chinese people]. *Huasheng Bao* 29 March 1994.

Huikan 1994a. *Huikan* 25 (31 May 1994), p. 10.

Huikan. 1994b. "Zhongguo Minzu Yishutuan Jianjie" [A brief introduction of the Chinese Folk Art Troupe]. *Huikan* 25 (31 May 1994), p. 14.

Jingxuan. 1995. "Beijing Lianyihui Zai Choubei Zhong" [Beijing Friends Society in preparation] *Ouzhou zhi Sheng*, 7 August 1995, p. 1.

k.z.t. 1997. "Két és fél milliós adomány: Kínai támogatás a rendörségnek" [Two and a half million in aid: Chinese support to the police]. *Magyar Nemzet*, 14 February 1997.

Li Minghuan. 1995. *Dangdai Haiwai Huaren Shetuan Yanjiu* [A study of contemporary overseas Chinese organizations]. Xiamen: Xiamen Daxue Chubanshe.

Li Yiyuan. 1970. *Yi ge Yizhide Shizhen: Malaiya Huaren Shizhen Shenghuode Diaocha Yanjiu* [A transplanted township: A study of Chinese town life in Malaya]. Taipei: Institute of Ethnology, Academia Sinica.

Liu Guokai. 1995. "Yali xiade Kangzheng – Guangzhou Qi-jiu Minyunde Huiyi yu Sikao" [Resistance under oppression – Reminiscences and thoughts on the '79 Canton democracy movement]. *Beijing zhi Chun*, 1 (1995), pp. 65–70.

Liu Zhixian. 1996. "Zhi «Ouzhou Daobao» She Shezhang Ji Dongtian ji Zhao Xin Xianshengde Gongkai Xin" [Open letter to the heads of the Ouzhou Daobao office, Mr Ji Dongtian and Mr Zhao Xin] *Ouzhou zhi Sheng*, 21 August 1996, p. 1.

Mao Chun. 1992. *Zhongguoren zai Dongou (90 Niandai Xin Rechao Chuguo Taojin Jishi)* [Chinese in Eastern Europe (A chronicle of the new gold prospector emigration boom of the 1990s)]. Beijing: Zhongguo Lüyou Chubanshe.

Népszabadság. 1995. "Egyelöre nem lesz kínai kisebbség" [No Chinese minority for the time being], Népszabadság 21 October 1995, p. 12.

Nyíri Pál. 1993. "'Magyarországi' kínaiak a magyar piacon" ['Hungarian' Chinese on the Hungarian market], *Napi*, 31 July 1993.

Nyíri Pál. 1994a. "Kínai élet és társadalom Magyarországon" [Chinese life and society in Hungary]. In Endre Sik and Judit Tóth, eds, *Jönnek? Mennek? Maradnak?* [Are they coming? Are they leaving? Are then staying?]. 1993 Yearbook of the Research Group for International Migration. Budapest: Institute for Political Sciences, Hungarian Academy of Sciences,.

Nyíri Pál. 1994b. "Kínaiak Magyarországon. Egy diaszpóraközösség konszolidáló-dása" [Chinese in Hungary: The consolidation of an overseas Chinese community]. *Mozgó Világ* 10, pp. 101–2.

Nyíri, Pál. 1995. The PRC's Economic Growth and Overseas Chinese in Southeast Asia: A Look at Politics and Security. Paper presented at the Fifth Tun Abdul Razak Conference, "Growing into the 21st Century: Progress and Prospects for the Southeast Asian Region," Athens, Ohio, 21–23 April 1995.

Nyíri, Pál, 1996. "Wang Iván." *Mozgó Világ*, 2.

Nyíri, Pál, 1998. "New Migrants, New Community: The Chinese in Hungary, 1989–1995." In Gregor Benton and Frank N. Pieke, eds, *The Chinese in Europe*. Basingstoke: Macmillan, pp. 350–79.

Ouzhou Daobao. 1994. "Xuexi, Liaojie, Jiaoliu (Fakanci)" [Learn, understand, communicate (Opening words)]. *Ouzhou Daobao*, 11 May 1994.

Ouzhou Daobao. 1996a. "Zhongguoren You Shi Yong Wuqi Baohu Ziji" [The Chinese sometimes use weapons to protect themselves]. *Ouzhou Daobao*, 31 January 1996, p. 1.

Ouzhou Daobao. 1997. "Chuzhang Lin Hangwei Da Ben Bao Jizhe Wen" [Director Lin Hangwei answers our questions]. *Ouzhou Daobao*, 22 March 1997, p. 1.

Ouzhou zhi Sheng. 1994. "Zhongguo Minzu Yishutuan Jianjie" [A brief introduction of the Chinese Folk Art Troupe]. *Ouzhou zhi Sheng*, 22 August 1994, p. 4.

Ouzhou zhi Sheng. 1995a. "Tuanjie, Shi LüXiong Huaren Chenggongde Qizhi" [Unity is the banner of success for Chinese in Hungary]. *Ouzhou zhi Sheng*, 7 August 1995, p. 1.

Ouzhou zhi Sheng. 1995b. "LüXiong Shanghai Huaren Shangye Lianhehui Choubeihui Chengli" [Preparatory committee of the Commercial Association of Shanghai Chinese in Hungary established]. *Ouzhou zhi Sheng*, 21 August 1995, p. 1.

Ouzhou zhi Sheng. 1995c. "Zhang Manxin Deng Chuxi 'Zhejiang Lüwai Zhiming Renshi Juhui'" [Zhang Manxin, others to participate in the "Meeting of Zhejiang Leaders Abroad"]. *Ouzhou zhi Sheng*, 18 September 1995, p. 1.

Ouzhou zhi Sheng. 1995d. 'Hualianhui Fuzeren Kanwang Zao Xi Fu Shangde Zhongguo Tongbao" [HCA executives call on Chinese compatriots injured in surprise attack]. *Ouzhou zhi Sheng*, 2 October 1995, p. 1.

Ouzhou zhi Sheng. 1995e. Qing Guoqing, LüXiong Fujian, Sichuan Tongxianghui Juxing Jihui" [Hungary's Fujian, Sichuan tongxianghui hold get-togethers to celebrate national holiday]. *Ouzhou zhi Sheng*, 2 October, p. 1.

Ouzhou zhi Sheng. 1995f. "Huashang Jiang Xibo Beiou Zhong Shang" [Chinese merchant Jiang Xibo beaten, sustains serious injury]. *Ouzhou zhi Sheng*, 9 October, p. 1.

Ouzhou zhi Sheng. 1995g. "'Sihu' Shichang Ddarenzhe Shang Wei Quanbu Dedao Chuli" [Not all attackers at Józsefváros market have been dealt with yet]; "Benbao Dunqing Huaren Tigao Jingti, Faxian Keyi Jixiang Jishi Baojing" [We call on Chinese merchants to increase vigilance: if you notice anything suspicious, report to police immediately]; "You You Huaren Zao Daitu Baoli Xi Ji" [Another Chinese runs into ruffians, suffers violent surprise attack]; "Bu Neng Rang Baoli Fanzui Manyan" [We cannot let violence and crime spread]. *Ouzhou zhi Sheng*, 16 October 1995, p. 1.

Ouzhou zhi Sheng. 1995h. "Hualianhui Disan Zhou Nian" [HCA's third anniversary]. *Ouzhou zhi Sheng*, 18 December 1995, p. 1.

Pieke, Frank N. 1998. "Introduction." In Gregor Benton and Frank N. Pieke, eds, *The Chinese in Europe*. Basingstoke: Macmillan, pp. 1–17.

Pieke, Frank N. and Gregor Benton. 1998. "The Chinese in the Netherlands." In Gregor Benton and Frank N. Pieke, eds. *The Chinese in Europe*. Basingstoke: Macmillan, pp. 125–167.

Polonyi Péter. 1995. "'Békekötés' a Józsefvárosi piacon" ["Peace" at the Józsefváros market]. *Kelet* 1, p. 2.

Polonyi Péter. 1996a. "Kínainak lenni Magyarországon" [To be a Chinese in Hungary]. *Távol-Kelet* 9, p. 1.

Polonyi Péter. 1996b. "Kapcsolatok" [Contacts]. *Távol-Kelet*, 11, p. 21.

Skinner, G. William. 1958. *Leadership and Power in the Chinese Community of Thailand.* Ithaca, N.Y.: Cornell University Press.

Song Zhiming. 1995. "Bixu Zhizhi Kang Xiong Fangdongde Liexing" [We must curb the poor practice of opposing Hungarian landlords]. *Ouzhou zhi Sheng,* 21 August 1995, p. 1.

Tan-Co, Felicidad. 1996. "Chinese-Filipinos unite for Jiang." *Asia Times,* 29 November 1996.

Távol-Kelet. 1995. "Újvárosháza, 1995. október 20–21" [New City Hall, 20–21 October 1995]. *Távol-Kelet* 6, p. 3.

Távol-Kelet. 1996a. "Ünnepel a Magyarországi Kínaiak Egyesülete" [The Hungarian Chinese Association celebrates]. *Távol-Kelet* 1, p. 2.

Távol-Kelet. 1996c. 'Örzö-védö' [Protection]. *Távol-Kelet* 3, p. 2.

Távol-Kelet. 1996d. "Külföldön élö kínaiak" [Chinese abroad]. *Távol-Kelet* 3, p. 13.

Távol-Kelet. 1996e. "Zhang Deping." *Távol-Kelet* 4, p. 16.

Távol-Kelet. 1996f. "Még egy pénzalap" [Another fund]. *Távol-Kelet* 4, p. 16.

Távol-Kelet. 1996g. "Újabb szülöföldi szervezet" [Another native-place organization]. *Távol-Kelet* 12, p. 18.

Weiss, Melford. 1974. *Valley City: A Chinese Community in America.* Cambridge, Mass.: Harvard University Press.

Wong, Bernard P. 1982. *Chinatown: Economic Adaptation and Ethnic Identity of the Chinese.* New York: Holt, Rinehart & Winston.

Xue Hong. 1996. "Women Yao Tao Hui Gongdao" [We shall demand justice]. *Ouzhou Daobao,* 12 June 1996, p. 1.

Yiwen. 1994. "Xibanya Huaqiao Huaren Xiehui Daibiaotuan Fang Xiongyali Huajie" [Spanish Overseas Chinese and Chinese Association's delegation visits Chinese in Hungary]. *Ouzhou zhi Sheng,* 22 August 1994, p. 1.

Zheng Qi. 1997. "*LüXiong Huabao Liu Hongyan Wu Xing Yu Hai*" [Our unfortunate Chinese compatriot living in Hungary, Liu Hongyan, meets with disaster]. *ZhongOu Shangbao,* 9 March 1997.

ZhongOu Shangbao. 1995a. "Xiongyali Zhonghua Gongshangye Lianhehui Chengli" [Hungarian Chinese Federation of Industry and Trade established]. *ZhongOu Shangbao,* 28 January 1995.

ZhongOu Shangbao. 1995b. *ZhongOu Shangbao* 20 December 1995, p. 2.

Notes

1 At one performance in 1996, Chinese children were wearing T-shirts commemorating the millecentennial anniversary of the Hungarians' "conquest of the homeland."

2 Li Minghuan points out that the latter two of the three types of institution central to overseas Chinese communities – organizations, schools, press – tend to be directly or indirectly affiliated with one of the former (Li 1995). The case of the Hungarian Chinese confirms this as far as the press is concerned. Of the five enduring Chinese periodicals in Hungary, *Ouzhou zhi Sheng* is published by HCA; *Ouzhou Daobao* is supported by the Association for the Promotion of Chinese-Hungarian Friendship; the Hungarian Chinese Federation of Industry and Trade launched first the *ZhongOu Shangbao,* then the European edition of *Gongshang Bao* (though in this case it acted on behalf of its mother organization, the Gongshanglian of the PRC).

3 Some of the advisor-interpreters who help customs authorities determine the value of Chinese goods and clear them through customs are relatives of HCA's

president and are rumoured to collect bribes in collaboration with customs officials.

4 Campaigns around these initiatives were, as HCA's statements of commercial aims generally tend to be, phrased not in business but in moral terms (Nyíri 1993).

5 According to Victor Yuan (personal communication), the PRC Gongshanglian has also been active in contacts with "migratory businesspersons" within mainland China. The Rui'an Migratory Businesspersons' Commercial Chamber (RMBPCC), an organization formed by a group of Wenzhounese in Beijing's Zhejiang Village, is supported by the Rui'an Gongshanglian. Beijing authorities have so far refused to register RMBPCC, but it has the potential to become the most powerful structure of Zhejiang Village, believed to be the largest contiguous migrant community in China (see the chapters by Xiang Biao, and Luigi Tomba in this volume). It is worth noting that, just like HCA's legitimation has relied on a combination of a show of relations with PRC authorities and traditional moral rhetoric, RMBPCC's organizers have enlisted the Rui'an government's official backing while facing the reluctance of Beijing authorities and have declared that they aim to provide public services to members and maintain the good image of Rui'anese. Other declared purposes of RMBPCC (providing business information; protecting the rights of members; establishing of a public security committee) are all shared by HCA.

6 There are no more than a few dozen Chinese from Xinjiang in Hungary. The Xinjiang tongxianghui consists, of course, of Hans. There is no indication that these people would be former cross-border traders who migrated farther afield to Hungary.

7 Alexander Maslov reports a conversation with a PRC Ministry of Public Security official who claimed that the sect was actually financed by Chinese in Malaysia and the United States via third parties in Japan and Taiwan. The sect is also active in mainland China itself. Maslov further reports cases of Xiantian Dadao activity among Chinese in Moscow, as well as rumours of such activity from Habarovsk and Vladivostok in the Far East (A. Maslov, personal communication).

8 Its vice-chairwoman distinguished herself by a particularly strong-worded appeal for Chinese unity after a Chinese merchant was bitten by a security guard's dog at a Budapest market; she stated that the security guard "was insulting [all of] us Chinese; he despises the Chinese merchants... today it is just a security guard who sets his dog off to bite a person; what will another Hungarian do to other Chinese tomorrow?" (Xue Hong 1996).

9 Examples are the Association of the Hungarian Chinese Cultural and Arts Circles (*Xiongyali Zhongguo Wenhua-yishujie Lianhehui*) and the Chinese-Hungarian Friendship Association (*ZhongXiong Youhao Xiehui*).

10 The embassy had apparently been instrumental in ensuring that Jiang met the delegates of HCA and no other organization. It is possible that HCA's delegates were invited to the embassy without Jiang's previous knowledge. The ambassador himself had warned APCHF's president to stay away from Jiang's scheduled programme.

11 The use of the term "anti-party elements" (*fandangfenzi*), rarely used since the Mao years, reflects both the HCA president's reliance on his association with the PRC party-state to gain legitimacy and his willingness to use this association to eliminate rivals. It also illustrates that he – a city Revolutionary Committee member during the Cultural Revolution – is occasionally out of tune with the latest ideological developments in the PRC.

12 *Ouzhou Daobao* reacted to the company's establishment by reprinting – without comments – an article titled "The Chinese Sometimes Use Weapons to Protect Themselves" from the Hungarian daily *Népszabadság*, in which the event was mentioned (Ouzhou Daobao 1996a).

13 In December 1995, the CCP's chief ideologue Li Ruihuan stressed at a Bangkok conference that the Chinese government, while respecting international law, wants to protect the interests of Chinese nationals overseas (*huaqiao*) (Távol-Kelet 1996d), raising concern in the region. Although the statement does not contradict the PRC's long-standing policy that declares the interests of Chinese nationals overseas a matter of its legitimate concern, enforcement of this policy would be an altogether new development in the PRC's Southeast Asia policy.

14 Tongxianghui have been particularly active in this field, presumably to garner credibility with officials in their home provinces.

15 Similar arguments were voiced in the Netherlands in 1988 when the Dutch Chinese community debated the possibility of a minority status (Pieke and Benton 1998:156–61).

16 Currently, Hungarian authorities are beginning to take an interest in the integration of the Chinese. A draft legal amendment allowing non-citizens to not only vote but run in municipal elections may make it easier for Chinese to find a voice in local politics. It will be interesting to see how this proposal will be received by the HCA.

17 *Ouzhou zhi Sheng* even suggested – probably erroneously – that most Chinese in Hungary were members of one organization or another (Ouzhou zhi Sheng 1995h).

18 An explanation for this is given in Pieke 1998.

19 The earliest commonly known example of these organizations are the Overseas Chinese Club of France (*LüFa Huaqiao Julebu*), formed by Wenzhounese in 1972, and the General Chinese Association in the Netherlands (*Lü Helan Huaqiao Zonghui*), also established by Wenzhounese in 1965.

20 In Belgium there already are two of them: the Belgian Overseas Chinese Association (*LüBi Huaqiao Lianhehui*) and the Belgian Chinese Association (*Bilishi Huaren Lianhehui*), the latter founded in 1996.

21 A fourth model positioning the Chinese as a member of the host socio-political community is perhaps rightly excluded from Li's approach, since in this model a Chinese would figure as an individual citizen rather than as a member of a dialect group.

22 In 1996, the old, influential, mostly Cantonese Belgian Chinese Chamber of Commerce (*LüBi Huashang Xiehui*) in Antwerp also sponsored the publication of a magazine devoted to "strengthening the motherland's ties with Chinese in Belgium and across Europe" (*Bi-Zhong Qiaosheng* 1996). When it co-organized a Chinese festival in Antwerp with the Belgian Overseas Chinese Association, the (Cantonese) *Nanshun Tongxianghui*, the *Antwerp Chinatown Protection Association* and the PRC ambassador were present as co-sponsor (see Bi-Zhong Qiaosheng 5, 1996, p. 22).

23 Bi-Zhong Qiaosheng 5, 1996.

24 Bi-Zhong Qiaosheng 5, 1996, p. 23.

25 This was the sixth top title collected by HCA's president, who was already serving as president of the Hungarian Chinese Chamber of Commerce, honorary president of the Hungarian Gongshanglian and the Chinese Patriotic Enterprises Group, and chairman of the Representative Committee of Hungarian Chinese Organizations. Although in the Gongshanglian, for

example, he is not the actual leader because he does not have the contacts to key organizational patrons in the PRC, the titles exemplify what Skinner calls "interlocking leadership" and point to the possible transnationalization of such leadership (Skinner 1958). Skinner's hypothesis that leaders who hold "interlocking" positions in several associations are influential holds true, for, as we have seen, HCA's honorary president and vice-president both hold titles in other groups as well. Most tongxianghui and "new-type" organizations lack the phenomenon of interlocking leadership; attempts to introduce it, as we have seen, have largely failed.

26 The process appears to resemble one that has taken place earlier within communities of post-1949 migrants from Taiwan in the United States. A recent study of migrants from Taiwan in Queens, New York, showed that, by the nineties, their most significant community structures were either "community service providers," such as the Chinese Immigrants Service Centre (*Huaren Yimin Fuwu Zhongxin*) that cut across the social layers of workers, small merchants, and professionals, or else organizations including both Chinese and non-Chinese local residents (Chen 1991).

27 An example is the participation of waishengren, including former Kuomintang officials from the mainland, in pro-PRC organizations in Belgium.

Chapter Thirteen

Exporting the "Wenzhou model" to Beijing and Florence: Suggestions for a comparative perspective on labour and economic organization in two migrant communities*

Luigi Tomba

Introduction

Two geographically and socially distant urban areas have been extensively modified in recent years by a flow of migrants from the Chinese province of Zhejiang. The first area, described at length by Xiang Biao in his chapter in this volume, is located in the southwestern suburbs of Beijing where a large community of migrants have earned the place the name of "Zhejiang Village" (*Zhejiang Cun*). Zhejiang Village has recently attracted considerable attention both at home and abroad, in particular for its *de facto* administrative independence from Beijing municipality and degree of self-organization in production and social services. The second area is the Chinese (mainly Zhejiang) community in the Florence region in Italy, where a flourishing leather industry attracts thousands of Chinese, whose self-organization recalls that of Zhejiang village in Beijing.

To what degree are the two communities, their migration and their social and economic organization at the destination comparable? Can observed similarities be traced back to a common cultural and economic background rather than similarities between the areas of settlement?

* I am indebted to the colleagues of the Department of Social Sciences of Florence University for introducing me to the world of Chinese migration in Tuscany and to Alberto Tassinari and Nedo Baracani for their willingness to cooperate and share information.

Finally, is it possible to consider Zhejiang migration as an aspect of an emerging economic model of private and family business?

The Wenzhou model

Much has been written about the "Wenzhou model" (*Wenzhou moshi*) of reform era economic development (Fei 1987; Gold 1990; Lin et al. 1987; Liu 1992; Nolan and Dong 1990; Parris 1993; Yuan 1987; Zheng 1991). The major ingredient of the Wenzhou model is the development of the private economy, and Wenzhou has been singled out as a pioneering example of the re-emerging spirit of Chinese entrepreneurship. What struck observers was the high rate of privatization of the economy of Wenzhou already in the early 1980s, long before the growth of private and collective enterprises in the rest of China. Equally intriguing was the tolerance of informal unauthorized economic practices that violated central policies of the time. This suggested that the local authorities played an important role in fostering the Wenzhou model, although several other factors have repeatedly been mentioned to answer the questions of Why Wenzhou? Why so fast?

While Chinese authorities generally credit Wenzhou's economic success to the post-Mao reform policies, historical, economic and geographical conditions have also contributed to the phenomenal development of Wenzhou. Historical causes include not only the tradition of private handicraft production and commerce, but also a strong independence of the local bureaucracy from the central authorities, due mainly to the geographic isolation of the area and the lack of central investment during the Maoist period (Liu 1992). Economically, Wenzhou suffered from poor agricultural conditions (almost eighty per cent of the territory is made up of mountains), forcing farmers to supplement agriculture with sideline productions from an early date on. Quite surprisingly, some of the reasons for Wenzhou's current development seem to lie in its former backwardness.

The introduction of a family responsibility system in the Chinese countryside in the early 1980s assigned to families the role and status of basic economic units. This stressed individual entrepreneurship as a way to deal with the high rates of unemployment inherited from the turbulent years of Cultural Revolution; subsequently, business in Wenzhou began to flourish again. The re-emergence of private business was also a result of strong pressure from below to get rid of the major bureaucratic constraints to private entrepreneurship. This pressure, however, found accomplices in the local leadership, as economic practices began to develop, such as business affiliation (the practice of using the name of a state enterprise to enter the market), underground financial organizations (using such practices as floating interests rates), and informal and unauthorized land transfer among peasant families. Quite interestingly, all these practices were later accepted and legalized in central policies.

Quickly, thousands of small commercial enterprises, workshops and other economic activities developed, lighting the fire of the so-called "shadow economy" (*yinxing jingji*). Although Zhejiang is the smallest Chinese province (about one per cent of the total area of China), its 1.5 million private and individual household enterprises are greater in number than those of other coastal provinces, such as Guangdong or Fujian, that are at the forefront of the reforms. These enterprises officially employ about three millions people, seventy-eight per cent of whom are registered as individual entrepreneurs (*getihu*) (Guojia Tongjiju 1996).

The large proportion of private household enterprises is one of the key features that make Wenzhou's fast development different from other provinces. Southern Jiangsu, for example, also experienced rapid development, but based its economic system on collective enterprises (although at the managerial level the two property forms differ much less than one may expect). The larger availability of state and public capital, the proximity of Shanghai and a much more developed agricultural basis have contributed to this pattern in Jiangsu.

Wenzhou, by contrast, suffers from geographical isolation and poverty and instead capitalized on the new freedom accorded to families. Family business Wenzhou style is characterized by extensive commercial networks, high labour intensity, low capital intensity, low mechanization of productive processes and "competitive solidarity."

It can also be inferred, although no statistical evidence is as yet available, that remittances and investment of well positioned Zhejiangese migrant also played a role in Wenzhou's development. Migration, in other words, in itself is a constituent feature of the Wenzhou model.

Confirming the ability of Wenzhounese to trade their products across the nation from the beginning of the reform period, is the boom of mail order trading. As Fei Xiaotong once said, Wenzhou enterprises are based on "one couple of hands, two legs, three stamps and four products" (Fei 1987). Wenzhou family enterprises used the postal service to bypass the need for an established commercial network. As a result, the profits of the local post offices increased from 63.000 yuan in 1978 to 1.83 million in 1985 (Fei 1987).

Neither direct personal links nor a continuity of familial migration strategies seem to exist between the communities in Beijing and Florence, yet the shared background of the Wenzhou experience has produced some striking similarities in their economic and cultural integration in the host society. Below, I compare the two communities on the basis of long term research (separately and using different methods) by Chinese and Italian researchers,[1] supplemented by my own observations.

282

Florence: A privileged arena for migrant business

Very few Chinese lived in Tuscany until the early 1980s, when larger numbers arrived in the Tuscan municipalities of Campi Bisenzio and Signa as well as the western suburbs of Florence (Brozzi and Peretola). It was only in the mid-1980s that a "silent" flow of migrants began to fill the Tuscan peripheries. The visibility of the Chinese community was greatly enhanced with the 1986 regulations (law no. 943/86) that allowed irregular immigrants to obtain legal residence. Non-EC citizens, who had entered Italy without a regular permission, were entitled to a residence permit provided that they could demonstrate to have a job and be economically self-sufficient. The number of Chinese migrants in Tuscany that obtained a residence permit in this way was 1,239 in 1989 (a significant ten per cent of the entire estimated non-EC population). In the following two years, an additional 2,254 residence permits were issued to Chinese, also in connection with a second regularization law of 1990, the final term of which was the end of 1991 (law no. 39/90). In 1995, 3,228 officially registered Chinese lived in the Florence-Prato area,[2] although a rough estimate following a third regularization in 1996 put the real number at over 10,000 (on the regularization laws, see also Carchedi and Ferri 1998).

The real number of Chinese migrants is still uncertain, but what is clear is that they own 711 regularly registered enterprises.[3] Chinese migrants have established an ethnic economy based on family enterprises that manufacture garments and leather handbags. The community is characterized by concentrated settlement,[4] mutual help, limited integration with the local population and resistance to administrative interference.

Some statistics further illustrate the importance of private enterprise. During the second regularization in 1990 and 1991, forty-five per cent of residence permits given to Chinese were for "autonomous work," that is, to run an private enterprise (a dramatic increase from the previous insignificant 0.1 per cent of 1989[5] – see table 13.1). In the municipality of Campi Bisenzio in 1993, sixty per cent (132 out of 223) of the officially registered enterprises engaged in leather production was Chinese.

The majority of the Chinese in Tuscany live in Florence and Prato (eighty-two per cent).[6] About ninety per cent of them are born in the Wenzhou region in southern Zhejiang (Wenzhou municipality, Qingtian county, or Rui'an county, Marsden 1994). While similar in outline to overseas Chinese groups around the world, the community's familism, migration paths and the nature and informality of their productive activities also bear the stamp their Wenzhounese heritage.

Similarly to Beijing's "Zhejiang Village," Wenzhou people in Tuscany have migrated as families. About twenty per cent of the residence permits issued to Chinese in Tuscany between 1987 and 1989 were for family members, which is a much higher percentage than for any other non-EC

Table 13.1 Chinese migrants: Reasons for issuing new residence permits

	27/1/87–1/11/89		2/11/89–2/12/91	
	Number	%	*Number*	%
No reason	11	0.8		
Tourism	23	1.8	38	1.4
Employment	906	73.1	122	4.7
Commerce and self employment	2	0.1	1,154	45.1
Study	43	3.4	38	1.4
Family	253	20.4	181	7.0
Waiting for employment*			1,010	39.5
Total	**1,239**	**100.0**	**2,554**	**100.0**

*Registered at the local job centre.

Source: : Istituto di Ricerca Economica e Sociale (IRES), Tuscany and Questura di Firenze (Bortolotti and Tassinari 1992).

migrant community. Men are only a slight majority of fifty-eight per cent, suggesting that family members are a part of the migrants' human capital already at the moment of migration. We are clearly not facing a migration flow mainly composed of individual men escaping their own countries for economic or political reasons. The Tuscan Chinese are an organized flow of potential small entrepreneurs who carefully choose a better place to invest their resources.

Tuscany, in this respect, is a very specific area. Small enterprises have been an extremely strong component of post-war economic development and modernization. During the 1980s, technological upgrading and restructuring of local workshops allowed Chinese producers to enter this sector, especially at the bottom end of the market. Chinese generally arrive in Florence and Prato not directly from the Wenzhou area, but from other European countries, particularly France and the Netherlands (Campani et al. 1994), in search of better business opportunities.

The enterprises of the Chinese community are characterized by informality. Enterprises, in particular after the 1991 regularization, are duly registered, but workers (in most cases family members or more distant kin) are not on the books. This practice is illegal but cannot be rooted out through administrative means. Relations between employer and worker are generally not formalized through written contracts or agreements.

High labour intensity and the use of second hand equipment characterize Chinese enterprises producing leather products and clothing, a fact that has dramatically changed the shape of this sector. The emergence of industrial districts during the post-war years is generally considered to be one of the most successful features of the economic development of the region. The "industrial district" (Becattini 1987; Pyke, Becattini and Sengenberger 1990) is an agglomeration of enterprises that draws on skills and personnel released by the crisis of "mezzadria"[7] agriculture. The enterprises emerging in this environment were based on family cohesion, kinship networks, high labour intensity, limited need for investment in fixed assets, and overlap of work and residence, in other words, all the elements that also make up the Wenzhou experience. When rising wages and technological upgrading created an opening in the 1980s, the Chinese could simply replace the original Italian entrepreneurs. The economic and social conditions of industrial districts in Tuscany fitted the Chinese, steeped in the Wenzhou tradition, like a glove.

The development of Chinese business in the area was greatly facilitated by the fact that Chinese could enter an existing economic system, which left some market niches free for low quality and cheap products, and made some basic technology available. The entry of Wenzhou entrepreneurs boosted competition, but also opened up opportunities for an ethnic division of labour. In Prato, for example, most of the Chinese enterprises became subcontractors to the renowned tailoring firms of that city.

Beijing: An independent ethnic economy[8]

"Zhejiang Village" is the name given to a large community of Wenzhou migrants, who settled in the southeastern suburbs of Beijing. Settlement commenced in the early eighties, and a large scale, concentrated, integrated and specialized economy developed around 1985–1986. At that time, a larger flow of migrants entered Beijing, while the reform of the city's commercial system offered more room to the Wenzhou community and their products (Xiang 1993).

The growth of the community, its concentration in certain areas and the subsequent extension of commercial activity to markets in southern Beijing favoured the development of a network of producers in Zhejiang Village itself. The hundreds of workshops are mainly involved in leather and clothes production. Their products (and especially the principal article, leather jackets) are today sold at most large garment markets in the capital. Although reliable statistics in this field are not available (Xiang 1993),[9] it is certain that Zhejiang Village has gained control over a large part of the distribution and production of shoes (Huang 1996)[10] and other leather products and clothes.

The workshops run by families frequently involve kin or friends as well. The ethnic and family connections make workers accept long working hours, poor living conditions and low pay. The ethnic link is also instrumental in the recruitment of labour from the Wenzhou area (Xiang 1993).

Some of the capital necessary to set up a new business in Beijing is generally raised in Wenzhou before migration. This is one of the regular features of Wenzhou one of business-oriented migration. Money can be borrowed from private banks, usurers, credit associations, or directly from family members (see also Giese, this volume; Xiang, this volume).

Investment in equipment has recently become increasingly necessary due to growing competition, and often increases the dependence of the workshops and families on loans. A second hand multiple sewing machine, for instance, can cost up to 130,000 yuan.[11]

The area where Zhejiang migrants settled had the advantage of limited administrative interference and the availability of housing. It was located in an area between the city and the countryside, where most of the resident population was not entitled to a full urban registration. On the other hand, the area lacked any infrastructure for the great number of people and enterprises that was about to arrive. This boosted speculation and led to a spiralling cost of housing: generally, up to ten people now share a room that is both workplace and residence.

Furthermore, the status of migrant made it very difficult for Zhejiang villagers to use services such as medical care or schooling. This situation, which is a result of the household registration system (*hukou*, see Chan, this volume), forced the migrants to rely on self-organization and mutual help. Inside the village, clinics providing basic medical care and nurseries have been set up. When a child reaches school age, the choice is between paying several thousand yuan per year for a private school, or sending the child back to Wenzhou (Xiang 1993).

The village seems to be an almost fully independent unit inside Beijing municipality. Officials whom I interviewed said that the Beijing government considers Zhejiang Village an "urban district" (*shiqu*), and the state will only intervene in its internal affairs when it endangers public security. The late 1995 clean-up was only the last of such emergency interventions, revealing the absence of any kind of medium or long term policy to integrate Zhejiang Village into the city.

For the sake of the comparison with the Chinese in Tuscany it is worth noting some of the differences between Zhejiang Village and other migrants in Beijing. There are at least three other major communities of migrants in the city, namely from Henan, Xinjiang and Anhui. The one most strikingly different from Zhejiang Village is "Henan Village," located in Liulitun, east of the Sanlitun diplomatic compounds in northeastern Beijing. Henan people (about 30,000 in 1995) are mainly employed in the construction industry, while a large number of them live by collecting garbage along the city's roads. The "village" itself, in contrast to relatively well organized and orderly Zhejiang Village, looks like a huge garbage dump, with a survival (Huang 1996) economy resembling South American urban slums, and based on organized work teams.[12]

In general, one major difference is immediately clear when comparing Zhejiang Village with other Chinese migrant communities. The Zhejiang settlement seems to be a complete economic system of production, trade and services. For this reasons it creates opportunities for upward mobility almost independently from the surrounding economic system. Other migrants generally depend on the local labour market for employment, mainly in construction. The role of the community is generally limited to mediation between individual migrants and local employers. When the community succeeds in finding autonomous sources of income, it is usually at the margins of the local economy, such as the garbage collection of Henanese in Beijing.

Evaluation

Below, I shall discuss the commonalities between the Beijing and Tuscan communities under four different headings: 1) the economic nature of migration and the forms of economic activity; 2) the role of the family in migration as well as in production and social organization; 3) the community's role and structure; 4) visibility and relations to local institutions.

Economic migration

First of all, the development of communities of Zhejiang migrants in the area around Florence and Prato is the result of an entrepreneurial choice of a favourable economic environment, characterized by 1) the development of a local leather and clothing industry based on small and family workshops and 2) the growth of an inward looking ethnic economy based on mutual help, which is nonetheless able collectively to enter the market.

The Zhejiang migrants are, in Beijing as well as in Tuscany, business migrants. The pull factor of the possibility to make money through business activities or employment in businesses of fellow ethnics is generally more relevant than the push factor of a poor, rural economy (Wenzhou is in fact among the fastest growing economies in the world). Wenzhou people move in search of the best opportunity to invest their capital, both financial and human (family members, tradition, training, skills, and entrepreneurial expertise). This is, for example, why the Zhejiang migrants tend to leave their hometown together with their family members (this is even more pronounced in case of international migration), who are an integral component of the "capital" to be invested in the enterprise.

Family

The Chinese community in Tuscany is organized as an economic system of which families are the basic components. Each workshop generally carries out the whole production process and no significant division of labour takes place among the Chinese factories. Competition does not affect cooperation or mutual help inside the community. All the workshops need

287

the community to organize services, reduce costs, and mediate the relations with the outside world. This kind of "cooperative competition" is fostered by strikingly similar (and therefore directly competing) products. A division of labour is nevertheless emerging. Groups of families specialize in specific activities, such as transportation, commerce, or certain other services. The economy of the village is becoming a mature and integrated economic system that is largely independent from local society. This evolution has recently led to the construction of higher quality markets places that partially changed the perceptions of the area by Beijing residents (Xiang, this volume).

Community

In both Beijing and Tuscany informality and mutual help are the best way to resist administrative pressure. In Tuscany employment, financial help and some services (Chinese self-managed clinics are a common phenomenon in this area) are mainly provided within the community, and mutual trust is strengthened by hierarchical organization and labour practices. Nonetheless, the Tuscan economy has not become an "enclave economy", as its dependence on local markets is great and many fundamental services (including mediating the difficult relationship with the Italian bureaucracy) are still provided by Italian intermediaries: sixty per cent of the entrepreneurs employ Italian consultants (Bortolotti 1992).

In Beijing, the migrant community, once formed, facilitated access to skilled labour, capital and markets. More recently, the growth of a more mature economic system required that outsiders also be employed in workshops of the village: about one third of the 100,000 migrants in the village today are from Anhui, Hubei and Henan, thus producing an ethnic division of labour between the different migrant communities.

Host society

Chinese communities abroad are generally perceived as closed and unwilling to integrate. Several cultural reasons may strengthen this attitude (language, customs, misperceptions, cultural diffidence of the local population), but economic considerations and the need to exploit all the advantages of ethnic cohesion are probably the basic explanation. Integration is not *a priori* rejected, but rather expressly slowed down in order to preserve the economic system. The level of labour intensity necessary for the Chinese enterprises to be competitive can only be maintained through family and ethnic participation, and no outsider is to be found in the Chinese workshops.

A division and specialization of economic functions, comparable to that described by Xiang Biao for Beijing, has not yet taken place in

Tuscany at this point. The cultural isolation of the Wenzhou community in Tuscany (due to a large extent to language problems) is higher than in Beijing.

The second generation that is currently growing up (Baracani 1994) will in future give a new face to the Chinese presence in the area. As result, the community may integrate more into local society and possibly develop into a more mature (while always ethnic) economy.

The characteristics of the economic system are also relevant when evaluating the visibility of Chinese communities in the local context. The Chinese community in Hungary described by Pál Nyíri is this book is mainly engaged in commercial activities which require a higher visibility and closer relationship with local society, in addition to a higher level of institutionalization. Quite the contrary, the Tuscan Chinese are producers, who prefer as little attention as possible from the local authorities and society.

Table 13.2 shows the distribution of Chinese enterprises in Tuscany by area and activity. Despite a significant presence of restaurants in the capital city of Florence, the predominance of productive activity is quite clear in all other areas. This situation will probably change as many Chinese leather workshops are experiencing a transition from production for wholesale distribution to production directly for retail trade; this may in time also increase the visibility of the community.

The Wenzhou model exported?

A couple of conclusions emerge from the comparison between the Tuscan and Beijing Wenzhou communities. First of all, a methodological observation. The researchers who studied the Wenzhou communities in

Table 13.2 Geographical distribution by sector of Chinese enterprises in the Florence-Prato area

	Florence	Prato	Campi Bisenzio	Empoli	Sesto	Signa	Lastra a Signa
Leather factories	124	2		1	67	8	
Clothing factories	14	261	81	9	4	11	8
Other factories		2			1	1	
Total industry	**138**	**265**	**81**	**10**	**72**	**20**	**8**
Trade (leather and clothes)	2	3	51				
Restaurants	27			1			
Other commercial activities	8	2					
Total services	**37**	**5**	**51**	**1**	**0**	**0**	**0**
Total	175	270	132	11	72	20	8
Number of registered Chinese migrants	1141	1483	349	63	15	53	51

Source: Anagrafi Comunali and Florence Chamber of Commerce, February 1995.

Beijing and Florence have used different methods and had very different objectives. Zhejiang Village has been thoroughly investigated from an anthropological viewpoint, while the researchers in Tuscany were either interested in issues of entrepreneurship and employment or wanted to facilitate policy making. Although their results are to a certain extent compatible, our knowledge would nevertheless greatly benefit from further coordinated research efforts.

The analysis presented suggests that the two communities are different expressions of a common migration strategy. They are moreover the result of the export in search of higher profits of the Wenzhou model to alien and more hostile environments. Somewhat speculatively, I suggest that migration is not merely an outcome, but an integral part of the Wenzhou model. The Wenzhou economy is boosted by migrant remittances, and Wenzhou is the hub of several national and international trade and business networks. Viewed from this angle, Beijing's Zhejiang Village is a tool for Wenzhou commercial penetration of the distant markets of northern China and Russia.

Far from having an all-encompassing explanation of this phenomenon, I would like to suggest some partially disconnected ideas. One set of comparative issues is the development strategies of the two communities. Their features can be traced back to the original imprinting of the model: business migration, internal markets for production factors (ethnic economy), family enterprises, labour intensity, competitive cooperation, commercial independence. All of these are found in the two communities, albeit at very different stages of development with the Zhejiang Village economy definitely as the more mature one.

Both communities seem to have already reached the phase when the structural problems of the take off phase become acute, problems that are mainly linked to environmental or administrative constraints. In Beijing, the independent nature of the village has led to an increasingly contradictory relationship with Beijing municipality, as demonstrated by the showdown of late 1995. Similarly, racial tension in Italy in the early 1990s contributed to the closure of the Chinese communities.

In Tuscany racism inspired by fear of economic competition from Wenzhou business played a similar role to the fear of political turmoil in Beijing. Yet, Chinese immigration is now generally recognised as highly valuable and is considered far less problematic in terms of social and racial tension than North African immigration. Even the popular notion of the transformation of the Florence peripheral belt into a "Chinatown" is generally associated with a positive evaluation of the organizational and commercial skills of the Chinese migrants.

Nonetheless, the Tuscan Chinese community is still facing significant constraints on the development of a solid ethnic economy that have not yet been overcome. Communication with the outside world is often even more difficult for the Chinese than for other migrants; the economy is still exploiting an economic niche, mainly producing cheap, low quality commodities.

A second set of comparative issues are those of preliminary *conditions* of migration. Long distance migration is a choice that requires much capital, both in financial terms and in terms of relationships. It also faces great constraints and risks, but potentially yields equally high returns. The choice of target area is therefore extremely important for families who want to start a business.

In Beijing *commercial* activities with limited or no capital investment formed the basis of the first immigration of Wenzhounese. In Tuscany, by contrast, the crisis of local workshops was the major pull factor that attracted *productive* investment from migrant families. Workshop owners now gradually consider entering trade themselves, but the core of the community is still engaged in production at different levels of integration with the local economy.

The arrival of business migrants to Tuscany was stimulated by the availability of second hand equipment and a greatly developed local market for garments and leather products. Businesses were established in suburban areas where housing was readily available and cheap. Similar factors operated in Beijing. Scarcity of affordable clothes attracted Wenzhou traders. The commercial activities made capital and goods available for production in Beijing itself; the area chosen by the first families coming to Beijing was in the semi-agricultural belt with low rents.

The final factor affecting the development of the two communities are bureaucratic and administrative practices. The Chinese economic reform of the 1980s turned the previously illegal activities of migrant businessmen into legal enterprises, which however continue to rely on informal practices. Currently, ninety per cent of the workshops are still not registered and virtually none of them adheres to the labour regulations on security, workers' rights and working hours, creating a "shadow economy" beyond the fiscal and administrative reach of the state. In total, this shadow economy was estimated to produce twenty per cent of the total output of Chinese urban economy in 1996 (Huang 1996).

The Chinese workshops set up in Italy after 1986 are generally registered, also as a result of the agreement between the two governments on the reciprocal protection of economic activities, but most of the fiscal obligations and labour protection regulations are still ignored, and the overlap of kinship and economic ties favour the emergence of informal labour practices.

The two migrations have many features in common and refer directly (through personal connections) and indirectly (as a cultural reference) to the economic experience of the land of origin. At the same time, their differences attest to a considerable flexibility in economic organization and adaptation to administrative pressure.

Future research into the Wenzhou experience will probably discover much more stable and clearer economic links between the Wenzhou homeland and Wenzhou migrant communities than we are able to establish today. This first overview presented here has however already provided some interesting glimpses of a complex transnational economic system of which migration is only one component.

References

Baracani, Nedo. 1994. *La seconda generazione nella migrazione cinese in Toscana: scuola e integrazione sociale* [The second generation of Chinese migrants in Tuscany: Schooling and social integration]. In Giovanna Campani, Francesco Carchedi, and Alberto Tassinari, eds, *L'immigrazione silenziosa. Le comunità cinesi in Italia* [The silent immigration: Chinese communities in Italy]. Turin: Fondazione Giovanni Agnelli, pp. 127–46.

Becattini, Giacomo. 1986. "Riflessioni sullo sviluppo socio-economico della Toscana" [On the social and economic development of Tuscany]. In Giorgio Mori, ed. *Storia d'Italia. Le regioni dall'Unità a oggi – La Toscana*, [Tuscany, history of Italy: Regions since reunification]. Turin: Einaudi, pp. 901–24.

Bortolotti, Franco. 1992. *Un distretto etnico? Le imprese cinesi della via Pistoiese* [An ethnic district? Chinese enterprises on Via Pistoiese]. Florence: Istituto di Ricerca Economica e Sociale (IRES) Toscana.

Bortolotti, Franco and Alberto Tassinari. 1992. *Immigrati a Firenze: il caso della collettività cinese* [Immigrants in Florence: The case of the Chinese community]. Florence: Istituto di Ricerca Economica e Sociale (IRES) Toscana.

Campani, Giovanna, Francesco Carchedi and Alberto Tassinari, eds, 1994. *L'immigrazione silenziosa. Le comunità cinesi in Italia* [The silent immigration: Chinese communities in Italy]. Turin: Fondazione Giovanni Agnelli.

Carchedi, Francesco and Marica Ferri. 1998. "The Chinese in Italy: Dimensions and Structural Characteristics." In Gregor Benton and Frank N. Pieke, eds, *The Chinese in Europe*. Basingstoke: Macmillan, pp. 261–77.

Colombo, Massimo et al. 1995. *Wenzhou – Firenze: Identità, imprese e modalità di insediamento dei Cinesi in Toscana* [Wenzhou – Florence: Identity, enterprises and settlement of Chinese migrants in Tuscany]. Florence: Angelo Pontecorboli Editore.

Fei Xiaotong. 1987. "Wenzhou Xing" [Travel to Wenzhou]. In Lin Bai et al. eds, *Wenzhou Moshide Lilun Tansuo* [Theoretical explorations of the Wenzhou model]. Nanning: Guangxi Renmin Chubanshe, pp. 45–62.

Gold, Thomas B. 1990. "Urban Private Business and Social Change." In Deborah Davis and Ezra Vogel, eds. *Chinese Society on the Eve of Tiananmen: The Impact of Reform*. Cambridge, Mass.: Council on East Asian Studies, Harvard University, pp. 157–78.

Guojia Tongjiju. 1996. *Zhongguo Laodong Tongji Nianjian 1995* [China labour statistical yearbook 1995]. Beijing: Zhongguo Tongji Chubanshe.

Huang Weiding. 1996. *Zhongguode Yinxing Jingji* (China's shadow economy]. Beijing: Zhongguo Shangye Chubanshe.

Lin Bai et al. eds. 1987. *Wenzhou Moshide Lilun Tansuo* [Theoretical explorations of the Wenzhou model]. Guangxi Renmin Chubanshe.

Liu, Yia-ling. 1992. "Reform from Below: The Private Economy and Local Politics in the Rural Industrialization of Wenzhou." *The China Quarterly* 130, pp. 291–316.

Marsden, Anna. 1994. *Cinesi e Fiorentini a confronto* [Chinese and Florentine face to face]. Florence: Firenze Libri.

Nolan, Peter and Dong Furen, eds. 1990. *Market Forces in China: Competition and Small Business – The Wenzhou Debate*. London: Zed Books.

Parris, Kristen. 1993. "Local Initiative and National Reform: The Wenzhou Model of Development." *The China Quarterly* 134, pp. 242–63.

Pyke, Frank, Giacomo Becattini and Werner Sengenberger. 1990. *Industrial Districts and Inter-firm Co-operation in Italy*. Geneva: International Institute for Labour Studies.

Solinger, Dorothy J. 1995. "The Floating Population in the Cities: Chances for Assimilation?" In Deborah S. Davis, Richard Krauss, Barry Naughton and Elizabeth J. Perry. eds, *Urban Spaces in Contemporary China: The Potential for Autonomy and Community in Post-Mao China*. Cambridge: Cambridge University Press, pp. 113–39.

Tassinari, Alberto and Luigi Tomba. 1996. *Zhejiang – Pechino, Zhejiang – Firenze: due esperienze migratorie a confronto* [Zhejiang – Beijing, Zhejiang – Florence: Two migratory experiences compared]. *La Critica Sociologica* 117, pp. 27–38.

Xiang Biao. 1993. "Beijing You ge 'Zhejiang cun': Shehui Zhuanxing zhong yige Zifa Chengshihua Quntide Chubu Yanjiu" [Beijing has a "Zhejiang Village": Preliminary research on a spontaneously urbanizing colony in the midst of social transformation]. *Shehuixue yu Shehui Diaocha* 1993, no. 3, pp. 68–74; no. 4, pp. 48–54; no. 5, pp. 51–54 and 48.

Yuan Enzhen ed. 1987. *Wenzhou Moshi yu Fuyu zhi Lu* [The Wenzhou model and the road to prosperity]. Shanghai: Shanghai Shehui Kexue Yuan.

Zheng Datong. 1991. *Wenzhou Gaige* [Wenzhou reform]. Shanghai: Fudan Daxue Chubanshe.

Notes

1 Chinese research on Zhejiang Village relies mainly on the work of Peking University's Department of Sociology and on Xiang Biao's fieldwork in the village, while in Italy most research has been carried out by the Department of Social Sciences of Florence University and local non-governmental organizations working on the issue of foreign migration.

2 This is the area comprising the belt around Florence, Tuscany's major city, and the city of Prato, located just 15 kilometres from Florence. This has historically been identified as a concentrated industrial district, specializing in textiles and leather products.

3 To illustrate the proportion of registered enterprises and the number of resident Chinese, an official of Campi Bisenzio, one of the municipalities where the Chinese arrived already in the early 1980s, said that when 246 Chinese were registered in 1990, 270 Chinese children were attending the local schools. He estimated that there were at least three thousand irregular Chinese migrants. See Colombo et al. 1995, p. 58.

4 Attempts to move part of the community to less congested areas have repeatedly failed.

5 A change in the regulation on self-employment for non-EC residents was the main factor leading to a rise in the number of permits for self-employment. See Carchedi and Ferri 1998:269–71.

6 In Prato the Chinese constitute a full sixty-five per cent of non-EC residents. The total number of officially registered Chinese in Italy was 22,875 before the 1996 regularization, making them the eighth most numerous nationality.

7 Mezzadria is the name for traditional sharecropping in central Italy.
8 Please refer to Xiang Biao's chapter for a fuller account of Zhejiang Village.
9 The official figure for the output value is about 200 million yuan a year, but this should be taken only as a very rough indication, also because of the growing export of products to northern Chinese markets and abroad.
10 A survey of the underground economy in 1991 revealed that among "irregular" goods (*lailu buming*), shoes had already surpassed in importance traditionally smuggled goods such as liquor (Huang 1996).
11 Interviews, June 1995.
12 Field visits and interviews in 1995 and 1996.

Part III

Migration, identity and belonging

Chapter Fourteen _____

Female autobiographies from the Cultural Revolution: Returned *Xiaxiang* educated women in the 1990s*

Nora Sausmikat

Introduction

When migration becomes a mandatory revolutionary and patriotic duty, state history begins to blend with individual lives, and individual life stories merge into the story of the collective. This implies further that both the state and the individual have a stake in the recollection and reconstruction of history in the formation of personal identity. Transformation processes within a state determine the social parameters for the reflection on individual life stories, and what happened twenty years ago can only be seen in the light of today.

The research presented here is part of a project which examines the effects of the mass migration of the *Shangshan Xiaxiang* movement (Up Mountains and Down the Villages movement; Xiaxiang movement in the remainder of this chapter) during the Great Proletarian Cultural Revolution (*Wenhua Dageming*; hereafter Cultural Revolution) on today's social identity, status, and self-perception of its female participants.[1] The long term consequences which this mass migration had on the individual lives of participating *zhishi qingnian* (educated urban youths; *zhiqing* for short),[2] and the social implications for today's outlook of Chinese urban

* Author's Note: The fieldwork and research for this project was supported by the Women's Studies Sponsorship Programme of the Administration for Women and Employment of the Berlin Senate and the Free University of Berlin. This work would never have been possible without the help of my Chinese colleagues and the informants who agreed to let me record their life stories. The arguments and interpretations offered here are my responsibility alone.

297

society are the focus of this research. Today, many former zhiqing have become influential people in politics and the economy, and now the time seems to have come for a fresh discussion on the zhiqing, or the "lost generation" as they are often called. Consequently, many former zhiqing have published memoirs and autobiographical essays in recent years.

Many interesting questions can be asked about the perception of this state-ordered mass migration, which re-settled some fourteen million educated urban youths in the countryside.[3] I shall concentrate here on the perception of the movement at a personal level, trying to show how women remember and explain it. I will first summarize the necessary historical facts and events one has to know about the Xiaxiang movement and the return to the cities in the 1970s, 1980s and 1990s. Following this I will give a brief overview of the discussion and changing perceptions in the 1980s and 1990s. In the analysis I shall show how personal memories and patterns of identification depend on the present social status of the individual. Specifically, I shall focus on the connotations which the term "zhiqing" gained in the 1980s and 1990s, and how these women managed (or did not manage) to reinterpret the events that were so central to their self-definition.

Why especially female zhiqing? At first it would seem that there should be no difference between the way in which young men and women experienced and reminisce about their relocation. The first time I became aware of the great importance of gender was when I did research on women studies in China. I found that many former female zhiqing got involved in women studies projects because of the importance of gender in shaping one's experiences in the countryside. Nowadays, special hot lines have been established to help other women reintegrate in the city.

More than anything else, however, have publications such as *Memoirs of Fifty Female Zhiqing from Beijing* (Liu Zhonglu et.al. 1995) drawn my attention to the specific situation of resettled women. Living in remote areas in order to be "re-educated" challenged these women's gender-specific behaviour, the assumptions they had been brought up with in the city, and most importantly, their personal autonomy. Many women were seduced, mistreated, or even raped by rural cadres, and the fate of some of these women became a symbol of tragedy for a whole generation.[4] Moreover, women had to assume masculine revolutionary roles. These roles conflicted not only with traditional rural expectations of women, but also with the revived femininity in urban China in the 1980s.

For this chapter I draw on a combination of narrative interviews with female zhiqing and information gathered during interviews with zhiqing scholars, and new publications from China, Taiwan and Hong Kong. Over a period of a year and a half, I interviewed seventeen female zhiqing in repeated sessions of three to four hours.[5] All of them had managed to return to the city, some of them as soon as after six years, some others only after twenty-one years in the countryside.

Oral history research, in the sense of "remembered history" (Steinbach 1980), investigates the institutionalization of history and the process of memory reconstruction, illustrating historical processes through individual biographies. The life records in the interviews are not treated as a realistic reproduction of the past. They are not the present of bygone days; they are actually a "present past."[6]

Outline and development of the *Xiaxiang* movement

Politically motivated resettlement programmes existed long before the Cultural Revolution.[7] From 1955 onwards, the first five-year plan sent thousands of town-dwellers to poor regions. The aims and forms of such resettlement policies changed several times in the course of the 1950s and 1960s. In the early 1950s, and again in the 1960s, resettlement programmes were a way to alleviate urban unemployment. From 1955 onward, sent-down urban educated youth *(xiaxiang zhiqing)* were also mobilized for the establishment of the new rural collectives, which needed millions of accountants.[8] But this group of urban born youths was small in comparison to the number of rural-born youths who were forced to return to the countryside since 1953 *(huixiang zhiqing)*. Like their Russian predecessors,[9] these rural educated returnees took part in production and land reclamation. Urban born educated youths did not face a lifelong stay in the countryside, whereas for rural born zhiqing it was their duty and obligation to return to the countryside. For rural and urban born youths alike, their contribution to the development of socialism in the hinterland was considered a highly revolutionary deed, but for many rural born youths it lost the quality of a free decision and was accompanied with a taste of overdetermination, since they were not given a chance to survive in the cities anyway.

The resettlement of the 1950s and early 1960s was pursued far less rigorously than the Xiaxiang movement of the Cultural Revolution. Urban zhiqing were generally given the guarantee that they would be able to return to an urban job, as a rule after four years. But even during this period, some found "backdoor" (illegal) ways to return to the city. This, together with bad living conditions and, from 1964 onwards, increasing propaganda for permanent settlement in the countryside, provoked protests and discussions (Rosen 1981:28ff).

Tens of millions of young Red Guards were mobilized during the first years of the Cultural Revolution between 1966 and 1968. As the Cultural Revolution drew to a close, they became a serious liability. The economic situation (high urban unemployment), the ideologization of society since 1962 (class struggle, dictatorship of proletariat) and the re-organization of the educational system made urban or academic careers more and more impossible. The Red Guard movement, moreover, had been seriously factionalized almost from the very beginning, and many Red Guards ultimately lost out in the violent power struggles that raged throughout China in 1967 and 1968 (Chan, Rosen and Unger 1983; Lee 1978; L. White 1989). Rural resettlement of former Red Guards promised a quick, cheap and permanent solution to all of these problems.

After 1966, and especially after 1968, resettlement therefore became much more an ideologically sponsored and controlled mass movement. Re-education of urban educated youth and class struggle were now the chief concerns; national economic development and the security of frontier areas would henceforth be only of secondary importance (Xinhua Ribao, 18 July 1969). Urban youths could thus no longer be recruited on a voluntary basis. Participation became mandatory in 1968 for all urban youths with a school education, while resettlement became permanent. In 1967, some Red Guards could still debate whether the Xiaxiang policy was Liu Shaoqi's[10] line (Chan 1985:180); after 1968, Mao himself made clear that resettlement was the future for all urban youths (Renmin Ribao, 22 December 1968).

The resettlement policy was thus turned into a programmatic educational policy and mass movement of class struggle, which mobilized some fourteen million young people between 1968 and 1976. Some of the zhiqing were motivated by a combination of idealism, awe of Mao Zedong's personality and a thirst for heroic action. Others were subjected to various forms of coercion.

Official accounts in the 1980s and 1990s

After Deng Xiaoping's rise to power in 1978, "speaking out bitterness" about the Cultural Revolution was encouraged, creating leeway for general literary criticism of mass rural resettlement. In 1982, the name "zhiqing fiction" was adopted for such literature, whose main issues and protagonists developed in different directions during the 1980s and 1990s. The "literature of the wounded" (*shanghen wenxue*) of the late 1970s and early 1980s portrayed local cadres as villains and zhiqing as their victims, describing the latter's unhappy marriages, suicides, or sexual frustration (Leung 1994:xxxvii; Liu Xiaomeng et al. 1995:213–218) The 1980s witnessed a general shift from more philosophical discussions of human relationships and the meaning of love and friendship to the description of realities in "reportage literature" (*baogao wenxue*) or memoirs. Yet for several reasons it has remained difficult to judge or condemn the resettlement movement in general.

First, in 1981 the CCP published its resolution *On Some Questions Concerning the Development of the Chinese Communist Party*. The Cultural Revolution was reduced to an ultra left mistake, and the investigations into crimes committed during the Cultural Revolution were put to a halt. The mass resettlement of urban youth remained undiscussed at the political level, because it was not seen as a product of the Cultural Revolution. Instead, Cultural Revolution resettlement was linked to its predecessors of the 1950s and early 1960s that were primarily predicated on development politics (Zhang Hua 1987). This link prevented a mass return to the cities, which could have occurred had the whole movement been condemned as a leftist mistake during the "ten years of chaos." It also prevented a re-interpretation of resettlement as a thinly veiled form of political exile or punishment, akin to the "reform through labour" that political prisoners are sentenced to. This latter issue was publicly discussed for a short period in 1986, when zhiqing from Shanxi province condemned their "reeducation" in the countryside and asked for the permission to return to the cities. At the initiative of zhiqing living in Shanxi, reports on their living conditions were compiled in Tianjin, Beijing and other cities. However, during the presentation of those reports, Hu Qili, Member of the Central Committee of CCP, and Hao Jianxiu, Secretary of the State Council, again unambiguously re-affirmed the party line:

> The Shangshan Xiaxiang movement is not a product of the Cultural Revolution. Even if one totally condemns the Cultural Revolution, one cannot therefore condemn the Shangshan Xiaxiang movement; this would be a great mistake. The importance of life lies in the willingness to make sacrifices. The meaning of luck lies in struggle (Renmin Ribao 29 January 1986).

In the 1980s, the government thus incorporated rural resettlement in its general policy of the Four Modernizations, insisting that zhiqing stay in the countryside to contribute to China's modernization, protect the border areas and provide patriotic education for the next generation. Wang Nianyi argues that this was intended to give the necessary recognition to the zhiqing's contributions to the revolution (Wang 1989:343). But since Wang is also one of the rare historians who openly name the great losses and bad consequences of these politics, this could be interpreted as a cautious critique of the government's positive attitude towards the Xiaxiang movement. The recognition of zhiqing as contributors to the revolution was merely a veil covering a much harsher truth: zhiqing who returned to the cities in the early 1980s were unwanted competitors on a tight job market. They were discriminated against and looked down upon as "people with problems," who cannot really contribute to the Four Modernizations because they lack the relevant skills.[11]

Since the suppression of the demonstrations of the People's movement on 4 June 1989, the perception of the Xiaxiang movement in "zhiqing fiction" has continued to develop in two directions. Currently, long term effects on the relationships between men and women are portrayed in semi-autobiographical essays. These are accompanied by a remystification of the countryside and heroic descriptions of zhiqing characters.[12] Yet the same restrictions continued to apply, and these found their way through the massive propaganda on the heroic perception of zhiqing. It is possible to talk about problems which evolved during and after the resettlement movement, but it was made clear again that it is taboo to denounce the original movement as a mistaken policy of the Cultural Revolution. In Spring 1991, some zhiqing cadres from Chengdu in Sichuan Province organized a large exhibition to commemorate the twentieth anniversary of their resettlement to Yunnan. The general title "Youth has no regrets" (*Qingchun wuhui*) characterized the way in which the zhiqing should reminisce on resettlement. Since then, this slogan has become an ideological guideline.

The labels "zhiqing" and "laosanjie"

The research reported on here concentrates on a special zhiqing group called *laosanjie* ("three old school classes"), who would normally have graduated from middle school in 1966, 1967, or 1968, but whose schooling was abruptly stopped short by the outbreak of the Cultural Revolution. The older laosanjie were the main protagonists of the Red Guard movement, and they are now at the forefront of the official and public discussion on rural resettlement.

Born between 1947 and 1952, the laosanjie went to the countryside during the first years of rural resettlement, especially between 1967 and 1969, setting them apart from youth who were resettled during the 1970s. Most of the laosanjie returned to the cities in the late 70s and early 80s. They are dominant today in defining the term "urban zhiqing." Already during rustication, this label was decisive for the future lives of sent down youths, since it set them apart from the "huixiang" rural zhiqing (see above). The label of urban zhiqing entailed a claim to state financial support for settling down.[13] It also represented their hope of an eventual return to the city: a short note attending to their original urban *hukou* (household registration) was attached to their personal file that travelled with them to the countryside. Rural youth being sent back to the countryside after their study in a city, on the other hand, forfeited their city registration completely and permanently.[14] Consequently, during the Cultural Revolution the relationship between these two groups was very tense.

Female laosanjie

Having grown up in a big city, the majority of female zhiqing counted on going to university or at least on getting a job in town. Having learned at school to be selfless, patriotic communists, propaganda after 1966

302

preparing them for resettlement urged them to emulate pre-cultural revolution models like Xing Yangzi and Hou Jun, both female zhiqing. The main element of the propaganda were slogans urging sent down youths to "establish roots" (*zhagen*), which for the female zhiqing meant marrying local peasants.

Especially zhiqing with bad class backgrounds[15] were pressurized to prove their dedication to the revolution. Many of them wrote "blood letters" in order to be recognized as "revolutionary zhiqing" and be allowed to go to the countryside. But when signing the application for resettlement, meaning the honour of participating in the revolution, almost none of these girls knew what the concrete meaning was of terms like "reeducation" (*zaijiaoyu*), "establishing roots," "developing one's talent to the full" (*da you zuowei*), or "changing the backward appearance" [of the countryside] (*gaibian luohoude mianmao*). Furthermore, the city educational system had little to offer, while those with bad class backgrounds had the added incentive of escaping class discrimination in the cities.

The departure to the hinterland is one of the most contradictory points in the narrations of former zhiqing. In what I would like to call the "officially sponsored memory", the departure for the countryside became a purely voluntary act, full of trust and belief in Chairman Mao and the revolutionary, glorious and patriotic nature of the act. Yet the majority of the autobiographers still get very emotional when talking about the departure as a separation from their parents, sisters and brothers. This ambivalence is very understandable. Resettlement had many functions and meanings at that time. It was a flight from the chaotic cities, where one was confronted with brutality and warfare. After 1968, going to the countryside became a duty; moreover, it promised a new future to those who had gone one or two years without work, or had been Red Guard activists who ultimately achieved no results. At the same time it was also an opportunity to engage in revolutionary activity in which everybody wanted to play a part.

During the first years in the countryside, zhiqing were confronted with a "reality shock:" the poor hinterland was much less romantic than they had imagined. They often were confronted with a different language, inadequate housing, no safety measures during hard and often dangerous labour, hunger and malnutrition. Especially in the villages zhiqing could rely only on themselves, which turned out to be very difficult for most of the girls.

Yet, in the autobiographies the memories of the first impressions of the countryside are very different. Some concentrate on the confrontation with staring peasants and the general strangeness of the environment. More commonly, however, the autobiographies narrate the poor living conditions and life of the other zhiqing. The experience of moving and living with a group of other zhiqing seemed often more significant than the confrontation with a radically new environment. In particular housing conditions were important in the urban youths: having to live with peasants of *both sexes* in their houses or tents, or sleeping with more than ten other zhiqing in one small room (Liu Xiaomeng 1995:93ff).

The zhiqing found that the reality of life in the countryside consisted of monotonous hard labour, the struggle for survival and the endurance of hardship. Some girls managed to work even harder than their male colleagues, but many lost their motivation and belief in their revolutionary merit of resettlement after the death of Lin Biao and the start of the Worker-Peasant-Soldier movement in 1971. The fall and death of Mao's hand-picked successor Lin Biao disillusioned the majority of zhiqing, many of whom had up till that point believed in the infallibility of Mao. The Worker-Peasant-Soldier movement reopened the universities for students of worker, peasant or soldier background, but in actual fact was used by many children of high cadres as an back door opportunity to return to the cities. In the early 1970s, hard physical labour, renewed relevance of study, and pressure to marry culminated in a biographical turning point for many female zhiqing. They either decided to marry, or tried to get a factory job in a nearby town, or committed suicide out of desperation (Liu Xiaomeng et al. 1995:630–33 and 648–650). In the early 1970s, girls who had left the cities between 1967 and 1969 rapidly reached the age that they would be considered too old for marriage. In this period, moreover, the procedures for admission to university provided ample opportunity for power abuse, ranging from rape, blackmail, and intimidation to forced marriages with handicapped workers who were a burden to the local community (Liu Xiaomeng 1995:57–65). Some of these cases have in fact been dealt with in the 1970s. In April 1973, a conference of the State Council chaired by Premier Zhou Enlai discussed two cases of rape and forced marriage by military teachers. Some cadres were shot for the sake of deterrence, but others are still in powerful posts today.

Only a small number of zhiqing managed to gain admission to university, but after the Zhang Tiesheng incident, all hope for zhiqing with a bad class background of enrolling in universities on the basis of academic excellence was squashed. Zhang handed in his examination paper empty with the declaration that he was a loyal revolutionary fighting against the bourgeois tendency of stressing knowledge over ideology (Renmin Ribao, 19 July 1973 and 18 August 1973).[16]

Henceforth, for many women the satisfaction in continuing to sacrifice their lives for the development of the rural hinterland (no longer for the revolution) shifted to aspiring to the promotion to leading posts. Gaining such promotions was decisive for their future destiny and evaluation of their past migration to the hinterland alike: migration became at this point the connecting link between their past and present lives. These women watched the "back-to-the-cities" craze of the late 1970s with resentment and despair. Today, they consider resettlement an effective measure that continues to help the development of the hinterland.

Other strategies to cope with the difficulties were either a retreat into marriage and raising children, or else seeking psychological support inside the zhiqing group. Female zhiqing were an attractive match for peasants, because they did not need to pay brideprice for them. Furthermore, peasants gained through these marriages a tie to a family in a big city. Female zhiqing who married peasants were suddenly confronted with gender roles totally unknown to them. Having learnt to act and work like a man, they were suddenly expected to be good housewives and caring mothers. In their recollections, most women married to local men remember the separation from their peers and their exclusion and isolation from the activities in the production brigade[17] as a source of high psychological stress. But the greatest burden for many of these women was the pressure to give birth to healthy sons. On the other hand, they have very positive memories of the solidarity among rural women. The situation for male zhiqing was very different: they were under pressure to become hard working peasants before they could marry rural women and, in addition, had to pay a brideprice without the benefit of family support.

Another problem was the lack of hygiene and medical care for women in the countryside. Either they had to rely on local doctors with only rudimentary medical knowledge (often themselves untrained zhiqing), or travel very long distances for treatment. Many women were infected with abdominal illnesses caused by sleeping on unheated, earthen *kangs* or working in the fields.

Resentment and frustration came to a boil with the demonstrations and protests after the death of Xu Lingxian in Yunnan province. The conditions of the zhiqing in Yunnan were extremely hard. State and military farms were governed in an authoritarian manner and hygiene did not really improve during the 1970s. The death rate (including suicides) rose so much that in 1976 a commission was established to examine the living conditions of zhiqing. Yet ultimately nothing really changed. In August 1978, the young female Shanghai zhiqing Xu Lingxian died because of wrong medical treatment while giving birth to a son.[18] Yunnan zhiqing gathered in large numbers to carry her remains to the provincial capital Kunming. The death of Xu Lingxian became a symbol for the suffering of all zhiqing and a vehicle for appeal to the government to care for the zhiqing who had remained in the countryside and help them return to the city (Liu Xiaomeng et al. 1995:665–675).

After the fall of the Gang of Four in 1976, waves of returned educated youths flooded the cities. In 1977 the government attempted for the first time to restrict this return migration, but with the start of the reforms in 1978, nobody cared any longer about bureaucratic niceties like "return licences for illness or family difficulties" (*bingtui, kuntui*). The slogan of that time "It is better to sweep the streets or clean toilets than return to remote areas" adequately summarizes the mood among zhiqing (Liu Xiaomeng et al. 1995:684). Many years of accumulated frustration erupted in a outpouring of demands, voiced in the liberal atmosphere of the Democracy Wall movement going on in Beijing at the time. The government first refused to give in to the demands. At a national work conference from 31 October to 10 December 1978, the Xiaxiang movement was confirmed rather than criticized. But on 21 January 1979 the government retreated, making limited concessions by offering jobs for zhiqing in provincial cities and by loosening the restrictions on return to the cities (Liu Xiaomeng et al. 1995:688ff). The Democracy Wall movement lasted until September 1979, during which time zhiqing continued to flood to the cities. Gradually, the protests became less forceful while the government re-established its political control; simultaneously, the legitimacy of the Xiaxiang movement was restored (Gold 1980:762). After 1980, most of the female zhiqing who had not yet managed to return had to wait until the end of the 1980s, when special laws and regulations facilitating return migration were promulgated.[19]

In the late 1970s and early 1980s most laosanjie women were in their late 20s or early 30s. Those who returned to the city were unemployed and either single or divorced, or else married to another zhiqing who was also unemployed. A common way of getting (or restoring) the desired city hukou, especially for married women still living in the countryside,[20] was to divorce the rural partner and marry an urban man. The new marriage law of 1980 allowed divorce if only one partner declared that "mutual misunderstanding" existed between the partners, thus granting more or less complete freedom of divorce also to women who had been forced to marry a rural partner (Liu Xiaomeng et al. 1995b:57–65).

In escaping from one marriage to a new one, many female zhiqing were considered immoral egoists by neighbours, relatives, or colleagues. The ability to confront this condemnation in many cases determined the success of reintegration into the city environment. Respondents described the return procedures and the "second fight" to find one's place in society as much more difficult and traumatic than the first migration out of the cities. For many it was difficult to find an urban partner, even for those who had not been married before with a rural spouse. Returned zhiqing started out with no social relationships in the city. In the early 1980s, a nationwide campaign tried to propagate "marriages with the old maids" in order to solve the problem of many single female zhiqing living in the cities. However, in the mid-1980s the campaign changed and established the "single independent modern woman" as a positive socialist model. Such women are pathologized in public opinion: a single woman over thirty is traditionally seen as a socially marginal "mad" person.

Female returned zhiqing had to learn from the very beginning what it meant to be a woman, sometimes even taking lessons in how to behave, dress and apply make up. Beginning academic studies at thirty, looking after children,[21] not being used to the roles of housewife, sexual partner and mother, living in very small flats and having to depend on parental financial support after ten to fifteen years of hard physical labour – these are only the most obvious of the innumerable problems of reintegration that returned female zhiqing faced. Most of them suffered from an inferiority complex, because even at the age of thirty they could not meet the usual social expectations and had difficulties making up for the education they had missed.

Because the state's lack of concern, the zhiqing network has become an essential factor for survival, as well as for finding a job, a partner, and psychological support. Female zhiqing in particular have built up emergency telephone networks for psychological support needed when confronting all these problems after returning to the cities. They hold regular meetings and engage in support for rural women or former schoolmates who are moving to the cities.

Mass migration – mass reflections

Most zhiqing in their reflections stressed the positive aspects of their rural life. Through resettlement they tempered themselves to be strong enough to face the full harshness of reality. Women who married in the countryside, on the other hand, strongly rejected the idea that life in the countryside was a valuable experience. They saw nothing good in being peasants and only wished to give their children an urban education. Yet others, especially those who had left behind a good job in the rural district town, were less negative about their life in the countryside. Unable to find similar employment in the city, they considered their return a big loss. We see how the individual career determines the meaning that is attached to migratory experiences today. Some who successfully returned to the city continued to refer fondly to their rural identity, while others who were fully integrated in their rural environment continued to long for urban life. However, the majority of returned female zhiqing kept on identifying themselves first of all as working women rather than housewives or mothers.

Female zhiqing in the 1990s can be described as a stigmatized group (Goffman 1976). A collective fractured biography and damage to the normal course of life create the need to restore a complete biography. The patterns of integration and assimilation – or the lack thereof – in new surroundings, first rural, then urban, should be interpreted as attempts to repair such biographical damage, or, to use Goffman's phrase, "spoiled identity." Damage to what is considered to be a normal biography started when these young people were separated very early on from their parents and were forced to live in a collective of "patriotic soldiers." Their upbringing had not prepared them for rural life where they continually felt incompetent. Upon their return to the cities they had to shift focus, once again feeling hopelessly incompetent.

Memories of mass migration, resettlement, rural life and remigration to the city are biographical tools to come to terms with these frustrations and feelings of incompetence. In other words, they are elements of a "healing biography." One only remembers those things that are biographically relevant today, while what is relevant varies from one standpoint to another (Bertaux and Bertaux-Wianne 1980:108; Niethammer 1980; Riley 1988).

Yet these memories and consequent biographical healing are not constructed in a social vacuum. Remembering is stimulated by official story lines as well as by the story lines produced by established returned zhiqing.

The party continues to distinguish between memories which can be officially accepted and others which do not "draw a clear border between then and now" (Rofel 1991 cited in Watson 1994:12). As long as the bad memories blame the "Gang of Four" or Lin Biao for the sufferings, and characterize the violence during the Cultural Revolution as senseless, the legitimacy of the present government is not questioned and the "telling of the truth" through memories can be accompanied by selective public amnesia. When examining the Xiaxiang movement, one thus has to be aware of the influence that official history has on individual biographic healing.

Similarly, the label of zhiqing is increasingly monopolized by those who have made a successful career after their return to the cities. Successful laosanjie now present themselves as the "real" zhiqing, (and therefore "real" revolutionary heroes), once stereotyped as fanatical and idealistic, but now successful exactly because of their willpower and ability to endure hardship (see for example Zhang Yongjun 1996). Businessmen and businesswomen among the laosanjie today make use of the zhiqing network for their businesses. They have their own publications and exclusive restaurants, appear on television and put together melancholic radio programmes. This excludes zhiqing who have remained in the countryside, and implies that the term zhiqing only applies to those who managed to return to the cities and build up careers.

Perceiving the revolutionary resettlement in the light of today's preoccupations, most of the women were still fighting against being discriminated as "cut-price goods" (*chulipin*) or useless old maids, who are looked down upon because they are either unmarried, or divorced, or otherwise do not conform to current expectations from women. Their special connection with the hinterland and their former participation in a once patriotic movement makes them official heroines and social victims at the same time; their memories are caught between these two stereotypes.

Against this background, we can better understand how difficult it often is to accept the label and stigma of "zhiqing" in one's biography.

> Looking from a distance, one can better judge who oneself in fact really is. At that time I wouldn't have called myself a zhiqing, but today, from a distant point of view and with a relatively secure and affluent livelihood, it can now be said that I belong to the generation of zhiqing (Lecturer).

> Now that you are asking me, and I know you are interested in my experience as a zhiqing, I naturally feel like a zhiqing (Housewife).

Both statements show how an identification with "zhiqing" is determined by the extent to which one concurs with the actual conception of values connected with this term. The latter informant actually wants to point out her feeling of distance towards the term "zhiqing", whereas the former informant identifies herself with this peer group in the terms of living conditions and stability.

One interesting shift in zhiqing publications in the 1990s has been that the collective of zhiqing as a group becomes much more important than the details of individual life stories. Zhiqing try to restore the good name of their generation as a whole, and gain recognition for their collective contributions, rather than come to terms with the vicissitudes of one's individual past. This trend in zhiqing literature is a manifestation of a concern not to be forgotten by history and sometimes even amounts to a careful "counter-narration" of official history. More and more "authentic" and "true" stories about the "real events" are written by high cadres who formerly were involved in the Xiaxiang movement and who now claim to have privileged access to secret documents. The large amount of zhiqing "oral" history on the Chinese literature market similarly is a sign that the battle for the truth only now has begun in earnest.

Conclusion

For the one it was a "big loss," for the other a "great achievement." The ability to establish continuity throughout a lifetime and combine past and present in today's identity determine one's self-perception. What is significant for all interviewees is the exclusion of a gender specific identity. They do not talk about female identity or female needs. Marriage or the birth of a child seem to be byproducts, marginal events in their lives' story. The need to cast off the negative stigma of "cut-price goods" after their return to the cities has translated itself in efforts to find a good job and get recognition in society as contributors to China's modernization. Becoming a good mother and a happy wife are much less relevant; perhaps the need to be "revolutionary soldiers" continues to run deeper than we think.

The meaning of "victim" lies not in past sufferings but in a destroyed standard biography. During the 1980s and 1990s, the term "zhiqing" became a politically clean, morally purified term for a generation as an alternative to negative labels, such as the "disturbed" or "lost generation."[22] The accounts presented by female zhiqing are profoundly contradictory. On the one hand we can see the ambition to fight against collective amnesia,[23] and on the other hand the desire to be free from the status of victims. They want to be recognized as individuals, who are able to continue their lives independently, looking to the future with hope despite all the disappointments in their lives.

The case of zhiqing migration, settlement and return migration shows that migration is not a static or completed event, but rather an ongoing process continually reworked in the biography of migrants; migration is a story that can be rewritten, re-invented and re-enacted time and again. Sometimes migration is a traumatic experience best forgotten entirely; at other times, the same trauma becomes the basis of bonding, group formation and collective action. Nowadays, zhiqing are discovering the latter aspect of their experiences. The time they spent in the countryside, the return to the city and finding one's place in society have made the network of fellow zhiqing in the 1990s – despite all the differences and conflicts – a loyal support group. Such networks are a real advantage in China's fast changing world.

References

Barmé, Geremie and John Minford, eds. 1989. *Seeds of Fire: Chinese Voices of Conscience*. New York: Noonday Press.

Bernstein, Thomas. 1977. *Up to the Mountains Down to the Villages: The Transfer of Youth from Urban to Rural China*. New Haven: Yale University Press.

Bertaux, Daniel and Isabell Bertaux-Wianne. 1980. "Autobiographische Erinnerungen und kollektives Gedächtnis" [Autobiographical and collective memories]. In Lutz Niethammer, ed. *Lebenserfahrung und kollektives Gedächtnis: Die Praxis der Oral History* [Life experience and collective memories: The praxis of oral history]. Frankfurt a. M.: Syndikat, pp. 108–22.

Bude, Heinz. 1987. *Deutsche Karrieren: Lebenskonstruktionen sozialer Aufsteiger aus der Flakhelfer-Generation* [German careers: Constructions of life of upwardly mobile members of the *flakhelfer-generation*]. Frankfurt a. M.: Suhrkamp.

Caoyuan Qishilu. [Notes from the Grassland]. 1991. Beijing: Zhongguo Gongren Chubanshe.

Chan, Ming K. and Arif Dirlik. 1991. *Schools into Fields and Factories*. London: Duke University Press.

Chan, Anita. 1985. *Children of Mao: Personality Development and Political Activism in the Red Guard Generation*. Seattle: University of Washington Press.

Chan, Anita. 1992. "Dispelling Misconceptions about the Red Guard Movement: The Necessity to Re-examine Cultural Revolution Factionalism and Periodization." *Journal of Contemporary China* 1, no. 1, pp. 61–85.

Chan, Anita, Stanley Rosen and Jonathan Unger. 1983. "Students and Class Warfare: The Social Roots of the Red Guard Conflict in Guangzhou." *The China Quarterly* 83, pp. 397–446.

Deng Xian. 1993. *Zhongguo Zhiqing Meng* [The dream of Chinese educated youth]. Beijing: Renmin Wenxue Chubanshe.

Goffman, Erving. 1976. *Stigma: Notes on the Management of Spoiled Identity.* Harmondsworth: Penguin.

Gold, Thomas B. 1980. "Back to the City: The Return of Shanghai's Educated Youth." *The China Quarterly* 84, pp. 755–70.

Gold, Thomas B. 1982. "China's Youth: Problems and Programs." *Issues & Studies* 18, no. 8, pp. 39–63.

Guo Dong. 1996. "Miandui Chaduide Rizi." [Reflections on the time working in the countryside]. *Wenyi Bao*, 29 March 1996.

Halbwachs, Maurice. 1980[1950]. *The Collective Memory.* New York: Harper & Row.

Heike, Irmtraut. 1995. "Johanna Langefeld: Die Biographie einer KZ-Oberaufseherin"[Johanna Langefeld: The biography of a female guard in a concentration camp]. *Werkstattgeschichte* 12, pp. 7–20.

Lee, Hong Yung. 1978. *The Politics of the Cultural Revolution: A Case Study.* Berkeley: University of California Press.

Leung, Laifong. 1994. *Morning Sun: Interviews with Chinese Writers of the Lost Generation.* Armonk, N.Y.: M.E. Sharpe.

Liu Xiaomeng. 1995. "Xiaxiang Nü Zhiqing Hunyin Pouxi" [An analysis of marriages of female urban educated youths]. *Ershiyi Shiji* [The twenty-first century] 30, pp. 57–65.

Liu Xiaomeng, Ding Yizhuang, Shi Weiming and He Gang. 1995. *Zhongguo Zhiqing Shidian* [Encyclopedia of Chinese urban educated youth]. Chengdu: Sichuan Renmin Chubanshe.

Liu Zhonglu et.al. eds. 1995. *Zhiqing Fangcheng Shi – Wushige Beijing Nü Zhiqingde Zishu* [Urban educated youth, a result of history – Accounts in their own words from fifty female urban educated youths from Beijing]. Beijing: Beijing Daxue Chubanshe.

Niethammer, Lutz, ed. 1980. *Lebenserfahrung und kollektives Gedächtnis: Die Praxis der* Oral History [Life experience and collective memories: The praxis of oral history]. Frankfurt a.M.: Syndikat.

Riley, Mathilda White. 1988. "Notes on the Influence of Sociological Lives." In Mathilda White Riley, ed. *Sociological Lives: Social Change and Life Course.* Volume 2. Beverly Hills: Sage, pp. 23–42.

Rofel, Lisa. 1991. "Violence in the Quotidian: Fragments of a Cultural Revolution Memory." Paper presented at the annual meeting of the American Anthropological Association, 20–24 November 1991, Chicago.

Rosen, Stanley. 1981. *The Role of the Sent-Down Youth in the Cultural Revolution: The Case of Guangzhou.* China Research Monographs No. 19. Berkeley: Center for Chinese Studies, University of California.

Rosenthal, Gabriela. 1988. "Geschichte in der Lebensgeschichte – Leben mit dem Dritten Reich gestern und heute. 10 Beiträge" [History in life history – Life in the Third Reich yesterday and today: Ten contributions]. *BIOS* 2, pp. 3–102.

Rosenthal, Gabriele. 1993. "Reconstruction of Life Stories: Principles of Selection in Generating Stories for Narrative Biographical Interviews." In Ruthellen Josselson and Amia Lieblich, eds, *Narrative Study of Lives.* Volume 1. Beverly Hills: Sage, pp. 59–91.

Scharping, Thomas. 1981. *Umsiedlungsprogramme für Chinas Jugend 1955–1980* [Resettlement programmes for China's youth 1955–1980]. Hamburg: Institut für Asienkunde.

Schwarcz, Vera. 1996. "The Burden of Memory: The Cultural Revolution and the Holocaust." *China Information* 11, no. 1, pp. 1–13.

Shi Weimin and He Gang. 1996. *Zhiqing Beiwang Lu* [Memorandum on urban educated youths]. Beijing: Zhongguo Shehui Kexue Chubanshe.

Shi Xiaoyan, ed. 1990. *Beidahuang Fengyulun* [Reports on stormy times in the Great Barren North]. Beijing: Huagong Chubanshe.

Steinbach, L. 1980. "Lebenslauf, Sozialisation und 'erinnerte Geschichte'" [Life course, socialization and "remembered history"]. In Lutz Niethammer, ed. *Lebenserfahrung und kollektives Gedächtnis: Die Praxis der* Oral History [Life experience and collective memories: The praxis of oral history]. Frankfurt a.M.: Syndikat, pp. 291–322.

Thurston, Anne F. 1984/1985. "Victims of China's Cultural Revolution: The Invisible Wounds." *Pacific Affairs* 57, no. 4, pp. 599–621 and 58, no. 1, pp. 5–27.

Thurston, Anne F. 1987. *Enemies of the People: The Ordeal of Intellectuals in China's Great Cultural Revolution*. Cambridge, Mass.: Harvard University Press.

Wang Nianyi. 1989. *1949–1989 Niande Zhongguo: Da Dongluande Shidai* [China from 1949 to 1989: The epoch of the great turmoil]. Zhengzhou: Henan Renmin Chubanshe.

Watson, Rubie S. 1994. *Memory, History, and Opposition under State Socialism*. Santa Fe: School of American Research Press.

White, D. Gordon. 1974. "The Politics of Xiaxiang Youth." *The China Quarterly* 59, pp. 491–517.

White, Lynn T. III. 1979. "The Road to Urumqi: Approved Institutions in Search of Attainable Goals During Pre-1968 Rustication from Shanghai." *The China Quarterly* 79, pp. 481–510.

White, Lynn T. III. 1989. *Policies of Chaos: The Organizational Causes of Violence in China's Cultural Revolution*. Princeton: Princeton University Press.

Yin Hongbiao. 1992. "Hongweibing Yundongde Liang Da Chaoliu" [Two major trends in the Red Guard movement]. *Ershiyi Shiji* [The twenty-first century] 30, pp. 26–38.

Zhang Hua. 1987. "Shilun Wenhua Dageming zhong Zhishi Qingnian Shangshan Xiaxiang Yundong" [Discussion of the Rural Resettlement movement of urban educated youths during the Cultural Revolution]. In Tan Zongji and Zheng Qian, eds, *Shi Nian houde Pingshuo: Wenhua Dageming Shilunji* [Commentary and evaluation after ten years: A collection of papers on the history of the Cultural Revolution]. Beijing: Zhonggong Zhongyang Dangshi Ziliao Chubanshe, pp. 141–55.

Zhang Yongjun. 1996. *Zhongguo Baiming Youxiu Qiyejia Fendou Shi* [A history of the struggle of one hundred excellent Chinese managers]. Beijing: Zhongguo Wenlianban Gongsi.

Notes

1 The approach here is therefore very different from existing research, most of it dating from the 1970s and early 1980s, which evaluated the movement as a political movement and development policy. Two excellent standard works are Bernstein 1977 and Scharping 1981. Gold 1980 and 1982, Rosen 1981, G. White 1974 and L. White 1979 discuss the basic mechanisms of this mass movement and its impact on city youth at that time. But the most valuable and

recent research is collected in Liu Xiaomeng et al. 1995 and Shi Weimin and He Gang 1996.

2 The Term "zhiqing" is translated in different ways, such as "urbling" (Barmé and Minford 1989), or simply as "urban youth" (Rosen 1981). It is used only for middle school students who were resettled from the cities to the countryside during the Cultural Revolution. Many of the older zhiqing were Red Guards, but the term "Red Guards" included a large variety of groups, and many Red Guards were not zhiqing. For Red Guards see especially Yin 1992; Chan, Rosen and Unger 1983 and Chan 1985.

3 Today it is still difficult to give the exact number of zhiqing who were sent to the countryside, because the material is incomplete and subject to many political restrictions. Scharping (1981) speaks of 17 million, Bernstein (1977) estimates that 12 million urban youth were resettled between 1968 and 1975. Liu Xiaomeng et al. (1995) mention a number of 17 million between 1962 and the end of the 70s, while during the Cultural Revolution period from 1967 until 1976 it is thought that 14 million urban educated youths were transferred.

4 See the case of Yunnan zhiqing Xu Lingxian below.

5 The interviews were conducted in Beijing in Autumn 1994 and March 1996.

6 In my analysis I have borrowed from the tradition of oral history research through the application of concepts such as "collective memory," (Halbwachs 1980, Bertaux and Bertaux-Wianne 1980) "life reconstruction" (Rosenthal 1993) and "meaning-reconstruction" ("Sinn-Rekonstruktion," Bude 1987). In the field of oral history many scholars concentrate on biographical reflections on the Second World War (Niethammer 1980; Rosenthal 1988; Heike 1995). In a few Chinese memoirs, the experiences from the Cultural Revolution are linked with experiences under German nazism, but there have been until now no systematic examinations of this comparison. Western studies of the Cultural Revolution treat it mainly as a traumatic experience (Thurston 1984/1985 and 1987). Vera Schwarcz (1996) recently confronted the question of comparison of the monumentalized history of the Second World War with the fractured memory of the Cultural Revolution.

7 Combining education with physical labour is in fact not an original idea of the Chinese Communist Party (CCP). The intellectual anarchistic elite in Tokyo and Paris during the 1920s, inspired by the Russian Narodniki and Kropotkin's anarchism, spawned the idea of transforming society through the combination of mental and physical education.

8 For Mao Zedong's call for the recruitment of rural accountants among the middle school students, see Zhang Hua 1987:142. At the same time Mao coined the slogan: "The countryside is vast, that is the place where you are needed," a slogan which became of great importance during the Cultural Revolution. It is interesting to note that many of Cultural Revolution female zhiqing later became accountants.

9 See Chan and Dirlik 1991.

10 Liu Shaoqi was Mao's main enemy and chief victim of the Cultural Revolution.

11 One informant told me that at the beginning of the 1980s there was a real criminalization of zhiqing. Conductors on public buses for example announced the return of zhiqing over a loudspeaker, warning the passengers to take care of their belongings.

12 Especially the publication of *Beidahuang Fengyunlu* (Reports on stormy times in Beidahuang) in 1990 (Shi 1990) sparked many zhiqing publications (for instance, Caoyuan qishilu 1991).

13 There was no guarantee of financial support, and many urban youth who were sent to the villages to settle down did in fact not get any such support.

14 For further information see Liu Xiaomeng et al. 1995.

15 Children of former "capitalists, bad elements, rich peasants, counter revolutionaries, rightists."

16 In the contemporary context being a "loyal revolutionary" meant having a good class background. Zhang was imprisoned in 1977, released in 1991 and has now become a successful businessman.

17 Brigades were rural collectives, composed of either one village, or a collection of hamlets, or a neighbourhood in a exceptionally large village.

18 In the 1990s the incident of Xu Lingxian again became an emotional topic among the now established zhiqing community (Deng 1993:1–15), who used the sorrows especially of female zhiqing for a re-evaluation of the entire resettlement movement. A strong demand for an open discussion of the political errors committed during the Xiaxiang movement is made by using again the tragic figure of Xu Lingxian.

19 In 1986 and 1987 the central government allowed most of the "older zhiqing" (send down in the 1960s) to return to the cities (first only zhiqing from Tianjin and Beijing, later other cities followed). In the same year, a new law was passed, allowing one of the children of those zhiqing who remained in the countryside to move to the cities for education. In 1988, the scope of this law was broadened, now allowing these children to receive a city hukou (Liu Xiaomeng et al. 1995:693).

20 The discussion about "settle down and establish roots" (*anjia luohu zhagen*) did not necessarily imply marriage with rural partners in the first years of the movement. In particular, Zhou Enlai, among others, propagated late marriage in the late 1960s and early 1970s for reasons of population planning. In addition, there was no money to build houses for married couples. But at the same time there was strong propaganda in favour of "revolutionary marriages" in order to decrease the "three big differences" (city-countryside, mental-manual labour, worker-peasant), and female zhiqing were presented with models of other female zhiqing who had married peasants. Furthermore, female zhiqing with bad class backgrounds often married peasants out of desperation.

21 It would require a separate article to discuss the difficult situation of the children of former zhiqing. Some were sold to peasants or left alone with the peasant mother. Others grew up with their grandparents in the cities and either never saw their mothers again or did not get to know them until they had reached adolescence.

22 Images which were widely used by western scholars as well, see Gold 1982 and Leung 1994.

23 Guo 1996.

Chapter Fifteen

Separation, reunion and the Chinese attachment to place

Charles Stafford

Introduction

This essay draws on material from anthropological fieldwork in Dragon-head, a Han Chinese village located in the southern part of the three northeastern provinces (*Dongbei*), i.e. in the "Manchurian" region which has been completely transformed in the last several centuries by migration from elsewhere. As Shepherd notes, the history of migration and settlement in this region is highly complex, involving as it does droughts and famines across north China, Qing Dynasty policy towards the "Manchurian frontier" in general and towards Mongols and Manchus in particular, the use in the region of different agricultural techniques by Han and non-Han populations, etc. (Shepherd 1993:403–7). But the question I shall ask is not how or why people ended up in the village of Dragon-head; instead I shall ask why the people who are there now – the descendants of migrants – feel that Dragon-head is where they belong. What produces this sense of attachment?

In order to address (although of course only in part) this question, I shall later outline a group of Chinese idioms and practices – observable in Dragon-head – which I shall gloss as "separation and reunion." Across China, many moments of "parting" and "return" – involving both the living and the dead and found in a very wide range of social contexts – are symbolically elaborated. I shall suggest that these various moments, when viewed together, have important implications for the production of Chinese identifications and attachments to place. In short, people in Dragon-head (and elsewhere in China) develop a sense of who they are, with whom they belong and where they belong, partly through experiencing processes of separation and reunion at particular historical moments. Given the redundancy of these processes and the wide distribution of their associated practices and idioms, it is in fact hard to see how people could fail to be influenced by them in some way.

By extension, the study of culturally-elaborated separations and reunions – and the identifications they help produce – should have direct implications for the study of migration in China. It is often assumed that Chinese migrants, having moved, continue to feel strong attachments to ancestral lands, native places, etc. – and perhaps they do. But if so, why? What (if anything) produces these feelings of attachment to place and to localized communities, and what effects do such feelings have? Might, for instance, the difficulty for long-distance migrants of participating in the annual cycle of family reunions constrain the movement of populations in China? I should stress from the outset that my own ethnography has focused on what might be seen as forms of non-migratory mobility (e.g. seasonal movements of friends and gods) rather than on long-term or even short-term migration, as such. My hypothesis, however, is that the culturally-specific notions of separation and reunion (expressed with reference to non-migratory mobility) help produce attachments to place, which by definition have an impact on histories of migration. The psychological and socio-cultural problems posed by human migration are a subset of the problems posed by human mobility.

I should also make it clear from the outset that I am not proposing a culturalist explanation of Chinese migration (or of any other social process); my point is certainly not that these idioms on their own determine histories of migration or of anything else. I am simply noting, first, that the idioms of separation and reunion are a significant product of Chinese history, and, second, that they may have significant historical effects, including effects on processes of migration. In noting this potential I am echoing the recent call of Helen Siu and David Faure for culturally-informed studies of Chinese society and history. In a volume (discussed below) which examines the Chinese "territorial bond" in historical and regional context, they call for a framework which "highlights the ways human agency, cultural meaning and political economy interpenetrated at crucial historical moments to produce local society" (Siu and Faure 1995:209). In the context of Chinese studies, one implication of this framework is to give greater attention to cultural variables, including popular beliefs and values (e.g. those expressed through popular religion), and to culturally-constituted emotions, all of which unquestionably influence the course of Chinese history. "Separation and reunion" is an important aspect of Chinese culture – a manifestation of popular values and emotions – which has never, to my knowledge, been addressed in a systematic way.

But, as the work of Siu and Faure also makes clear, taking such cultural forms, however important, as ahistorical and unlocalized variables is potentially very misleading. Here I shall argue that although Chinese attachments to place may partly be built up through processes of separation and reunion, the ahistorical assumption that such attachments are generically strong and directed towards the past, is unfounded. Instead I shall stress the role of separations and reunions in structuring identifications in the present and the priority of this present-orientation – at least for those now living in Dragon-head – over reproducing ties to the past.

Anthropological studies of migration and the attachment to place

Before turning to the case of Dragon-head, I want very briefly to mention three anthropological studies – on the surface very different from any conceivable Chinese case – involving Hausa religious pilgrims, Pintupi hunter-gatherers and Malay fishermen, which highlight important issues related to migration and the movement of human populations. These examples show, among other things, the variety of ways in which an attachment to place may be conceived and enacted.

First, the religious pilgrims, whose sense of attachment is to a destination rather an origin. C. Baba Yamba has described Hausa Muslims who, fulfilling religious duty, went on pilgrimages from West Africa to Mecca and yet never, or only exceptionally, arrived. Instead they ended up in the Sudan – "closer to Mecca" – where they "...put up temporary villages and refrained from the construction, say, of brick houses lest they be seen as abandoning their ideology as temporary sojourners" (Yamba 1992:112). Here they resided for generations "they were on their way" (1992:111) and indeed, with the passage of time, they arguably were in fact "getting there", in the sense that their temporary villages were becoming more sacred (more Mecca-like). In any case, they were obliged to live for generations in the Sudan. In order to be employable by Sudanese they had to show "reliability" through achieving "stable residence within a pilgrim community" (1992:113). In short, having stopped in mid-pilgrimage, the Hausa lived in relatively stable, increasingly sacred and yet ideologically "temporary" communities. In effect, the process of "going there" – whether through notional pilgrimage or the sacralization of villages (described as "moving closer to Mecca") – seems to have been as important for them as ever actually "getting there." And the ideological attachment to this future place, a destination for the most part never seen, had crucial implications for their sense of belonging to a present-day community of "migrants". (Note that from a Chinese perspective, which emphasizes places of origin, this orientation will perhaps seem almost backwards.)

The second example involves Pintupi Aborigines from the Australian Western Desert. Because of their hunting and gathering livelihood and because of recent displacements, the Pintupi have often been on the move, i.e. they have been perpetual migrants. Against this background, Fred

Myers has described the complex relationship in Pintupi thought between sentiment, community and place. For the Pintupi, he notes, "land and people are inseparable" (Myers 1986:25) and furthermore the "...inseparability of people and place makes territorial boundaries highly flexible if not insignificant" (1986:93). (From a Chinese perspective, the flexibility of Pintupi boundaries, identities and attachments seems quite remarkable.) The point is that a Pintupi place, for example a "camp", *ngurra*, is not constituted simply through its geographical existence, nor through its mythical origins in the Dreaming, but also through human action – including the cooperation in time of those who share it as a "camp." In Pintupi thought, the mythical meanings of place (which relate to the Dreaming) are layered with meanings produced now, and in the recent past, by collective human action. As Myers puts it, "The way of thinking that enables a people to make a camp almost anywhere they happen to be, is a way of thinking that creates a universe of meanings around the mythologized country" (1986:54). In short, among the Pintupi the sentiment of attachment to place is inseparable from relatedness, i.e. from attachment to the community which produces place. And to go to a different place is, by extension, not to be part of the community which remains behind. This explains why, among the Pintupi, people who have gone away – thus distancing themselves (in both senses of the expression) from relatedness – may be greeted angrily on their return (Myers 1988).

Finally, I want to mention Janet Carsten's (1995) discussion of Pulau Langkawi, Malaysia, a fishing community in which, because of past migration, there is a "great diversity of origins". Carsten has discussed the processual nature of relatedness in Langkawi, where "...identity and kinship are acquired throughout life through the process of living together in houses, sharing food, engaging in relationships of different kinds, marrying and having children and grandchildren" (1995:1, see also Carsten 1997). Because of the emphasis on these processes, and on the "horizontal" ties of siblingship rather than on "vertical" ties of descent, the origins of the community in migration are often conveniently forgotten:

> (...) what is important is producing kinship in the future. To a considerable extent, the details of past diversity are gradually obliterated. In this sense, forgetting this past is part of an active process of creating a new and shared identity (Carsten 1995:8).

The production of relatedness in the present and future is here more important than remembering histories of migration, the ancestors and the past. In Langkawi, "Differences of origin are always in the process of being converted into similarity; they are best forgotten" (1995:14). (Again, these Malay notions of kinship and identity, which imply a "forgetting" of history, may seem very different from Chinese notions, in which relatedness is meant precisely to be given by a patrilineal past.[1])

These three cases – Hausa pilgrims who never reach their idealized destination, Pintupi hunter-gatherers whose fluid concept of place is inseparable from present-day activity, and Malay villagers who conveniently "forget" their places of origin – might obviously illuminate questions of attachment to place in different ways. The contrast with Chinese perspectives on place – often assumed to be directed to the past, to be centrally concerned with the reinforcement of boundaries, and to involve a "long historical memory" – will perhaps seem very striking. In any case, what is arguably most important in each of the three examples is the creative production, albeit in very different forms, of present-day and future relatedness. That is, the "cultural" imagining, making and forgetting of place is central to the reproduction of these communities and to the production of the sense of attachment (to places and/or communities) among those who live in them. In this sense, I shall argue, the experience of Hausa, Pintupi and Malay people is not very different from the experience of the people I have known in Dragon-head. Of course, this is a distinctly functionalist way of putting the matter ("ideas about place function to produce solidarity"). It remains to be asked why, in certain historical contexts, the same "ideas about place" might have entirely different effects and be deployed in different ways. I shall return to this question below, but first let me turn to Dragon-head.

A Chinese case of migration

As I noted at the beginning, northeastern China, the region in which Dragon-head is located, has been completely transformed in the last several centuries by migration from other parts of China. This is an historical fact of defining significance and it seems impossible to understand the region without taking it into account. And yet many of the people who live there now can say rather little on the subject and normally say nothing unless asked. After all, it is perfectly possible for a village or region to be the historical product of migration without, for all that, the subject manifesting itself in the activities and conversations of everyday life in any explicit and obvious way.[2]

Nevertheless, on a visit in 1996 to Dragon-head I did discuss migration with, among others, an elderly farmer. He estimated, when prompted, that fully ninety per cent of the local population are the descendants of migrants, primarily from Shandong Province. He recalled, from his own childhood, having heard his father discuss the matter. Forced to leave Shandong due to economic hardship, his father's great-grandfather had walked all the way to the Northeast with his younger brother in search of a better life. During the journey the two brothers, obliged to beg for food in order to survive, became separated and never saw each other again. I asked the farmer if any contact had been sustained with the home province and he replied that "from early on there wasn't any". He knew the name of the county from which his great-great-grandfather had set out, but expressed no interest in visiting that place where, as he put it, he would be without relatives or friends.

Conversations of this kind might, of course, tell us a great deal about the history of migration to Dragon-head, especially in combination with other kinds of evidence which might be gathered during fieldwork. But this conversation in particular quickly ran into certain dead-ends. The farmer was unclear about the political and economic conditions in Shandong which prompted the exodus, he couldn't remember being told how his great-great-grandfather had managed to find work and establish a family in the Northeast, he couldn't think of anything else to say on the topic and soon we were discussing something else. Why this should happen is perhaps not a great mystery. This man does not think of himself as having significant ties to Shandong, nor is being "from Shandong" a significant element in his contemporary identity. His life is lived in the fields and farmhouses of Dragon-head and among the people who live there. He talks much more, and much more spontaneously, about his children and grandchildren and about current concerns (e.g. the price of fertilizers) than about the ancestral past.

Anthropologists often have difficulty in addressing the history of identification with a place (or the history of anything) purely through participant-observation fieldwork. What living people now say about the past, if they say anything at all, often sits oddly with the past as traceable through documents, archives, official histories and even through earlier ethnographies. This is not necessarily because people are ignorant of what happened in the past, although they may be that as well, but also because the "making of history" (here meaning the individual and collective production of historical narratives)[3] is subject to many forces: political meddling, aesthetic conventions, cognitive constraints and so on. It follows that a given history of migration, or a given history of belonging to a place, e.g. one told by an elderly farmer in a village such as Dragon-head, might raise as many questions about the past as it answered.

But the point I am getting at is not that people in Dragon-head are bad at narrating truthful or complete histories of the past – in which case a fieldworking anthropologist might be better off leaving migration to the historians. Instead I want to stress that these people are good at producing history in the present and precisely micro-history of a kind which is at times overlooked by historians. Villagers may find it difficult and somewhat unnatural to relate explicit histories of migration. But the collective production of identification with place – which is surely central to the understanding of migration – is everywhere to be seen and almost all the time. Among other things this involves, as I will describe in the next section, the perpetual movement of persons and spirits, a process which both builds up and expresses the sense of belonging to particular communities and places. By examining through participant-observation the way in which this aspect of Chinese history is made, anthropologists, I suggest, have an important contribution to make to our understanding not only of Chinese migration, but also of Chinese history more generally.

Separation and reunion

As I mentioned at the beginning, in Dragon-head, as in other Chinese communities, considerable attention is given, in many different contexts, to various moments of "parting" and "return". One of the clearest rules of etiquette, for instance, expressed in everyday practice, is that guests, having been properly greeted (*jie*), should be properly sent off (*song, songbie, songxing*), even if this only means walking them to the outside gate (*waimen*) of a farmhouse compound. It often suffices to simply apologize for failing to do this: "I won't see you off" (*wo bu song ni*); and in many cases a guest will make it clear that his host should not bother: "Do not send me off!" (*bu song!*) But what ideally should happen with guests – polite sending off – is clear. When truly "outside" or especially important guests are involved, the etiquette I refer to may be taken to considerable lengths. They may be sent on their way with banquets, gifts, speeches and tears.

The routine arrival and departure of close relations and friends, by contrast, is sometimes dealt with casually or even abruptly – it would be strange to treat such insiders too "politely." Neighbours and relatives often walk in and out of each others' houses without comment or fuss. But at certain times of the year, for example during festivals of reunion, the comings and goings of even the closest kin and friends are also symbolically elaborated (for instance, through cycles of reunion banquets). At the very least it is hard for anyone – relative or friend – to leave Dragon-head for a substantial period of time without being invited by various households to eat *jiaozi* (dumplings), a food which symbolizes reunion. On such occasions the talk often turns to the possibility, however remote, of future meetings, just as formal banquets routinely end with arrangements being made for further collective meals. Moments of separation (when commensality ends) are sometimes even said to be desirable, because of the joy which a future reunion will bring.

The things I am superficially alluding to here – the way in which people are greeted and sent off, the kinds of meals eaten with various types of people on various occasions of parting and return, the comments which are routinely made during such meals – are, for the most part, completely taken for granted in Dragon-head, i.e. they are "naturalized" social behaviour. And my point is that in Dragon-head it seems perfectly natural to articulate the value attached to certain kinds of human relationships in this way: by emphasizing the bittersweet moment of departure and the joyous moment of return. And both types of event, departure and return, require a public marking. The individual occasions are sometimes minor, but I want to draw attention to the potential cumulative effect – which is surely not trivial. In fact, at times it seems as if these moments of going away and coming back again are more important, *vis-à-vis* the conceptualization of certain relationships in Dragon-head, than any fixed state of being together.

A similar observation could be made concerning relationships with ancestral spirits and Chinese deities, whose mobility is also taken for granted and whose movements are a regular source of speculation and concern. For example, some of the most important rituals in Dragon-head involve greeting (*jie*) and sending-off (*song*) the ancestors. On the last day of the last lunar month (*chuxi*) the family dead are invited to leave their graves (an exit made possible by the small brick archway or door (*men*) found on each burial mound). At the homes of their descendants, these ancestral spirits are subsequently greeted by volleys of firecrackers and invited to enter through the farmhouse door (especially decorated) and to partake in a family-reunion meal of jiaozi (reunion dumplings, again). This rather straightforward reunion, and the reaffirmation of family hierarchy and cosmic order it implies, stands at the very centre of Chinese ritual life. Then, after the new year has begun, the ancestors are collectively, noisily, and properly sent back to their graves, at least for a while.

In similar fashion, the gods of Chinese popular religion, equally mobile, are invited to (*qing*) and greeted at (*jie*) particular households in Dragon-head. Once they have arrived (*dao*), and been welcomed with offerings of various kinds, devotees hope they will remain and provide blessings and stability. However, when they depart, as does routinely happen, they must be properly sent on their way (*song*). Again, this is accomplished with respectful offerings, in the hope that the gods will eventually return – something they usually do, at times more or less immediately. In sum, a substantial proportion of Chinese religious ritual is focused explicitly on the arrival and departure of spirits – moments which help define the relationships of families and communities with their ancestors and gods.

Now the examples of separation and reunion I have sketched out so far – drawn from the etiquette of everyday life and of special occasions, from festivals and banquets, and from routines for dealing with spirits – are easily observable in Dragon-head. But of course nobody claims them as local inventions. These are ideas and practices reproduced from a Chinese conceptual world, one which emphasizes flux: the mobility in space and time of both people and spirits. In other words, it emphasizes the spatial and processual nature of human and spiritual relationships. Separation and reunion, in this sense, is an important and widespread idiom not only in

Dragon-head, but also in China. To be more exact, there exists in China a whole cluster of idioms and practices which share a family resemblance and which may be glossed as "separation and reunion." At times invested with great emotion, these idioms and practices are expressed in various interrelated domains, including kinship, etiquette and religion, but also in fields as diverse as literature, politics and architecture. For instance, a great many classical Chinese verses – which often also contain implicit or explicit political references – focus precisely on moments of departure and on the agony of separation (Excellent examples of this are found in the work of Du Fu [Tu Fu], e.g. in his highly political "Dreaming of Li Po", which concerns the separation between two of China's greatest poets, brought about when Li Po was sent into exile[4]). The architectural elaboration of Chinese doors and gates (through which persons and spirits move), and their near-universal decoration with auspicious markers and charms, also conceivably reflects and helps reproduce the focusing of interest on moments of parting and return.

In Dragon-head, these various idioms of separation and reunion are concretely expressed in widely differing contexts: a child recites a Tang dynasty verse about separation, the village head politely sees a visitor to his outside gate, a woman sits on a stool rolling jiaozi for a departing guest, a poster announces the "arrival" of the God of Wealth, the host at a banquet makes long-winded arrangements for future meals, a farmhouse door is decorated with auspicious *duilian* poetry,[5] and so on. Very much more could be said about each of these diverse expressions, but my hypothesis is that they are connected.

History as seen from a *kang*

But what is the significance of these expressions of the Chinese attachment to place? In part through reference to them, I will suggest, people in Dragon-head construct their sense of temporal and physical placement in the world. One's personal experience of history is partly framed in Dragon-head by sequences of separations and reunions. This is because movements of persons and spirits through space are also patterned in time, as is, for example, made very explicit during *Zhongqiujie* (the mid-Autumn festival celebrating harvest and reunion) and *Chunjie* (the lunar new year). This latter festival, the high-point of the lunar calendar, is centrally structured around a complex sequence of departures and returns. As I have mentioned, ancestors are welcomed back from their graves (to reunite with their descendants) and then are sent away. Gods – and very importantly the Stove God[6] – are sent away (to meet amongst themselves) and then are welcomed back. Brothers reunite, daughters return to their natal homes, and various categories of kin, friends, colleagues and neighbours come together – if only for brief, but nevertheless very

323

systematic, visits – in order to reaffirm connections which transcend separation. A historic trace of these connections is produced, every year, by the (temporally and spatially) structured cycle of visits, each of which ends with a dispersal.

People thus learn to place themselves in historic communities, and to situate themselves in places, against the background of these separations and reunions. This is, in short, an aspect of identification and the attachment to place which is constantly being produced through human action, and which is therefore observable in the making. As I have noted, the idioms used in this process are borrowed from a traceable Chinese tradition. But the local production of identification involves the complete remaking of this tradition in new historical communities such as contemporary Dragon-head, and through new mental representations, not least through those developed by children. Although I cannot convincingly prove the existence of this process in an essay of this length, I shall briefly indicate what I have in mind.[7]

Children in Dragon-head are born into a symbolically-structured learning environment. This environment includes, among other things the *kang*, the fire-heated brick platform bed which is the social centre of farmhouses in north China. The kang – a place where children are conceived, and where they spend much of childhood – is warm because it is (literally) connected to the stove. Women, at stoves, produce everyday meals (often eaten on the kang), but also food for banquets and festivals, including the new year celebration of reunion and renewed fertility. During weddings, the kang explicitly becomes an emblem of fertility: the bride and groom are teased about sex while sitting on the kang (*naofang*) and "pressing the kang" (*yakang*) with a boy is said to help ensure that newlyweds will have a son. A woman who has just given birth is meant to sit on the kang almost literally doing nothing for one month (*zuo yuezi*) and this is therefore the place where infants are first breastfed. In this and other ways, the kang – as one learns in the process of becoming an adult – is associated with warmth from the stove and with food, women, fertility, conception, nurturance and children. Needless to say, the emotions which might attach to these associations are various, but also potentially crucial in terms of identity.

The experiences and emotions of children in Dragon-head, growing up in the kang-centred learning environment, are also, as I have been saying, framed by separations and reunions. For example, infants hear (and are often terrified by) the firecrackers which greet returning ancestors on the last day of the last lunar month. They also experience the socially chaotic period after the first day of the first month. This is characterized by the "stringing together of doors" (*chuanmenr*), during which relatives and friends come together for day-long banqueting and gambling. These activities take place on, or directly adjacent to, the *kang*. The communities of persons on which a child's family most directly depend throughout the year are explicitly reaffirmed during this period. Naturally, some of these people come from other places, and one must sometimes travel to other places in order to see them, thus complicating the social landscape. So the "place" of attachment is multiple and loosely-bounded; it includes one's own kang and farmhouse, but also a neighbourhood and a village and the connected "places" of one's relations and friends. The "attachment to place" merges with attachments to the various communities which produce various places (in the Pintupi sense, see above), not least through processes of separation and reunion.

I am not, of course, suggesting that children necessarily see this, or see it in this way, only that they are growing up in a world in which it is there to be seen. During the new year festival, the idioms of separation and reunion are evoked in specific places, such as on kang in Dragon-head, and acted out by specific persons – and all of this within the learning environment of the child. It goes without saying that this seemingly coherent process (of connecting sentiments and emotions with persons and places) is embedded in the shambolic flow of festive life. Children run in and out of houses, shooting off firecrackers, eating new year delicacies and watching – often with considerable frustration – seemingly interminable games of *majiang* (i.e. "mahjong"). Their mothers play and join in the eating and drinking, but they also work throughout the festival period, gathering and chopping firewood and preparing and presenting food. These women and children (while going about their business) are embedded in complex relationships with, and have complex attitudes towards, the people who surround them during the festival and who come and go. They also have complex relationships with, and attitudes towards, the places through which these people move. What I am suggesting is that within this overall environment (including symbolically-loaded kang, and symbolically-loaded separations and reunions) the seemingly minor activities of women and children – work, thought and play – should be seen as productive, producing effects in the world.[8] Their activities which relate to separation and reunion may, I have been suggesting, help produce (in themselves and in others) the feeling of having a place in specific historical communities and feelings of attachment to specific places. I would also argue, beyond this, that the traceable connection between these small productive effects – the production of emotional attachments – and larger patterns in Chinese history should be taken more seriously.

Remembering, forgetting and recreating the past

This brings me back to the subject of migration. What is *not* easily observable in Dragon-head, at least not on the surface, is that the community was produced in the past through migration, although of course it was. Ancestral "place of origin" was undoubtedly a crucial aspect of identity for the migrants themselves and also presumably for many of their descendants. But it is nevertheless possible for people now living in Dragon-head to speak of the "place of origin" as an unfamiliar land, bereft of relatives and friends. What one sees, instead, is a present-day community which is partially reproduced through a form of "perpetual migration," i.e. the ongoing separations and reunions of persons and spirits. This is a process which helps people see where and with whom they belong, and indeed which helps make these senses of belonging seem mostly natural and obvious. This is not to say that the identifications, places or communities thus produced are themselves necessarily straightforward or neatly bounded, but simply to stress that they are made, not given. In this sense, material from Dragon-head bears comparison with the ethnographic examples of migration (Hausa, Pintupi and Malay) outlined above. In those examples, the conceptualization of place (in relation to an imagined future, a constructed present, or a forgotten past) is not really constrained by the factual history of migration, although it may be partly shaped by it. Instead, the conceptualization of place is one means of getting by in the present and producing present-day communal solidarity.

The same could be said of Dragon-head and the separations and reunions, which help attach people to places and communities. But remember that precisely this same function – even within China – might be fulfilled by a variety of conceptualizations of history, place and community. For example, Rubie Watson has clearly shown that the constructed history of one south China lineage, explicitly directed towards an ancestral past, conveniently helps reproduce particular kinds of relationships in the present. This case, obviously very different from the Hausa, Pintupi or Malay examples, involves a backward-looking "long memory." In present-day relationships within the lineage, the imagined (if inaccurately imagined) ancestral past helps naturalize both unity and inequality. But, as Watson makes clear, this process must be seen in the flow of history, where both politico-economic factors (such as the changing possibilities for class affiliations) and cultural variables (such as concepts of "lineage" and "equality") merge. More precisely, ways of conceptualizing this particular lineage are inseparable from the political-economic history which produced it (Watson 1985).

In sum, both an imagined past (e.g. a mythical lineage history) and an imagined present (e.g. an ongoing sequence of separations and reunions) may contribute to history, partly through evoking emotions of attachment and belonging which have real effects in the world. But these effects need contextualization. In the case of Dragon-head they should be placed alongside a more general politico-economic history which might stress the impact of, for example, natural disaster, including the famine in Shandong which prompted an enormous exodus and resettlement in the Northeast. Obviously, I have not done this in my essay, but I hope to have drawn attention to a cultural variable which is arguably of considerable importance, and which should be taken into account by those studying Chinese migration.

Chinese "territorial bonds"

By way of conclusion I will briefly outline why, in the context of modern Chinese studies, I consider this an important way of proceeding. At the outset, I mentioned the recent (and excellent) historical and anthropological volume concerning lineages, ethnicity and "the territorial bond" in south China, edited by Helen Siu and David Faure. In their introduction, the editors note the significant contribution of William Skinner to Chinese studies (Siu and Faure 1995). Both the history and anthropology of China have been influenced by Skinner, and especially by his emphasis on "regional systems." Skinner encouraged historians away from conceptualizing Chinese history in primarily imperial or dynastic terms. But he also encouraged anthropologists of China away from village-based studies and towards the examination of, for instance, the role of regional marketing centres in the rural political-economy. The regional approach – which sees China neither as an imperial whole, nor as a series of isolated villages – clearly has many implications for the study of Chinese identities and of the Chinese attachment to place.

Siu and Faure, in their attempt to illuminate the territorial bond, follow Skinner in taking "the starting position that a regional approach to the historical process in China is necessary" (1995:1), and they focus on the unique histories of the Pearl River Delta. But they also seek to extend his argument in a "cultural" way. That is, they see the region as "a conscious historical construct that may be captured in the cultural expressions of those involved in creating it" (1995:1). In other words, regions do not simply exist. They are conceptualized as existing, and created in part culturally through the symbolic practices of lineage, local community and the state. They also link the development of territorial bonds to histories of migration and inter-ethnic relations. These involve patterns of displacement, inclusion and exclusion which are, again, culturally conceived. As Siu and Faure note, their approach implies taking seriously certain aspects of Chinese culture, such as popular religion, which may formerly have been relegated to the historical margins (1995:8).

I suspect that most anthropologists of China would endorse the position of Siu and Faure – making the regional cultural – not least because of the weight it attaches to processes which they themselves have been studying for some years. The anthropology of China has often focused on the relationships between kinship, popular religion and locality; and has consistently examined what it means in China to belong to a family, a community and a place.[9]

Here, however, I want to suggest that the anthropological history of Siu and Faure should be taken even further, in part by descending – contra Skinner – below the level of regions, and even below the level of lineages or villages. If we hope to understand the Chinese attachment to place, and by extension to illuminate Chinese migration, the potential contribution of micro-ethnography (that is, the micro-ethnography of childhood) should be taken more seriously. Siu and Faure note, in their Introduction, the possible discomfort of historians with anthropological interpretations which are not backed up by "hard documentary evidence" (1995:19). But ethnographic fieldwork helps us grasp emotions, sentiments and attachments, which are in part produced and made manifest at the level of everyday experience. These manifestations often precisely do not make it into "documentary evidence" of any kind, and yet they are surely crucial to the production of history, which is after all a collective enterprise.

All people produce history, but only some make it into historical accounts. It is striking that the volume edited by Siu and Faure, which is very ambitious in its attempt to provide a coherent and synthesizing analysis of the dynamic of Chinese regional history, makes virtually no mention of children or women. This is partly because lineage histories and ideologies, official accounts and political discourse all tend to ignore the role of children and women in history. By contrast, I would argue that children and women are absolutely crucial to the production – partly within themselves and partly through separation and reunion – of the Chinese territorial bond (the attachment to place), which is in turn obviously crucial to the flow of local and regional histories. Anthropological research can illuminate the connections between the ordinary lives of seemingly unimportant people in seemingly unimportant places and the wider historical patterns they both respond to and help produce.

References

Bloch, Maurice. 1991. "Language, Anthropology and Cognitive Science." *Man* 26, no. 2, pp. 183–98

Borofsky, Robert. 1987. *Making History: Pukapukan and Anthropological Constructions of Knowledge*. Cambridge: Cambridge University Press.

Carsten, Janet. 1995. "The Politics of Forgetting: Migration, Kinship and Memory on the Periphery of the Southeast Asian State." *Journal of the Royal Anthropological Institute* 1, no. 2, pp. 317–35.

Carsten, Janet. 1997. *Kinship and the Heat of the Hearth*. Oxford: Oxford University Press.

Chard, Robert. 1990. "Folktales on the God of the Stove". *Chinese Studies (Hanxue yanjiu)* 8, no. 1, pp. 149–82.

Hawkes, David. 1967. *Little Primer of Tu Fu*. Oxford: Clarendon Press.

Myers, Fred R. 1986. *Pintupi Country, Pintupi Self: Sentiment, Place and Politics among Western Desert Aborigines*. Berkeley: University of California Press.

Myers, Fred R. 1988. "The Logic and Meaning of Anger among Pintupi Aborigines." *Man* 23, no. 4, pp. 580–610.

Sangren, P. Steven. 1987. *History and Magical Power in a Chinese Community*. Stanford: Stanford University Press.

Shepherd, John Robert. 1993. *Statecraft and Political Economy on the Taiwan Frontier: 1600–1800*. Stanford: Stanford University Press.

Siu, Helen F. and David Faure. 1995. "Introduction." In Helen F. Siu and David Faure, eds, *Down to Earth: The Territorial Bond in South China*. Stanford: Stanford University Press, pp. 1–19.

Stafford, Charles. 1995. *The Roads of Chinese Childhood: Learning and Identification in Angang*. Cambridge: Cambridge University Press.

Stafford, Charles. forthcoming. "Patriliny and the Cycles of *Yang* and *Laiwang*: Rethinking Chinese Relatedness." In Janet Carsten, ed. *Cultures of Relatedness*.

Watson, Rubie. 1985. *Inequality among Brothers: Class and Kinship in South China*. Cambridge: Cambridge University Press.

Yamba, C. Bawa. 1992. "Going There and Getting There: The Future as a Legitimating Charter for Life in the Present." In S. Wallman, ed. *Contemporary Futures*. London: Routledge, pp. 109–123.

Notes

1 I have recently argued, however, that this is a misleading way of thinking about Chinese kinship. Alongside formal patrilineal ideologies in China, one finds notions of relatedness which are considerably more fluid and incorporative, and thus comparable to those described by Carsten and others working on Southeast Asian systems of kinship. These include the cycle of *yang*, involving mutual nurturance and support between generations, and the "cycle of *laiwang*", involving mutual nurturance and support between friends and acquaintances (Stafford, forthcoming).

2 This is partly because cultural phenomena in general are not necessarily formulated explicitly or linguistically. See Maurice Bloch's discussion of the generally non-linguistic nature of cognition and cultural knowledge, and the implications of this for anthropology (Bloch 1991).

3 See Borofsky 1987.

4 Translated in Hawkes 1967:87ff.

5 *Duilian* are auspicious poetic couplets which are often displayed in two vertical lines on opposite sides of door frames and gates. Each new year fresh duilian are posted at farmhouses in Dragon-head – in part as conventional decoration, but also, at least in theory, to ensure the auspiciousness of what arrives through the door.

6 The Stove God, *Zaojun*, is seen as a kind of house policeman who observes family behaviour throughout the year. He returns to Heaven during the new year festival to report his findings. His sending off is thus said to be especially important because it may influence his report, and he is often given a kind of sticky candy on departure so that he will be unable to say bad things (see Chard 1990).

7 My current research and writing is focused on these issues, which are discussed more fully in an unpublished essay entitled "The Firecracker: Children and History in Post-Mao China." There I address the complex relationship between

separation and reunion, Chinese conceptualizations of time, and the learning of conventional history.

8 I have previously discussed, based on research in Taiwan, the significance of the relationship between mothers and children for processes of identification (Stafford 1995).

9 One obvious example, also directly influenced by Skinner's notion of regional systems, is Sangren's investigation of ritual and the production of local history in Taiwan (1987).

Part IV

Conclusion

Chapter Sixteen ⎯⎯⎯⎯⎯⎯⎯⎯⎯⎯⎯⎯

Conclusion: Of exceptionalisms and generalities

Ronald Skeldon and Graeme Hugo

As the most populous country in the world, the great tradition with the longest continuous history of civilization and the largest economy in the world until the first half of the nineteenth century, China seems to be in a strong position for consideration as exceptional with respect to its migration experience. However, many other countries can also claim to be exceptional. For example, nativist American thinking has regarded the experience of the westward movement of the frontier as having instilled an exceptional character in the people and society of the United States. Viewed in comparative perspective, the American experience can be seen to have been different but not unique (see Nugent 1992). Similarly, we would argue that there are many aspects of the recent history of migration in China which are different, but, when placed in a broader context of contemporary migration, especially in the wider Asian region, not necessarily unique. While accepting the variations explicit in the Chinese patterns, we feel that, rather than retreating into sterile relativism, it is more profitable to view those patterns from a comparative perspective. We are mindful of the extent to which the China development model, as perceived by outside observers in the 1960s and 1970s, was seen to be exceptional. However, in general terms, it fell within the orthodoxy of the centrally planned economies of the time, with its emphasis on heavy industry and, despite the rhetoric, a pro-urban bias based upon the squeezing of the rural producer. Equally clear, though, were deviations from the general model which gave particular "Chinese characteristics" to the model: the Great Leap Forward and the Cultural Revolution, for example.

The sheer size and diversity of China clearly generate very particular conditions. Movements across comparable distances, and between culturally very different groups, in most other parts of the world would encompass international migrations whereas, in China, these are internal within a single state. However, the magnitude and complexity of the Sinitic world have more important implications: the time and effort required to become an authority on China does not encourage scholars, or even allow them, to divert their attention to cases elsewhere. Certainly, irrespective of the region studied, there is always a temptation to consider one's own area to be "unique." Nevertheless, a lack of consideration of the broader perspective appears to be particularly the case for scholars of China where a justification for a separate world appears strong. In work on migration, studies such as those by Goldstein (1987) and by Roberts (1997), which compare China with other countries, are rare indeed. This volume has attempted to redress the balance somewhat by examining migration among several different parts of China and among several different types of overseas Chinese community and, in this concluding chapter, we attempt to extend the comparative perspective more widely.

Let us start with a consideration of what indeed appears to be a critical feature that has given migration in China over the last fifty years apparently unique characteristics. This stems from a fundamental practical, as well as methodological, issue that overshadows almost every aspect of recent migration studies in China: the household registration system (hukou). Systems of household registration in China go back centuries, reflecting the long tradition of centralized control, but they have been implemented with varying degrees of success. Even under the Communist authorities, who formalized the hukou system from 1958, its effectiveness varied and, since 1979, it has perhaps been more honoured in the breach than in the observance. Nevertheless, Chan finds the system useful in identifying what he considers to be two fundamentally different systems of mobility in migration in China in the post-Mao period: those more permanent shifts that have merited going to the effort of changing one's place of registration, and those more short term movements that are not captured by the system at all. Irrespective of whether Chan's dualistic interpretation may draw too sharp a line through what appears to be a very grey area, this debate highlights familiar territory for migration scholars worldwide: the difficulty of identifying a migrant in time and space. The task of differentiating circulation from other more long term forms of mobility remains a major challenge for all migration specialists, and it is instructive to see how the problem is approached in China. One of the editors of this volume engages in this debate in his introductory chapter.

Chan also draws attention to another issue that often typifies migration studies in other parts of the world. He notes the richness of many of the existing data sources in China for the study of migration in the post-reform period. Rather than continually bemoaning a lack of data and calling for yet more surveys, the emphasis should be more upon utilizing fully the existing data sets, despite their weaknesses. In other parts of the world, too, there is a virtual chorus for the collection of more migration-related data, but the existing data are never fully analysed. It is often relatively easy to collect further information but much more difficult to complete meticulous analysis. There is an unfortunate tendency among many migration analysts to have relatively short collective memories (see Skeldon 1995). While one has to look ahead, one also has to be aware of what has gone before. Chan's chapter is a refreshing attempt to present to us an assessment of a wide array of available data sources for the study of migration in China.

Unquestionably, the hukou system, in association with the system to distribute subsidized grain in which an individual was only entitled to his or her grain in the area in which he or she was registered, was of fundamental importance in controlling mobility at certain times during the Maoist period. Urbanization would have been much faster during this time had the controls not been in existence. Banister (1987:327), for example, estimated that the urban population of the early 1980s would have been more than double without the policies to limit migration and reverse the flows from the cities through some well-publicized campaigns. During the Communist period to the late 1970s, there was virtually no movement either into or out of China. International movements were limited to a few thousand students, perhaps 11,000, who, until the Sino-Soviet split of 1961, went to the then Soviet Union to study, and several thousand technical personnel who were sent to assist other socialist countries. More than 13,000 engineers went to Tanzania in the early 1970s, for example. With these few exceptions, China was totally isolated from the rapidly evolving global migration system, and its internal mobility was restricted or punctuated by officially sanctioned programmes of movement. No other developing country has been able successfully to control its mobility to achieve state objectives in quite the same way. From this point of view, the recent history of migration in China has indeed been exceptional.

However, after the implementation of the reforms from 1979 onward, the patterns of mobility both within and from China have come to take on a much more familiar hue to those who have worked on population mobility in other parts of the developing world. The date 1979 must be taken with some degree of caution as it is likely that there were greater continuities than a sharp break before and after that date. Lynn White (1994) has already clearly shown that gradually increasing mobility in the hinterland of Shanghai can be traced back well into the mid-1970s. As we learn more and more about migration in the Maoist period, it is likely that, as with the interpretations of China's economic development, the exceptionalist elements will become less and less stark and we will see, as Lary in her chapter maintains, much greater mobility than was originally thought.

Taking 1979 for the moment as a convenient cut-off date, what we have seen since then has been a marked resumption of rural-to-urban movement, including a massive increase in circulation, which in the Chinese context is termed the "floating population" (*liudong renkou*).

There has also been a resumption of emigration, although this is still relatively small by historical standards and in terms of China's vast population. These international movements include migration for permanent settlement, the movement of labour, the movement of students and increasing clandestine or illegal flows (Skeldon 1996). The studies in this volume have examined aspects of both the internal and the international flows and some interrelations between them.

Only a few selected aspects of the increasing flows could be covered in this volume. The focus is upon internal movements and on but one of the emerging international flows, that to Europe, which, while relatively small compared with flows to North America and Australasia, remains the least known. Moreover, the flow to Europe is somewhat different from the other larger outflows. It originates primarily in Zhejiang province, whereas migrants to North America and to Australasia come primarily from the southern provinces of Guangdong and Fujian. The detailed micro-level studies of Chinese migration to Europe illustrate important aspects of the whole process of migration, which may have relevance to emigration from southern China. Thunø shows the clear continuities between past and present migration and the interrelation between internal and international movements. The traditional regional trading networks of Wenzhou were progressively extended to incorporate international destinations which led to later, more permanent movement. This evolution of a trading diaspora to a settler diaspora has relevance for those concerned with transitions in population mobility in a wider context.

The studies presented in this volume not only illustrate many other commonalities between the Chinese patterns of migration and those elsewhere but also reflect research themes and approaches among the researchers that are becoming common in many parts of the world. As outlined by Pieke in his introduction, the selected studies cover a range of approaches to migration in China from the more traditional, formal demographic analyses to the more subjective, situational and biographical approaches. The most notable common areas of concern, as evinced in the chapters in this volume, include the following ten major themes that represent critical topics in the study of migration in and from China, as well as in migration studies more generally. These themes emerged not only from the formal papers but also from the debate, which was at times vigorous, that followed the various presentations and summaries during the conference.

1 A concern with networks was apparent: how these not only facilitate further movements between origins and destinations, but also help to incorporate migrants into the societies and economies of destination. This is seen particularly in the several studies of migration from Zhejiang and in the concerns about the development of ethnic economies and their

expression in occupational specialization and segmented labour markets. The analysis of rural-urban linkages and of the development of informal activities fall very much into this area. Only with the reforms in China and the development of free markets for goods and housing has the whole issue of an informal sector emerged. This perhaps reaches its most obvious expression in Zhejiang Village on the outskirts of Beijing (see the chapter by Xiang Biao), which strikes a familiar chord in those who worked in Latin America in the 1960s and followed the literature on barriadas in Peru or favelas in Brazil. With the wave of floating population directed at the major cities, Chinese authorities are now facing the problem of providing adequate housing, transportation and employment, the solution to which may lie in small private initiatives in an informal sector (see de Soto 1989). Clearly, these issues revolving around networks focus on that one major aspect of migration in China that has typified its history since 1979: the massive increase in circulation.

While there is strong recognition of the centrality of social networks in facilitating much of the internal and international migration and the adjustment of migrants at their destinations, our understanding of precisely how these networks operate is limited. How wide a kinship group do they encompass? How much can one expect from relatives and friends at the destination? Do they attenuate with time? To what extent are they becoming interrelated with some of the institutions influencing migration, such as recruiters? To what extent do they operate to encourage migration regardless of economic reality and to what extent are they conduits of information about the opening up of new opportunities in some places and the diminution of opportunities in other places? Several of the studies in this volume begin to answer these and other questions about the significance of social networks in the migration and settlement processes, but in China, as elsewhere in Asia, our knowledge in these areas remains incomplete.

What is clear, however, is the importance of family in the organization of migration and in the establishment of networks, albeit in different configurations. The networks spread information and make migration and/ or circulation a possibility. They are a form of social capital which allows families to spread their risk and take advantage of a broader range of possibilities and, as these networks develop, so too may we expect the spatial movement of the population to increase (see also Roberts 1997). In addition, as new relationships are created among increasingly diverse groups of people in new situations and locations, so too are ethnic identities redefined. The analysis of ethnicity and changing identities through networks, as Pieke makes clear in his introduction, will be an intrinsic part of any attempt to "rethink" migration.

2 Concern was also shown at the impact of migration on origin and destination areas, particularly through the transfer of remittances to

origins, and the contribution of migrants to social ills such as unemployment, overcrowding, pollution and crime at destinations. As in so many other areas, migration tends to be seen in a negative light as an uncontrolled element in society. Migrants are blamed for increases in unemployment and in crime, although reliable data are scarce and a collective prejudice develops towards the floating population, as seen in the work of Ding and Stockman on Shanghai.

The remittances that are sent back to communities of origin, either from the city or from overseas, are seen to be used for consumption rather than investment, another social evil. Migration is thus seen to undermine the rural communities of origin. However, evidence from other countries suggests that a sharp difference between the impacts of consumption and investment may be false: increased consumption is likely to stimulate investment. Consumption, as expressed in new house construction, will stimulate local industries, and even expenditure on weddings or other festivals is likely to have an impact on local agricultural production, and so on. The contemporary literature on the impact of remittances indicates that the second- and third-round impacts of consumption expenditure are important in local job creation. Moreover, the fact that migrants tend to come from particular regions strongly focuses the economic impact of remittances, so that potentially they are an important source of scarce capital for local and regional development. However, more detailed research is needed on the precise nature of the impacts of remittances on outmigration regions, not only in China but elsewhere in Asia. A related issue, especially with respect to international migration, is the extent to which the overseas-based communities act as "beach heads" for the export of the products of the origin communities. For example, it is apparent that the Korean communities established in California and elsewhere in the United States were a crucial element in the initial penetration of the North American market by South Korean manufactured goods in the 1970s and 1980s. It would seem that some Chinese communities in Europe are operating in the same way.

The view apparent among policy makers in China (reflected in some of the chapters in this volume, Ding and Stockman for example) is that the net impact of the massive rural to urban migration occurring in China is negative. However, the consensus emerging elsewhere in Asia is that the effects of rapid urbanization are more complex. While there are significant problems created by burgeoning pressure on services, job opportunities etc. in major urban areas, there are substantial net benefits not only for the migrants themselves and their families but also for the national economy. With the economies undergoing such rapid structural change and the associated massive displacement of labour from agriculture and expansion of industrial and service activity, massive rural to urban migration is a necessary corollary.

3 There is the impact of migration on the migrant himself or herself. The study of migrant selectivity and migrant characteristics has always been central to the work of migration researchers and is given expression here in the chapter by Hoy on fertility and family planning amongst short-term migrants, although it is also explicit in several other chapters. The analysis of migrant fertility is not only relevant to migrant/non-migrant differences, but also to the broader interrelationship between migration and fertility. We still do not fully understand how one might impact on the other in a truly integrated model of a demographic transition (Zelinsky 1971; Skeldon 1990).

A related issue here, which is alluded to in several of the chapters, is the increasing participation of women in both internal and international migration. The feminization of migration is in fact a worldwide trend of the 1980s and 1990s (Chant 1992; Zlotnik 1993) and has been especially pronounced in Asia. Women make up a greater proportion of most migration streams, while the amount of autonomous movement in which they have been the key decision makers is increasing exponentially. This raises a number of important issues, which have not been fully addressed either in this volume or elsewhere in the literature on Asia, in particular the question in what way migration is related to the empowerment of women and the changing roles and status of women. Caroline Hoy, in her chapter, however, well illustrates how migration can provide young women with a greater sense of freedom than could be found within the traditional bounds of Chinese village society.

4 The use of China's vast supply of labour, internally as well as internationally, has clear parallels with the situation in other parts of the world. The role of the broker and labour recruiter appears as ubiquitous in China as in other parts of the world from which labour migration occurs. Contract labour certainly did not begin with the reforms but appears to have been common before 1979 (Blecher 1984). However, it has proliferated since, as private rather than state recruitment has become dominant in the supply of labour for joint ventures in the Special Economic Zones and beyond in the south of the country. State and provincial recruitment agencies also began to recruit labour for overseas contracts from 1979. The numbers working overseas increased almost sixfold between 1983 and 1993 to 173,000 contract workers in more than one hundred countries, although the majority were in what might be called the "near overseas" in Hong Kong and Macau. Just how the brokers operate and their arrangements with regional as well as national authorities, as well as with overseas employers, will be an important research area in Chinese migration studies and can be informed by comparative international perspectives.

The chapters in the present volume offer some important insights into the institutionalization of migration processes in China and its significance initiating and perpetuating emigration flows, especially international movements. This issue remains a neglected area of study elsewhere in Asia where the significance of the "migration industry" is no less important. In the present volume the pivotal importance of the labour contractor (*baogongtou*) and the snakehead (*shetou*) in shaping migration flows within and from China, historically as today, is well established. While the roles of contractors, as well as those of other institutions such as provincial labour export companies, are significant in the legal emigration, they are especially active and crucial to the burgeoning smuggling of people and the growth of undocumented migration currently occurring out of China. Research into such organizations clearly sets new challenges for migration researchers not only theoretically but also methodologically.

5 Although many recent interpretations of migration and the migrant in China tend to be negative and to see migration as creating more problems than it solves, it is also possible to see the migrant as victim. The expulsion of people from their homes and their exile is a very strong theme in much current thinking on migration. The "sending down" of so many young people in China during the Maoist period lends itself particularly to this type of interpretation and Sausmikat adds to this a sensitive gender dimension. Throughout studies of human movement, the emphasis on the individual experience of migration provides a balance to the many socio-economic interpretations at the macro level. Movement, however, needs to be set against non-movement and concerns about attachment to place, how that is built up, and how it is modified by migration. An example of such micro-level, qualitative work in China is given in the chapter by Stafford.

The issue of protection of the rights of migrants is emerging as one of the pre-eminent themes in migration policy in Asia. It is clear from several chapters in the present volume that migrants are often placed in vulnerable situations because of their "foreignness," language barriers, illegal status or other markers as an outsider. They are often made scapegoats for various ills at the destination, ranging from crime and unemployment to the spread of disease. The lack of institutional support has meant that migrants have often created their own formal and informal systems to provide protection for themselves. Several of the chapters here have demonstrated how such formal and informal associations operate, not only to protect migrants, but also to ease their adjustment to the destination and facilitate the maintenance of strong linkages with the place of origin. The operation of these formal and informal associations needs to be investigated in greater detail since there often appear to be tensions between the roles.

6 Another important theme relates to the interrelationship between migration and the labour market, especially in the destination areas. The

chapters in this volume indicate three modes of incorporation of Chinese migrants into local destination labour markets as is the case elsewhere in Asia. First, a small number of educated professionals are able to enter highly paid, highly skilled sectors of the labour market by virtue of their formal qualifications. Second, large numbers of entrepreneurs, usually operating at a relatively small scale, become established, often with the assistance of friends and family already at the destination. Third, many migrants enter the so-called 3D (dirty, dangerous, difficult) lowly-paid, low-status jobs at the destination which are eschewed by the local labour force.

In almost all these cases migration is strongly associated with the segmentation of labour markets at the destination. While this pattern has been common in most free-market countries of the developing world, it is relatively new in China where, until recently, employment was dominated by a unified job allocation system. We need to know more about the means by which migrants enter the new evolving labour markets and how the migrant groups articulate with employers and other labour market players at the destinations. In this respect the function of migrant enclaves in destination areas needs elucidating. To what extent they facilitate entry to the labour market and act as a seed-bed for new ethnic entrepreneurs has been little investigated. The whole involvement of migrants in informal sector activity, both within China and in Chinese communities overseas requires careful analysis.

7 These qualitative interpretations lead to one of the major emerging concerns in the social sciences generally, not just in migration studies, and one that is implicit in many of the chapters. This is the issue of identity, ultimately of "Chineseness", but also of migrant identities within the Chinese world. Most obvious in an overseas context, identities are nevertheless present in cities in China, often expressed through the *huiguan* or homeplace associations, but also through other markers such as occupational specialization. This discussion takes us back to issues raised above relevant to ethnic enclaves (see the chapter by Nyíri). Felt, or perceived, differences between migrant and non-migrant, between migrants from different parts of China and, more clearly, between foreigner and Chinese migrant, lie at the heart of group definition. Migration, by bringing peoples from different groups together, in essence creates group tensions. These issues are not explicitly addressed in the studies in this volume but they lie very much in the background, and the chapters provide insight into what is clearly becoming a much more complex society in China.

8 Identity leads to issues associated with nationalism and national security. Migration and security have emerged as major themes in

contemporary migration studies, most obviously in studies of international migration (see, for example, Weiner 1993), but also in internal movements. One of the most important planned migrations during the Maoist period that can be interpreted in this light is the movement into Xinjiang, Tibet and other peripheral areas sparsely populated by Han Chinese. Once again, these planned movements have their counterparts in many other parts of the world as governments have striven to extend the areas under their effective control. Movements into the upper Amazon basin in South America, into the dry zone of Sri Lanka, into border areas in the central highlands of Viet Nam and, the largest, the transmigration from Java and Bali to the peripheral islands of Indonesia, can all be interpreted in this light.

Apart from concerns of domestic security, these movements to colonize border areas raise another issue which has widespread implications: environmental degradation. All of these environments are fragile and the influx of many thousands of settlers who may have had no prior experience in managing a similar type of landscape is likely to create severe problems. Most of these environments can support relatively low population densities, and the destruction of the tropical moist forest and the overworking of marginal semi-arid grasslands are likely to have repercussions that extend far beyond the local areas.

9 In the international arena, there are security concerns of a very different kind: the fear of large-scale emigration from China. Far eastern Russia, the countries of Southeast Asia, and many countries in the West fear an uncontrolled influx from the massive population that is China. Partly, these attitudes reflect xenophobic and "yellow peril" attitudes of the past, but they are also partly grounded in the realities of the present emigration from China. Illegal migration is increasing from China. Official Chinese sources have estimated that there were up to half a million Chinese in transit to the West in cities in Southeast Asia, Russia, eastern Europe and Latin America, and American sources put the number of illegal migrants entering the United States alone from China in the early 1980s at over 100,000 a year. The sources are reviewed in Skeldon (1996:452–3). It is not the issue of illegality of movement alone that is of concern. This movement is associated with organized criminal groups and with the production of and international trade in drugs. While only a small number of Chinese migrants, legal and illegal, are involved in criminal activities, the financial power of these groups means that they indeed represent a threat to many societies. The threat has developed to such an extent that some countries are run by, or for the benefit of, drug cartels. In Asia, Cambodia, and almost certainly Myanmar, fall into this category and the implications of having these countries as full members of regional organizations have yet to be understood. This issue is, however, rapidly

becoming of global significance and will be of major concern to governments in the developed and developing world as we move into the twenty-first century.

10 The previous topic leads on to the final concern, although some might say this is the most important concern, that of policy. Quite clearly, during much of the 1960s and 1970s, the Chinese authorities were remarkably successful in curbing migration, if not actually stopping movement totally, profoundly influencing the direction and limiting the volume of that movement. Since the reforms, that control has been eroded and internal migration seems virtually out of control. Can order be re-established in the context of a more open economy without imposing repression? A major point of debate at the conference was whether there should be a free movement of labour within China's huge labour market, or whether that flow ought to be subject to some form of control. Social engineering, after all, has been a major characteristic of the demographic management in socialist societies. The experience of countries in other parts of the developing world with attempts to restrict migration has largely been a history of failure. Policies that accommodate to the flows and attempt to improve the quality of life in origins and destinations are more likely to achieve some measure of success. China may therefore have much to learn from other parts of the developing world in implementing the kinds of policies that can help to incorporate migrants into the economic and social fabric of cities, as well as support the areas of origin of the migrants. Finally, as alluded to above, China and countries around the world will need to develop coordinated policies to control the influence of international criminal groups.

Many other parallels can be drawn between migration in China and migration in other parts of the world and between the approaches used in the study of migration in China, of which this volume provides many examples, and those used in other parts of the world. The risk-minimizing rather than income-maximizing interpretation of the reasons for migration, for example, seems singularly appropriate for the analysis of population movements in the largest peasant society in the world. Again, dualistic interpretations appear to characterize so many approaches to the study of migration in China, just as they do elsewhere. Hukou/non-hukou migrants, floating migrants/permanent migrants and state enterprise/free market enterprise all strike a familiar chord to the outsider looking at interpretations of migration in China. Yet again, with regard to the development of the spatial pattern of migration in China, the movements seldom originate among the poorest people in the country, as has been shown to be the case in many places elsewhere. The list of parallels can go on and on. Yet, the sheer size and diversity of China unquestionably introduce variations not found elsewhere. What would normally be international migrations in most parts of the world in terms of linear and social distance crossed are, in China, internal migrations. Again, with rising provincial controls, internal migration in China may have greater parallels with international movements elsewhere.

The exceptionalism of the Chinese world is an appealing vision to the many who have been able to penetrate its mysteries. However, when viewed in a comparative perspective, the generalities of more universal experience begin to emerge. This applies, we feel, particularly to the recent trends of migration both within and from China. That migration, for all its diversity, has much in common with the process in other parts of the world. The studies in this volume are among the new wave of research carried out by young scholars working on population movement among the Chinese peoples. It was important to examine their findings in a broader context and this appears to have revealed the similar themes identified above. Migration in and from China is not unique. There are differences but these, rather than giving rise to exceptional migration patterns, are but variations on common themes with Chinese characteristics. In turn, these studies of Chinese migration provide insights that deepen our understanding of population mobility in general and move us forward towards the editors' objective to "rethink" migration.

References

Banister, Judith. 1987. *China's Changing Population*. Stanford: Stanford University Press.

Blecher, Marc. 1984. "Peasant Labour for Urban Industry: Temporary Contract Labour, Urban-Rural Balance and Class Relations in a Chinese County." In N. Maxwell and B. McFarlane, eds, *China's Changed Road to Development*. Oxford: Pergamon Press, pp. 109–23.

Chant, Sylvia. 1992. *Gender and Migration in Developing Countries*. Belhaven: London.

Goldstein, Sidney. 1987. "Forms of Mobility and Their Policy Implications: Thailand and China Compared." *Social Forces* 65, no. 4, pp. 915–42.

De Soto, Hernando. 1989. *The Other Path: The Invisible Revolution in the Third World*. New York: Harper and Row.

Nugent, Walter. 1992. *Crossings: The Great Transatlantic Migrations, 1870–1914*. Bloomington: Indiana University Press.

Roberts, Kenneth D. 1997. "China's 'Tidal Wave' of Migrant Labor: What Can We Learn From Mexican Undocumented Migration to the United States?" *International Migration Review* 31, no. 2, pp. 249–93.

Skeldon, Ronald. 1990. *Population Mobility in Developing Countries: A Reinterpretation*. London: Belhaven.

Skeldon, Ronald. 1995. "The Challenge Facing Migration Research: A Case for Greater Awareness." *Progress in Human Geography* 19, no. 1, pp. 91–6.

Skeldon, Ronald. 1996. "Migration from China." *Journal of International Affairs* 49, no. 2, pp. 434–55.

Weiner, Myron. ed. 1993. *International Migration and Security*. Boulder: Westview Press.

White, Lynn T. 1994. "Migration and Politics on the Shanghai Delta." *Issues and Studies* 30, no. 9, pp. 63–94.

Zelinsky, Wilbur. 1971. "The Hypothesis of the Mobility Transition." *Geographical Review* 61, no. 2, pp. 219–49.

Zlotnik, Hania. 1993. "Women as Migrants and Workers in Developing Countries." *International Journal of Contemporary Sociology* 30, no. 1, pp. 39–62.

Index

A Dong 255
ABC study 50–1, 62
Amin, S. 73–4
Anhui province 79, 88, 119, 288
Anti-Japanese War (1937–1945) 40
Arnold, F. and Liu Zhaoxiang 140
Asian Games (1990) 231, 339
Association of the Hungarian Chinese
    Cultural and Arts Circles 277
Association of Hungarian Chinese
    Entrepreneurs from Shanghai 261
Association for the Promotion of
    Chinese-Hungarian Friendship
    (APCHF) 257–8, 260, 276; conflict
    with HCA 263–5
attachment to place 315–17; and
    anthropological studies of migration
    317–19; significance of expressions
    of 323–5; and territorial bonds
    327–8

Baimen town 170, 171–2, 175
Banister, J. 143, 335
Banks, M. 15
Banyuetan 94
Bao Ruo-Wang, J.P. and Chelminski, R.
    41
Baotou city 222
Baotou Iron and Steel Plant 39
Barmé, G. and Minford, J. 313
Barth, F. 10
Becattini, G. 284; and Sengenberger,
    284
Beijing 38, 42, 49, 60, 87, 104, 105–6,
117, 119, 149, 162, 222, 223, 224–5,
    226; Chaoyang district 250; Fengtai
    district 218; see also Zhejiang Village
    (Beijing)
Beijing Bureau of Industry and
    Commerce 231
Beijing Municipal Construction Team
    Management Office 108
Beijing Municipal Urban Construction
    Management Department 106
Belgium 269, 270, 272
Bernstein, T.P. 134, 312, 313
Bertaux, D. and Bertaux-Wianne, I.
    308, 313
Bi-Zhong Qiaosheng 253, 278
Bilsborrow, R. and UN Secretariat 71
Blecher, M. 119, 339
Bloch, M. 329
border settlements 35–7
Borofsky, R. 329
Bourdieu, P. 160, 172–5, 177, 200; and
    Wacquant, L.J.D. 174, 175
Boyd, M. 15
Brown, A.A. and Neuberger, E. 67

Cai Wenmei et al 145
Caldwell, J.C. 136
Campani, G. et al 284
Campbell, E.K. 137, 138
Carchedi, F. and Ferri, M. 189, 283,
    293
Carsten, J. 318
chain migration 9, 10, 16, 19, 188, 190,
    223–5

Chan, A. 300, 313
Chan, A. *et al* 300
Chan *et al* 313
Chan, K.W. 34, 50, 52, 60, 67, 71, 134
Chan, M.K. and Dirlik, A. 313
Chaney, R. 74
Chant, S. 339
Chant, S. and Radcliffe, S.A. 71
Chard, R. 329
Chaudhuri, J.R. 74
Chefoo Treaty (1876) 161
Chen 279
Chen Bin 164, 165
Chen Hansheng 164
Chen Jinyong 67
Chen Lite 162, 163, 164, 167
Chen Murong 162, 163, 164, 165, 176
Chen Sanjing 164
Chen Xuewen 161
Chen Yuanfeng 162–4
Cheng, C. 134
Cheng, T. and Selden, M. 51
China General Construction Company 107
China Labour Bulletin 79
China News Analysis 140
China News Digest 272
China Overseas Exchange Commission 253, 262
Chinese Academy of Social Sciences (CASS) survey 50–1, 62, 75, 77, 79–80, 81, 85–6, 101–2
Chinese Exclusion Act (1882) 163
Chinese Immigrants Service Centre 279
Chinese Investment Group of Hungary Rt 267
Chinese People's Political Consultative Conference (CPPCC) study 51, 61, 64
Chinese-Hungarian Friendship Association 277
Choe, M.K. and Wu Jiaming 145
Christiansen, F. 74
Civil War (1946–1949) 33, 40
Clarke, G. 5
Cleland, J.G. and Shen Yimin 143, 145, 150
Coale, A.J., and Chen Shengli 78; *et al* 145
Cohen, R. 18
Colombo, M. *et al* 293

construction team migration 103–4; case studies 112–17; migrant workers in contracting teams 109–12; peasants within establishment 104–9
contract labour teams 12–13, 20, 30; competitiveness of 105–6; control over 106–8; and education/training 108, 110–11, 116; emergence of 104; fees levied on 106; Lin Da team 113–15; management of 105; migrant workers in 109–12; Old Hu's free contracting team from Wuwei 112–13; organizational structure of 108–9, 117; and quality 107; social image of 104–5; social life of 117; unified management/associated teams distinction 109; wages/benefits for 111; Yazhu team 115–17
credit associations 249
Crissman, L. 10
Cultural Revolution (1966–1976) 34, 40, 42, 43, 45, 48, 219, 281, 297, 299, 300–1, 333
Czene, G. 265

dam building 38
Dangdai Zhongguo Congshu 38
Daqing Oil Fields 35
Davies, C.B. 137
Daxing'anling Mountains 35
De Soto, H. 337
De Tinguy, A. 2, 41
Demko, G.J. and Fuchs, R.J. 67
Deng Xian 314
Deng Xiaoping 226, 232, 300
Deng Zhenglai and Jin Yuejin 241
Dependents of Overseas Chinese Commission 262
Ding Jinhong 61; *et al* 119
Domenach, J.-L. 38, 39, 43, 45
Dong Bingdi 162, 163, 174
Dongguan 49
Dragon-head village 315, 319; children in 324–5; construction of personal history in 323–5; and migration 319–21; remembering, forgetting, recreating the past in 325–7; and separation/reunion 321–3; and territorial bonds 327–8
Du Fu 323
Du Toit, B.M. and Safa, H.I. 74
Duara, P. 17

Eades, J. 15
Elias, N. and Scotson, J.L. 119
emigration *see* international migration
Europe 227, 228, 336; Chinese
communities in 269–71, 272–3;
illegal immigration to 166, 189–90,
199; institutionalization of
emigration to 165–7; as migrant
destination 162–4, 169, 171;
number/distribution of Qingtian
Chinese in 164–5, 176; reasons for
choosing as destination 187–91

family planning *see* fertility/family
planning
Fangshan town 167, 174, 177
Far Eastern Economic Review 79, 94
Fawcett, J.T. 15
Feeney, and Wang 145
Fei Xiaotong 31, 184, 189, 218, 249,
281, 282
female zhiqing 298; children of 314;
coping strategies of 304–5;
discrimination against 308–9; and
marriage 305, 306; networks 310;
and problems of reintegration 307;
and reality shock of the countryside
303–4; as revolutionary 302–3; as
stigmatized group 307–8
Fengtai Bureau of Industry and
Commerce 232, 233, 249
Fengtai Public Security Bureau 233,
234, 240
fertility/family planning: adaptation
model 138–9; and birth intervals
145–8, 150; data collection on 135–6;
disruption model 139; effects of on
migration 139–41, 143–4, 149, 150–1;
measures for 134–5; new regulations
148–9; and opportunity costs of
children 150; population background
135–6; rural/urban differences 137;
selection model 138; sex ratios
139–41, *142*, 143–4, 149–50;
socialization model 138; structural
influences/cultural conditions 136–7;
subpopulation survey 151; theories
concerning 137–9
Findley, S. 74
Five Year Plans 39, 41
floating population 52–3, 55, 75, 215,
216, 217, 335–6; attitudes towards

120–1; and crime 125–6; described
119–20; and education 127–8, 129,
131; and employment 127, 130;
environmental impact of 126–7, 128;
factors influencing residents'
attitudes 129–31; fertility/family
planning in 134–5; gender attitudes
towards 129; generational attitudes
towards 130–1; influence of on
community 124–7; as new form of
urbanization 120; and opportunities
for contact/extent of interaction
123–4; and property 125; residents'
acceptance of 127–8; survey of
relationships towards 121–32; and
transport 125; *see also* non-hukou
migration
Florence 280; as privileged arena for
migrant business 283–5; racism in
290; Zhejiang migrants in 287–9
Florence/Zhejiang Village
commonalities: community 288; and
development of communities 290–1;
economic migration 287; and
exporting of Wenzhou model
289–92; family 287–8; host society
288–9; *see also* Zhejiang Village
(Beijing)
Forbes, D. and Thrift, N. 67
Foshan/Shenzhen survey 74–6; and
backward/forward remittances 92–5,
102; and comigration/home visits 87,
91–2, 98; and information flow/job-
searching avenues 88–91, 97–8; and
migrant selectivity 76–85; and
reasons for migration 86–8, 96–7
Four Modernizations 301
Fujian province 87, 188, 336

Gallin, B. and Gallin, R.S. 25, 132
Gang of Four 305
Gansu province 39, 43, 226, 264
General Chinese Association
(Netherlands) 269
Georges, E. 71, 240
Germany: as land of milk and honey
207–9; life of migrants in 210–12;
migration to 199–200, 204, 205–7
Giese, K. 75
Goffman, E. 307
Gold, T.B. 312, 314
Goldring, L.P. 217

Goldstein, S. 334; *et al* 134; and
    Goldstein, A. 50, 53, 137, 138, 139,
    146
Gong'an Bu 49
Goodman, D.S.G. and Segal, G. 253
Gottschang, T. and Lary, D. 47
Great Leap Forward (1958–1961) 30,
    34, 38, 90, 333
Greenhalgh, P. 167
Gu Hua 45
Gu Shengzu and Jian Xinhua 74, 94
Guangdong province 33, 60, 188, 216,
    336; rural/urban migration in *see*
    Foshan/Shenzhen survey
Guangxi province 60, 85
Guangzhou city 49, 119
Gui Shixun 134, 135
Guizhou province 181
Guo Dong 314
Guomindang 33, 36
Gurak, D. and Caces, F. 71
Guxi Construction Company 110, 111

Hai Ming 255
Hainin city 229
Hajdú János 260
Halbwachs, M. 313
Hamilton, G.G. 10
Han Chinese 1, 11, 36
Hangzhou 161
Hausa Muslims (West Africa) 317,
    319
Hawkes, D. 329
Heaton, T.B. *et al* 136
Hebei province 44, 45, 113–15, 229
Heberer, T. 36
Heike, I. 313
Heilongjiang 35, 43, 227
Henan province 39, 85, 106, 115, 119,
    288
Heshenqiao village 220
Hirschman, A.O. 73
Hong Kong 8, 19, 44–5, 203–4, 205–6,
    339
Hongqiao town 220, 226, 229
Honig, E. and Hershatter, G. 145
Hoy, C. 134, 135
Hu Yiren 253
Hua Sheng Bao 254
Huang Weiding 285, 286, 291, 294
Huangqiao Construction Company 110
Huaren Tongxun 254

Hubei 60, 288
Hugo, G. 137, 138
Huikan 253, 254
hukou migration 5, 11, 43; compared
    with international migration 55;
    described 51–3; employment
    characteristics 59–60; geography of
    60–2, *63*, 64, *65–6*; reasons for
    56–7; recent mobility trends 53–5;
    socio-demographic characteristics
    57–9; theoretical implications of
    64, 67–8; *see also* internal
    migration
hukou system 50–1, 119, 334–5; and
    migration 51–3; as quasi-passport
    ("green card") system 51–3; 64, 67
Hull, T.H. 140
Hunan province 45, 85, 119, 229
Hungarian Chinese Association (HCA)
    277, 278–9; commercial section of
    256–7; dispute with APCHF 263–4,
    265; establishment of 252–3; and
    fight against crime 262–3; leadership
    of 254–6, 257, 268; loyalty to Beijing
    253; as organizer of charitable/
    cultural events 253–4; political
    muscle of 261–2; and politics 257–8;
    reason for growth 256; relationship
    with Hungarian authorities 265–8;
    strengthening role of 267–9; threats
    to 260–1
Hungarian Chinese Catering
    Association 257, 266–7
Hungarian Chinese Chamber of
    Commerce 256
Hungarian Chinese Federation of
    Industry and Trade 256, 276
Hungarian Chinese Patriotic
    Enterprises Group 267
Hungarian Vietnamese Association 256
Hungary: consolidation of Chinese
    community in 252; and crime 262–3;
    and establishment of HCA in 252–8;
    identity of Chinese community in
    269; and links with China 264–5,
    269–73; migration to 251–2;
    professional/other interest groups in
    259–60; proposal for residential
    Chinatown in 266; relationship with
    Chinese migrants 265–8; religious
    associations in 258–9, 260
Huzhou 161

illegal immigration 166, 189–90, 199,
203, 204–5, 213
Inner Mongolia 36, 37, 39, 44, 227
internal migration 2–3, 18, 29, 45–6,
336; age factor 57, 58; antecedents of
29–30; educational factors 58;
employment characteristics 59–60;
for escape 44–5; family reasons for
56–7; for famine 43; for flight 34;
gender factors 57–8, 60; geography of
60–2, 63, 64, 65–6; and industrial
relocation 39–40; and marriage 57,
58; for organized labour 40–1; for
punishment 34, 41–2; and relocation
for socialist progress 37–9; and rise in
mobility 49–50; socio-economic
duality in 57–62, 64, 67–8; as
spontaneous 43–4; stages of 33–5; in
the "static" decades 30–3; and
strengthening of borders 35–7;
see also hukou migration
international migration 2–3, 18, 336; and
fertility 149; from Zhejiang province
160–72; information concerning
200–1; institutionalization of 339–40;
negative aspects of 201; and neo-
classical theory 159, 184; new
economics of 159, 173; organization
of/trafficking in 202–3, 205–7, 211,
213, 214, 339–40; reasons for 201–2;
and remittances 338; and role of
employer 207–9; routes taken 203–6;
and social improvement 187; as
temporary 175; and theory of social
practice 160, 172, 174–6, 177; and
valid documents 204, 206–7; and
wage-differentials 159, 173; and
world-systems model 160, 173
International Soong Qingling
Children's Foundation 253
Italy 189–90, 228

Japan 40, 165, 168, 175, 188
Ji Dangsheng et al 247, 248
Ji Meikai 163
Ji Zhaojun 163
Jiang Zemin 255, 260
Jiangsu province 43, 60, 87, 122, 123
Jiangxi province 85, 181, 229
Jinan study 61
Jingwen Garment Wholesale Centre
231–2, 233, 239

Jinhua 161
Johanssen, S. and Nygren, O. 140

Kane, P. 43
Kanto earthquake (1923) 168
Kasarda, J.D. 150
Kearney, M. 216
Keji Ribao 149
Kelliher, D. 49
Kemper, R.V. 139
Keqiao town 230, 249–50
Kipnis, A.B. 198
Korea 40
Kunming 204

Labour Bureau 108
Lanzhou city 39, 264
Lary, D. 30
Lavely, W. et al 137
Lee, B.S. and Farber, S.C. 138
Lee, H.Y. 300
Leung, L. 300, 314
Li Fan and Han Xiaoyun 51, 79, 80
Li Haoran 181
Li Jiali and Cooney, R.S. 140
Li Mengbai, et al 119, 133; and Hu Yin
50, 53, 71, 79
Li Minghuan 180, 188, 252, 270, 276
Li, R.M. 36, 134
Li Yiyuan 269
Li Zongling et al 249
Lianyungang 43
Li'ao town 170, 171, 172, 175, 176,
181
Lin Bai et al 218, 281
Lin Biao 304
Lin Maoxiang 163
Linzhou city 106–7
Lipton, M. 73–4
Liu, A. 50
Liu Banmu 164
Liu Guokai 263
Liu Qiming 51
Liu Qiuhua 247
Liu, X. 16
Liu Xiaomeng et al 300, 304, 305, 306,
313, 314
Liu Yia-ling 249, 281
Liu Zheng et al 79, 85, 89
Liu Zhixian 266
Liu Zhonglu et al 298
Long, H. 55

Ma, L.J.C. 67
Ma, R. 11
Mabogunje, A. 13, 15
Macao 44
MacDonald, J.S. and MacDonald, L.D. 223
McGee, T.G. 139
Mallee, H. 50, 51, 74, 90, 119, 120, 134
Manchuria 29–30, 31, 33, 36, 39, 47, 204
Mao Chun 252
Mao Zedong 300
Marsden, A. 283
Marseilles 162–3, 166
mass migration 226–7; and capital market 230; and itinerant flow 229; and labour market 229; and proliferate flow 228–9; and raw materials 229–30
Massey, D.S. 18–19; et al 8, 25, 160, 173, 179, 184, 187, 188
Meillassoux, C. 216
Merton, R.K. and Kitt, A.S. 186
migration 1; anthropological studies of 317–19; and attachment, separation and reunion 315–28; and backward/forward remittances 92–5, 102, 210–11; as biographical event 16, 17; characteristics of 1–2; Chinese 333–44; comparisons of 3–4; data on 334–5; debate concerning 2; definitions of 4–6; and family 337; fear of 342–3; feminization of 339; and home comunities 7–9; and identity 341; impact of 337–9; integrated/global approach to 19; and labour market 339–41; legal/semilegal/illegal distinction 203; methodology 6–7; and migrant as victim 340; and nationalism/security 341–2; and networks 336–7; organization of 9–12; and policies/policy making 19–22, 343–4; political issues concerning 132; and problem of assimilation 21–2; and protection of rights 340; relevance of 12–19; remittances 228; and "rich" returnees 191–4; role of family in 7, 9; shared experience of 17; and social networks 336–7; social/political contexts 15–16; state initiated 31–3; time frame 4

migration configuration 14–15, 18
migration system 13, 15
Ming dynasty 161
Ming Tombs Reservoir 38
Ministry of Agriculture see Nongye Bu
Ministry of Agriculture (MOA) study 51
Ministry of Construction (MOC) study 50, 53
Montanari, A. and Cortese, A. 189
Mookherjee, H.N. 136
Mosher, S.W. 149
Mote, F.W. 21
Myers, F.R. 318
Myrdal, G. 73

Nanjing 162
Nanjing Treaty (1842) 161, 163
National Association of Overseas Chinese 262
Nationalist period (1912–1949) 35
Naughton, B. 40
Netherlands 228, 268; emigration to 185–6, 189, 190, 192–3
New York United Federation of Chinese Associations 272
Newell, C. 145
Niethammer, L. 308, 313
Ningbo 161
Nolan, P. 50; and Dong Furen 184, 281
non-hukou migration 5–6, 56, 57, 58, 60, 67, 215–17; and discrimination/exclusion 11–12; state/non-state space 240–4; three-circle structure 244; and underground market 220; see also floating population
Nongcun Xingyu 51
Nongye Bu 77, 79, 80, 88, 90, 94, 95
Northeast see Manchuria
Norusis, M.J. 143, 146
Nugent, W. 333
Nyiri Pál 251, 253, 261, 262

Oi, J. 93
Ong, A. and Nonini, D. 25
Orientalism 167
Ostergaard, C.S. 241
Ouzhou Daobao 278
Ouzhou zhi Sheng 253, 254, 255, 256, 260–1, 263, 266, 271, 278
Overseas Chinese Affairs Bureau 262
Overseas Chinese Association (Belgian) 269

Pan Zhifu 34
Parkin, D. 14–15
Parris, K. 249, 281
Patterson, 10
Pearl River Delta 61, 75, 327
peasant migration 32, 34, 36, 43–4, 50
Peng Xun 32, 33, 35, 37, 38, 42
People's Political Consultative
   Conference (PPCC) 255
People's Republic of China (PRC,
   1949-present) 32, 47–8, 251; and
   links with Hungarian Chinese
   community 253–6, 258, 260, 262–3,
   265–6, 269–73
Petersen, W. 226
Philippines 273
Pieke, F.N. 3, 9, 16, 17, 25, 160, 217,
   278; and Benton, G. 278
Pintupi Aborigines (Australia) 317–18,
   319
Piore, M.J. 67, 71
PLA 36
Polonyi Péter 256, 267
Poston, D.L. Jr. and Yaukey, D. 51
Pulau Langkawi community (Malaysia)
   318, 319
Putuo Mountain 162, 179
Pyke, F. 284

Qianjiayang village 220, 226
Qianlong Emperor (1736–1795) 41
Qianyan 176
Qiao Xiaochun and Chen Wei 145
Qing dynasty (1644–1911) 1, 29, 31,
   33, 35, 40, 41, 161, 162, 168
Qinghai 43
Qingtian city 3
Qingtian County 228; emigration from
   161–4, 177, 180; institutionalization
   of emigration from 165–8; number/
   distribution of Chinese in Europe
   164–5; soapstones from 162–4, 167,
   173–4, 177
Qingtian xianzhi 162
Qiushan village 167

Redding, G. 25
Representative Committee of Hungarian
   Chinese Organizations 260
Republic (1911–1949) 31, 165
Returned Overseas Chinese 262
Riley, M.W. 308

Roberts, K.D. 334, 337
Rofel, L. 308
Ronnas, P. and Sjoberg, O. 67
Rosaldo, R. 217, 240
Rosen, S. 299, 312, 313
Rosenthal, G. 313
Rouse, R. 217, 240
Rowe, W.T. 21
Rozelle, S. et al 64, 71
Rui'an city district 181; emigration
   from 170–2, 175, 176
Rundquist, F.-M. and Brown, L.A. 139
rural/urban migration 32, 43–4, 73–4,
   338; and age 76–7; demographic
   indicators 77–85; and economic
   situation 82–5, 87; and education
   80–2; and family 87, 97; and gender
   78–80, 87–8, 97; and household size
   77–8; and marriage 79–80, 87, 92,
   97; see also Foshan/Shenzhen survey

Sabagh, G. and Sun Bin Yin 138
Sanmen Dam 38
Scharping, T. 42, 76, 312, 313; and
   Schulze, W. 75, 94; and Sun
   Huaiyang 75, 94
Schoenhals, M. 42
Schoppa, R.K. 179, 180
Schwartz, V. 313
seasonal migration 53
Second Leap (1960–1961) 34
Shaanxi 43
Shandong province 29, 35, 36, 37, 40,
   44, 47
Shanggutou village 249
Shanghai 39, 43, 44, 60, 87, 119, 162,
   166, 335; and survey of relationships
   towards floating population 121–32
Shanghai City Overseas Chinese Affairs
   Bureau 253
Shanghai Friends' Society (Belgium)
   269, 270, 272
Shanghai Municipal Police Bureau 125
Shankou 174, 177
Shaoxing city 230
Shen Jianfa 134
Shen Yimin and Tong Chengzhu 33,
   41, 44
Shenzhen see Foshan/Shenzhen survey
Shepherd, J.R. 315
Shi Songjiu et al 119, 133
Shi Weimin and He Gang 313

Shiba, Y. 161
Shijazhuang city 226
Shimonoseki Treaty (1895) 161
Shryock, H.S. and Siegel, J.S. 141
Siberia 40
Sichuan province 60, 79, 85, 88, 119, 181
Siu, H. and Faure, D. 316, 327–8
Siu, P. 210
Sjaastad, L.A. 67
Skeldon, R. 7, 12, 15, 52, 55, 56, 101,
    160, 335, 336, 339, 342
Skinner, G.W. 279
Smith, C. 49
Solinger, D.J. 21, 56, 60, 120, 134, 242
Song Dynasty (960–1279) 168
Song Naigong 39, 44
Song Zhiming 268
South Africa 40
Soviet Union 48, 163, 166, 204, 205,
    227–8
Spain 270–1
Special Economic Zones 75, 84, 339
Stafford, C. 329, 330
Standing, G. 74
State General Bureau of Industry and
    Commerce 231
Steinbach, L. 299
Strand, D. 21, 241
Su Runyu 39, 43
Summerskill, M. 40, 164
Sun Mingquan 175

Taiwan 44, 272–3, 279
Taiyuan city 226
Tan Xiaoqing 138
Tan-Co, F. 273
Tanzania 335
Taubman, P. and Wachter, M.L. 67
Thailand 203–4
Third Front (1964–1971) 40, 41
Thompson, R.H. 10
Thunø, M. 9
Thurston, A.F. 42, 313
Tianjin 162
Tibet 36, 205
Tirasawat, P. 74
Todaro, M.P. 67
Tongji University (Shanghai) 110
Tu Ping 143, 145
Tu Wei-ming 25

United Nations 52

Urban and Rural Construction
    Committee of Beijing 107
urban zhiqing 302
urban/rural migration see rural/urban
    migration

Veblen, T. 193, 198
Voets, S.Y. and Schoorl, J.J. 25

Wakabyashi, K. 119
Waley-Cohen, J. 41
Wang Chunguang 218
Wang Jianmin and Hu Qi 71
Wang Nianyi 301
Wang Wuding et al 123, 127
Wang Zhongming 170, 184
Watson, J.L. 15
Watson, R. 326
Watson, R.S. 308
Wei Jinsheng 32, 48
Wei Qiao 161, 175
Weiner, M. 2, 168, 342
Weiss, M. 259
Wencheng county 228; emigration from
    169–70, 176
Wenzhou 162, 180, 181; conspicuous
    consumption in 191–4, 198;
    described 182; expectations of
    emigrants from 184–7; migration
    from 168–72, 218, 225; motives for
    emigration from 182–4; reasons for
    choosing Europe as destination
    188–91; relationship with Europe
    187–8; relative deprivation of
    emigrants from 185–7
Wenzhou Bureau of Industry and
    Commerce 232, 233
Wenzhou city 3, 10, 228, 229
Wenzhou model 281–2; export of
    289–92
Wenzhou Public Security Bureau 233,
    234
White, G. 312
White, L.T. III 25, 132, 300, 312, 335
White, M.J. et al 138
Williams, R.M. 186–7
Wimberley, D.W. et al 138
Wong, B.P. 259
Woolf, S. 6
Woon, Y.-f. 134
Worker-Peasant-Soldier movement
    304

World Exhibition, Paris (1899) 163
Wu, H.H. 41–2
Wu, H.X. 134
Wu Yulin 43, 44
Wuhai 221, 222, 249
Wuhan 162

Xia Weizhong 241
Xiang Biao 216, 240, 285, 286, 294
Xiao Gongqing 241
Xiaxiang movement 297–9; female
   laosanjie 302–7; mass migration/mass
   reflections 307–9; official accounts
   (1980s/1990s) 300–2; outline/
   development of 299–300; "zhiqing"
   and "laosanjie" 302
Xinjiang 36, 37, 41–2, 48, 204
Xiong Yingwu 35
Xu Gang and Yu Jingwei 140
Xu Lingxian 305, 314
Xu Zhong 79, 80
Xue Hong 277

Yamba, C.B. 317
Yan Xinli 168, 188
Yang, M. M.-h. 198, 241
Yang Yunyan 56, 60; and Chen Jinyong
   54
Yangzi River 38
Yangzi Valley 36
Ye Zhongming 162, 163, 166, 176
Yellow River 38
Yin, A. 26
Yin Hongbiao 313
Yongjia county 220, 228
Young, J. 45
Youzhou 162, 174, 177
Yuan Enzhen 281
Yuhu town 181
Yunnan 204
Yunxiang Yan 198

Zelinsky, W. 339
Zeng Yi; et al 140, 141; and Vaupel,
   J.W. 136
Zhang Chunyuan 79, 80
Zhang Hua 301, 313
Zhang Kaimin 44, 79, 85
Zhang Qingwu 53, 79
Zhang Tiejun 248
Zhang Tiesheng 304
Zhang Xiaohui et al 51

Zhang Zhicheng 168, 169, 171–2, 175,
   184, 187, 197; et al 169, 170, 176
Zhao Renwei 50
Zhejiang Province 3–4, 8, 10, 11, 85,
   87, 122, 123, 166, 176, 182, 229–30,
   255, 336; described 161; emigration
   from 160–1; emigration from
   Qingtian County 161–8; emigration
   from Wenzhou area 168–72; living
   conditions in 201–2
Zhejiang Provincial Overseas Chinese
   Affairs Bureau 271
Zhejiang Village (Beijing) 20, 280, 283,
   337; broker in 237–8; and chain
   migration (1984–1986) 223–5; and
   changes in government behaviour
   230–4; and completely marketized
   migration in small groups
   (1982–1984) 222–3; and covert
   migration in small groups
   (1970–1980) 218–20; described
   217–18; development of 240–4; elder
   in 236–7; and formation of "business
   space" 227–34; history of 218–27; as
   independent ethnic economy 285–7;
   and mass migration (1987–1995)
   226–7; and mature market system
   228–30; and over migration in small
   groups (1980–1982) 220–1; and
   people with power 234–40; public
   leader in 238–40; silent rich man in
   235; and undertaking of international
   trades 227–8; see also Beijing;
   Florence/Zhejiang Village
   commonalities
Zheng Dajiong 249
Zheng Datong 281
Zheng Qi 266
Zhengzhou city 39
zhiqing fiction 300–2
zhiqing migration see female zhiqing
Zhou Chongjing 36, 42
Zhou Enlai 304, 314
Zhou, K.X. 49, 149
Zhou Liuxian 163
Zhou Nanjing 179
Zhou Wangsen 161, 163, 174, 176
Zhou Xingquan 44
Zhuxi village 175
Zlotnik, H. 13, 15, 339
Zou Junyu et al 34
Zou Lanchun 79